Habitat Creation and Repair

Habitat Creation and Repair

Oliver L. Gilbert

Reader in Landscape
The University of Sheffield

and

Penny Anderson

Consultant Ecologist
Penny Anderson Associates

OXFORD NEW YORK TOKYO

OXFORD UNIVERSITY PRESS

1998

Oxford University Press, Great Clarendon Street, Oxford OX2 6DP

Oxford New York

Athens Auckland Bangkok Bogota Bombay
Buenos Aires Calcutta Cape Town Dar es Salaam
Delhi Florence Hong Kong Istanbul Karachi
Kuala Lumpur Madras Madrid Melbourne
Mexico City Nairobi Paris Singapore
Taipei Tokyo Toronto Warsaw

and associated companies in
Berlin Ibadan

Oxford is a trade mark of Oxford University Press

Published in the United States
by Oxford University Press, Inc., New York

A catalogue record for this book is available from the British Library

Library of Congress Cataloging in Publication Data
Gilbert, O. L.
Habitat creation and repair / Oliver L. Gilbert and Penny Anderson.
Includes bibliographical references (p. 246) and index.
1. Habitat (Ecology)—Great Britain.   2. Wildlife habitat
improvement—Great Britain.   3. Restoration ecology—Great Britain.
4. Habitat conservation—Great Britain.   5. Habitat (Ecology)
6. Wildlife habitat improvement.   7. Restoration ecology.   8. Habitat conservation.
I. Anderson, Penny.   II. Title.
QH541.G53   1998   639.9'2—dc21   97-44755
ISBN 0 19 854967 9 (Hbk)
ISBN 0 19 854966 0 (Pbk)

Typeset by Best-set Typesetter Ltd., Hong Kong

Printed in Great Britain by
Bookcraft (Bath) Ltd
Midsomer Norton, Avon

Preface

This book provides a practical guide to habitat creation, taking the reader through the ethics, the principles, and then the detail of designing habitats that will eventually contribute significantly to the total natural resource for nature conservation. The aim is to condense the existing widely scattered literature, add our own experience from working in this field, and combine them into a readily accessible, up-to-date account of this rapidly developing subject.

Habitat creation needs to be separated from habitat restoration. We have taken as our starting point ground recently bared by earth moving, demolition, ploughing, and other events, or sites dominated by communities of low wildlife value such as improved pasture or conifer plantation. If a site is already occupied by semi-natural vegetation with a complex structure or high species diversity, habitat creation is not normally appropriate—what may be required in such a case is habitat management or restoration. It should be noted that while this book separates habitat creation from habitat restoration in America both activities are included under the latter name.

Following the introductory chapters the book is arranged by habitat. For each it takes the reader through options and solutions, reveals problems to look out for, and gives good and bad examples of habitat creation in practice. While the majority of case studies come from the UK, some are from abroad; for example, the Dutch are leaders in coastal defence and the North American achievements on tundra sites damaged by oil-related development and on prairie grassland recreation are unrivalled. We would stress that the principles of habitat creation are the same wherever they are being applied.

Habitat creation is not a universal panacea to be applied indiscriminately to sites as an alternative to tended open space. Frequently a gardenesque or naturalistic approach will be more appropriate. If mature, self-maintaining communities occupy the site, habitat management is the correct option. Increasingly, however, the wish is to create a particular vegetation type and structure that will attract local animals and other plants, and be of value for nature conservation. To be properly integrated, sites should reflect the local geology, soils, and land uses, and enhance regional distinctiveness. New habitats of wildlife value also help mitigate the impact of the enormous loss of meadows, ancient woodlands, downland, hedgerows, and wetland that has occurred over the last 50 years. Our book gives guidance on deciding when habitat creation is the correct path to follow and takes the reader through site survey to the final design, getting the scheme on the ground and following it up with monitoring. It has proved impossible to do full justice to every topic so we have had to be selective with an emphasis on personal experience.

During the writing of this book, and throughout the preceding years of research, we have been sustained by support and advice from numerous colleagues and friends. Space not ingratitude precludes the naming of everyone who has made a contribution of value. Particular thanks are due to Rob McInnes and Peter Worrall who wrote most of the text on wetlands, prepared figures, and loaned photographs, and to Jala Makhzoumi who, with patience and skill, produced the majority of the line drawings, while Nick Gibbons delineated many of the maps and graphs. Julia Watson is thanked for her tolerance in converting illegible scrawl into typewritten text. Others, thanked for providing illustrations or other material include the following: Dr Eleanor Cohn, Wolverhampton University; Dr A. J. Davey, University of East Anglia; Nuclear Electric plc; Berkshire County Council Highways Agency; and Alistair Cameron of the National Trust, Cornwall. We are also indepted to the following for help in various ways: Jeremy Cotton; Katherine Hearn, National Trust; Chloe Palmer; Miranda Plowden, Dearne Valley Groundwork Trust; John Redmayne; Peter Sibbley; and Ian Trueman of Wolverhampton University.

August 1997
Sheffield   O. L. G.
Chinley   P. A.

Contents

1 Introduction 1
  The ethics of habitat creation 1
  The role of habitat creation 3
  Types of habitat creation 5
  Strategic habitat creation 7
  Some problems 10
  Achievements to date 13

2 Designing new habitats: general principles 16
  Setting objectives 16
  Site context 18
  Site survey 21
  Ground preparation 31
  Choosing the right plants 33
  Long-term management and monitoring 37

3 Promoting natural succession 38
  Principal factors controlling succession 40
  Kick starting the succession 44
  Natural reversion 47
  Comparative rates of natural reversion 48
  The technique in action 50

4 Grasslands 54
  Introduction 54
  Natural colonization 57
  Sowing a seed mix 59
  Creating grasslands for animals 79
  Management 83
  Diversifying existing dull grasslands 87
  Monitoring 91

5 Woodland, scrub, and hedgerow 92
  Positioning the wood in the landscape 92
  Designing the wood 93
  Establishment options 95
  Species selection 99
  Introduced species 104
  Planting layout 105
  Establishment 107

Introducing woodland herbs   111
Fauna   115
Scrub   121
Hedgerows   124

6 Heath and moor   130
Introduction   130
Ecological issues   134
Heathland creation techniques   145
Economic heathland establishment   155
Heath and moor creation for animals   156
Adding dwarf shrubs to existing vegetation   156
Post-establishment management   157

7 Montane and submontane habitats   160
Introduction   160
Repair and creation techniques: seed bank, turfing, transplants   162
Repair and creation techniques: seeding   164
Vegetation and soil reinforcement   171
Conclusion   172

8 The coast   174
Sand dunes   175
Saltmarshes   180
Intertidal sand and mudflats   183
Shingle structures   184
Saline lagoons   185
Maritime cliff grassland   187
Coastal heaths   188
Unprotected soft cliffs   189
Summary   190

9 Farmland   191
Changes in lowland farming since 1945   191
The opportunities   192
Arable land   194
Pastures and meadows   199
Heathland/scrub creation on rough grazing   201
New farm woodland   201
New hedgerows and farm trees   202
The farm conservation plan   203

10 Wetlands   204
The issues   204
The design and construction of wetlands   205
Ponds and lakes   214
Reed-beds   220
Wet grassland and duck marsh   221
Rivers and floodplains   223
Constructed wetlands   232
Summary   235

11 **Getting it right** 236
     Project planning and design 236
     The importance of using local genetic stock 238
     Control of the contractor 241
     Management, monitoring, and interpretation 243
     Whole environment management 244
     The benefits of habitat creation 245

     References 246
     Glossary 265
     Index 269

1 Introduction

The ethics of habitat creation

It is necessary to start by considering the ethics of habitat creation. Habitat creation is regarded in certain areas as a universal remedy for mitigating adverse human impacts on the environment. However, this view is counteracted by some nature conservationists who consider that 'faking nature' is largely ineffectual and to be discouraged. A well-publicized example, where the arguments for both sides were given wide exposure, involved Oxleas Wood in south London. This large, ancient oak wood lay on the proposed route of a major road that would have cut the wood in half and resulted in the destruction of 8.3 ha of high forest. The Department of Transport, which was sponsoring the road, offered, in mitigation, to plant 10.2 ha of new trees on farmland adjacent to the wood. The Department of Transport suggested that this 'exchange land' would more than make up for the lost woodland. The assurances were that the loss of value would be only temporary and that full value would be recreated. In short, the Department of Transport was claiming that the destruction of this Site of Special Scientific Interest (SSSI) would be compensated for by habitat creation.

In many previous cases similar proposals had undermined the arguments of conservationists. In other words, habitat creation promises have carried weight against environmental objections. However, in the case of ancient woodland that has occupied a site for centuries and evolved a rich and complex structure, the claim that revegetation, rehabilitation, or re-creation can restore value can be strongly contested. It is not possible ecologically or feasible economically; too many species are involved and there are too many unknowns. It is important to realise that, even if a very high level of habitat creation had been achieved, Oxleas Wood would still have lost something of value; namely, it would no longer be a natural feature. Taking a notion from aesthetics, the Department of Transport were proposing that a fake or forgery was equivalent to the real thing. Fakes lack the value of the genuine article, even when the genuine article includes an element of past use by man.

However, habitat creation cannot fully restore value for an additional reason; we value parts of our environment because they are natural to a high degree and have evolved over many decades if not centuries. A newly created

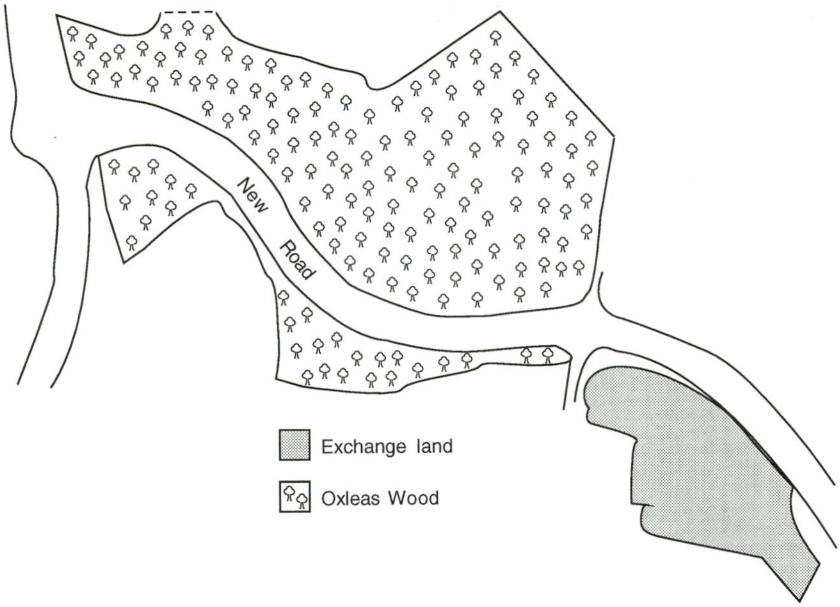

Fig. 1.1 A public inquiry refused permission for this major road through Oxleas Wood. The inquiry considered that mitigation proposals, to replace the woodland destroyed with new planting (exchange land), were inadequate.

area of forest would be no substitute; it is the product of contrivance—origin and evolution are important. Continuity has been lost and with it, the ability of the community to explain itself. Sites such as ancient woodland are enjoyed as more than pretty scenery; ecological knowledge transforms them into an enthralling experience just as a knowledge of art history or painting technique sharpens aesthetic evaluations and alters aesthetic perceptions. The case of Oxleas Wood (Fig. 1.1) went to public inquiry and permission for the road was refused on the grounds that the proposals did not meet the Government's current environmental standards. The inadequacy of the mitigation proposals, which would have caused a severe loss of amenity to users of the wood, was central to the defeat.

The principles illustrated here are equally applicable to other long-established habitats. The crucial point to be made about habitat creation is that it is never a substitute for the genuine article; as indicated above, it fails to deliver the goods on at least three fronts: naturalness, continuity, and complexity. Ethical arguments for and against habitat creation are explored further by Elliot (1995). Where there is a straight choice between preserving or recreating a valuable habitat, preserving it will always be the ecologically preferred option.

The role of habitat creation

Where does this leave habitat creation? Habitat creation still has an enormous role to play in areas where the natural environment has already been extensively damaged by deforestation, agriculture, land drainage, mineral extraction, or civil engineering projects. At the smaller scale it has a role in recreating farm ponds, hedgerows, areas of scrub, or flowery road verges. But even this role undersells the importance of habitat creation. It is not merely a tool for the repair of damaged areas, or a method of providing patches of aesthetically pleasing, wildlife-rich habitat in country parks; it provides a philosophy and a means of reversing long-term trends of habitat loss over huge areas that have become monotonous through overexploitation.

There is an interesting difference between the concepts of habitat creation/restoration in North America and Europe. In the former, the aim is to re-establish habitats that were widespread prior to European contact. There has been a general perception of these as being natural habitats, unaffected by man. However, it is beginning to be recognized that traditional practices by the different Amerindian tribes over centuries has probably had a major role in shaping them (Rogers-Martinez 1992). This brings the practice (even if not the concept) of habitat creation/restoration closer to the European approach, which focuses more on the rehabilitation of habitats that have evolved over many centuries of land management. Restoration in Western Europe, therefore, tends to be geared more toward reinstating the conditions prevailing in the cultural landscape 50–100 years ago, before the intensification of agriculture, widespread afforestation, and the post-war surge in habitat destruction caused by drainage, ploughing, hedgerow clearance, and urban development. Simulation of pristine habitats is not often attempted, though for a time, in Germany, under the influence of R. Tuxen, it was fashionable to try to recreate the potential natural vegetation of a region using pollen data to provide the model.

The potential for habitat creation is prodigious owing to the huge habitat losses experienced in recent decades (Nature Conservancy Council 1984). More recently, the 1990 Countryside Survey (Department of the Environment 1993) suggests a slowing down of losses in Britain during the period 1978–90, though moorland grassland declined 3%, while coniferous woodland increased 5%. However, this survey detected a considerable further decline of hedges in arable and pastoral landscapes; increasingly, boundaries with fences were coming to dominate the countryside. Most worrying was an overall loss of diversity in the vegetation. For example, in pastoral landscapes, semi-improved grassland showed a significant decline in species, especially those typical of unimproved mesotrophic meadows. Floristic diversity also declined in hedge bottoms, verges, and along stream sides. Verges had become more overgrown and featured an increase in coarse grasses. Stream sides had fewer species indicative of aquatic margins and wet meadows. Woodland showed a decline in species number, evidence of disturbance, and a trend towards a more grassy ground flora. The loss of meadow species, which were once an important component of these pastoral landscapes, further reduced an already depleted resource. With regard to arable landscapes, this survey revealed a 38% decline nationally in species number over the 12 years.

The findings of the 1990 Countryside Survey point to a failure of current conservation policies, and was one reason why English Nature developed their idea of 'Natural Areas', which gives habitat creation a proactive rather than a defensive role in reversing trends of habitat decline and loss. In many parts of lowland England, SSSIs are almost the last remaining places rich in wildlife and natural features. As small isolated sites have no buffering capacity they are easily harmed, and this can lead to losses from which they are unlikely to recover. A recent survey of threats to SSSIs in England and Wales revealed that over 10% are currently experiencing significant damage (Friends of the Earth 1994). The Natural Areas Programme aims to integrate them into the countryside as a whole by paying more attention to their context and to link them up, thereby offering opportunities for key species to spread. For example, in the Chilterns Natural Area, one aim is to increase the total area of short sward chalk grassland through reversion of arable land; by doing this, populations of key species, such as wild candytuft (*Iberis amara*) and the silver-spotted skipper butterfly (*Hesperia comma*) (Fig. 1.2) can recover.

A similar approach, reversing trends of habitat loss in order to upgrade the environment, is being explored by local authorities; for example, Peterborough (Peterborough Environment City Trust 1995) has recently announced its aim to expand the area of quality semi-natural habitat in their district to 15% by the year 2010 using appropriate habitat restoration techniques, includ-

Fig. 1.2 A programme of habitat creation has been proposed to reverse the decline of the silver-spotted skipper (*Hesperia comma*) in the Chilterns Natural Area (drawn by J. Makhzoumi).

ing natural regeneration. A likely result of the Countryside Commission sponsored landscape character maps of Britain is that regions will adopt policies that strengthen local character through habitat creation. Cambridgeshire County Council, alarmed at the decline and increasing blandness of the local countryside, has already published landscape guidelines that do this (Cambridgeshire County Council 1991). Other countryside policies and initiatives, such as long-term set-aside, Countryside Stewardship, the National Forest, the Community Forests, the Environmentally Sensitive Areas (ESA), and the UK Biodiversity Action Plan will be using habitat creation to achieve this. By mid-1995, the Countryside Stewardship scheme and ESAs had been responsible for the creation of 13 300 ha of new grassland from cultivated land. This high level of activity demonstrates that habitat creation is becoming central to the activities of planners, landscape architects, and conservationists. There is, however, plenty of room for improvement; for example, much of the grassland mentioned above is very poor in plant species—its effectiveness would be increased if there was also management for breeding birds and other nature conservation benefits.

Types of habitat creation

New habitats can be established in different ways, at different scales, and to satisfy various objectives and functions, including non-ecological ones. The *Peterborough natural environment audit: consultation document* (Peterborough Environment City Trust 1995) provides a good example of a multiple, integrated approach, which sets its plans for habitat creation in a framework of land uses. First, there are the non-recreatable sites considered essential for the maintenance of biodiversity in the area; these are akin to nature reserves and designated the 'critical natural capital'. Buffer areas adjacent to the above, which are needed to sustain them, are known as 'supportive capital'. Next in significance are 'constant natural assets', which are important for maintaining the ecological framework of the district; these formerly widespread communities provide much of the local character and will be recreated on a large scale using one of the following methods.

1. Natural colonization. Allowing natural processes to determine the habitats developing on an unmodified site.

2. Framework habitats. Engineering restoration is undertaken on the topography, soils, drainage, etc., with or without some planting to provide key desired features and to provide a framework within which natural colonization can take place. If a particular habitat or mosaic of habitats is required this method is usually the best option.

3. Designer habitats. This method involves complete landscaping to a pre-determined design; trees are planted, scrub established, and grassland sown to a precise scheme, and managed to ensure conformity with the original plan. These are also known as facsimile habitats.

4. Political habitats. These are colourful, interesting and attractive habitats created for people in urban areas. They have an educational and propaganda role and do not attempt to reproduce any particular target habitat (Baines 1989).

It should be remembered that habitat creation is only one of a palate of techniques that can be uses to increase the nature conservation interest of an area. Habitat creation needs to be distinguished from habitat restoration, which attempts to restore existing degraded semi-natural vegetation. Often altering the management regime is all that is required. For example, in the Chilterns Natural Area, many of the nature conservation objectives can be achieved by scrub removal and the reintroduction of grazing, or by managing old coppice woodland. Alternatively, habitat transplantation, where an original habitat is moved from a donor to a receptor site, can be employed. This book is concerned primarily with habitat creation on sites that are bare or support a simple community, such as an arable field, an area of rye-grass (*Lolium perenne*), or a site where extensive earth moving has taken place; all such sites have a low conservation interest. These other reconstruction techniques, also known as habitat enhancement or habitat diversification, are dealt with by Buckley (1989), Byrne (1990), and Sutherland and Hill (1995). It is possible, within a single scheme, for the three approaches to be used in combination.

By definition, habitat creation involves creating a dynamic community of interacting plants and animals that should increase in diversity over time. Can it be applied to a single species? It is a very different activity from English Nature's Species Recovery Programme, which has the principal short-term objective of reversing the decline of populations of the rarest plants and animals in England. This is species rehabilitation; occasionally the promotion of a single species may be dependant on a very precise habitat creation or restoration scheme, such as for the sand lizard (*Lacerta agilis*) or natterjack toad (*Bufo calamita*)—a subject we do not cover in this book.

Habitat repair may involve a single spectacular species. For example, the black poplar (*Populus nigra* ssp. *betulifolia*) (Fig. 1.3), requires near-natural river dynamics to provide seasonally flooded bare ground for seed germination. British rivers no longer provide these conditions, so natural regeneration does not occur. There are only a few thousand of these magnificent flood plain trees left; unless the practice of taking cuttings (truncheons) and planting them to replace senescent trees is revived, numbers will continue to decline.

Fig. 1.3 The only way the native black poplar (*Populus nigra* ssp. *betulifolia*) can be maintained in the British countryside is through habitat repair (drawn by J. Makhzoumi).

The same is true of the pollarded willows (*Salix* spp.) that line dykes in Cambridgeshire fenlands, adding character to the flat landscape.

Strategic habitat creation

Most habitat creation to date has been piecemeal and on a small scale. For example, 75% of purchases of wild flower seed in Britain involve less than 8 kg, sufficient for only 0.2 ha (Brown 1989). Wild flower meadows are often included in landscape schemes to provide variety from the horticultural approach, a splash of colour, or perhaps to cover a steep bank that would be difficult to mow regularly. This, however, is only playing at habitat creation; people with vision see it as offering the opportunity to upgrade huge areas of countryside, a way of rescuing large areas from mediocrity and a method of restoring regional and local character.

Used strategically, habitat creation can help to buffer and link the increasingly fragmented, isolated, and diminishing habitat patches of high value that remain. For some time, conservationists have been looking for a means of extending nature conservation from small protected areas into the wider surroundings, and this offers just such an opportunity. Habitat restoration and creation have a vital role to play in buffering sites from incompatible adjacent land uses and in linking older fragments together, thus, facilitating the dispersion of the more mobile plants and animals. To be effective this needs tackling at a strategic level rather a site level.

This linking function is the most exciting aspect of the Natural Areas concept (English Nature 1993) and of other initiatives, such as the Cambridgeshire Landscape Guidelines, Hampshire County Council Planning Department Strategies and the Peterborough Environment Audit. These are strategic aproaches that propose an integrated approach to habitat creation over large areas and with long time scales. On a national scale, Pye and French (1993) estimated the current average rates of net loss or gain for each major coastal habitat in England, and these authors used this information to predict possible trends over the next 20 years. Estimates that predict future losses have been converted into target figures for the recreation of these habitats. Due to forecasted increases in sea-level, all the habitats studied are threatened with widespread erosion; the recommendations were for 13510 ha of coastal habitat creation to be undertaken in order to maintain the *status quo*. The benefits of accepting and funding these proposals are projected major savings in coastal defence costs and the amenity value of having a relatively unspoilt coastline. At Northey Island on the Essex coast, the cost of restoring a short stretch of the original sea wall was estimated at £55 000. This figure compared unfavourably with that for a managed retreat scheme (£25 000), which, when implemented, resulted in the creation of nearly 1 ha of new salt-marsh (Turner and Dagley 1993).

Habitat creation is equally applicable to urban areas where it has come a long way since the small, purpose-designed ecology parks of the early 1980s. These attempted to imitate the countryside by producing a hay meadow, calcareous grassland, a thicket, a small woodland, a marsh and a pond, sometimes all in an area of under 2 ha. People appreciated these familiar communities but they were expensive to maintain and perhaps would have been better harbouring urban wildlife. In a number of towns, Victorian parks are being redesigned along ecological lines, combinations of unmown grass, woodland, and scrub are replacing tended open space. Large though many of these schemes are they are still site-based and would benefit from an integrated approach on a broader scale.

An example of the integrated ecological approach is a project adopted by the Sheffield Development Corporation (SDC) who were responsible for rejuvenating a highly urban, run-down valley covering 800 ha (Sheffield Development Corporation 1994). The ecology of this valley derives from two main attributes; the underlying natural features that pre-date urbanization, and an overlying layer of human impact. Together these attributes provide a source of local distinctiveness that has arisen from interrelationships between the valley's structure and its cultural history. The SDC's approach to the landscape has been to use the existing pattern of relict and more recent habitats to form the basis of designs that enhance local character, both in terms of ecology and industry. The distribution of the spontaneous vegetation used as models is strongly related to landscape and includes oak–birch woods and acid grassland on high ground, an ash–hawthorn woodland on the valley sides, an urban scrub of buddleia (*Buddleia davidii*), cotoneaster (*Cotoneaster* spp.), goat willow (*Salix caprea*), and orchard apple (*Malus domestica*) on the valley floor, and willows, poplars (*Populus* spp.), alder (*Alnus glutinosa*), and wild figs (*Ficus carica*) beside the river (Fig. 1.4). The latter are already present where the water was warmed by thermal discharges. This provides a frame-

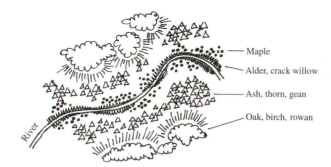

(a) The natural pattern related to topography and soil

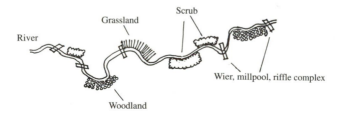

(b) Important wildlife sites beside the river

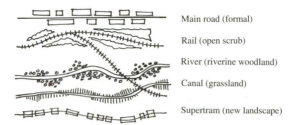

(c) Human impact: each transport corridor is characterized by a different habitat

Fig. 1.4 Examples of how habitat creation is being used to reinforce local character in the Lower Don Valley, Sheffield (drawn by M. Plowden).

work into which planting schemes can be fitted, each zone with its own scale and preferred planting mix.

In contrast to habitat creation elsewhere, the post-industrial base has been taken as the starting point; these communities are well matched to current conditions in the valley and so have lower implementation and maintenance costs. In addition to echoing existing features, the SDC introduced a new element by the use of maples (*Acer* spp.) to characterize the main road corridor and to highlight prestige modern developments. Maples were chosen because of their visual interest and formality, and because valley bottoms are one of their major natural habitats in North America. Further details of this approach are provided in Fig. 1.4.

Some problems

Use of non-native plant material

Habitat creation is most successful in areas where the environment is still rich in wildlife. This is because the surrounding habitats provide a steady influx of colonizing material. However, in areas that have been intensively farmed over a long period there is no longer a reservoir of species to invade in this way; they need to be introduced. The accepted way of achieving this, especially with designer habitats, has been to purchase the basic plant material. A recent survey (Akeroyd 1994) has revealed that a high proportion of so-called native wild flower seed being sold in Britain is non-native in origin. A major source seems to be central and southern Europe where it is surplus to agricultural and horticultural requirements. If such seed is used in habitat creation schemes, then, far from helping the British flora, it is threatening it through competition and hybridization, which could lead to an erosion of native genetic variation.

The genetic base of the British flora has already suffered from introductions. Last century it was widely believed that, as a timber tree, continental *Quercus robur* was superior to our native strains; for this reason, foreign material was extensively planted, even in the remote areas that were the traditional stronghold of *Q. petraea*. The result has been massive introgressive hybridization; in many parts of Scotland, for example, it is now difficult to find a pure specimen of either species (Cousens 1963). A comparison of the growth of native and commercially obtained continental European hawthorn (*Crataegus monogyna*) showed that the genotypes were morphologically distinct and that the foreign material, because it displayed a lower growth rate coupled with a higher mildew score, had a lower establishment rate (Jones and Evans 1994).

The variants to beware of in modern commercial seed mixes are robust and gross compared to their native counterparts. They include agricultural red clover (*Trifolium pratense* var. *sativum*), fodder bird's-foot trefoil (*Lotus cor-*

niculatus var. *sativus*), kidney vetch (*Anthylis vulneraria* subsp. *carpathica*), hybrid ox-eye daisy (*Leucanthemum* × *superbum*), and fodder burnet (*Sanguisorba minor* subsp. *muricata*). It is believed that introduced varieties of sanfoin (*Onobrychis vicifolia*) and white clover (*Trifolium repens*) now far outnumber native populations. Worryingly, hybridization has started to occur between native and alien bird's-foot trefoil; the upright character of the fodder plant appears to be dominant.

Nurseries and seed merchants that guarantee native plants are now appearing and should be used preferentially. Alternatively, techniques such as hay strewing, using locally harvested material, are an excellent method of perpetuating regional plant communities; this has been demonstrated on a commercial scale at Wolverhampton (Jones *et al*. 1995). One firm now specializes in collecting seed from SSSI grassland and distributing it for use within the natural area from which it was collected. This has the major advantage that both herb and grass seed is of local provenance—most suppliers still have great difficulty in locating native British grass seed. Despite Akeroyd's findings, seed mixes have greatly improved since 1970 when Nickersons advertised a 47-species 'Conservation mix' (Fig. 1.5), which, in all probability, contained not a single native wild flower seed. See also Chapter 4.

The fauna

In most habitat-creation schemes the fauna is left to arrive by itself—a function that some of it is well able to perform. Many groups are extremely mobile; certain invertebrates, for example, begin to arrive on an area of bare ground as early as the first plants, if not before. A survey of urban demolition sites, 1–6 years old, which had been left to colonize naturally, showed high densities of ground beetles, grasshoppers, harvestmen, spiders, woodlice, slugs, centipedes, millipedes, ants, and Lepidoptera (Gilbert 1989; Lott and Daws 1995). Within a few years, a third of the total number of species of British dragonflies visited a newly created pond near Peterborough. Local birds and most mammals also arrive as soon as food sources or cover are sufficiently developed. What has impressed workers is the rapidity, and often the rarity, of the early invaders of post-industrial sites (Eyre and Luff 1995). There are of course other, less mobile, species, which fail to colonize, but unfortunately too little is known about their specific requirements to be able to introduce them.

It is possible, through design, to encourage certain groups of organisms and this is occasionally attempted. Davis and Coppeard (1989) were asked to develop grassland habitats that would attract butterflies onto a landfill site in Essex. They approached this assignment through introducing appropriate larval food plants, including nectar-producing flowers for the adults, and by diversifying the structure of the vegetation to provide different degrees of

Fig. 1.5 A seed merchant's leaflet from the early 1970s advertising a 47-species 'Nature Conservation Blend', which probably contained not a single native wild flower seed.

shade and shelter, by varying sward height, and by ensuring there was bare ground for basking. Eighteen species of butterfly were recorded during the first five years, the majority establishing strong breeding populations. The use of fertilizers was beneficial to the Essex skipper (*Thymelicus lineolus*). So, if there are interesting butterflies on an adjacent site, they can be induced to expand into newly created habitats by providing appropriate conditions.

Well-funded habitat creation schemes sometimes cater for vertebrates (for example, through the provision of bat tunnels, prefabricated badger sets, badger gates, pipe drains to encourage water voles, or underpasses to provide toads with a safe passage across roads). There is considerable scope for further innovation, except in the case of designing some kinds of wetlands for birds, which is now a well-known art.

Anyone contemplating designing for invertebrates should consult Kirby (1992) and Fry and Lonsdale (1991). Many of our 30 000 species of invertebrate are in decline, and action is needed to reverse this. Information on how to provide for invertebrates is included in relevant chapters in this volume, but there are a few principles that can be applied widely. For example, the importance of bare ground has only recently been recognized; vegetation structure is important in every aspect and at every scale; a mosaic of several different habitats adjoining one another on a single site is more valuable than equal areas of the same habitats on separate sites; also, seemingly insignificant or trivial features such as a seepage line, a stony area, or a sunny bank can have a high potential for the group. It is time that more attention was paid to the faunal aspects of habitat creation.

Achievements to date

To many people, habitat creation is synonymous with the sowing of wild flower meadows or the restoration of flooded gravel pits. Of course, it is far wider than this, but habitat creation schemes do not always attract publicity, partly because of the high degree of failure. A questionnaire survey (Jones 1990), showed that the main thrust with respect to terrestrial schemes is still the creation of species-rich neutral grassland, with woodland, heathland, and a miscellaneous category following well behind (Fig. 1.6). Full intervention (e.g. designer habitats to produce a target community) has been more popular than allowing natural colonization; however, the success rate of these schemes has generally been low. A more recent assessment (Parker 1995), concluded that many projects fail because they are not well enough thought out at the planning stage and because precise objectives are not set. Other projects are too ambitious for the resources available. Ecological misjudgements are rife, particularly regarding soil fertility and the source of the plant material. The need for aftercare had often not been addressed and site monitoring was inadequate. Parker goes on to give guidance by breaking habitat creation into a series of stages and advises on the preparation of a 'project plan', which should contain the following: (1) objectives; (2) resources; (3) methodology and implementation; (4) the fauna; (5) initial (short-term) management; and (6) management plan and long-term objectives. Wetland habitat creation techniques are considered to be ahead of the rest, particularly regarding long-term

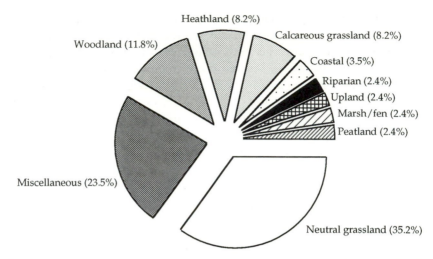

Fig. 1.6 Habitat creation activity in the UK, as assessed by a questionnaire survey (from Jones 1990).

management. In contrast, relevant techniques for woodlands, which are very complex habitats, are relatively underdeveloped.

If new habitats are to be successful they must succeed socially by looking attractive, by helping to consolidate the landscape, and by contributing to local character. They must, in addition, satisfy nature conservation objectives and be ecologically sound so they do not fail or necessitate high management costs. Relevant ecological experience is essential for assessing existing site value, interpreting environmental constraints, selecting the right species, and manipulating the new vegetation through appropriate management. But habitat creation is seldom just an ecological exercise. It needs to heed visual and amenity requirements, observe archaeological constraints, and involve local people at every stage, especially in urban fringe areas. Ecologists therefore need to work alongside other professionals and the local community.

This approach is exemplified by the Peterborough initiative which includes 'A strategy for people and wildlife' with projects such as establishing a 'Wild-flower way', a 'Barn owls, bats and buildings' initiative, a 'Woodland link-up scheme', 'Project otter', 'Operation hedgerow', and 'Damsels and dragonflies'. The same is happening in Sheffield, Leicester, London, and a dozen other cities; there is a growing and popular demand for habitat creation as an alternative to the horticultural approach in urban areas. Some of the newly created habitats already have local names such as the 'Flower Fields' and the 'Mouse Field' in Liverpool. An awareness of the importance of people is particularly well developed in the UK, compared with the continent or the United States.

Habitat creation has a longer history than might be expected. Two-hundred years ago Richard Payne Knight and Uvedale Price (Andrews 1989) published books advocating a style of landscape gardening that had many principles in common with those promoted by ecologists today in that it was sympathetic to nature conservation. Their style, known as 'picturesque', emphasized the conservation of variety, intricacy, irregularity, roughness, ruggedness, and the sense of place. They expressed a preference for making the most of the existing natural landscape, which was contrary to the smooth, formulaic works of the professional improvers, 'Capability' Brown and his successor Humphry Repton. Building on 200 years of history, modern principles of habitat creation are outlined in the next chapter.

2 Designing new habitats: general principles

Long before seeds are sown or plants selected, successful habitat creation depends on the careful consideration of several basic factors. These factors can be grouped into several general topics. Site context is important and relates to the nature of the adjacent habitats and how the site functions in the wider ecological landscape. The next relevant consideration is the location of a site, how it is to be managed, and its potential use by people. Of critical concern are the nutrient status and nature of the soils or water in, or on, which the plants are to be established. Evaluation and analysis of these permits the selection of suitable objectives for the new habitat. Once objectives have been set, the design process has to consider questions of shape, scale, habitat type, species, and implementation (see Fig. 2.1). This chapter deals with these all-important considerations.

Setting objectives

The setting of objectives is an essential prerequisite to habitat creation. It assists in the design of the most-appropriate set of habitats and provides an all important reference point against which the degree of success can be judged at a later stage.

Various objectives may be adopted, but not all will be wholly compatible—priorities will need to be identified. Parker (1995) considers that many habitat creation projects fail through lack of carefully thought out and precise objectives at the planning stage.

Nature conservation objectives are likely to be central to any habitat creation project. These may be related to establishing a well-structured and diverse grassland, woodland, pond, or other habitat, or they could target specific groups such as butterflies, amphibians, or wintering geese. Such objectives are being adopted on a wide scale, from school grounds, parks, and gardens to ESAs and Natural Areas where large-scale buffering and extension of fragmented habitats is being planned (for example, the Stiperstones Upland in Shropshire; English Nature, undated).

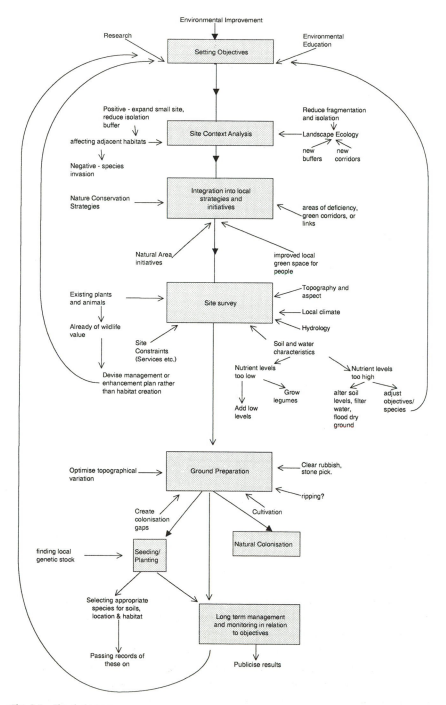

Fig. 2.1 The design process.

Other important objectives will include amenity, environmental education, issues of safety and access, and proximity to people. The need for rapid establishment of vegetation to give a green cover for visual reasons (which will coincidentally reduce eventual diversity through too much competitive growth) and an aesthetically pleasing and interesting habitat and site will also play an important role in the design process. In such situations, the design itself will benefit from public consultation and local involvement. A number of habitat creation schemes, and associated research into techniques and designs, have had, as one of their objectives, the provision of mitigation or compensation to reduce the impact of particular development projects. Although such habitat creation cannot fully replace the complexity and historical value of long-established communities, it has a value in contributing to new areas for nature conservation.

Some of the earliest attempts at creating new swards were principally for research purposes (e.g. Wells *et al.* 1981). The various factors influencing habitat creation are still far from fully understood, so incorporating research and monitoring into a variety of schemes can only assist future projects, provided, of course, that the results are made available to others.

Site context

In most instances, the site is earmarked before a project begins. However, where there is choice, an analysis of the context of the wider area would be constructive. First, it is productive to consider the landscape ecology of an area: the pattern, linkages, relative size, and dispersion of existing habitat patches of different types. A knowledge of habitat quality and of the principles of landscape ecology (see for example: Griffith 1995; Vos and Opdam 1993) would identify the more valuable patches and the priorities for establishing new habitats. For instance, if there is a scatter of widely dispersed small woods with a good hedgerow network and little else, or fragments of heathland, then the best approach might be to enlarge some of the smaller patches. In other circumstances, establishing new patches or linkages could be more beneficial. Some options are shown in Fig. 2.2.

Expanding existing small habitat patches will provide an important buffer and reduce the edge effect, which tends to dilute the core species characteristic of the habitat and introduce many catholic, non-specialist ones, as shown by Webb and Hopkins (1984) in heathlands and Butcher *et al.* (1981) for woodland birds, at least in the United States. In such situations, reducing fragmentation results in a reduction of the edge-to-area ratio.

Adding new habitat patches could involve, for example, creating new ponds to fill in 'gaps' in a pond cluster, thus assisting connectivity between subpopulations of amphibians and other animals. If, for instance, great crested

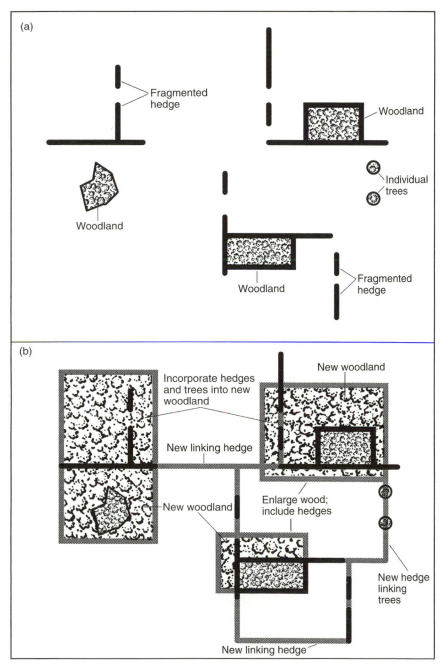

Fig. 2.2 Enhancing the ecological landscape: (a) before habitat creation; (b) after habitat creation.

newts (*Triturus cristatus*) form metapopulations and travel, on average, between 250 m and 500 m from a pond (Oldham 1994; Oldham and Nicholson 1986), then creating new ponds suitable for this species within a cluster of other ponds could assist in population spread, provided the habitat in between is suitable.

How the site might fit into the landscape ecology of its surroundings needs analysis, so that the most appropriate habitat to establish can be identified. A survey might reveal that the site already supports valuable species, so a habitat enhancement scheme might be most appropriate. It is important not to decide on a habitat that could create problems for adjacent ones that are already valuable. For example, establishing woodland adjacent to ungrazed heathland can result in the unwanted colonization of trees into the dwarf-shrub heath. In addition, an inappropriate habitat choice could provide a barrier to species that need to disperse across adjacent areas.

The site context analysis needs to be carried out by an ecologist knowledgeable about and sensitive to the kinds of habitats, species, and dispersion patterns that occur in the area.

There is also the opportunity at the planning stage to integrate the habitat creation into local strategies and initiatives. Many local authorities have developed nature conservation, green, or landscape strategies. Most strategies not only describe the habitats of value in their areas and set out policies for wildlife protection and enhancement, but also outline opportunities for creative conservation. Wildlife corridors, green wedges or chains, linkages, and areas of deficiency are variously identified. In many instances, the green wedges are fragmented and in need of strengthening (as in the Gloucester City and the Tyne and Wear Nature Conservation Strategies), whereas areas of deficiency, as adopted by the London Ecology Unit, are those where people have no local access to green sites. With urban decay and regeneration, there are real opportunities to introduce wild space into these areas. Reference to English Nature's developing Natural Areas profiles or the Countryside Commission's Landscape Character project would also assist in selecting the most appropriate habitats to emphasise local character.

Once a site is selected, further analysis of its context is important, that is, its location in relation to the needs of people requires appraisal. If enjoyment by local people is to be one of the key objectives for the site's establishment, practical considerations (such as the likely numbers of visitors expected, the seasonal variation in use, access points, possible trampling problems, and the visitors' desires, fears, expectations, and activities on the site) all need review, preferably through public participation and consultation. At the same time, any possible problems of vandalism, rubbish dumping, or other corollaries of human presence can be identified. All these factors will play a part in the eventual site design.

Site survey

A site survey is essential prior to habitat selection and design. Such a survey does not need to be detailed or expensive. The following are the essential features to identify:

1. General topography and aspect, including whether slopes are accessible to different machines or not.

2. Site hydrology—not forgetting that an area that is dry in summer can be waterlogged or flooded in winter.

3. Local climate—just identify the extremes, such as frost hollows, sunny sheltered areas, exposed ridges, etc.

4. Existing plants and animals on the site and their current nature conservation value, including a map of the main vegetation types showing the different plant communities.

5. Soil or water characteristics in terms of pH, main nutrients, hardness (of water), and any potentially limiting feature (e.g. heavy metals, salinity, compaction of soil).

6. Adjacent habitat types, species composition, and nature conservation value.

7. Any site constraints, such as underground services or overhead power-lines.

Some of the above are self-evident and need no further explanation, but an understanding of others is of critical importance and merits amplification.

Topography and hydrology

A variable topography and hydrology on a site will provide for equally vari-able and, therefore, probably more interesting habitats. Such variation could include shallow and deeper soils, rock outcrops, wet, damp, and dry areas, and warm or shaded slopes, each of which would develop a different flora and fauna over time. If the topography is being created, then the diversity can be designed, but it does need to be compatible with future public use and man-agement. In general, damp and wet areas need to be emphasized, not drained away.

Local climate

It is not vital to collect local statistics on climate; however, where available, they can be very useful. In general, it is profitable to talk to local gardeners on the character of the area. Are late springs, summer droughts, frost pockets, biting easterly winds, or storms a feature of the area? Such local knowledge is invaluable for selecting suitable species and habitats.

Soils and water

The failure of many habitat creation schemes can be attributed to a lack of understanding of the soils and water characteristics of site (Parker 1995). There are a number of aspects to consider.

Nutrient status

The nutrient levels in soils or water determine the productivity of plants and whether particular species become dominant or not. An understanding of Grime's stress-tolerance model (Grime 1979; Grime et al. 1988) will assist in an appreciation of the ecological issues involved. In short, Grime developed a model that explained the relative competitive ability of plants. The basic features of this are shown in Box 2.1. Although the extremes of Grime's triangular model are described, it is more instructive to think of these as end-points along a continuum of variation. Thus, stresses can vary in their severity, and disturbance in its scale and regularity. Grime et al. (1988) show the location in the model of a wide variety of grassland species, which is particularly useful when considering soil fertility issues.

In the average British environment, where extremes of pH, climate, etc., are less important, soil fertility will be the main determinant of the capacity for plant productivity. This, linked to soil depth and hydrology, will therefore be the chief factor dictating the community composition of the habitat being created.

It is fundamental to Grime's theory, and clearly observable in the field, that soils where competitive species dominate are characterized by a low plant diversity and richness (see Box 2.2). These are typical on deep or disturbed soils with adequate levels of available nutrients for vigorous plant growth. If these soils are compared with those found in long-established semi-natural habitats such as calcareous grassland, ancient woodland, marshes, or dwarf-shrub health, as Gough and Marrs (1990) and Marrs (1993) have done, then the low levels of nutrients, especially of phosphorus, are notable (as evident in Table 2.1).

It is important to note that many competitive species are not completely excluded from stressed environments, but occur often as isolated plants in poor condition. If the stress factors are reduced, they rapidly expand and become dominant. This can be seen in diverse grasslands where management ceases and the more competitive species gradually take over at the expense of the stress tolerators (Grime et al. 1988; Marrs 1993).

The implications for habitat creation are clear. If a diverse, rich plant com-

Box 2.1 Competitors, stress tolerants, and ruderals

Grime (1979) and Grime *et al.* (1988) identify two main factors that limit a plant's ability to grow: stress and disturbance. Stress might include low fertility, low light, drought, anaerobic conditions, high exposure, 'thin' soils, or other factors. Disturbance may be small or large-scale, occasional or regular and could be imposed on a stressed or un-stressed environment. Ploughing a field or weeding a flower bed regularly are obvious signs of disturbance, but molehills, flooding and scouring by streams, land slippage, grazing, and trampling all provide bare ground at different scales, seasonality, and regularity.

Plants have generally failed to develop a strategy to cope with high levels of disturbance combined with extreme environmental stress. However, with little or no stress or disturbance, a competitive strategy has evolved characterized by a peak of rapid, robust, vigorous summer growth and producing a high, dense canopy of leaves and extensive lateral spread above and below ground.

On dry, fertile soils, the favourable conditions are exploited by competitive plants such as rosebay willowherb (*Chamerion angustifolium*), creeping thistle (*Cirsium arvense*), and couch grass (*Elymus repens*). On wet soils, the equivalents are common reed (*Phragmites australis*), great hairy willowherb (*Epilobium hirsutum*), and purple loosestrife (*Lythrum salicaria*) whilst, in water, reed-mace (*Typha latifolia*) and reed sweet-grass (*Glyceria maxima*) are characteristic competitors. It is more difficult to identify the equivalent species in a wood since, under the tree canopy, light is reduced and therefore acts as a stress factor, whilst the trees and shrubs, being woody and long-lived, have a different growth pattern. Nevertheless, the faster, more competitive growth of sycamore (*Acer pseudoplatanus*), many willows (*Salix* spp.), and elder (*Sambucus nigra*), relative to species like hazel (*Corylus avellana*) and holly (*Ilex aquifolium*) is easy to detect.

In contrast to the competitive environment, stressed conditions are exploited by plants that are characterized by an evergreen, perennial, long-lived, slow-growing habit. They flower and set seed irregularly, and take a long time to establish; the longevity of individual roots and leaves is considerable. Typical examples include the common cottongrass (*Eriophorum angustifolium*) on wet peat, stonecrops (*Sedum* spp.) on walls and cliff ledges, and sheep's fescue (*Festuca ovina*) in grasslands. Ruderal plants (the nomads of the plant world) have developed a strategy best suited to respond to disturbance. They are typically short-lived ephemerals, annuals, or biennials, which establish and complete their life cycle rapidly, producing quantities of well-dispersed seeds. Typical species include chickweed (*Stellaria media*), groundsel (*Senecio vulgaris*), sow thistles (*Sonchus* spp.), and grasses like sterile brome (*Bromus sterilis*) and black twitch (*Alopecurus myosuroides*).

munity is the desired objective, whether on soils or in water, the nutrient levels must be low and competitive species must be constrained. Phosphorus seems to be the key nutrient in soils, nitrogen being less critical (provided that the availability of phosphorus is low). However, the situation is not as simple as

Fig. 2.3 Hogweed, a potentially competitive plant, constrained by stress on a limestone quarry floor dominated by stress tolerating plants.

Box 2.2 Diversity and richness

It is important to differentiate between diversity and richness. Richness simply relates to the overall list of species without taking their relative abundance into consideration, whereas diversity embraces the latter. In calcareous grassland, an average of 30–40 plant species/m² over a whole enclosure illustrates a high diversity; in contrast, a field containing 40 species, of which one is dominant and the rest scarce, with only 2–3 species/m² on average, may be rich but is not diverse. Richness and diversity are relative to a community type, with some types, such as well-managed chalk grasslands, being naturally more diverse and rich than others, such as dwarf-shrub heath.

---

this. More research is needed on the relationship between different soil nutrients and plant diversity, particularly in relation to habitat creation. 'Low' levels need to be more clearly defined for different plant communities, and the relative importance of the various nutrients needs evaluation. The

Table 2.1
Comparative levels of main soil nutrients in different situations

		Extractable phosphorus (ppm)	Potassium (ppm)	Mineralizable nitrogen (ppm)	Total nitrogen (%)
Arable					
Clay[1] (not cropped for 10 years)		22.8 (range 7–62; $n = 20$)	386.7 (range 225–860; $n = 20$)	ND	ND
Sandy[2]	Site 1	12	ND	24	ND
	Site 2	293	ND	66	ND
Limestone[2]		16	ND	132	ND
Semi-natural grassland					
Clay[1]		4.7 (range 3–6; $n = 3$)	125.7 (range 102–147; $n = 3$)	ND	ND
Neutral[3]		56.6 ($n = 3$)	174.4 ($n = 5$)	ND	0.85 ($n = 5$)
Calcareous[3]		15.7 (range 6.5–37; $n = 12$)	226.5 (range 110–620; $n = 20$)	ND	0.67 range 0.3–1.44 ($n = 12$)
Limestone[2]	Site 1	6	1010	97	ND
	Site 2	3	1130	162	
Sandy[2]	Site 1	13	250	34	ND
	Site 2	5	462	28	

[1] Standsted Airport, unpublished data collected by PA.
[2] Various sites given in Gough and Marrs 1990.
[3] Various sites given in Duffey *et al.* 1974.
ND, not determined.

interaction of soil types, productivity, and management is also important. Furthermore, the extent to which careful management can mask fertility is not clear.

Results from the available research suggest that if high diversity and richness are objectives, then desirable nutrient levels in soils for habitat creation should be within the following range: total nitrogen, <10000 ppm (<0.1%); extractable phosphorus (P), 0–45 ppm; extractable potassium (K), 0–400 ppm; and extractable magnesium (Mg), 0–100 ppm (Highways Agency 1993).

For P, K, and Mg, the figures are equivalent to the soil fertility indices of 0–3 used by ADAS. However, the figures given in Table 2.1, and the habitat creation attempts described in the following chapters, suggest that significantly lower levels of phosphorus (and probably potassium) would be more suitable.

However, the availability of the nutrients and of a plant's ability to utilize them also depends on the pH and the hydrology. The limed and unlimed plots in the long-term park grass experiments at Rothampsted (e.g. Tilman *et al.* 1994) show that, with constant nutrient levels, differences in pH result in clear differences in species composition. Differences in soil moisture and water-logging, irrespective of nutrient levels, would also determine the botanical composition, as a product of the differences in the nitrogen cycle (de-nitrification being a major factor in waterlogged soils).

Similarly, the chemical character, especially the nutrient content, of water can have a profound effect on the nature and diversity of aquatic systems. The trophic status of a water body, as reflected in levels of total phosphorus and total nitrogen will significantly control its plant and animal assemblages. For this reason, the relative levels of phosphorus and nitrogen have to be taken into account when setting objectives for a wetland habitat creation scheme; the levels of these elements would characterize the processes that would occur in the wetland and therefore the habitats that would be supported. The relationship between the trophic status of lakes and nutrients is described in Table 2.2. In addition, Vollenweider (in Mason 1991) has identified the permissible loading levels for phosphorus and nitrogen in water bodies of different depths (Table 2.3).

Although an understanding of the nutrient levels of water is essential in order to establish the habitat framework for a wetland scheme, the situation is further complicated by the effect of other factors, such as the ratios between nitrogen and phosphorus and the pH level of the water. However, as will be described in Chapter 10, when creating ponds or lakes using a water resource with a nutrient status that may compromise the habitat creation objective, it may be possible to construct the wetland so that part of it provides a buffer or attenuation zone for the incoming water supply.

Nutrient levels in river channels also have an effect on habitat structure (Haslam 1992; Ward *et al.* 1994). However, in all wetland systems, the physical (e.g. sediment size, water levels), hydrological characteristics (e.g. flow rates, depths of flooding) and bio-geochemical processes (e.g. plant uptake of nutrients, biomass production) have an equally significant influence on the potential structure and quality of created habitats.

In non-open water type wetlands, such as fens and mires, a complex inter-relationship exists between nutrient levels and availability, and the chemical processes are determined by the stability of water levels, redox potential, and pH (Hughes and Heathwaite 1995). For example, as soils become progressively waterlogged and reduction processes begin to dominate, phosphorus may be released into a soluble, available form, whilst nitrogen is lost through de-nitrification. Such understanding can be critical in evaluating the

Table 2.2

Characteristics of lake trophic status

Trophic category	Mean total phosphorus (mg m⁻³)	Mean yearly chlorophyll (mg m⁻³)	Chlorophyll maxima (mg m⁻³)	Mean yearly Secchi disc transparency (m)	Secchi disc transparency minima (m)	Oxygen (percentage saturation[1])
Ultra-oligotrophic	4.0	1.0	2.5	12.0	6.0	<90
Oligotrophic	10.0	2.5	8.0	6.0	3.0	<80
Mesotrophic	10–35	2.5–8	8–25	6–3	3–1.5	40–89
Eutrophic	35–100	8–25	25–75	3–1.5	1.5–0.7	40
Hypertrophic	100.0	25.0	75.0	1.5	0.7	10

[1] Percentage saturation in bottom waters; this will vary depending on the mean depth of the water body. However, there can also be pronounced mesolimnetic oxygen maxima or minima depending on thermal stratification.
Source: OECD (1982).

Table 2.3
Vollenweider's permissible loading levels for total nitrogen (N) and total phosphorus (P)

Mean depth (m)	Permissible loading (g/m²/year)		Dangerous loading (g/m²/year)	
	N	P	N	P
5	1.0	0.07	2.0	0.13
10	1.5	0.10	3.0	0.20
50	4.0	0.25	8.0	0.50
100	6.0	0.40	12.0	0.80
150	7.5	0.50	15.00	1.00
200	9.0	0.60	18.00	1.20

Source: Mason 1991.

appropriateness of a site and in anticipating initial changes to soil and water chemistry that may occur in the early phases of wetland habitat creation.

Dealing with nutrients

If the soil or water contains undesirably high nutrient levels for the selected habitat, there are four possible options. First, the plants can be carefully selected to be competitive and compatible. The resulting plant diversity would not be high, but with careful, sustained, long-term management, an attractive and useful community for nature conservation can be developed. It is worth thinking positively and considering the value of vigorous plant communities for small mammals (and therefore their predators), for litter- and ground-dwelling invertebrates, and for birds that need cover, rather than the species of sparse, open, flower-spangled swards. Gilbert (1991) has shown how vigorous tall-herb communities on a top-soiled motorway embankment can survive for at least 20 years without management. Working with existing nutrient levels is an ecologically sound option, since manipulating soil fertility may be expensive in terms of money and resources.

A second alternative for nutrient rich soils is to flood the area and plant iris (*Iris pseudacorus*), purple loosestrife (*Lythrum salicaria*), meadow-sweet (*Filipendula ulmaria*), bur-reed (*Sparganium erectum*), meadow rue (*Thalictrum flavum*), or whatever is locally native instead. It is ironic that the tall, competitive herbs of dry soils, such as rosebay willowherb (*Chamerion angustifolium*) or stinging nettle (*Urtica dioica*) are often labelled as weeds, whereas the same competitive growth in marsh and emergent species is seen as desirable.

Fig. 2.4 Applying sulphur to reduce soil alkalinity in the Brecklands (ADAS copyright).

A third, and often more difficult, solution is to reduce the nutrient levels or their availability. There may be time to wait for natural leaching in soils to reduce available phosphorus. The length of time will depend on the levels and the natural leaching rates in the soil. Gough and Marrs (1990) suggest depletion rates in clay soils under grass of 1–3 ppm/year; in sandy soils, rates are possibly as high as 20 ppm/year. They also calculated that phosphorus levels in a recently grassed field might fall from 19.6 ppm to the 5.4 ppm of an older grassland in 5–15 years. This process can be accelerated by depletion cropping—that is, by using arable crops known to be high nutrient demanders (e.g. rye) and even enhancing their growth with nitrogen fertilizers to augment their phosphorus uptake (Marrs 1993). This approach has been successful in reducing phosphorus after 5 years of cropping on arable land at Minsmere, Suffolk (Owen *et al*. 1996), and Marrs (1985) used it for the same purpose for 2 years on Roper's Heath, also in East Anglia.

Excessive acidification or liming is another way of reducing nutrient availability in soils. However, a pH over 8 or under 4.5 needs to be maintained by adding lime or sulphur, respectively. Experiments under way to reduce pH for the creation of heathland (see Chapter 6) have been successful at Minsmere using bracken litter or sulphur (Owen *et al*. 1996), and sulphur has been applied for the same purpose in the Brecks, East Anglia (Chambers and Cross 1996).

An alternative way of reducing nutrients is to remove the topsoil (and, hopefully, sell it—some schemes have paid for themselves in this way). It is important to note that soil stripping will require planning permission from the Local Authority, as described in the *Code of good agricultural practice for the protection of soil* (MAFF 1993). Soil stripping could also entail considerable lorry movements if the whole profile were removed. Any stripping needs careful assessment of nutrient loadings at different soil horizons to decide on the amount to remove. Note also that, to an engineer, the topsoil is usually the whole profile down to the C horizon, whereas to biologists, the topsoil is normally only the A horizon. Contract documents must make this clear!

When dealing with wetland systems where continuous nutrient input is a problem, filtration, using a constructed wetland or just a patch of reeds or reedmace, may be the answer (see Chapter 10). However, it may be possible to use an understanding of soil processes to encourage the removal of phosphorus through controlled flooding of an area. When a field becomes water-logged, the saturated conditions lead to a low redox potential in the soil (i.e. reducing as opposed to oxidizing conditions). This encourages phosphorus to dissolve and thereby become potentially mobile in the soil. Should there be the capacity to control the nature and extent of this waterlogging, it may be possible to flush or leach out the phosphorus using the hydrological gradients created by drainage of the site. This is a complex process which would only be adopted if sufficient information was available about the soil chemistry and hydrology. This flushing process does not remove the phosphorus, it simply moves it downstream to another habitat.

The fourth and final option is to find another site!

pH

pH plays a major part in determining the plant communities that can be established. It may vary significantly over a site, and must be tested—even approximate measurements using a cheap gardener's test kit are better than none. Opportunities to establish communities typical of either acidic or highly calcareous conditions need to be sought and grasped—habitat creation currently focuses too much on mesotrophic communities, although several large-scale projects are currently helping to address this imbalance, particularly in the creation of heathland (see for example: Davey *et al.* 1992; Evans 1992; Chapter 6).

Hydrology

The general aim should be to maximize the benefits of hydrological variation on the site. This might depend on creative engineering, and does not need to concentrate on the extremes of wet (ponds, ditches) or dry, but to include both seasonally and permanently wet ground—again, the neglected communities.

Wet areas on a site are a bonus and should be carefully fostered (as described in Chapter 10).

Ground preparation

Whether natural colonization, seeding, or planting are to be utilized, the ground usually needs some sort of preparation. Again, homogeneity should be avoided, but sensitivity to future management requirements, types of machines to be used, and desired growth rates will dictate the need for different forms of ground preparation. The obvious requirements might include site clearance of rubbish and other alien materials, stone picking, ripping, and seed bed preparation.

The first may be too obvious to mention, but inadequate contract supervision during a project can leave unwanted wire, lumps of concrete, or metal waste, which can result in expensive damage to cutting machines. It may be worthwhile retaining some rubble, etc., rather than removing it all, since it can harbour important invertebrate populations and amphibians (Lott and Daws 1995). Stone picking to various minimum sizes is standard practice, but before valuable money is allocated, consider its need. On several mountain-top restoration schemes, the stones, some quite substantial, in the respread topsoil–subsoil mixture were purposely retained to hold down the soil and

Fig. 2.5 Stones left on the surface on the summit of Great Dun Fell (Cumbria) helped stabilise the soils during seeding operations.

successfully helped the seed and young plants survive the rigours of wind and rain (Fig. 2.5). This was acceptable as rough grazing was the future planned land use.

For successful tree and shrub growth on compacted soils, ripping is essential (Buckley and Insley 1984). This needs to be deep (>45 cm), to be carried out under dry conditions, and to consist of two passes of a tyned machine at right angles, a task which is difficult on steep slopes, especially when these are engineered structures. However, the poor growth of trees on such sites is evidence of the need.

Where herbaceous vegetation is required, and shallow rooting plants are available, ripping may not be necessary and, indeed, may provide a welcome stress in a too fertile environment. Any resulting reduction in the speed of establishment and subsequent growth would foster greater diversity over time as more species could colonize more slowly into the gaps. On the other hand, where a plant cover is required quickly for reasons of, say, stabilization, compromises will need to be made. Perhaps parts of the area could be left unripped.

Soil preparation for seeding is essential, although this may not always mean the fine tilth generally prescribed. Whatever the soil type, good cultivation (using, for example, power harrows) is as important for habitat creation as for establishing a crop. However, there are exceptions. On some particularly inhospitable slopes, seeds tend to establish where moisture is trapped in small gullies or cracks, and it may be useful to focus on creating a small-scale microtopography, possibly along the contour, to minimize erosion. In other situations, where one community is to be changed to another, sowing may be into existing vegetation. Details of techniques are described in the relevant chapters, but the essence is always to provide suitable colonization gaps for long enough for the new species to germinate and establish.

Problems may arise if seed bed preparation takes place well before seeding; this may allow a cover of other species to colonize first. The standard approach is to spray this off before seeding, but it is worth identifying whether the plants involved would add value to the scheme or not. If there is prodigious growth of undesirable species (only likely on fertile soils with an abundant seed bank), herbicides or further cultivation may be needed to remove the competition. However, on many sites, the adventists could be highly desirable or, at least, neutral and add variety and protective micro-habitats to the scheme. In this case, the decision would have to be taken whether to harrow lightly to knock them back temporarily, or to seed directly into them. The important point is that these options are worthy of consideration and effective, given the appropriate circumstances. This makes contract specifications more difficult, of course, but habitat creation is most successful when working with nature.

On steep banks and quarries, cultivation will not be feasible, and hydroseeding the easiest means of sowing. Both substrates, however, need a similar approach, which involves manipulating the slopes or faces so that they can support plant growth while, at the same time, avoiding application of over-fertile materials, such as sewage sludge, which encourage nettle patches rather than a diverse sward. The restoration blasting research work (Gagen and Gunn 1988) has shown the way forward in the Derbyshire limestone quarries where, by selective blasting, new tors, outcrops and scree slopes can be formed to develop the character of the nearby dale slopes. Establishing an appropriate wild flower mix subsequently onto a subsoil base selectively placed on the new slopes, gives the desired patchy green cover. A similar re-creation of pertinent geological features is adopted on some steep road cuttings, with plant growth on soils on ledges and in fissures.

Choosing the right plants

With the site and its preparation decided, selection of species is the next task. Assuming that natural regeneration/colonization is not adequate (see Chapter 3), there is a strong case for trying to establish new plant communities that resemble as closely as possible the vestiges of the semi-natural communities in the area. English Nature's Natural Areas initiative or the Countryside Commission's Character Area project (or their equivalents in other countries) provide the contextual framework that then has to be refined to suit the soils and other site characteristics. The aim should be to enhance the distinctiveness and identity of the area, using locally native species and stock, and to avoid the overwhelming tendency towards homogeneity, which can be seen in so many landscape schemes. As Nan Fairbrother (1970) so clearly put it:—

> We ought to know where we are in the natural landscape. We should be conscious of the difference between the Midland clays, or the chalk, or the farming loams, or the sand and gravel country, or the sterner rocks of the uplands. Not only could the vegetation change with the different types of landscape, but so could the style of design and maintenance for different types of landscapes, so could the land-forms of different soils, and in cuttings the rock itself be left exposed.

The extent to which this aim can be achieved is questioned by Scott (1995) who points out that creative conservation projects cannot be directly compared with the long-established sites of high nature conservation value. They are different; a product of a different time under different conditions.

Species selection should be based on the soil fertility as the lowest common denominator—only those species capable of competing successfully in the ambient conditions and under the expected management regime will survive. If local character is used to identify the appropriate species, locally native ones, suited to the geology, hydrology, and soils, must be chosen. The British flora has developed in relative isolation from the Continent for 7000 years.

ASH/HAZEL MIX

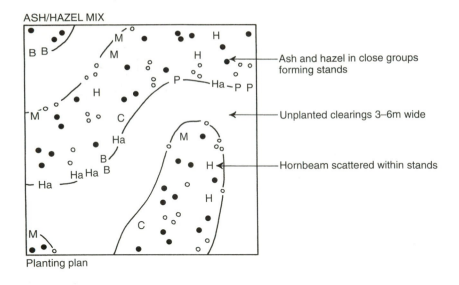

Ash and hazel in close groups forming stands

Unplanted clearings 3–6m wide

Hornbeam scattered within stands

Planting plan

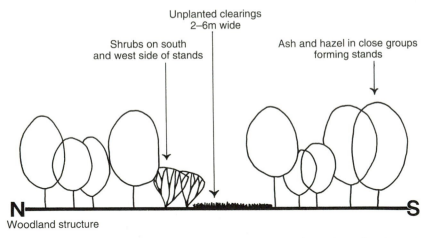

Unplanted clearings
2–6m wide

Shrubs on south
and west side of stands

Ash and hazel in close groups
forming stands

N   S

Woodland structure

Fig. 2.6 A woodland mix used on base-rich clays at Stansted Airport designed to reflect the nearby ancient woodland tree and shrub community.

Many species are genetically distinct from their counterparts on the Continent and both behave quite distinctly and are adapted to local conditions. Indeed, there is evidence of much smaller scale genetic variation and adaptation (Worrell 1992) and it may be possible sometimes to tap this resource.

Many species have a very clearly defined national and local distribution, and much effort has been expended in recording this. The restricted distributions of some species, such as stemless thistle (*Cirsium acaule*), bird cherry (*Prunus padus*), and dogwood (*Cornus sanguinea*), have been attributed to

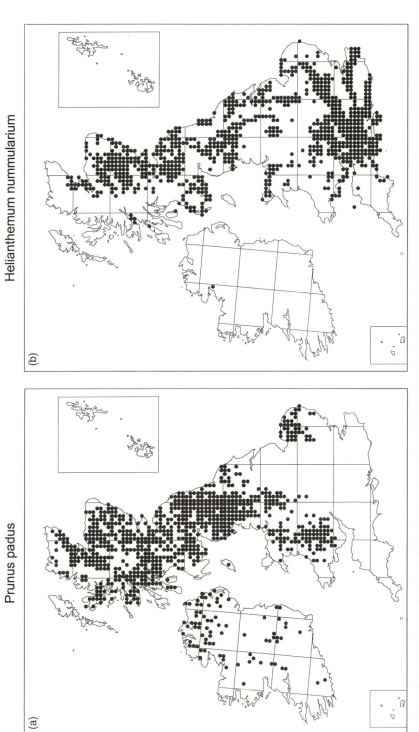

Fig. 2.7 Distribution in Great Britain and Ireland of (a) bird cherry (*Prunus padus*) and (b) common rockrose (*Helianthemum nummularium*) showing distinctive patterns related to climate or base-rich soils.

climatic factors working either through high rainfall inducing grey mould (*Botrytis*), and hence decreasing viable fruit production, or drought inducing wilting (Jarvis 1960; Piggott 1974). Other distributions are clearly related to soil pH, such as rockrose (*Helianthemum nummularium*) and horseshoe vetch (*Hippocrepis comosa*), although, as might be expected, several interrelated factors are usually involved. For many species, however, geographical patterns are unexplained; for this reason, it seems sensible, for the most part, to copy them. To do so both ensures long-term viability of a population and also local distinctiveness, thus fulfilling Nan Fairbrother's dream. This approach is doubly important in order to protect national distribution patterns and avoid introducing species into the 'wrong' environment where they may spread in an undesirable fashion or hybridize with close relatives.

It may be straightforward selecting locally native species, but it can be difficult to obtain them. First, it is advisable not to buy ready-made mixes—these do not generally show any affinity with national vegetation types nor with local communities, nor do they show any geographical variation, although some are moving in this direction. Furthermore, it is essential to obtain native British stock and to avoid agricultural, non-British and amenity variants. Many agricultural legumes, for example, grow tall and vigorously. Take the robust variety of bird's-foot trefoil; it is a pale-flowered, short-lived perennial, quite unlike its wild counterpart. Furthermore, the wild form seems to attract common blue butterflies (*Polyommatus icarus*) much more successfully than the non-native strains. Obtaining locally native stock is even more important adjacent to existing high-value sites.

Obtaining native British stock of trees and shrubs can be a major problem. Such stock need to be ordered in advance, and is perhaps best grown from locally collected seed. This is often feasible for community based projects where the county wildlife trust and local schools grow material for projects, but it is more problematic for larger schemes.

There is also a potential issue concerning whether to establish a wide range of species suited to a community, or to leave out the rare ones. In general, the consensus is to establish locally common species, but where plants are clearly rare as a result of habitat destruction rather than for other, often poorly understood reasons, it may be desirable to reintroduce them. However, advice from the relevant county wildlife trust, the Botanical Society of the British Isles, or an equivalent body, should preface such a step. Information on the species used and those that establish should be passed on to the local biological records centre.

In general, nurse species are unnecessary, both in herbaceous and in woody communities. They often cause later management problems, and are not usually recommended in grassland any more (Chapter 4). However, it may be necessary to use nurse species in extreme situations where growth is very slow. For example, various grasses can assist in providing a suitable environment for slow-growing species like heather to establish (Chapter 6), or in montance areas (Chapter 7) or derelict land such as worked-out quarries (Chapter 4).

Once the species have been chosen, mixes may well need modification according to their availability and cost. Collecting seed from existing habitats is one possibility.

Long-term management and monitoring

Too often, management requirements are an afterthought, whereas they need consideration at the earliest stages of project planning. The availability of management will dictate the habitat types that can be established. Not only do measures need to be identified, but the type of machinery, accessibility of a site, its long-term security of tenure, and, most importantly, a commitment to finance ongoing maintenance all need to be planned.

There are situations where little or no vegetation management will be needed, or at least for some years, but this should be a positive decision rather than a *laissez-faire* result. Most vegetation types will need some kind of attention, on various time scales. Grassland may need regular grazing or cutting, a hay crop may be feasible, and cuttings may require safe disposal. Woodland could require coppicing, pollarding, or thinning, nurse species (if used) will need controlling and, at the very least, physical structures such as fences or groynes, will have to be repaired. A commitment of long-term resources, both funds and labour, is a prerequisite for all habitat creation projects.

It is essential to provide adequate feedback through project appraisal and monitoring to benefit the detailed development of the community, to fine-tune its management, and to apply to new schemes. Habitat creation, after all, is still in its infancy, and project monitoring from ecological, practical, social, and economic viewpoints, which is then not only fed back to the scheme and its supporters, but also widely broadcast, will add to the sum of knowledge on the subject.

3   Promoting natural succession

This is the approach to habitat creation that, where it is appropriate, appeals most strongly to ecologists. In its purest form it entails leaving the site to nature, so that a secondary succession can develop, which involves local plants and animals colonizing by natural dispersal methods. Some control may be exerted over the course succession takes through mowing or grazing, to arrest the development of woodland, but the exact outcome is not known in terms of eventual species composition, structure of the vegetation, or time scale. Not all sites are suitable for such an open-ended approach to design, but increasingly succession is being employed on parts of sites where recreation and wildlife conservation are the proposed end use. As this is a relatively recent approach, many of the mature examples are the product of neglect or failure of the planning system, which has, for example, allowed sites where mineral extraction took place to escape restoration work. A recent questionnaire to mineral planning authorities (Mills *et al.* 1995) revealed a trend in favour of natural colonization as a method of establishing ecological interest, so it is starting to be used as a positive technique.

Despite the existence of numerous examples—for example, a recent survey found that 14% of biological Sites of Special Scientific Interest (SSSIs) had special features resulting from the natural colonization of land that had been subject to mineral working (Mills *et al.* 1995)—there is still considerable apprehension surrounding this technique of re-establishing communities. To help resolve this fear, factors influencing succession need to be identified (so that it is possible to be more predictive) and good examples need to be publicized. The approach is equally relevant for sites with nutrient deficient soil or sites with fertile soil. A classic example can be seen at Rothamsted Experimental Station at Harpenden in Hertfordshire.

In 1882, Sir J. B. Lawes, director of the Experimental Station told the 39th wheat (*Triticum* sp.) crop occupying the top end of Broadbalk Field, 'I am going to withdraw all protection from you, and you must for the future make your own seed bed and defend yourself in the best way you can against the natives, who will do everything in their power to exterminate you' (Lawes 1884). The sequence of events on this fenced 0.2 ha area, now called the Broadbalk Wilderness, has been recorded from time to time (Brenchley and Adam 1915; Hall 1905; Lawes 1895; Thurston 1958; Witts 1964). The last wheat plant

Fig. 3.1 This woodland resulted from natural colonization when a field of beans was left unharvested in 1886. No tree was planted, and the area has never recieved any management. Geescroft Wilderness, Rothamsted, Harpenden, Hertfordshire. (Photo 1995).

was seen in 1886; then, after progressing through a neutral grassland stage, the site was described in 1913 as a dense thicket of trees and shrubs. It is now occupied by mixed deciduous high forest 25 m tall, in which the leading species is ash (*Fraxinus excelsior*), with lesser amounts of oak (*Quercus robur*), sycamore (*Acer pseudoplatanus*), gean (*Prunus avium*), field maple (*Acer campestre*), holly (*Ilex aquifolium*), and hawthorn (*Crataegus monogyna*); ivy (*Hedera helix*) is dominant in the field layer. The composition is still changing as hawthorn and hazel become shaded out.

A larger wilderness area, Geescroft (1.3 ha), was established nearby in 1886 when a field of beans was deliberately left unharvested. Succession here was slower and via a grassland dominated by *Deschampsia cespitosa*, but this site too is now an area of high forest dominated by oak and ash (Fig. 3.1). Inside it is very shady, the floor being littered with dead wood, deep leaf mould, and moss; patches of woodland plants such as enchanter's nightshade (*Circaea lutetiana*), ground ivy (*Glechoma hederacea*), bluebell (*Hyacinthoides non-scripta*), and stinking iris (*Iris foetidissima*) have started to appear.

Kenneth Mellanby, when director of Monkswood Research Station, Huntingdonshire, started a 4 ha wilderness in 1964 by letting a barley field run wild (Mellanby 1968). Monitoring appears to have been minimal but within six years the site had become well colonized by young, even-aged oaks. Today it is a thick wood with an oak canopy at 12–14 m standing over a dense understory of dogwood (*Cornus sanguinea*); the floor is largely bare but there is a lot of dead wood around and it supports thriving populations of deer, moles (*Talpa europaea*), birds, and butterflies. Noteworthy features are its natural appearance, local character, and the abundance of animal life; the botanical composition is sufficiently varied for there to be landmarks such as birch clumps, a bent ash tree, and a large crooked goat willow.

These examples are clear evidence that in lowland Britain areas of land left to themselves revert naturally to broad-leaved woodland. This can happen on a large scale; nearly a sixth of the whole of Surrey turned spontaneously into woodland in the mid-nineteenth century (Rackham 1986), while in the eastern United States an area of farmed land much greater than the British Isles has 'tumbled down' to woodland since 1800. It should be remembered that these secondary woods lack many common herbaceous woodland plants and that they are not always located where a designer or a nature conservationist would like to see them; for example, they may be in a position to invade heathland or chalk downland. It is still beyond the ability of ecologists to predict the composition of secondary woods, except in a general way.

Principal factors controlling succession

Many years ago the North American ecologist Clements (1916) recognized the following subprocesses of succession: (1) initiation (nudation); (2) immigration of new species; (3) establishment; (4) competition; (5) site modification (reaction); and (6) stabilization. Landscape architects normally speed up the process by planting sites so by-passing immigration and establishment, and through careful species selection and management, the influence of stages 3 and 4 are moderated so that invasions and extinctions are minimized. In comparison, techniques that involve natural colonization are slow and less certain as all five stages have to take place (Miles 1979). When deciding whether a site, or parts of a site, are suitable for employing natural colonization as a method of revegetation, the following factors need to be considered.

Nudation

Engineering restoration involves machinery that grades sites out to their final designed land-form, taking care of factors such as stability and drainage. The condition in which a site is left is important regarding the succession. For example, older mineral workings used gunpowder blasting and this process resulted in shattered quarry faces with large quantities of loose stone fragments tipped into spoil banks and a lack of compaction. This provided a varied topography and microclimate and a corresponding range of niches and habitats for wildlife. Colonization proceeded fairly rapidly in such environments, producing a mosaic of communities.

In contrast, modern quarries do not have piles of waste stone, the floors tend to be bare bedding planes, which may remain uncolonized for years as rates of soil formation can be very slow. In general, an uneven surface of loose material that provides good contact between seeds and the substrate (important for water uptake) and an adequate rooting depth of soil with a bulk density of <1.6 promotes the best conditions for a succession to start. So, the condition in which a site is left is crucial to the initial stages. Harrowing or ripping of the surface, if appropriate, can be highly beneficial. For example, Mellanby (1968) noted that in a recently cultivated field adjacent to Monkswood the comparatively light acorn crop of 1964 gave rise to numerous young oaks, while the bumper crop of 1965 encountered harder, unbroken soil and hardly any converted to young trees; the state of the soil surface was more important than the number of acorns.

Migration

Colonization is largely controlled by the propagule pool of seeds, spores, rootstocks, bulbs, and other plant fragments that are available in the surrounding landscape. This has the advantage that local genotypes will be involved and local species assemblages perpetuated. If a site is adjacent to ancient, species-rich vegetation there is every chance of it quickly becoming colonized by ecologically interesting communities; if it is set in arable farmland then there is likely to be an influx only of common weedy species. This is borne out in practice. The vegetation establishing in disused limestone quarries in the Peak District National Park is much more like ancient calcareous grassland than that colonizing Magnesian limestone quarries in the intensively farmed arable plain to the east where there is no longer a suitable reservoir of propagules (Hodgson 1982). An extreme example is Ferriby chalk quarry at the edge of Hull, which after many years still lacks 25 of the commonest chalk colonizers (Davis 1982).

The initial pioneer species of calcareous spoil tend to lack specificity to that habitat; they are common, mobile species with a wide ecological amplitude, such as cock's-foot grass (*Dactylis glomerata*), creeping red-fescue (*Festuca rubra*), Yorkshire-fog (*Holcus lanatus*), rough hawkbit (*Leontodon hispidus*), ragwort (*Senecio jacobaea*), and dandelion (*Taraxacum officinale*), with significant numbers of legumes and annuals. The more demanding species such as orchids, rockrose (*Helianthemum nummularium*), horse-shoe vetch (*Hippocrepis comosa*), salad burnet (*Poterium sanguisorba*), and wild thyme (*Thymus polytrichus*) come in later.

A further striking example of how natural colonization reflects the flora of the surrounding area involves the succession on urban wasteland. This habitat

can develop locally distinctive vegetation in which every stage is characterized by a high proportion of garden escapes, such as snapdragons (*Antirrhinum majus*), lupins (*Lupinus polyphyllus*), golden rod (*Solidago* spp.),
buddleia (*Buddleia davidii*), cotoneasters (*Cotoneaster* spp.), and Swedish
whitebeam (*Sorbus intermedia*) (Gilbert 1989).

The distance over which effective migration can occur has been the subject
of a few investigations (Gibson *et al.* 1987). A 10 ha field in Oxfordshire, which
had been under arable cultivation for over 20 years, was left to revert to grassland under a regime of light sheep grazing. After five years, 43 (of 75) vascular plant species restricted to patches of old calcareous grassland within 2 km
of the site had colonized the field and were spreading. Six had come from a
long way away and one was a national rarity (*Galium pumilum*). Colonization was much faster than had been expected, proceeded downhill against the
prevailing wind, and there was no particular tendency for one type of seed
dispersal to be predominant. Significantly the propagules had originated from
only small remnants of adjacent permanent grassland. This establishes the
mobility of many species. A further study demonstrated that sites can derive
their flora from localities up to 40 km away. Alkaline wastes left by the Leblanc
process in north-west England provide specialized soil conditions that are not
represented nearer than the coast. However, after 80 years a considerable
number of species, including several orchids (Table 3.1) appear to have made
the journey successfully from coastal calcareous dunes (Bradshaw 1983;
Greenwood and Gemmell 1978).

With respect to acid soil conditions, heather (*Calluna vulgaris*), round-
leaved wintergreen (*Pyrola rotundifolia*), and many species of sphagnum moss
have efficient methods of long-distance dispersal. Self fertility is an advantage
to species colonizing over a long distance, as populations can be formed from
a single individual. Examples of self-sterile species, which have a reduced colonizing ability, are heath bedstraw (*Galium saxatile*) on acid sites and quaking
grass (*Briza media*) on calcareous ones. However, a good dispersal capacity
is the key to successful colonization.

Establishment

Once propagules have arrived the next step is establishment. Establishment
involves selection of those species adapted to the chemical and physical conditions of the site. Park (1982) and Skaller (1977), who studied events following the arrival of seeds on the soil surface, suggest that these events rather
than seed input are the major limiting factors in colonization. Physical
processes, such as wind, water, erosion, and frost (which lead to burial and
overturning), caused enormous losses of seed and seedlings in their experimental plots; dyed seeds were noted to move down the soil profile, while des-
iccation, both direct and indirect, was the most frequent cause of seedling

Table 3.1
Species that have colonized alkali waste heaps in Lancashire through
long-distance dispersal (Greenwood & Gemmell 1978; Bradshaw 1983)

Species	Nearest source[†]	Dispersal[*]
Anacamptis pyramidalis	Coast	W
Anthyllis vulneraria	Coast/Mersey	B,A
Blackstonia perfoliata	Coast	W
Briza media	Mersey	W,B,A
Carlina vulgaris	Coast	W
Dactylorhiza fuchsii	Coast/grassland	W
D. incarnata ssp. *coccinea*	Coast	W
D. purpurella	Coast/mosses	W
D. praetermissa	Coast	W
Daucus carota	Coast	B,A
Echium vulgare	Coast	B,A
Erigeron acer	Coast	W
Gymnadenia conopsea	Coast	W
Linum catharticum	Coast	W,B,A
Orchis morio	Mersey valley	W
Orobanche minor	Coast	W
Salix repens ssp. *argentea*	Coast	W
Senecio erucifolius	10 km away	W
Vicia lathyroides	Coast	B,A

* W, wind; B, birds; A, animals.
† Minimum distance from coast, 30–40 km; minimum distance from Mersey valley, 10 km.

mortality, though grazing and predation by insects could also be very damaging. A year after sowing wild marjoram (*Origanum vulgare*) survival was down to 1–3%, losses due to frost-heave having been particularly severe.

Experimental work by Humphries (1982) showed that the rate of establishment of all species could be increased by raising the resource level (water and nutrients) as this enabled the young plants to attain the critical size for survival quickly. Resource levels correlated with the amount of root growth, and the production of the first or second true leaf. Both Park (1982) and Humphries (1982) found that a light mulching with sawdust aided establishment.

Competition and reaction

The end result of succession is normally a very distinctive vegetation, particularly if succession has taken place on subsoil. If the substrate continues to provide stressed conditions the vegetation will remain open and receptive to incoming propagules for many years and it is probable that the site will eventually form a refugium for rare plants (Ratcliffe 1974). Bradshaw (1983, 1984)

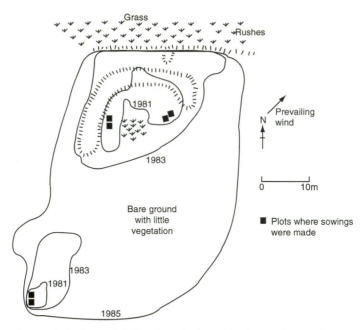

Fig. 3.2 The spread of yellow rattle (*Rhinanthus minor*) on a blast furnace slag wasteheap in Lancashire following sowings made in autumn 1979 (After Ash *et al.* 1994).

has repeatedly emphasized the crucial role that nitrogen plays in controlling succession and has shown how the addition of nitrogenous fertilizers or the entry of legumes speeds it up. This is not always desirable as on infertile soils it promotes rapid closure of the sward. Diversity can also be delayed by the availability of species; when missing taxa such as yellow-wort (*Blackstonia perfoliata*), eye-bright (*Euphrasia nemorosa*), Autumn gentian (*Gentianella amarella*), and yellow rattle (*Rhinanthus minor*) were introduced artificially onto abandoned mineral workings they spread rapidly (Ash *et al.* 1994) (Fig. 3.2).

Kick starting the succession

In practice there has been much trepidation about using natural colonization techniques, which many still regard with suspicion and as only suitable for small sites or parts of sites that are inconspicuous. The public complain if large scars remain visible in the countryside, engineers require fast stabilization of slopes to prevent fines washing off, and planning conditions frequently require money to be spent on revegetation. For reasons such as these, techniques have been developed that 'kick start' the succession by sowing an initial nurse

Table 3.2
The numbers, local rooted frequency, and cover of invading
species on adjacent areas of raw calcareous soil sown with a *Lolium*-based or
Festuca-based grass seed mixture, or left unsown; Longstone Edge, Derbyshire

	Lolium	*Festuca*	*Festuca*	Control
Age of grassland (years)	5	3	3	5
No. of unsown species (per unit area)	30	36	28	26
Rooted frequency of unsown species	10.64	43.16	109.00	7.98
Bare ground (percentage local frequency)	75.60	32.86	27.00	79.50

For method of calculating local and rooted frequency see Lloyd *et al.* (1971).
Source: Gilbert and Wathern (1980).

sward so that sites appears green and are sufficiently stable to satisfy engineering requirements.

The technique appears to have first been used deliberately in 1972 on a visually prominent Carboniferous limestone ridge in the Peak District National Park (Wathern and Gilbert 1979; Gilbert and Wathern 1980). The site, which carried a species-rich calcareous grassland, was being shallowly but extensively worked for fluorspar (fluorite). The resulting scar of raw soil was visible for miles and during heavy rain there was considerable movement of material downhill into hayfields at the foot of the slope. A restoration grass mix of slow growing, stress-tolerant species was formulated based on taxa that were dominant in the surrounding grassland. It was anticipated that if they were sown thinly they would stabilize the soil surface and green the site but the sward would remain sufficiently open to be receptive to incoming propagules.

The mix (*Festuca ovina*, 40%; *F. rubra* var. *fallax*, 20%; *F. rubra* var. *rubra*, 20%; *Agrostis tenuis*, 10%; *Poa pratensis*, 10%) was hand sown at a rate of $12.5\,\mathrm{g\,m^{-2}}$, which was higher than recommended. Results exceeded expectations. The resulting intermediate sward density provided a structure that was highly receptive to the influx of propagules from the surrounding species-rich vegetation, which, after 5 years, the sown areas closely resembled. Table 3.2 compares the floristics of two areas of limestone subsoil that had been sown down to the new mix for three years with an adjacent earlier type of restoration mix—a five-year-old rye-grass sward, and a 5-year-old unsown control plot. It can be seen that the total number of unsown species per unit area in each treatment are similar but the areas reinstated using the *Festuca*, despite being younger, contain up to ten times the density of colonizing species and have much less bare ground.

Many of the species recruited preferentially into the fescue sward were typical of older types of semi-natural calcareous grassland, e.g. carline thistle (*Carlina vulgaris*), eye-bright (*Euphrasia officinalis*), limestone bedstraw

(*Galium sterneri*), fairy flax (*Linum catharticum*), milkwort (*Polygala vulgaris*), salad burnet, wild thyme, and germander speedwell (*Veronica chamaedrys*). Semi-natural grassland surrounding the reinstated areas was presumed to be the seed source. The sown grassland took only six months to become sufficiently dense to be satisfactory on aesthetic and erosion-control grounds and remained open to the natural seed fall for over five years.

An experimental application of compound fertilizer (75 kg ha^{-1}), in addition to accelerating both sward height growth and closure, promoted a massive growth of thistles. The key to the technique is the ability of the thinly sown *Festuca* mix to establish relatively rapidly then close only very gradually to produce a sward of intermediate density that remains receptive to seed fall for many years. It acts as a nurse reducing the normally severe losses at the establishment stage, similar to the sawdust mulch that Park (1982) found increased survival in his experiements. The use of top soil, fertilizer, legumes, or a higher seeding rate would negate this by promoting competitive exclusion.

It is not always easy to get the sowing density right. When a similar grass seed mix was applied to an urban demolition site in Sheffield at *c.* 4 g/m^2, the resulting sward, even though it only achieved 50% cover after two years, was biologically 'closed' and did not allow recruitment of the urban ruderal flora to any significant extent (Table 3.3) (Gilbert 1995). Understanding the soils and the levels of stress, as explained in Chapter 2, is critical to this approach.

The same principles apply to many invertebrates colonizing new areas. Sowing grass seed onto top soil to give quick ground cover is very harmful to open-ground invertebrates, which often start declining once a closed sward has developed (Kirby 1992). Sowing onto subsoil is somewhat better, as there is an 'incipient grassland' stage that lasts for a few years. Best of all are conditions where there is a mosaic of ruderals, bare ground, and grassland plants. This can be achieved by allowing the natural colonization of parts of a site,

Table 3.3
The effect that sowing a grass seed mix on a recently cleared wasteland had on the subsequent establishment of a ruderal flora; vegetation was recorded after 21 months with twelve 1 m^2 quadrats in each area

	Sown	Control (unsown)
Total cover (%)	52	16
Cover ruderal spp. (%)	2	16
Number of ruderal spp. per m^2	2	10
Number of spp. per 12 m^2	17	43

which will prolong the early successional stages on which many invertebrates are dependent. If warranted, regular disturbance can be used to maintain open ground for important invertebrates at selected sites.

Natural reversion

Until the introduction of wild flower mixes (originally called conservation mixes) in the early 1970s, most landscape treatments were extremely simple: if grassland was prescribed, a grass seed mix of four or five species was sown onto top soil; if woodland was required a limited number of trees and shrubs were planted. Given decades, or even centuries, some of these horticultural associations diversify until they come to resemble semi-natural communities. Sown lawns that have never received lime, fertilizer, or herbicide applications illustrate this rather well. A series studied in the Midlands attained maximum diversity, as measured by the Shannon Index, after about 70 years. Then, as leaching of the upper soil horizons caused the pH to fall below *c.* 5.5, the plant species number started to drop (Wathern 1976). Through natural reversion, lawns such as those associated with stately homes, like the 'Capability' Brown lawns at Chatsworth, may come to resemble NVC classes CG 10 (*Festuca ovina–Agrostis capillaris–Thymus praecox: Trifolium repens–Luzula campestris* sub-community) and eventually U 1 (*Festuca ovina–Agrostis capillaris–Rumex acetosella*) with heather, heath-grass (*Danthonia decumbens*), mat-grass (*Nardus stricta*), heath milkwort (*Polygala serpyllifolia*), and tormentil (*Potentilla erecta*) in the turf (Gilbert 1983a, 1983b). The presence of the field woodrush (*Luzula campestris*) indicates that reversion has started and that early colonizers such as daisy (*Bellis perennis*), dandelion, and annual meadow-grass (*Poa annua*) are on the decline.

It is just as well that some sown communities diversify on their own, as the plant material needed to recreate many specialized habitats is never likely to become commercially available. Even with communities such as grasslands, where habitat creation has been a commercial success, the detail has to be filled in by reversion. An example of just how much of the diversity has to be provided by nature has come from a study of the grassland that was sown on the dam at Cow Green Reservoir in Upper Teesdale. Construction was completed in 1970 by spreading a thick layer of heavily limed and fertilized topsoil onto the sloping face of the dam, subsequently one of us (OLG) monitored the site, using permanent 2 m × 2 m quadrats. The prepared soil was sown with an engineers 'stabilization mix' of *Lolium perenne* 25%, *Festuca rubra* 50%, *Phleum pratense* 10%, *Agrostis capillaris* 10%, and *Trifolium repens* 5% at a rate of 15 g m^{-2}, this was then grazed by the local hill sheep. The results from one randomly sited permanent quadrat (4 m^2) shows how over the next 25 years it was colonized by a total of 43 species comprising 24 higher plants, 16

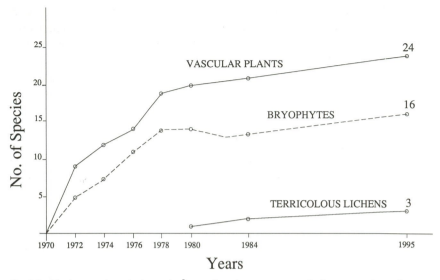

Fig. 3.3 The ingress of species into a 4 m² area of newly sown rye-grass (*Lolium perenne*) sward over 25 years. Cow Green Reservoir, Upper Teesdale, Yorkshire. (Gilbert previously unpublished data).

bryophytes, and 3 lichens (Fig. 3.3). The point to note is that none of the 19 cryptogams and less than a third of the vascular plants are available in commercial quantities, so it would have been impossible to sow the appropriate community at the outset. By chance, 35% (by weight) of the grass seed mix, which was intended to provide a 100% cover, was of unsuitable species, and this resulted in the sward rapidly opening up and becoming receptive to the local seed rain. Turfing using material from the bed of the reservoir would have been the soundest solution ecologically.

Comparative rates of natural reversion

The factors controlling rates of natural reversion are starting to be identified. Regularly mown grassland is slow to accumulate species because mowing promotes tillering and therefore a dense growth of the sown species. Mowing is also selective as only a few growth forms such as mats, rosettes, and the smaller monocotyledons with basal growing points are compatible with close mowing. Grazed grassland is more receptive to incoming propagules; trampling poaches the ground and breaks the sward creating gaps for establishment. This interpretation is supported by observations of recently created species-rich grasslands at Wolverhampton that are either cut or grazed (Atkinson *et al.* 1995). Unmanaged grassland can quickly become unexpectedly diverse as the species flower and set seed freely; this contradicts the commonly held belief that cutting is required to maintain species-rich grassland. An example involving unmown motorway verges is described by Gilbert (1990); here legumes that support themselves on tendrils, Umbelliferae, tall herbs with leafy stems, and the larger grasses are all well suited to survival in long grassland.

The mobility of many freshwater plants and animals was noted by Darwin (1859). As an example, Williams *et al.* (1997) have reported how a mosaic of new pools created on a 2 ha riverside site in Oxfordshire acquired 20% of all Britain's wetland plants and macro-invertebrates within five years of excavation; species richness in the largest pond was as great as that recorded from any pond in the county. The same effect can be seen at Rother Valley Country Park in Yorkshire where all water bodies have some connection with existing surface water. Enhanced rates of colonization also occur on river banks submerged in times of flood. There are, of course, plants and invertebrates that are slow to colonize ponds isolated from other wetlands; such species, if desired, may need to be introduced.

The poor dispersal ability of most woodland ground flora plants is responsible for their slow rate of spread into recently created woodland. Young woodland contains a transient flora of shade-bearing species that are not woodland plants e.g. greater burdock (*Arcticum lappa*), creeping thistle (*Cirsium arvense*), cock's-foot grass, American willowherb (*Epilobium ciliatum*), cleavers (*Galium aparine*), annual meadow grass, chickweed (*Stellaria media*), and stinging nettle (*Urtica dioica*). The first woodland species to arrive are often wind dispersed, such as the broad buckler-fern (*Dryopteris dilatata*) and male fern (*D. filix-mas*), or else ivy and bramble (*Rubus fruticosus*), which are dispersed by birds. Eventually isolated patches of additional common species like herb-robert (*Geranium robertianum*), red campion (*Silene dioica*), and hedge woundwort (*Stachys sylvatica*) appear. Woodland ground flora introduction is a priority in habitat creation schemes, it will otherwise take generations to develop.

Differential rates of colonization have been investigated at the 250 ha Rother Valley Country Park in South Yorkshire where a landscape consisting of several types of grassland, wetland, and woodland was established on an opencast coal site. An analysis of the vegetation 15 years later showed that diversification had taken place at different rates depending on the community and its management. Two aspects of diversity contribute to plant succession. First, with time, additional species invade so the 'species component' rises; secondly, the frequency of species increases and becomes more even as dominance by a limited number of aggressive taxa with high growth rates is lost. These two factors ('evenness of spread' and 'species diversity') can be combined into the Shannon Weiner diversity index (Greig-Smith 1983), which usually lies between 0.5 (early successional stages) and 3.5 (in older, semi-natural communities). Table 3.4 gives Shannon Weiner values for a range of

Table 3.4
Shannon Weiner diversity index scores for a range of 15-year-old plant communities and a relic grazed grassland over 50 years old, all at Rother Valley Country Park, South Yorkshire

Community	No. of quadrats	Shannon Weiner score
Regularly mown grassland	20	1.61
Unmown grassland	20	1.90
Pasture	20	2.00
River bank	20	2.30
Relic pasture	20	2.43

Data provided by C. Palmer.

these communities at Rother Valley Country Park and other opencast coal sites in South Yorkshire. Slowest to diversify are mown grasslands, followed by unmown/ungrazed grasslands, then grazed grasslands, while fastest of the communities investigated are river banks. From observations made elsewhere it is clear that woodland is the slowest of all to diversify, while aquatic habitats such as streams, pond margins, and salt marshes are among the fastest. These comparisons give some guidance as to where effort should be expended during habitat creation projects.

The technique in action

A number of organizations have declared their intention to use natural colonization to recreate habitats that have been lost. For example, English Nature has suggested the following minimum targets for coastal habitat recreation over the next 20 years: sand dunes, 240 ha; salt marsh, 2750 ha; intertidal flats, 10 000 ha; shingle structures, 200 ha; saline lagoons, 120 ha; maritime cliff top grassland, 150 ha; and coastal heathland, 50 ha (Pye and French 1993). The only satisfactory way these specialized habitats can be recreated is by allowing the natural processes of invasion to provide the flora and fauna, though this will need to be combined with the manipulation of topography and drainage (see Chapter 8). On a more local scale, one of the objectives of the Peterborough Environment City Trust (1995) is to restore at least two sizable areas (>10 ha) of bare limestone, associated with quarries or road corridors, to limestone grassland through natural colonization, and subsequently to manage these for nature conservation and public access. Woodland is to be expanded in the same manner.

Examples of intent are easier to come by than instances of the technique in action. However, Parish Quarry in Derbyshire is an almost perfect illustration (Fig. 3.4). This 7 ha limestone quarry lies within a National Park and

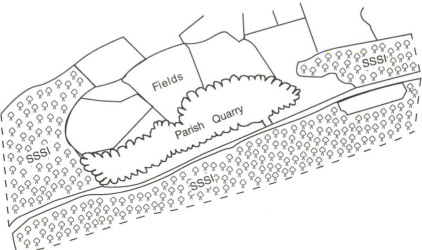

Fig. 3.4 This limestone quarry, which lies in a National Park and is surrounded by SSSIs, has restoration conditions that specify revegetation through natural colonization. Parish Quarry, Derbyshire (Photo 1995).

is surrounded on three sides by woodland SSSIs. When it closed in 1992, discussions between the owners, English Nature, and the National Park Authority led to a considerable simplification of the original restoration conditions, which had included tree and hedge planting, and the sowing of a species-rich wild flower meadow. The agreed strategy was some essential slope stabilization and tidying up, a little tree planting, and the quarry floor was to be surfaced with small chippings. It was then to be left to revegetate through natural colonization, the expectation being that it would eventually be added to the ash–lime woodland SSSIs that surround it. Waste heaps were left uneven to provide a varied environment, and it was decided not to plant small-leaved lime so as to safeguard the genetic purity of the local population. After three years, colonization has proceeded to the point where parts of the floor are turning into a wetland with rushes (*Juncus* spp.) and brooklime (*Veronica beccabunga*) prominent, and species like hairy St John's-wort (*Hypericum hirsutum*) are starting to colonize the wasteheaps.

Now this option has been taken once, other sites are being examined for the same treatment. For example, the adjacent limestone plateau is pock-marked with small-scale operations that involve the reworking of old heavy metal spoil tips for fluorspar. Following extraction, these are now being left to be colonized naturally, particularly where the site is a mosaic of bare and partly vegetated areas. This is very much to the benefit of the metallophyte flora, which includes mosses and lichens that require open conditions (Department of the Environment 1994).

Along the Cornish coast, the National Trust are experimenting with the phased reversion of arable fields to semi-natural grassland. At Predannack, on the Lizard Peninsula, a group of cliff-top fields, previously used for barley and turnips, were thinly sown with *Festuca rubra* 'Dawson' (50 kg ha^{-1}) and Westerwolds rye-grass (10 kg ha^{-1}) in 1988 and thereafter treated as rough grazing land with no use of agrochemicals. Today the vegetation is still very ordinary being dominated by the grasses *Festuca rubra* and *Holcus lanatus* with abundant daisies, dandelions, plantains (*Plantago* spp.), white clover (*Trifolium repens*), and annual meadow grass. This is a result of residual fertility. However, suffocated clover (*Trifolium suffocatum*) and buck's-horn plantain (*Plantago coronopus*) are invading on a broad front from the surrounding grassland and wet areas are turning over to rush–common fleabane (*Juncus–Pulicaria dysenterica*) flushes. More recent reversions have omitted the use of Westerwolds rye-grass and, very recently, the National Trust have experimented with leaving reversion fields unsown. The next logical step would be to try local topsoil stripping to overcome problems of residual fertility and encourage the stripped sites to evolve towards a species-rich squill (*Scilla verna*) grassland.

Frequently heard objections to the natural colonization option are that 'leaving it to nature' takes too long and is too unpredictable. Those who hold this view have probably been unduly influenced by the slow rate of colonization of pyrite-rich coal mine waste, which is inhospitable due its extreme acidity, or by some similar situation. Most soil raw materials are far more benign and develop a visually satisfactory vegetation cover in 2–5 years.

Unpredictability can be an asset. To illustrate this it is necessary to take examples of natural colonization that have taken place by default rather than design. Opencast mining for coal started as an emergency measure during the Second World War and sites were not always restored after abandonment. The old working called Seckar Lane, in the arable lowlands near Wakefield, was never restored as the contractor became bankrupt in 1950. Today it is a most remarkable place. It has turned into a dry heathland dominated by heather and wavy hair-grass (*Deschampsia flexuosa*) with a good range of associates such as crowberry (*Empetrum nigrum*), pill-headed sedge (*Carex pilulifera*), mat-grass, and tormentil. There is also an extensive area of wet birch–willow woodland containing several orchids, round-leaved wintergreen, and at least eight species of *Sphagnum*. The site is entirely surrounded by arable land. It would have been impossible to predict that long-distance dispersal would produce such vegetation types. The site was designated an SSSI in 1984.

Many similar examples in the Yorkshire–Nottinghamshire area are described by Lunn and Wild (1995). Over 40 years the disused Holbrook colliery has accumulated 11 species of *Sphagnum*, purple small-reed (*Calamagrostis canescens*), many orchid species and hybrids, a rich lichen flora, and numerous rare invertebrates. The lesson is that natural colonization is not only suitable for remote sites surrounded by species-rich vegetation. Ecologists who have monitored a range of examples have been astonished at the speed with which native species have invaded and the distances over which dispersal is effective. If there are remnants of appropriate communities in the neighbourhood, recolonization will be faster. However, for many vegetation types, a high proportion of the species will arrive and establish naturally provided that soil conditions are suitable, and, in particular, fertility is low. Most terricolous lichens, bryophytes, and many fungi require the reduced competition associated with low-fertility sites.

There is a further benefit of allowing natural processes to play a part in determining the vegetation and this is illustrated by the 20 ha Scholes Lane opencast site near Rotherham. This site was restored to a gentle slope and sown down to agricultural grasses in 1957. Since then the unproductive, poorly drained pasture has been subject to only light grazing, which has enabled the uniform grassland to develop into a mosaic of communities, the distribution of which are determined by subtle environmental variables. At least eight NVC types or sub-types are now present. This is a reason for not imposing designer communities on a site unless there is good cause; kick-starting the succession by sowing an open sward of small grasses will allow it to evolve into a mosaic of communities the pattern of which is determined by and therefore well related to the landscape, but in a subtle way that it would have been impossible to predict.

4 Grasslands

Introduction

More than any other community type, grasslands illustrate the difference
between 'designer' and 'political' habitat creation. Much of the substantial
wild flower grassland establishment, especially in urban areas, might be
classed as 'political', in that it is all about stimulating a public interest in and
appreciation of wildlife (Baines 1989). In contrast are the schemes where ecological design takes precedence in an effort to expand the dwindling resource
of flower-rich grassland, although on some sites attempts are made to combine
these objectives. There are examples where each has succeeded in its chosen
objectives and, equally, where many have failed.

One of the earliest attempts in Britain to establish flowers in a grass matrix,
specifically for both wildlife and people, was in the restoration of colliery shale
tips in the 1970s in Central Forest Park, Stoke-on-Trent (Cole 1986). The wild
flowers added were limited by availability (Table 4.1) at a time that was
well before the proliferation of seed merchants marketing the current wide
range of native species. Much earlier, however, in 1935, one of the finest prairie
reconstruction exercises in the United States commenced at Wisconsin University Arboretum. With seed collected by hand, the Conservation Corps were
responsible for clearing and sowing 24 ha, a project masterminded by the
renowned ecologist Aldo Leopold (Jordan *et al.* 1987a).

Contrast these efforts with the current situation, where off-the-shelf mixes
are available to suit different situations, and there are long catalogue lists of
native species and the potential to mix your own suite of species in an attempt
to emulate particular National Vegetation Classification (NVC) communities.
And all this in just 25–30 years.

The expansion of wild flower grassland schemes has largely been in tandem
with the increasing availability of native seed of appropriate species, stimulated, in the first place, by the extensive research at Monk's Wood Experimental Research Station (Wells *et al.* 1981, 1986, 1989). At the same time as
the former Ecological Parks Trust and others were establishing habitat complexes for educational use and enjoyment in urban areas, there was a move
to naturalistic landscape schemes, and another away from the bland restoration of derelict land to using visually exciting colourful flowers. This was the

Table 4.1

An early seed mix from Nickersons with a seed weight ratio
(grasses : wild flowers) of 73 : 27 and a recommended sowing rate of 62.8 kg ha^{-1}

Scientific name	Common name
Wildflowers and herbs	
Cytisus scoparius	Broom
Spartium junceum	Spanish broom
Lotus corniculatus	Bird's-foot trefoil
Trifolium hybridum	Alsike clover
Lupinus albus	White lupin
Medicago lupulina	Black medick
Trifolium dubium	Lesser trefoil
Coronilla varia	Crown vetch
Melilotus albus	White melilot
Trifolium pratense	Red clover
Trifolium repens	White clover
Polygonum esculentum	Buckwheat
Plantago lanceolata	Ribwort plantain
Urtica dioica	Stinging nettle
Dipsacus fullonum	Wild teasel
Dipsacus sativus	Fuller's teasel
Sanguisorba minor	Salad burnet
Chrysanthemum leucanthemum	Ox-eye daisy
Achillea millefolium	Yarrow
Cichorium intybus	Chicory
Petroselinum segetum	Corn parsley
Petroselinum crispum	Garden parsley
Carum carvi	Caraway
Digitalis purpurea	Foxglove
Calluna vulgaris	Heather
Salvia officinalis	Sage
Papaverum somniferum	Opium poppy
Papaverum somniferum album	White poppy
Grasses	
Lolium perenne	Perennial rye-grass
Festuca pratensis	Meadow fescue
Festuca arundinacea	Tall fescue
Festuca rubra	Creeping red fescue
Festuca rubra ssp. commutata	Chewings fescue
Festuca ovina	Sheep's fescue
Festuca tenuifolia	Fine-leaved sheep's fescue
Dactylis glomerata	Cock's-foot
Poa pratensis	Smooth-stalked meadow-grass
Poa trivialis	Rough-stalked meadow-grass
Cynosurus cristatus	Crested dog's-tail
Phleum pratense	Timothy
Phleum bertolonii	Smaller cat's-tail
Alopecurus pratensis	Meadow foxtail
Agrostis tenuis	Common bent
Agrostis stolonifera	Creeping bent
Deschampsia flexuosa	Wavy hair-grass
Bromus arvensis	Field brome
Bromus inermis	Hungarian brome

period of research into the value of legumes in restoring nitrogen starved soils (e.g. Bradshaw and Chadwick 1980), and the beginning of the movement to bring wildlife into the cities. The coincidence of all these forces inevitably led to the establishment of new grasslands on a large scale, and the initiation of research into some of the problems faced by these early practitioners.

Over the last decade or more, the impetus and successes of the earlier schemes together with the expansion of interest in the environment have led to an exciting explosion of opportunities. Not all of these opportunities are grasped perhaps as widely as they could be, but new flowery grasslands are now being established much more as a matter of course along road sides, around commercial and residential developments, in restoration and reclamation projects, and in parks, school grounds, and domestic gardens. With the expansion of the ESAs and Countryside Stewardship schemes, new grasslands are now being established on a large scale in rural areas too.

Exciting as these opportunities are, it should not be forgotten that few, if any, of the new grasslands match the complexity and diversity of old, long-established pastures and meadows (Gibson and Brown 1992), which are so important to protect. Notwithstanding this, the new communities have much to offer. Declining populations of once widespread plants and the more mobile animals that can reach the new sites are significantly boosted. New corridors are provided to link older fragments together and to buffer other habitats. Above all, the flowers and butterflies are a joy to see and stimulate basic emotions, providing welcome relief to the concrete jungle of everyday life.

From a cost effectiveness point of view, sowing flower-rich grasslands can be ten times cheaper than planting woodland but, compared with other grassland types, they are much more costly (Table 4.2). With the additional costs of regular maintenance (see p. 86), new grasslands need to be targeted where they will be most beneficial. Ecologically, this will be where they enlarge and connect existing diverse grasslands, provide edges to hedges, woods, and scrub, or constitute extensive swathes in their own right. Where the new grasslands are essentially for people, concentrating their establishment on banks, beside

Table 4.2
The relative cost of seed for creating different types of grasslands

	Sowing rate kg ha^{-1}	Seed cost per ha (1996 prices)
Typical wild flower seed mix	30*	£543–£1350
Amenity grass seed (includes rye-grass)	250–350	£877–£1228
Road verge grass	100	£207
Basic grazing mixture (6 grasses, includes rye-grass & clover)	40	£140

* See p. 72.

paths, and in other visually prominent positions, will maximize their amenity value. Wherever new grasslands are established, long-term security and protection from disturbance are essential. Flower-rich grassland, which is later excavated for a service line or planted with trees is a waste of money.

There are three basic approaches to establishing new flower-rich grasslands—encouraging natural colonization, sowing a seed mix onto a bared surface, or diversifying an existing ecologically dull grassy sward.

Natural colonization

Natural colonization is discussed in detail in Chapter 3, but it is worth highlighting some of the often highly valued grasslands that have colonized largely unaided. These have tended to be on disturbed and subsequently abandoned land, such as quarries and waste tips. A recent Department of Environment report (Land Use Consultants and Wardell Armstrong 1996) highlights the diversity of situations in which such circumstances can arise, and the variation in communities that can develop—from calcareous grassland to acid communities, including healthland. The keys to success are persistent open ground to provide colonization gaps and a source of propagules that can reach the site. The most promising conditions are on skeletal soils with a low nutrient base, on which seeds and spores can establish and grow.

This situation also provides a valuable habitat for invertebrates. Kirby (1992) notes that invertebrates begin to arrive on bare ground as soon as the plants, if not before. Some of these earlier colonizers are interesting and uncommon species. Since these species disappear as the sward closes, Kirby considers that the natural colonization of grasslands is far superior to the sowing of seed, so long as bare ground persists. On demolition sites with much rubble, Lott and Daws (1995) confirm the importance for beetles in the early stages of natural colonization; this contrasts with Morris's (1990a) view that Hemiptera are best encouraged by the removal of the initial weed stage and rapid establishment of a grass turf.

Natural colonization may not be so effective on nutrient rich soils, particularly when there is a dearth of native species in the locality. Fertile ground is likely to vegetate quickly, both from the on-site seed bank and from adventists. Growth will be rapid and competitive. Smaller, weaker species and most annuals will be quickly eliminated and a few aggressive species will take over. This process can be delayed by grazing, cutting, or other appropriate interference, but the eventual diversity will probably be low. Whether this matters depends on the scheme's objectives. Rank grassland may be excellent for a variety of breeding birds like skylark (*Alauda arvensis*), litter-loving invertebrates, and small mammals. Predators, including barn owls (*Tyto alba*), short-eared owls (*Asio flammeus*), and kestrels (*Falco tinnunculus*), would benefit from the food supplied by such areas.

Fig. 4.1 Natural colonization in an old limestone quarry—now a Site of Special Scientific Interest and nature reserve—Millers Dale, Derbyshire.

The natural colonization option has been taken in a variety of situations, some intentionally and others through neglect or serendipity. There will be hardly a county without an abandoned quarry resplendent with grassland species characteristic of the nearest semi-natural fragments, and many of them are now nature reserves. Colonization of other types of waste ground—pulverized fuel ash, waste from the Leblanc process, abandoned railway sidings—are famous for their masses of orchids (Shaw 1994) and unusual species (Gemmell 1982). In some areas, these former wastelands have become the only or main site for locally scarce plants such as clubmosses, which are now a feature of old sand pits on the Derbyshire limestone plateau and of Stoney Hill, an opencast coal and clay mine in Telford, Shrophire (Land Use Consultants and Wardell Armstrong 1996).

But will new quarries and waste tips acquire such a flora? There would have been a greater source of propagules from species-rich grasslands in the vicinity 40–50 years ago, which are now largely gone. Decisions on new sites must be cognizant of this, as the early colonists now are those of disturbed areas (often intensively used agricultural land) and these may not be suitable precursors to the desired grassland (Land Use Consultants and Wardell Armstrong 1996). There are examples, however, where recent reliance on natural colonization is paying dividends. The re-establishment of a limestone grassland flora under an experimental sheep grazing programme near Wytham Woods, Oxfordshire, has been well documented (Brown and Gibson 1993; Gibson *et al.* 1987) and is described in Chapter 3.

Where the spread of vegetation unaided might be too slow and unpredictable to suit the site's objectives, amelioration of the features limiting establishment can assist. Low levels of fertilizer may be useful (Davis *et al.* 1985), a sparse grass cover can be added as a thin matrix in which new species can find shelter, as described in Chapter 3. Gilbert and Wathern (1980) demonstrated this successfully on a relatively small scale, and a grass nurse is now being adopted more widely, particularly by the National Trust, some of the ESA projects, and certain derelict land restoration schemes.

Sowing a grass nurse is not suitable for nutrient-rich soils—the grasses take over and the other plants fail to find a foothold. This is illustrated by the South Downs ESA where, since 1987, some 5000 ha of arable land has been sown, mostly with perennial rye-grass (*Lolium perenne*) and white clover (*Trifolium repens*) (Peel *et al.* 1994). By 1993, these species were still dominant, despite the cessation of fertilizer applications. From 1992, a chalk grassland reversion option was offered, which required the sowing of at least 5 out of a list of 10 native grasses with or without a variety of broadleaved species at 15–30 kg/ha on arable land (ADAS 1996). The fields where the results were recorded all used cattle or sheep grazing to manage the swards. By 1995, the monitoring revealed that a range of unsown broadleaved species had colonized the grass-only sown fields, with annuals, including nationally declining species like Venus' looking glass (*Legousia hybrida*), featuring in the first year, and perennials increasing subsequently. Of the latter, 11 were included in the recommended seed list (Table 4.3). Although Gibson (1995) suggests that it takes about 100 years for chalk grassland to establish unaided on abandoned arable land, ADAS (1996) considers that the trials in the ESA of the sown grasses show encouraging signs of being suitable precursors to the development of chalk grassland in a shorter time-scale. However, the sown diverse grass mix plus broadleaved species had a greater potential to develop into chalk grassland; however, the cost was recognized as an overriding factor at this large ESA scale (ADAS 1996).

Sowing a seed mix

The first consideration, once the decision to sow a seed mix has been taken, must be that of matching the objectives to the site conditions. The soils, exposure, slope, and other ambient factors must, to an extent, dictate the objectives. It will be impossible, for example, to establish a colourful, species-rich, non-competitive turf on deep fertile soils and, equally, a vigorous grass sward suitable for geese grazing will not grow on infertile subsoils. The dilemma is

Table 4.3
List of approved species for Tier 3.1 Arable reversion to chalk grassland

Scientific name	English name
Agrostis capillaris	Common bent
Anthoxanthum odoratum	Sweet vernal grass
Briza media	Quaking grass
Bromopsis erecta	Upright brome
Cynosurus cristatus	Crested dog's tail
Festuca ovina	Sheep's fescue
Festuca rubra ssp. *commutata*	Chewings fescue
Phleum bertolonii	Smaller timothy
Poa pratensis	Smooth meadow grass
Trisetum flavescens	Yellow oatgrass
Anthyllis vulneraria	Kidney vetch
Achillea millefolium	Yarrow
Centaurea nigra	Common knapweed
Centaurea scabiosa	Greater knapweed
Clinopodium vulgare	Wild basil
Daucus carota	Wild carrot
Galium verum	Lady's bedstraw
Leontodon hispidus	Rough hawkbit
Leucanthemum vulgare	Ox-eye daisy
Lotus corniculatus	Bird'sfoot trefoil
Medicago lupulina	Black medick
Origanum vulgare	Marjoram
Pimpinella saxifraga	Burnet saxifrage
Plantago lanceolata	Ribwort plantain
Plantago media	Hoary plantain
Primula veris	Cowslip
Prunella vulgaris	Self heal
Sanguisorba minor	Salad burnet
**Helianthemum nummularium*	Common rock-rose
**Campanula rotundifolia*	Harebell
**Scabiosa columbaria*	Small scabious

* More expensive species that may be considered.
Source: ADAS (1996).

that it is easy to add nutrients to achieve high growth rates, but much more difficult to reduce nutrients and add stress to soils.

Soils

Having decided on a strategy, the first step is to select the type of grassland required. This should be largely dictated by the soils rather than by deciding on the grassland type and then finding the soils are unsuitable. It is much cheaper to work with nature than to make costly, and possibly short-lived, changes to the soils. It is also worth questioning whether the soils are suited

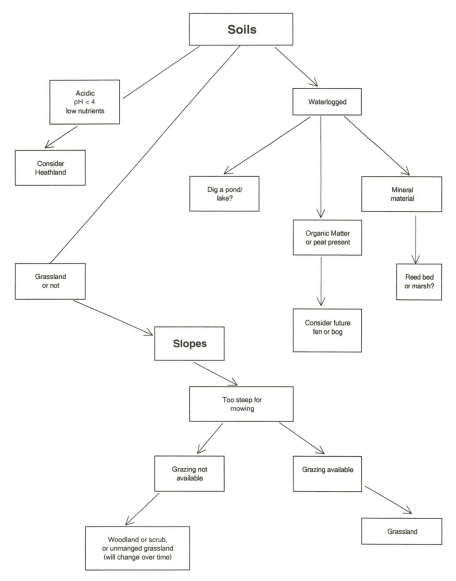

Fig. 4.2   Is grassland the most suitable habitat to create?

to grasslands at all, or whether other plant communities might be more appropriate (Fig. 4.2). Ash *et al.* (1992) provide a useful key for identifying soil types by the species present, but soil analyses will be safer and, obviously, necessary for bare soils.

There will be circumstances where ameliorative treatments are warranted. On highly calcareous substrates, where pH is extreme, lime levels can be reduced using sulphur or bracken litter (see Chapter 2). Extreme acidity can be ameliorated by adding lime. Only where the existing conditions are too severe for grass growth, or the objective is a particular community, would such treatment be warranted. On colliery shale tips, for example, where the pH can be less than 3, ripping in crushed limestone at a low rate can make the difference between a black or green appearance (Land Use Consultants and Wardell Armstrong 1996). On the whole, however, there will be a characteristic grassland type to suit the pH of most non-degraded soils.

Nutrient levels are another matter. The most common problem will be fertility levels too high to permit the development of a diverse sward. It is important to bear in mind that, naturally, soil depths, types, and nutrient levels would have covered a vast range from the thinnest, driest, and most infertile, to deep alluvial soils enriched with flood waters in the lowlands. The major difference now is the nutrient enrichment most lowland soils have experienced. We need to find ways of negating the effects of artificial nutrient enrichment without losing sight of the diversity of soils available. In other words, not all grasslands need infertile soils to produce a new habitat of wildlife value, but if your objective is a vista of colour and variety, low fertility is fundamental.

Phosphorus is widely believed to be a critical nutrient, with high levels being a problem in establishing flower-rich grassland (Gough and Marrs 1990). Some care is needed in interpreting soil analyses—a low available phosphorus level may mask a rapid turnover from the total phosphorus pool (which is insoluble) to the dissolved available supply. If high phosphorus levels are expected (as on intensively used ex-arable land) measuring the total phosphorus content would also be useful. If phosphorus is low, high nitrogen levels may not unduly influence the community. Nitrate-nitrogen is released from decaying organic matter fairly slowly and is probably in low supply if the site has been arable land or bared during construction works for a while. Ammonia-nitrogen is more likely to be a product of inorganic fertilisers, and usually leaches readily.

One nutrient that has not yet been examined in detail or experimentally in relation to new flowery grassland, is potassium. Ex-arable land frequently holds high quantities, with ADAS soil fertility index values of 3–5. Magnesium levels can be equally high. Personal observations (PA) suggest that high potassium levels, even with low phosphorus, may reduce the diversity of sown wild flower mixes over time (see the case study at Stansted Airport in Box 4.1).

The solution to high fertility is either to design a plant mix to suit the soils, an approach adopted on some sites by the organization Landlife (Ash *et al.* 1992), or to attempt to reduce the nutrient levels. In the former case, vigorous species, both native and naturalized, such as lupins (*Lupinus polyphyllus*), Michaelmas daisies (*Aster nova-belgii*), dotted loosestrife (*Lysimachia punctata*), and other mostly urban escapes, were used to create splashes of colour in a vigorous grass sward planted on topsoil covering a landfill site in Knowsley, Merseyside. Gilbert (1985) has shown how cow parsley (*Anthriscus sylvestris*), knapweed (*Centaurea nigra*), and yarrow (*Achillea millefolium*) all competed successfully and spread in a typical tall, unmanaged, false oat-grass (*Arrhenatherum elatius*) motorway verge on topsoil, just as they do on the many longer-established rural verges in England.

However, not everyone wants their new grasslands to resemble these examples. Many people prefer communities where the vegetation is shorter and less vigorous and where more species can thrive. Such slow-growing swards have the added advantage of being cheaper and easier to keep short, owing to their reduced maintenance requirements compared with more-vigorous grassland (see p. 86).

Since it is impossible to maintain a species-rich sward on nutrient-rich soils, in many cases soil fertility levels will need to be reduced. Basic methods and the limitations of topsoil removal and nutrient stripping by cropping are described in Chapter 2. Nutrient removal by cropping is probably not possible in urban areas where removal of topsoil may be the only practical solution. Topsoil stripping has the advantage of removing the seed bank, although there are occasions where this would be a disadvantage as it can hold an interesting assemblage. Ideally, seed bank tests should be conducted prior to a decision to strip. The soil may also be criss-crossed with field drains. Making the land wetter may be welcome, but remember that neighbouring landowners may object to their land being wetter! On low-lying ground, topsoil stripping in patches may provide a shallow pond instead of a seed bed. One stripped site flooded in winter and valuable seed was washed away (PA, personal observation).

It will also only be worth stripping the topsoil if nutrient levels in the lower horizons are significantly less than those in the surface layers. This is often, but not always, the case (Evans 1992); the depth that needs to be stripped can only be determined by sampling at different levels. The nutrient profiles will relate to soil texture (with less leaching in clays than sandy materials), flooding (as described in Chapter 2), and the depth of ploughing. It may be desirable to remove only the top 7–10 cm, or as much as 30–40 cm (3–4000 m³/ha), or the depth to which nutrient enrichment has occurred. The latter is a major earth-moving exercise, and trailer movements, noise, and dust (or mud) all need to be taken into account.

It may be feasible to use the topsoil to improve the agricultural value of adjacent fields where soils are too shallow. One of the discriminants between agricultural soil class 3A and 3B is too shallow a soil. Adding a second top horizon to a class 3B field could raise it to class 3A. The big mistake is to pile all the topsoil into the tree or shrub planting areas, which do better on low nutrients; flower beds and other horticultural areas are much more appropriate recipients.

Landlife (Ash *et al.* 1992) have experimented with other ways of reducing soil fertility. By removing half of the topsoil (10 cm) and mixing the

Box 4.1   New grasslands at stansted airport

As part of the overall landscape scheme, some 32 ha of wild flower grassland was sown at London Stansted Airport from 1986 to 1991 on subsoil and *in situ* topsoils. The same seed mix, harvested from a hay meadow, was used throughout, except that on the areas sown in 1986, it was diluted 50 : 50 with a secondary source derived from an earlier progeny, while this was changed subsequently to a 66 : 33 ratio as the secondary source proved less rich. An undiluted mixture was sown on a subsoil area.

Each area has been surveyed regularly since sowing, with extra quadrat data and soil analyses collected in 1996. Clear differences were manifest by this date and these were believed to be related to residual nutrient levels; however, analysis has failed to find any clear relationships, and many factors seem to be affecting the swards.

The table (p.65) shows the variability in plant richness and nutrient levels, but these are not significantly correlated. A Decorana analysis shows no clear differentiating factors between quadrats but suggests an increase in broad-leaved species on the first axis. The main differentiating factor seems to be the original seed mix, with the undiluted mix (MRC) still richer than the earliest 50 : 50 mix (F6a). The MRC mix was the only one sown onto subsoil. None of the new communities fit neatly into the National Vegetation Classification, but most show closer affinities with the neutral MG5— *Cynosurus–Centaurea* (crested dog's-tail–knapweed type) than any other. The less rich and grassy site (F6a) is developing into the neutral MG6 *Lolium–Cynosurus* (rye-grass–crested dog's-tail), while, despite regular annual cutting, F1d is approaching the MG1 *Arrhenatherum elatius* false oat-grass community.

The soil analyses (p. 65) reveal high phosphorus on only one site (F8a), moderate levels in 5 others and low levels (below 12 ppm) in the rest. The last group are either on subsoil (MRC) or on soils that had been stockpiled and respread. The rest are *in situ* ex-agricultural soils. The potassium and magnesium levels do not match this pattern and it is difficult to determine how the considerable variation affects the sward composition and diversity. In general, there is a tendency for plant diversity to be low and grasses more dominant where phosphorus and potassium levels are moderate or high.

remainder with a number of low fertility media (Table 4.4), they successfully reduced the vigour of the plants sown on a set of plots at Knowsley Community College, Merseyside. They have since extended the approach, positively seeking out low fertility urban soils in housing schemes, on landfill sites, and in parks, and establishing attractive grasslands with considerable success.

More problematic are new meadows sown onto imported soils or waste ground. This activity has contractual implications when specification precedes the known origin and nature of the soil. One possible way round this is to specify the maximum nitrogen, phosphorus, and potassium levels and pH range acceptable and to monitor the contract closely. Better still would be the identification of suitable on-site soils (top or subsoils) before any develop-

Site*	Total species recorded on site[†]	Total species in 30 0.25 m² quadrats	Av. nos. spp. per quadrat	Ratio grasses to broad-leaved plants	Av. pH	Av.[‡] P	Av.[‡] K	Av.[‡] Mg
F1a	60	35	10.17	1.25	7.9	18	409	921
F3a	45	37	11.10	0.68	7.9	8	434	472
F6a	52	29	8.27	1.77	7.9	11	298	110
F8a	50	41	13.67	0.52	7.0	48	384	124
F3b	64	38	11.33	0.83	6.9	16	324	113
F1d	54	29	9.00	2.08	7.8	19	327	153
F2d	49	31	10.43	1.39	7.9	21	377	87
F10d	78	38	9.90	0.81	7.8	12	269	72
F11d	72	48	10.20	1.16	7.7	10	289	107
STCP	70	41	11.83	0.86	7.9	12	356	106
MRC	90	35	10.47	0.39	7.4	5	136	104
Cowslip field[§]	42	NA	NA	NA	6.4	5	125	123

Wild flower grassland sown at Stansted Airport

* Management plan reference code.
[†] N.B. sites vary in extent.
[‡] Extractable ppm ($n = 3$ or 4).
[§] An old meadow for comparison.
NA, not available.
Source: Penny Anderson Associates, unpublished data collected 1995–6.

ment commences and ensure that these are separately stripped and stored ready for re-use later. This is the approach the Highways Agency have been taking recently where subsoils have been carefully earmarked for eventual grassland establishment and returned to their original geological formation on the cuttings or embankments of the new road (Robin Cure, personal communication).

Ground preparation

Whether the soil is a friable topsoil, stony waste, or sticky clay subsoil, wild flower grassland establishment requires a high quality tilth just like any other type of grassland. This means thorough stone and rubbish clearance if conventional agricultural machinery is to be used (but see Chapter 2, p. 31 for possible exceptions where some stone cover may be useful).

Compacted soils will need to be broken, at least in the upper horizon, using a power harrow, plough, or equivalent; frosts can help break down heavy clays. Cultivation is best carried out in dry conditions in summer. If undesirable invasive species are expected, the ground should be left fallow for a growing season and the weeds herbicided before wild flower seed is sown. If possible, the main cultivations should be conducted prior to this to avoid exposing a

Fig. 4.3 Experimental plots established by Landlife at Knowsley Community College where half the topsoil was replaced by various inert materials (see Table 4.4).

Table 4.4
Materials used to mix with topsoil and reduce fertility

Material	Properties
Crushed concrete	Fine grades rotovate in evenly and give a good calcareous soil.
Colliery shale	Gives an acid soil over time.
Ground limestone	Gives a calcareous soil, but not recommended since its extraction destroys somewhere else.
Subsoil	Very variable in pH and fertility. Infertile types best.
Sand	Results not as good as the materials above. Variable in pH.
Sulphur	Not recommended.
Road cold planings	Not recommended.
Metal tailings[1]	Not recommended.

[1] Mining waste material.
Source: Ash *et al.* (1992).

second cohort of weed seeds to the light. Hydroseeding can be used for certain sites, especially those on steep slopes and inaccessible to agricultural machinery, such as some road-side cuttings and quarry faces. In this situation, there is no special ground preparation, the mix is simply sprayed on as a slurry.

If the site supports desirable or neutral species already, it may be possible to encourage them in the new grassland. First, the species need to be assessed. Those with rhizomes or other vegetative structures, or which form part of the viable seed bank, would regrow after shallow cultivation. Long-established stress tolerators are unlikely to survive, but provided there are no vigorous, invasive species and the wild flower seed is added after cultivation, a mixture of pre-existing and new plants will establish. Several experiments have been conducted successfully where only broad-leaved seed was added to rotovated plots, grass growth being dependent on the re-establishment of the disturbed grasses (Derek Lovejoy Partnership and Penny Anderson Associates, in preparation). Where annual arable species are the main adventists, perennial grasses will need to be sown with the broad-leaved plants.

Selecting the right species

The very limited variety of grassland types currently being created in no way reflects the considerable diversity of communities found throughout the British Isles. Omitting agriculturally improved swards and specialist montane communities, the National Vegetation Classification recognizes 11 neutral, 6 acid, and 10 calcareous main grassland types, with 26, 23, and 42 sub-communities, respectively (Rodwell 1992). As each is characteristic of partic-ular soils and other environmental features, there will be at least one com-munity or main grassland type that will suit most habitat creation sites. Use of such vegetation classifications should provide the basis for more imagina-tive new grasslands better suited to their local environment.

Since some communities are very restricted in geographical distribution and localized (as demonstrated by the sweet vernal-grass–wood cranesbill com-munity (*Anthoxanthum odoratum–Geranium sylvaticum*) in Fig. 4.4), it is important to select a community appropriate to the area. Having identified the most suitable community, species regarded as weeds like creeping and spear thistles (*Cirsium arvense* and *C. vulgare*) or ragwort (*Senecio jacobaea*), and other widespread species likely to colonize unaided such as dandelion (*Taraxacum officinale*) should be omitted. Mixes will then need to be tem-pered by the availability and cost of species. Many of the specialist acid grass-land species in particular are not available commercially, but a good proportion of the main lists can be purchased, although few of the grasses are either the wild form or native to Britain. Future management must also play a part in selection, since, if grazing is to be employed or hay cut, poisonous species need to be avoided. Some species respond better to management for hay than others, and the composition of hay meadows and grazed swards on the same soil can be markedly different.

The basic community mixtures will need to be further modified in accor-dance with good practice guidance. This was first established by Wells *et al.* (1981) and later endorsed by others (Luscombe and Scott 1994), and

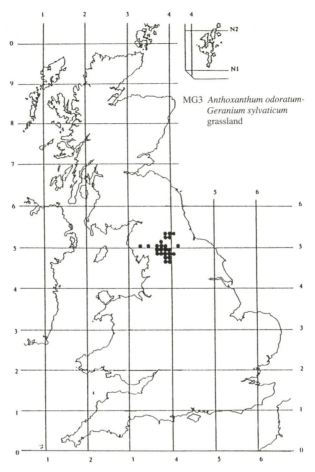

Fig. 4.4 The distribution in Great Britain of the sweet vernal-grass–wood cranesbill community. Reproduced courtesy of JNCC.

recommends that the species used should (1) be locally native to the geographical region of the site; (2) be common, widespread and typical of the area; (3) be suited to the soils; (4) be British in origin and native, not agricultural, strains; (5) establish readily, e.g. with no complicated dormancy; (6) include attractive flowers, especially where the site is designed for community use; and (7) be in a mix with a limited number of species.

Justification for these guidelines comes from both ecological and practical considerations. Locally native species are most appropriate because they are both adapted to the conditions and also responsible for providing regional distinctiveness. Furthermore, if, within this context, plants suited to the soils are also selected, these will accentuate the typicality of the community, which will then fit much better into the neighbouring ecological character. Plants not adapted to the soils and regional climate may survive for some time, but will eventually decline under extreme conditions—for example, particularly severe drought, prolonged frost, or winter waterlogging. The need for regionally adapted plants is another strong argument for using not only native seed but, preferably, seed from plants native to the region and soils.

Species that are common and widespread in an area are more likely to thrive in sown mixtures as they are not being so obviously limited by environmental factors. There is considerable concern from organizations like Plantlife and the Botanical Society of the British Isles (BSBI) about planting both rare species and those atypical of a region. Considerable research has been conducted into the geographical distribution of species and the factors affecting this. Planting species outside their natural range makes it much more difficult to determine natural distributions and controlling factors. On the other hand, if a species is rare in an area solely through habitat loss, and was once more widespread, there is less harm in reintroducing it, but all records of such introductions should be passed onto the local BSBI recorders and the biological records centres.

Using species that establish readily is common sense, and particularly important on the more nutrient-rich soils, where, unless they develop relatively quickly, they will be excluded. This is less critical on nutrient-poor ground where colonization gaps may persist for several years. Similarly, the advice to restrict species variety may be acceptable where simple, resilient, and colourful mixes—perhaps the 'political' swards—are being sown, but will not necessarily contribute significantly to attempts to re-establish facsimiles of old grasslands for nature conservation.

Commercially available species tend to be those that establish more easily, and these most readily fall into the central area of Grime's competitive-stress model (see Box 2.1). The species that do not establish easily and are less readily available commercially tend to be the more stress-tolerant ones which are, unfortunately, often the ones that give a distinctive flavour to a community such as thyme (*Thymus* spp.) and rockrose (*Helianthemum nummularium*). One possibility is to collect the seed of these species by hand. However, unless experienced in collecting seed at the appropriate time and storing it, hand collecting is only likely to be successful for those species without demanding germination requirements, which are generally available commercially anyway. Experimenting with collecting seed is certainly worthwhile—but permission needs to be sought from the landowner first.

There are excellent examples of fine new grasslands (mostly prairies in the United States) being established using hand collected seed, and a few have also resulted in new ecological discoveries. Noticing that some collected seed failed to establish in the new prairies, Steve Packard inferred that these were savannah species that were ecologically distinct from open prairie species, thus discovering a previously unknown community empirically (Jordan and Packard 1989).

Fig. 4.5 A typical mesotrophic ox-eye daisy meadow.

This discussion points towards the difficulties inherent in devising, obtaining, and establishing the species characteristic of distinctive, stressed habitats and accounts for the proliferation of ox-eye daisy meadows, which seem to be the 'norm' in wild flower grassland creation. It also emphasizes the importance, as with other habitats, of safeguarding the best of our existing diverse array of special grassland communities, since most are non-reproducible under the present state of the art of habitat creation.

Having selected the right species, the next step is to translate this into a new grassland. Alternative means of proceeding are to sow a proprietary seed mix, to mix and match from the catalogues, or to use hay as a seed source. Hand collected seed of particularly important species could be added to any of these, and special plants could also be established subsequently as plugs.

Off-the-shelf mixes

In general, these mixes should be avoided. They tend to lack distinctiveness and some include combinations of species with incompatible growth strategies and environmental requirements. For example, several pond edge mixes include cowslip (*Primula veris*) and meadow buttercup (*Ranunculus acris*), species that do not grow in waterlogged soils (Duffey *et al.* 1974; Grime *et al.*

1988). Some calcareous grassland mixes include plants like clustered bell-flower (*Campanula glomerata*), and traveller's joy (Clematis vitalba) is sold in a shaded area mix—in neither case is reference made to the limited, mostly southern, natural distribution of these species.

Furthermore, an evaluation of the different mixes offered for sandy, calcareous, alluvial, and clay soils in many catalogues shows a consistent affinity (although not always a close match) to the neutral grassland NVC type MG5, the *Cynosurus cristatus–Centaurea nigra* community. Even the very laudable attempt to create NVC mixes by one seed company fails to produce sufficient distinctiveness in all the options, and a number of mixes still key out as MG5 rather than their desired type. It is not surprising, therefore, that so many sown mixtures end up as very similar ox-eye daisy meadows.

Mix and match mixtures

Selecting the desired species is a better recipe for developing a suitable grass-land mix. The first requirement is to decide on the ratio of wild flowers (this conventionally refers to broad-leaved plants, but remember that grasses are flowering plants too) to grasses. As a rule, seed mixes are sold with an 80% grasses and 20% wild flowers ratio by seed weight, and this is stated in the catalogues as the normal ratio in grassland communities. This, in fact, hides a great deal of variation; some 'grasslands' support only a low grass cover, especially where rushes (*Juncus* spp.), sedges (*Carex* spp.), or even woodrushes (*Luzula* spp.) are abundant. Unfortunately, seed of most species of these genera are generally unavailable, although some, such as field woodrush (*Luzula campestris*), hairy sedge (*Carex hirta*), and most of the grassland rushes, are easily collected by hand and establish well.

Where soil nutrients are too high, reducing the level of competitive grasses in the mix would be advantageous (see Emery 1986 for advice on non-competitive grass species). In certain situations, grasses can be omitted altogether, for example, where there is either a copious seed bank or nearby seed sources of acceptable grass species. Consideration also needs to be given to the ratio of grass to wild flower seed number rather than percentage weight. Where grasses such as bents (*Agrostis* spp.) with 15000 seeds/g are used compared with fescues (*Festuca* spp.) at 1000 seeds/g, many more *Agrostis* plants would establish compared with *Festuca* (assuming equal chances of establishment).

The same consideration should be given to seed mixes where percentage by weight is given. The proportion of wild flower to grass seed by number may be quite different from the 80:20 ratio being offered. Table 4.5 demonstrates the differing ratios of seed by weight and number from two typical mixes. The proportional establishment of species from such a mix needs to take into account the very different viability of species and their equally variable ability

Table 4.5
The different ratios of seed by weight and number in two different clay mixes

	No. seeds/g	No. in 1 g of mix	Percentage by No.	Percentage by wt.
Mix 1				
Centaurea scabiosa	150	0.75	0.06	0.5
Centaurea nigra	400	1	0.07	0.25
Daucus carota	800	10	0.75	1.25
Filipendula vulgaris	1 000	5	0.37	0.5
Galium verum	1 600	16	1.20	1
Galium mollugo	1 500	15	1.12	1
Geranium pratense	100	1	0.07	1
Hypericum perforatum	10 000	25	9.34	1.25
Knautia arvensis	130	0.65	0.05	0.5
Leucanthemum vulgare	3 000	60	4.48	2
Leontodon hispidus	900	9	0.67	1
Malva moschata	500	2.5	0.19	0.5
Plantago lanceolata	300	3.75	0.28	1.25
Plantago media	2 000	10	0.75	0.5
Primula veris	1 000	5	0.37	0.5
Prunella vulgaris	1 500	22.5	1.68	1.5
Ranunculus acris	500	2.5	0.19	0.5
Ranunculus bulbosus	240	0.6	0.04	0.25
Rumex acetosa	650	6.5	0.49	1
Sanguisorba minor	300	1.5	0.11	0.5
Silene alba	700	3.5	0.26	0.5
Smyrnium olusatrum	30	0.3	0.02	1
Stachys officinalis	700	1.75	0.13	0.25
Taraxacum officinale	1 300	19.5	1.46	1.5
Total wild flowers			**24.16**	**20**
Alopecurus pratensis	500	5	0.37	1
Briza media	500	5	0.37	1
Cynosurus cristatus	2 000	200	14.94	10
Deschampsia cespitosa	7 500	75	5.60	1
Festuca pratensis	1 000	200	14.94	20
F. rubra ssp. commutata	1 000	200	14.94	20
F. rubra ssp. rubra	1 000	250	18.68	25
Poa trivialis	4 000	80	5.98	2
Total grasses			**75.84**	**80**

to survive in different competitive environments; nevertheless, the 80:20 grass to broadleaf ratio can look quite different when seed number is calculated.

Experiments established in 1973 on an ex-arable field near Royston, Hertfordshire, by Wells (1990) have shown that a richer, more colourful sward develops and persists for over 20 years if a 50:50 grasses:forb mix is used (PA, personal observation). The key issue is the cost of grass seed compared with many wild flowers and this unfortunately tempers most mixes.

A second consideration is the quantity of legumes to include. On soils defi-

Table 4.5
Continued

	No. seeds/g	No. in 1g of mix	Percentage by No.	Percentage by wt.
Mix 2				
Achillea millefolium	6 000	30	1.4	0.5
Centuarea nigra	400	20	0.09	0.5
Lathyrus pratensis	60	1.2	0.05	2
Leucanthemum vulgare	2 000	40	1.9	2
Lotus corniculatus	500	2.5	0.12	0.5
Lychnis flos-cuculi	5 000	25	1.2	0.5
Plantago lanceolata	300	7.5	0.36	2.5
Primula veris	1 000	20	0.96	2
Prunella vulgaris	1 000	15	0.7	1.5
Ranunculus acris	400	10	0.5	2.5
Rhinanthus minor	300	3	0.14	1
Rumex acetosa	2 500	25	1.2	1
Silaum silaus	500	5	0.24	1
Stachys officinalis	700	14	0.7	2
Trifolium pratense	150	0.75	0.04	0.5
Total wild flowers			**9.6**	**20**
Agrostis capillaris	1 500	900	43	6
Anthoxanthum odoratum	1 000	30	1.4	3
Briza media	500	5	0.24	1
Cynosurus cristatus	1 500	600	28.7	40
Hordeum secalinum	200	6	0.3	3
Festuca rubra ssp. *commutata*	1 000	100	4.8	10
F. rubra ssp. *pruinosa*	1 000	150	7.2	15
Trisetum flavescens	5 000	100	4.8	2
Total grasses			**90.44**	**80**

cient in nitrogen, legumes can kick-start the succession in an admirable and attractive fashion, and can contribute around 100 kg nitrogen/ha/year to the soil (Marrs *et al.* 1983). However, this is only advisable on soils that are also low in phosphorus (and possibly potassium too), since otherwise, once nitrogen levels increase, vigorous grasses and other species can then take over. On soils with adequate nitrogen and phosphorus, it is advisable to omit legumes altogether to avoid this problem. This is unfortunate because they are both colourful and the food plants for many invertebrates.

Working out the proportion of individual species needs to take account of seed size, viability, and the probable rate of establishment. The more reputable wild flower seed merchants can provide this advice on receipt of a list of species and their eventual desired abundance in the sward. Some suppliers sell their mixtures with species individually packaged. Hence, modification to improve customized mixtures is feasible. It is very important that you specify that no substitutions are to be made and any replacement species are negotiated to your satisfaction.

It is important to recognize that a wild flower seed mix does not and, indeed, should not, cover a site with a green blanket in its first year. If it does, the slower growing species are likely to fail. A blaze of colour can be expected in year two or even three. It is tempting in these circumstances to add a brilliant display of annuals for the rather dull first year, in the expectation that these will disappear as the perennials take over. This will only be effective if the newly developing grassland is on poor soils and the growth in the middle of the first year does not need controlling by cutting. On nearly all soils, except nutrient-poor subsoils or equivalent waste materials, the growing sward will need to be cut and the arisings (cut material) removed one to four times in the first year. In such circumstances, adding annuals is a waste.

Landlife has pursued an alternative approach in Merseyside where they have been sowing glorious single species stands of colourful annuals, often on temporarily vacant land in urban areas, so they can reap the seed. Their imaginative use of these flowery fields as a focus for community activities, especially involving children, is a key to their success (Luscombe and Scott 1994).

Seed quantities

After some experimentation (Wells et al. 1981), the quantity of seed recommended by most seed merchants for creating grasslands is between 30 and 40 kg/ha. However, further research has suggested that this may be higher than is necessary. Wild flower seed is expensive, some species much more so than others. To create large areas of grasslands, costs per unit area need to be minimized. Stevenson et al. (1995) have shown that chalk grassland can be created using seeding rates as low as 1 kg/ha. In this case, the seed used was a 50:50 grass to forb mixture. In small scale trials, 0.1, 0.4, 1.0, and 4.0g/m^2 were sown using part hand collected and part bought seed. After 2 years, there were no significant differences in the number of chalk grassland species between the three higher seed rates, and the swards under all four rates showed a similar level of affinity with the desired NVC community. The control plot, in comparison, remained weedy and unrepresentative of any chalk grassland type.

Furthermore, Stevenson et al. (1995) found that at the higher sowing rate, some species, including thyme (*Thymus polytrichus*) appeared etiolated and the cover of carnation sedge (*Carex flacca*) fell. In the 4g/m^2 (40 kg/ha) plots, bare ground had disappeared within the 2 years, whereas in the low seeding plots, it persisted at a significant level (60%) over the same time-scale. This is advantageous when it gives slow germinating sown species or desirable colonists a chance to establish, but may present difficulty where an early green cover is needed for amenity reasons, or to exclude vigorous ruderal species.

Fig. 4.6 Activities for local children in the brightly coloured annual plant seed crops in suburban areas in Merseyside.

The cost implications of different seed rates are significant. At 1996 prices, using an Emorsgate Seeds (Norfolk) mix, to establish 1 ha of calcareous grassland at a range of sowing rates would be costed as follows: cost of seed at 40 kg/ha, £1468; at 4 kg/ha, £160; and at 1 kg/ha, £40.

This is an 80% grass to 20% wild flower seed weight mix. If very low seed rates are to be adopted, then a greater ratio of broad-leaved plants compared with grasses and a 50:50 mixture becomes much more affordable. The 80% grass to 20% wild flower mixture would require 8 kg of wild flowers at 40 kg/ha, and 0.8 kg at 4 kg/ha. If a 50:50 mixture is used instead, only 2 kg of wild flower seed are needed for a 4 kg/ha application. The above mixture altered to a 50:50 grass to wild flower mix at 4 kg/ha would cost £290. Broad-leaved plants alone in the seed mix quoted above cost £125/kg.

When using very low seed application rates, extra care is needed to ensure the seed is well mixed as it is sown, and it should be bulked up with sawdust, sand, or barley meal to obtain an even spread. It is also sensible to sub-divide the area and the seed to avoid running out.

There will be occasions where much higher seeding rates will be needed, especially on particularly inhospitable soils. Helliwell (1996), for example, sowed 50 kg/ha of rye-grass to act as a nurse, to which was added locally collected seed species representing a cliff crevice, cliff grassland, or chalk grassland community onto Channel Tunnel spoil at Folkestone, Kent. This was a particularly stressed environment with low nutrient levels and at high risk from salt spray. In this case (a rare event in grassland establishment), fertilizers were needed as well.

Hay field mixes

An alternative to sowing a commercial seed mix is to use seed collected from a local hay field. This can be produced as a combined mixture by running seed collecting equipment over the hay before it is cut, or the hay can be cut and collected for strewing. The seed may contain considerable quantities of chaff, and sowing rates should take this into account. It is also sensible to have the seed mix tested for its species content and viability so that missing species can be added.

Several hay field mixtures are available commercially, or you can collect your own. Specialist machines can be hired, the best brush seed off without cutting the plants, thus providing the opportunity to collect in different seasons and obtain a more representative mix. The very basic heather seed brush and collecting box has been used successfully to collect wild flower seed.

It is important to consider the future of the donor field and its animals. Collecting should not endanger the future of the sward and the advice given by Crofts and Jefferson (1994) and Porter (1994) needs to be followed. Many of the plants are long-lived and no harm is done by harvesting on an occasional basis, but annual species like yellow rattle (*Rhinanthus minor*) have a short-lived seed bank (Grime *et al.* 1988) and could disappear in the donor site if collected too regularly. Similarly, collecting machines need to be modified to avoid taking significant numbers of invertebrates (Waring 1990). Collecting from different areas of a field, or different sites in consecutive years would help (Porter 1994). Drying seed on ground sheets at the edge of the field allows animals the opportunity to escape.

Seed harvested from hay fields can be sown in the same way as other seed mixes, but if a complete hay crop with seed intact is taken, this is spread out onto a prepared surface covering about twice its source area and then removed after a few weeks when the seed has dropped off (Trueman *et al.* 1991). Leaving a thick layer on the ground hinders germination. On the other hand, if hay is strewn much more thinly—so bare ground is showing through—without subsequent collection, less seed is spread and the sward will take longer to establish, but there is a saving in labour. The hay is usually spread straight after cutting to avoid losing seed.

The main advantage of using a local hay field seed source is that a closer match can be obtained between the new and longer established grasslands. A wider collection of species, many of which cannot be obtained commercially, are likely to be in the crop and, most importantly, the grasses will all be native, and sedges, woodrushes, and rushes will be included if in the original sward.

Although a considerable number of grasslands have been established using

Fig. 4.7 A diverse community sown on subsoils using a seed mix derived from hay at Stansted Airport (see MRC in the table in Box 4.1, p. 65).

hay field seed, few have been monitored in any detail and the results published. One exception is Ian Trueman's work at the University of Wolverhampton, which pioneered hay strewing with considerable success using a diverse MG5 *Cynosurus–Centaurea* mesotrophic grassland from Shropshire as the seed source. In one of Trueman's experiments, in which the effectiveness of hay strewing is compared with a seed mix containing an equivalent spectrum of species, the hay seed source scored more highly on the number of species per quadrat and total number of species (Jones *et al.* 1995). Hay strewing also proved cheaper, despite the considerable transport cost. The fluctuating abundance of the main species established in some of the 20 or so meadows that have been created in Wolverhampton are provided by Atkinson *et al.* (1995) and Trueman *et al.* (1991) who found significant differences in persistence, which related possibly to different management regimes or original fertility levels. Hay cutting plus aftermath grazing tended to favour species typical of the source meadow compared to a late hay cut with repeated subsequent cutting as an alternative to grazing.

A different approach was taken by MacDonald (1992, 1994) who sowed seed collected in 1986 on five separate occasions to maximize representation of different species from an alluvial hay meadow near Oxford. After three years, 39 species out of a possible 58 originating from the donor site had established and comprised 81% of the flora of the new meadow. MacDonald (1992) concluded that, despite the nutrient enrichment in the new site after arable cropping and the resulting favouring of rye-grass, the new sward was recognizable as a rather patchy version of a typical *Alopecurus pratensis–Sanguisorba officinalis* community (MG4 in the NVC—Rodwell 1992). This is one of the few published examples of an attempt to re-create a specific NVC grassland community.

The extensive (32 ha) new wild flower grasslands that have been integrated into the landscape scheme around London Stansted Airport illustrate the technique of using hay that has been collected using a combine harvester on the donor site. The richest and most diverse sward, which was sown on subsoil, has over 100 plant species recorded since 1986 and contains 69 that were definitely or probably from the original donor site (Anderson 1994*a*; Box 4.1).

Establishment

Sound advice on the mechanics of sowing is provided in a number of seed catalogues, but Luscombe and Scott (1994) also provide useful contract specifications. For successful establishment, a medium tilth is required, as for any other grass mix. Seed is best drilled, but effective distribution can also result from manual broadcasting (especially on small sites) or through the use of a hand-held seed fiddle. Manual application has the advantage of facilitating alterations to mixes to suit small scale topographical variation and allowing sowing in drifts. Whichever method is used, the seed will need to be bulked up with a carrier, regularly stirred to mix the different seed sizes evenly, and divided into sub-units to ensure even application across a site. The best time to sow new grassland is late summer/early autumn. Seedlings are killed by frost if sown too late, whilst drought is likely to affect spring sowings. The exception is at high altitude or latitude, when a spring sowing is probably most appropriate. An autumn sowing has the additional advantage of allowing vernalization for those species like cowslip that need it.

New grasslands change in appearance dramatically during the first few years (Wells *et al.* 1986). Ox-eye daisies (*Leucanthemum vulgare*) and legumes like red clover (*Trifolium pratense*), if they are included in the mix, produce a mass of exuberant colour in the second and third summers after sowing, and then decline, as a wider mixture of species take over. Common knapweed and carnation sedge take time to establish. Cowslips can continue to spread by seed if colonization gaps persist; after 5–6 years they can provide a substantial contribution to the sward.

Plants that fail in some trials may grow successfully in others. For example, pignut (*Conopodium majus*) has a poor reputation for establishment but grows easily if sown straight after collection in mid-summer (PA, personal observation). Similarly, eye-bright (*Euphrasia nemorosa*) failed in laboratory tests (Wells 1987) but established in chalk grassland trials (Stevenson *et al.*

1995). Carnation sedge has a ripening requirement (Wells *et al.* 1981) and establishes after several years provided there are still available niches.

Creating grasslands for animals

There are only limited examples of grasslands created for specific groups of animals. In most schemes, creating general biodiversity may be an objective, but there are few accounts of the colonization rates and range of animals present after establishment. Some of the farm headlands research (see Chapter 9) and the Wytham Woods work near Oxford are exceptions (Brown *et al.* 1990). These authors, in their investigations into the impact of grazing on naturally colonising chalk grassland, found that grazing, especially continuously, reduced the total abundance and number of species of leaf miners. Herbivorous Coleoptera and Heteroptera densities and species richness were enhanced by autumn grazing but reduced by spring grazing, although the reactions of individual species varied within this generality. In contrast, the successional trend of spiders was a gradual accumulation of species, especially on the ungrazed controls. Even after 7 years of colonization, only a third of the species regarded as typical of calcareous grasslands had appeared (Gibson *et al.* 1992).

A wide range of invertebrate groups were recorded using a variety of techniques in a small habitat creation scheme established by the Highways Agency at the intersection of two motorways in the English Midlands (Penny Anderson Associates 1993). The total number of species recorded (Table 4.6) from four surveys in 1992–1993, when the 1 ha site had been established for six years, shows a considerable range for such a small, isolated area. The greater attraction of the wild flower grassland to most groups is clear, but the tussocky grass proved particularly valuable for cover and hibernation. Groups of animals not well represented were litter dwelling and non-flying species. In general, the invertebrates recorded are common and widespread, and most are believed to have reached the site unaided. One weevil species, rare in Staffordshire (where the interchange is located) is thought to have reached the site as eggs in *Medicago* seed, while some of the gall wasps and moths could have been brought in on the planted trees. The only national rarity recorded was one fly, *Scoliocentra caesia*, but there were two regionally local Coleoptera.

As in the Highways Agency's study, Wheater and Cullen (1997) also found a dearth of woodlice, molluscs, orthopterans, and centipedes in restored limestone quarries in which a new wild flower grassland had been established compared with a natural daleside. Numbers of Coleoptera and Diptera were similarly high on the new site compared with the daleside, reflecting the more open conditions and differences in vegetation cover and structure.

Table 4.6
The number of selected invertebrate species recorded on a 1 ha, relatively
isolated habitat scheme between the M42 and M6 interchange north of Birmingham

Groups	Habitats present				Total No. of species
	Recent tree/shrub planting exposed	Better established tree/shrub planting	Wildflower grassland	Rank grass + broom	
Coleoptera					
Carabidae	14	15	25	14	35
Staphylinidae	27	25	53	25	65
Chrysomelidae	2	6	9	5	14
Apeionidae	4	11	15	11	33
Others	30	23	45	24	68
Total beetle species	77	78	148	79	215
Diptera					
Nematocera	7	14	15	8	23
Brachycera excluding Syrphidae	9	17	14	11	28
Syrphidae	10	16	20	13	24
Cyclorrhapha	29	44	55	38	78
Total Diptera species	55	91	104	70	153

Table 4.6
Continued

Groups	Habitats present				Total No. of species
	Recent tree/shrub planting exposed	Better established tree/shrub planting	Wildflower grassland	Rank grass + broom	
Hemiptera	9	16	26	23	41
Homoptera	5	11	17	15	31
Psylloidea	0	1	0	1	2
Lepidoptera butterflies	2	5	11	4	11
Lepidoptera moths[1]	7	12	10	5	26
Hymenoptera	14	14	16	10	35
Mollusca	0	0	1	1	2
Orthoptera	0	0	1	1	1
Crustacaea	1	1	1	1	1
Chilopoda	0	0	1	0	1
Total other species	38	60	84	61	151
TOTAL—ALL SPECIES	70	226	332	206	516

NB No Aranae recording was conducted.
[1] Day flying species only, no moth light trapping carried out.
Data unpublished, collected by Penny Anderson Associates, published with the permission of the Highways Agency.

Fig. 4.8   An abundance of cowslips sown beside new woodland planting.

Morris (1990a) considers that the proximity of semi-natural grassland is important in attracting Heteroptera and Auchenorrhyncha to new sites, and stresses the importance of using varied seed mixes with a wide range of grasses (on which most characteristic grassland Auchenorrhyncha feed) and characteristic herb species (Morris 1990b,c). Morris's studies on newly sown grasslands at Royston, Hertfordshire, show that the number of hemipteran species appearing in the early years of succession can be large, but that a mature fauna takes several years to colonize.

Grasslands for geese

Other grasslands may have precise zoological objectives that dictate special mixtures. For example, in areas where geese are damaging crops, blocks of grassland, preferably over 10 ha in extent, with 15–30 ha needed per 1000 geese, can be sown with a grass–clover mixture to provide an alternative feeding area (Andrews and Rebane 1994). The grass then needs to be reduced to 5 cm by cutting or grazing by the end of September ready for the arrival of the geese. If such grasslands are established under set-aside rules, compliance with the scheme regulations is necessary to obtain grant aid. However, adding 50 kg N/ha, irrespective of the grazing or mowing management, maximizes its attractiveness to geese (Vickery et al. 1994).

Grasslands for butterflies

Generally, grasslands are established with the expectation of attracting a variety of animals, but some have been designed principally to support viable populations of butterflies. One scheme, on a former landfill site in Essex, was sown in 1983 (Davis 1989). Eighteen butterfly species were recorded between 1983 and 1987, and the new grasslands contributed to substantial increases in some species in the locality (Table 4.7); however, all the species were common and mobile. Warren and Stephens (1989) could also expect this finding. Their habitat was designed to attract butterflies using hedges, ditches, banks, nettle patches, and acid wet grassland on a 9 ha ex rye-grass field in Dorset. Being close to populations of several uncommon and relatively immobile species such as marsh fritillary (*Euphydryas aurinia*) and brown hairstreak (*Thecla betulae*), it was hoped that these would be able to colonize the new site, and the design included special and detailed provisions for these species. However, Warren and Stephens (1989) provide sound advice for attracting the more common butterflies to new habitats (Box 4.2).

Management

The first year

On fertile soils up to 4 cuts should be allowed in the contract, taking the sward down to about 50 mm. Cuttings must be removed. On less fertile substrates (for example on subsoils), mowing may not be necessary at all, or only once or at the most twice in the first year. The aim is to prevent the weed or early grass growth from blanketing the slowly establishing desirable wild flowers. Application of a selective grass herbicide can assist in such situations and allow the broad-leaved plants to flourish if grass growth is too dense (Gilbert 1989). Grass growth retardants may also be useful in the establishment period and beyond, but evidence for their effectiveness is inconclusive. Mefluidide, applied in April–May before the main growing season, can inhibit grass growth, but has to be applied to a short sward. It is not clear whether it reduces broad-leaved plant diversity and is best used on a grass dominated ward.

If grazing stock are available, they can be used to tread in newly sown seed (Stromberg and Kephart 1996), but they are probably more valuable in subsequent years. There is little research on when grazing might be first introduced, but Jones and Haggar (1994) consider the first few weeks to be too early, as at high stocking rates broad-leaved plants in particular were lost to trampling or urination. It seems prudent to introduce stock in the second rather than the first growing season, as MacDonald (1994) reports on a new alluvial meadow near Oxford.

Table 4.7
Butterfly index values[1] on an Essex landifill site

Latin name	Common name	1983	1987	Comment
Thymelicus sylvestris/ Thymelicus lineola	Small/Essex skipper	76	236	Both species recorded, bred on couch and creeping bent grass in control plot
Ochlodes venata	Large skipper	0	1	
Pieris brassicae	Large white	+	10	
Pieris rapae	Small white	+	52[1]	
Pieris napi	Green-veined white	0	7[2]	May have bred on charlock, lack of crucifers affected all whites.
Anthocharis cardamines	Orange tip	0	5	
Lycaena phlaeas	Small copper	0	1	Not breeding despite Rumex spp. being present.
Polyommatus icarus	Common blue	5	313	Bred on Medicago.
Celastrina argiolus	Holly blue	0	0	Present in other years.
Vanessa atalanta	Red admiral	3	13	
Cynthia cardui	Painted lady	3	13	
Aglais urticae	Small tortoiseshell	4	382	Probably bred on nettle patch.
Inachis io	Peacock	3	8	
Lasiommata megera	Wall brown	0	3	
Pyronia tithonus	Hedge brown	5	48	
Maniola jurtina	Meadow brown	144	960	
Coenonympha pamphilus	Small heath	55	623	

[1] Index values as used in the standard butterfly recording methodology (Hall 1981).
[2] Actual numbers.
Data adapted from Davis 1989.

The second and subsequent years

Lack of management is one of the main reasons for the failure of new grass-lands. From an ecological viewpoint, management should maximize the opportunities for plants to flower and set seed, and for as wide a range of invertebrates as possible to establish viable populations on the site. At the same time, it should further the process of grassland establishment and prevent it from changing into scrub or woodland. Light grazing, with higher stocking densities through autumn into winter (if the soils can support it), or occasional cutting with the arisings removed, are best. Crofts and Jefferson (1994) provide good advice on grassland management. On most grasslands, cutting once a year in autumn would match the requirements, but this could be less frequent on subsoils where growth is slow and sparse. Such late cutting has the added advantage of giving the least time for regrowth over winter,

> **Box 4.2 Guidelines on attracting butterflies**
> **(After Warren and Stephens 1989)**
>
> 1. Identify the local habitats that are currently good for butterflies.
> 2. Which of these can be created on your site?
> 3. What butterfly species are resident in the locality?
> 4. Are these species mobile, capable of finding and colonizing a new site?
> 5. Are there any special needs for the expected colonizers that can be provided, such as tall grassland, south facing slopes, nettle patches?
> 6. Is it possible to cater for the less mobile, rarer, more demanding species? Seek specialist advice, e.g. from the British Butterfly Conservation Society or equivalent.

Fig. 4.9 A variety of machines are available which cut grassland and collect the arisings.

and thus starting with an open sward in the spring in which the annuals—yellow rattle for example—can re-establish. Cutting earlier, as when a hay crop is taken in July or August, will reduce the potential for invertebrates and small mammals, and give a longer period for regrowth during the growing season. In such situations, further cuts with the arisings removed, or grazing will be needed. Smith and Rushton (1994), for example, have emphasized the importance of aftermath grazing in old meadows where there is a loss of species if hay cutting in July is not followed by grazing.

If stock are unavailable, another alternative is to take an early cut with the arisings removed, but this needs to precede the bird breeding season, particularly since several birds of conservation importance (JNCC 1996a) may be benefiting from the new grasslands, such as skylark and grey partridge (*Perdix perdix*). The early cut can reduce grass vigour for up to 2 months, and two early cuts in April in small scale situations—such as in gardens or school grounds where ground nesting birds are not an issue—reduce eventual sward height and vigour significantly (PA, personal observation). For further advice on grassland management, the Lowland Grassland Management handbook (Crofts and Jefferson 1994) should be consulted.

The recommended cutting regimes can create practical management problems, so compromises are usually needed. Cutting grassland in late autumn yields little of feed value, so disposal of arisings is an issue, especially if they cannot be composted or used as animal bedding. Cutting a hay crop in July or August obviously overcomes this, and a subsequent autumn cut may still be usable for animal feed. Ash *et al.* (1992) have shown that cutting and removal of material up to 3 times a year is no more expensive and often much cheaper than traditional amenity grassland management with 8 to 16 cuts a year (Table 4.8).

Cutting without removing the arisings is only acceptable where growth is thin, the wind strong, or the slope steep so that the material does not blanket out the smaller species, but rather disintegrates or blows away rapidly. Removal of the material was once believed to contribute to a significant nutrient drain, but this is only likely through cutting at the height of the growing season, when most nutrients are in the foliage. The main functions of removing cut material are to avoid the development of a thick thatch that effectively

Table 4.8
Estimated comparative costs of cutting different grassland types

Grassland type	Approximate cost/ha/year[1]			
	Cuts/year	Small area (<0.2 ha)	Medium area (0.2–0.8 ha)	Large area (>0.8 ha)
Amenity, vigorous	16	£3000	£630	£350
Amenity, slow growing	8	£2800	£800	£440
Wild flower grassland vigorous[2]	2	£1334	£800	£232
Wild flower grassland slow growing[2]	1	£667	£400	£116

[1] Costs depend on machines used. It is assumed pedestrian mowers and hand raking are used for small areas, compact flails for medium areas, and 5 unit gang mower (amenity 16 cuts) or tractor flail for larger areas. Using forage harvesters is cheaper on medium and large areas.
[2] Costs include removing cuttings.
Source: adapted from Ash *et al.* (1992).

smothers weaker, smaller plants and to create colonization gaps. On the other hand, leaving some grassland uncut, perhaps around the edge of sites, would benefit shade- and damp-loving invertebrates, such as meadow brown butter-flies (*Maniola jurtina*), as well as amphibians and small mammals. A dense sward reduces colonization by trees and shrubs, and an occasional cut and clear to control scrub is all that is needed.

'Spring' and 'summer' meadows

The literature (for example, Emery 1986) and seed catalogues refer regularly to 'spring meadows' (cut from mid-summer onwards after spring flowering) and 'summer meadows' (cut until mid-summer then left to flower). There is no such thing as a 'spring' or 'summer' meadow ecologically. Most semi-natural grasslands contain a succession of flowers from early spring to late autumn which, in turn, support a plethora of invertebrates that might depend on roots, leaves, stems, buds, flowers, fruits, or seeds of different species. Without these various structures, the animals cannot complete their life cycles and will be no more than passing visitors. The distinction between 'spring' and 'summer' meadows is false and contrary to nature.

'Spring meadows' may have a role in urban areas where shorter grass is needed during the school summer holidays for intensive recreational use, or to avoid grass fires. There does not seem to be any sound ecological or socio-ecological reason for having a 'summer meadow', so why not try to create a year round grassland instead—its value would be infinitely greater.

Diversifying existing dull grasslands

Existing grassland can be diversified by oversowing, by rotovating and sowing flower seed, by slot seeding or by adding pot-grown or plug plants. Each method is suited to a particular set of conditions.

Rotovation and seeding

The sward can be lightly and shallowly rotovated or cultivated, and oversown just with broad-leaved species. This is a particularly appropriate technique on sites where the existing sward is in need of diversification but consists of a limited range of desirable species that are likely to regenerate after distur-bance. Rotovation creates the gaps in which the added seed can establish. This technique has been used with some success on the A55 roadside enhancement scheme in North Wales (Derek Lovejoy Partnership and Penny Anderson Associates, in preparation) and on other sites (PA, personal observation); however, it is always worth gauging the seed bank first. On one of the A55 sites there was concern that a flush of creeping thistle, which developed after disturbance, would swamp the newly establishing sward, however, the thistles declined without treatment in the second year. In contrast, on another plot a welcome show of field woundwort (*Stachys arvensis*) appeared.

Oversowing

Oversowing an existing grassland is only worthwhile if establishment gaps exist or can be created. This is most straightforward in long, uncut swards that have recently been burnt or closely mown with the arisings removed. Spreading wild flower seed (with no grasses) onto the surface and raking it in can be successful, but there has been little research on the subject. Trueman *et al.* (1991) have had some success strewing hay onto a closely cut sward and leaving it until the seed had fallen off. Yellow rattle is one species that can be successfully introduced by oversowing; this species is particularly useful in restraining grass vigour through its hemi-parasitic habit.

Slot seeding

Slot seeding uses agricultural machinery and was first researched by Wells *et al.* (1989) and Wells (1987). Its use for wild flower seeding requires technical knowledge, as Luscombe and Scott (1994) warn, if the desired sowing rate is to be achieved. There are different types of slot seeders, one has a spray attachment to herbicide a strip in which the seed is sown, a second rotovates a strip for the seed instead. The addition of slug pellets would be beneficial since Clear Hill and Silvertown (1994) found that the exclusion of slugs from plots where five common dicotyledonous plants had been seeded significantly increased seedling emergence. Both types of machine work equally well (Luscombe and Scott 1994). The seed is normally sown at $0.2–0.6\,g/m^2$, preferably in autumn (Wells *et al.* 1989).

The most suitable grassland in which to use slot seeding is one where grasses are not vigorous, fertility is not high, and there are no pernicious weeds. It is important to cut or graze the surrounding sward as low as possible before treatment, and to cut the re-developing sward in the subsequent spring, and possibly summer, as well as autumn in the first year to prevent smothering of the new seedlings (Wells *et al.* 1989).

There are few reports of slot seeding being carried out on a large scale, or of the subsequent rate of spread of the introduced species. Andrews and Rebane (1994) report on one farm in Lincolnshire where an old ridge and furrow hay field was first cropped without additional nutrients for one year and then grazed hard before slot seeding. All the 22 species introduced are present and flowering, and others have re-established with spotted orchid (*Dactylorhiza fuchsii*), ragged robin (*Lychnis flos-cuculi*), and meadow saxifrage (*Saxifraga granulata*) the most notable successes.

Wells *et al.* (1989) concluded that slot seeding is effective in introducing a wide range of species into established grasslands, provided those used were

Fig. 4.10 Slot seeding using a herbicide, at Monks Wood Research Station, Huntingdon.

carefully selected to match the soils and the sward received the necessary management to ensure their establishment. However, in Luscombe and Scott's (1994) view, slot seeding has as many failures as successes, and is not suitable for those wishing to avoid potentially wildlife damaging chemicals like slug pellets.

Adding potted plants

The final option is to introduce potted or plug plants. Wells *et al.* (1989) describe how 4–5 month old plants can be inserted into established grasslands using a bulb-planter. By using a mixture of species, micro-habitats can be accentuated using plants grown *en masse* using normal horticultural facilities (Ford 1984); in urban areas in particular, plants can be grown and inserted by children as part of community projects. These advantages have to be set against potential failure rates. Wells *et al.* (1989) recorded survival from none to 87.8% for 14 species 2 years after planting, while between 42% and 93% of planted individuals died after one year in a trial comparing the effectiveness of seeding with adding plant plugs on the A55 near Bangor (Derek Lovejoy Partnership and Penny Anderson Associates, in preparation).

Failure can mostly be attributed to drought after planting, or to mismatching species requirements to ground conditions, with plants like bulbous buttercup (*Ranunculus bulbosus*), kidney vetch (*Anthyllis vulneraria*), and clustered bellflower succumbing to winter waterlogging (Wells *et al.* 1989). Although many species in these trials flowered, no significant spread into the adjacent grassland, except for ox-eye daisy and meadow buttercup, was recorded after three years. Boyce (1994) recorded 76% survival of 19 species planted 1 m apart in a rye-grass sward after five years, but found reduced success where competition with white clover was most intense. The species that had spread most successfully in this period were red clover, self heal (*Prunella vulgaris*), bird's-foot trefoil (*Lotus corniculatus*), rough hawkbit (*Leontodon hispidus*), bugle (*Ajuga reptans*), meadow buttercup, ox-eye daisy, yarrow, and common knapweed. Cowslip and lady's smock (*Cardamine pratensis*) showed the lowest rates.

Bisgrove and Dixie (1994) suggest careful use of the growth retardant mefluidide to suppress grass growth for a couple of months during the establishment period. Evidence indicates that the plugs can tolerate some competition from grass, but are vulnerable to slugs if the tall grass collapses and lodges. Low rates of some graminicides could be used to knock grass growth back in this critical period too (Bisgrove and Dixie 1994). The same approach could be applied to establishment periods after rotovating or slot seeding.

The cost of inserting plants is now much reduced thanks to the application of plug plant technology developed for the vegetable industry since the late 1980s. Instead of 50–80 pence for potted plants, prices per plug are as low as 15 pence, based on a peat-free modular transplant system (Bisgrove and Dixie 1994). In the last few years, at least 350 projects have been completed using

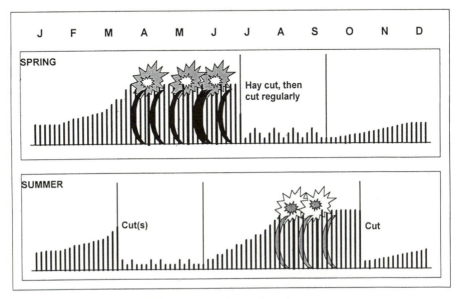

Fig. 4.11 Cutting regimes to produce 'spring' or 'summer' meadows.

this technique, with five for the Highways Agency, including the A10 at Melbourne and M32 at Bristol. The number of plants supplied typically range from 5000 to 50000 plugs/ha (Bisgrove and Dixie 1994).

Wells *et al.* (1989) considered the most appropriate use of potted plants was for species that are slow or difficult to establish, or very expensive as seed, and that would subsequently spread vegetatively. But the spread of potted species requires regeneration gaps, which are difficult to engineer in a dense grass sward. Sensitive management will be the key.

Monitoring

Although recommended as an essential part of any grassland creation project (Parker 1995; Luscombe and Scott 1994), the general lack of monitoring of developing grassland contributes to the unnecessarily high failure rate. Monitoring does not have to be hugely time-consuming or rigorously scientific, although detailed quadrat-based monitoring provides the most useful feedback information. An examination of the developing sward in different seasons, keeping a record of its appearance, relative growth rate, height, density, species composition, and their relative abundance (plants or animals, depending on the objectives), are an essential part of the feed-back mechanism. Such information should inform management decisions and provide a long-term data-base for sharing with others and for subsequent schemes. New grasslands take time to stabilize (Anderson 1994*b*; MacDonald 1994) and monitoring should continue for up to 10 years, although perhaps less intensively in the later ones. Even then, especially in open swards, new species will continue to appear. Only with proper monitoring can the developing sward be assessed against the original objectives, and the level of success in meeting these be evaluated.

5 Woodland, scrub, and hedgerow

Woodland habitat creation entails creating woodland communities that have a diverse structure and contain a wide range of tree, shrub, and ground flora species. It involves making many desisions, one of the most important of which concerns the origin of the material to be used. Here there is a range of choices (Peterken 1995), which become progressively less rigorous:

Species and genotypes locally native $\longrightarrow$ Species locally native $\longrightarrow$ Species nationally native but not locally native $\longrightarrow$ Species introduced

Purists advocate the use of local genetic stock; however, this is rarely available in the quantities required, so the second definition has to be employed using commercially obtained nursery material. The realities of imposing the strictest policy in relation to major timber species, such as oak (*Quercus* spp.), which have been widely planted in the past, need to be recognized and not allowed to hinder woodland creation.

When creating new woodland many more skills are required than a knowledge of forestry and woodland ecology. Just as important as the species composition of the wood is its location in the landscape, its size, shape, and relationship to other semi-natural habitats. It has been argued, from an ecological viewpoint, that since many woodland plants and animals are slow to colonize, an appropriate approach is to cluster new woods to produce districts with 25–30% woodland cover, which would then diversify more quickly. Areas suitable for this treatment might be the Weald, the Chilterns, Deeside, and the Welsh borders. The Community Forest programme is an example of this approach.

Positioning the wood in the landscape

Woodland has many roles to play in the landscape, and nature conservation is only one of them. To the public, and to bodies such as the Countryside Commission, its function in providing regional and local distinctiveness is equally important. In any one area the pattern of woodland is determined by natural features, such as land-form or intractable soils, acting in combination with cultural factors, which might favour hilltop plantations, shelter belts, or groups of small woods laid out to facilitate pheasant shooting. These patterns should be fully understood so that new woodland habitat is sited sensitively and plays a multifunctional role in the countryside.

An example of the important role that woodland plays in determining landscape character comes from Cambridgeshire, where guidelines have been produced for the design and management of the rural landscape so that change can be more responsive to place (Cambridgeshire County Council 1991). Following extensive survey work, the county was divided into nine character areas and, for each, recommended plant species and design guidelines were prepared. These largely involved manipulating woods, hedgerows, and individual trees. For example in the south-east clay hills the principles for landscape improvement were to (1) manage ancient semi-natural woods and create edge area; (2) create new woods, ideally linked to existing ones; (3) plant woodland belts and widen hedgerows to link woods; (4) manage hedgerows; and (5) screen unsightly village edges. In the chalk lands character area the recommendations were different: (1) plant new beech hangers on high ground; (2) manage existing shelter-belts; (3) plant new mixed woodland and shelter-belts to emphasize land form; (4) reinforce hedgerows; (5) promote chalk grassland; and (6) create a number of intimate landscape corridors picked out by small woods, lines of trees, and scrub.

Many of these primarily aesthetic proposals coincide with good practice from a habitat creation angle (particularly woodland extension and the linking of woods). Conservationists also like to see the woods nucleated.

Designing the wood

A thorough ecological survey of the site and its surroundings (see Chapter 2) should precede any planting so that species can be matched to soil type (e.g. texture, pH, wetness) and climate, and, if necessary, different types of woodland introduced on different parts of the site. At the survey stage it may also be possible to identify optimal precursor vegetation whose herbaceous species can give a head start to developing a woodland ground flora (Rodwell and Patterson 1994). These are often areas of heathland or wet flushes and will involve 'trade-offs' such as an alder wood with an appropriate ground flora at the expense of wet ground. Areas of high nature conservation interest that are valuable in their own right need to be recognized so they can remain unplanted. The history of the site may also be important and a survey of existing woods can give a local context when it comes to selecting suitable tree, shrub, and ground flora species.

Often the reasons for planting trees are ill-defined, such as a belief that it is a good thing to do, or a grant becomes available. Clarifying objectives and deciding on priorities can help resolve most questions of woodland design. Popular reasons for planting native broad-leaved woodland include the promotion of nature conservation, timber production, sport, and for landscape improvement; less-common objectives are the enhancement of a particular species, education, and bio-fuel; creating ancient woodland is not a realistic objective—it is well beyond our abilities. Several of these objectives conflict, but perhaps a unifying theme might be the promotion of biological diversity.

New woods need to include open ground. This has been recognized by the Forestry Commission whose Woodland Grant Scheme currently allows up to 20% of an area to remain unstocked. Glades, wide rides and unplanted margins are of particular importance to mammals, birds, and invertebrates and may warrant sowing with grassland/heathland species. Another feature of amenity planting grants is that 10% of the stock can be shrubs—so there is an opportunity to start building up habitat mosaics. In practice this is a grey area, sometimes the under-shrub hazel (*Corylus avellana*) is classified as a tree, to allow the shrub component to reach 40%. If there is room, an unplanted buffer zone around woods is a good idea, it will develop into an ecotone, and in intensively farmed areas will reduce the effects of agrochemicals. At Stansted Airport, marginal strips of wild flower grassland were sown to provide a buffer and a nectar source for hoverflies and other insects (Fig. 4.8).

To sit well in the landscape the shape of a wood should be determined by land-form or by enclosure patterns. Ancient landscapes comfortably accept irregularly shaped woodlands, while more regular shapes are most acceptable in planned (enclosure) landscapes. The size of a woodland is often determined by its function. Large scale for timber production, small scale for shooting, narrow for wind-breaks, while for nature conservation it is difficult to generalize. The recommendation with regard to birds is that the landscape should hold woods of a variety of sizes (Ford 1987). The thinking behind this is that birds differ in their requirements; the optimum habitat for species such as nightingale (*Luscinia megarhynchos*), treecreeper (*Certhia familiaris*), goldcrest (*Regulus regulus*), chiffchaff (*Phylloscopus collybita*), marsh tit (*Parus palustris*), nuthatch (*Sitta europaea*), woodpeckers, and jay (*Garrulus glandarius*) is the interior of large woods, while small woods with rich external edges, are preferred by turtle dove (*Streptopelia turtur*), finches, buntings, and most warblers. In contrast, Moore and Hooper (1975) provided compelling evidence that large woods were best, after surveying 433 sites they showed that with every tenfold increase in size the number of breeding birds approximately doubled. Large woods are more likely to include habitat mosaics, more NVC types, and will be buffered against change so the rarer species have an assured future. Small, newly planted, isolated woods are the least successful for nature conservation.

The ideal shape has been debated at length (Spellerberg 1995). Though

---

Box 5.1   Beech House Farm Wood, South Yorkshire: design philosophy

---

The Woodland Trust commissioned an ecological survey of this 21 ha site and its surrounding fields and woods. The subsequent design (see Fig. 5.1) was driven by the following requirements. First, the planting had to attract the maximum Forestry Commission grant, which was a major constraint (for example, open areas could not exceed 20% or shrub planting 10%). The pattern of open areas was determined by the presence of transmission lines and service ducts, a request by the local population to maintain views of certain well-known landmarks, and the ecological survey which had identified acid banks carrying betony (*Betonica officinalis*), mat-grass (*Nardus stricta*), tormentil (*Potentilla erecta*), and devil's-bit scabious (*Succisa pratensis*), which are uncommon species in the agricultural lowlands. The locals also wanted wide rides so that they felt safe, and a bridleway. Species selection mirrored existing woods but with a greater presence of ash (*Fraxinus excelsior*) to the north, a wetland mix for boggy ground and two compartments given over to natural regeneration. Crab apple (*Malus sylvestris*) appears to be over-represented, since it occurs singly in woods of this type, and alder (*Alnus glutinosa*) may prove to be a problem in the 'main mix'. The shrub areas were mostly sited along the margin facing Birdwell village. Wherever possible the wood boundary and ride edges follow existing hedgerows. It is anticipated that the farmer who previously owned the site will take a hay crop off the rides using a forage harvester but scrub will be allowed to develop along south facing ride margins. By chance, the final design has the appearance of a medieval hunting forest.

---

there is no strong evidence that linear corridors facilitate colonization, most conservationists feel happier if their woods are connected to other habitat blocks from which flora and fauna can be 'trawled'. Consequently, the optimum shape may be a compact wood where interior conditions of shade and humidity can develop, with arms radiating outwards to connect with other woods and riparian corridors. Opdam (1993) recommends a minimum core of 2 ha to be functional and viable for woodland birds. Figure 5.1 shows a planting plan for an area of naturalistic woodland in a semi-rural part of South Yorkshire, the design philosophy is provided in Box 5.1.

Establishment options

Natural colonization

In their hearts, most ecologists would like to see woodland established by natural colonization, the site going through a natural succession of a grassland–scrub mosaic stage, then to scrub with invading trees, and eventually passing over to woodland of unpredictable composition. Such a wood will

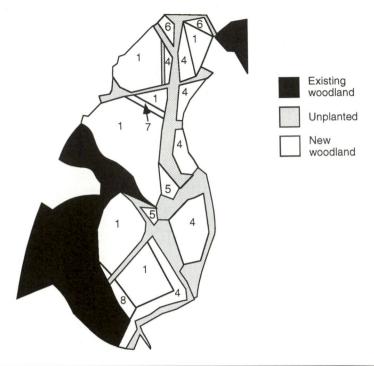

Existing woodland

Unplanted

New woodland

Species	Main mix (1)		Wood edge (4)		Trees/shrubs (5)		Wet (6)	
Quercus robur	40%	4630	35%	1780				
Fraxinus excelsior	25%	2890			30%	1670	20%	280
Alnus glutinosa	20%	2310					20%	280
Prunus avium	14%	1620	20%	1020				
Ilex aquifolium	1%	120			2%	110		
Malus sylvestris			15%	760				
Crataegus monogyna			10%	510	30%	1670		
Prunus spinosa			10%	510				
Rosa canina			10%	510	10%	560		
Acer campestre					10%	560		
Corylus avellana					18%	1000		
Populus tremula							15%	210
Salix fragilis							15%	210
S. caprea							10%	140
Betula pendula							20%	280
Area (ha)	5.14		2.26		2.48		0.61	

Planting density 2250/ha (2 m spacing). Compartment 7: *Corylus avellana* 100% 1000 plants (under power lines). Compartment 8: natural regeneration.

Fig. 5.1 Section of a new woodland created by the Woodland Trust as part of the South Yorkshire Forest. See also Box 5.1 (designed by C. Crayke).

be composed of local genotypes and the distribution of the trees will be matched to site conditions. The new community will require a minimum of management and appear natural, which is an elusive character (Ratcliffe 1977). So why are so few woodlands established in this way?

The Forestry Commission Research Division under took a survey in 1993 to evaluate natural colonization as an option for woodland creation (Hodge and Harmer 1995). It involved 47 sites that had been abandoned for between 10 and 41 years. Ash (*Fraxinus excelsior*), birch (*Betula* sp.), goat willow (*Salix caprea*), and hawthorn (*Crataegus monogyna*) made up 85% of the coloniz-ing woody vegetation with an average of three species per site. Colonization tended to be either very sparse or very dense, but on average only 19% of the land was adequately stocked (though this might be more than adequate for nature conservation purposes). There was a positive link between infertility and woody plant colonization. The conclusion was that natural colonization was too slow and unpredictable to be a suitable method of establishment (pre-sumably for forestry purposes). Also it was concluded that the woody veg-etation was species poor and there was no control if woodland with particular characteristics was required.

Despite these disadvantages natural colonization is still the preferred option for extending existing semi-natural broad-leaved woodland of high nature conservation value. Sites adjacent to existing woods experience a heavy seed fall and colonization can be promoted by cultivation, harrowing, and weed control to create a seed bed and reduce initial competition. If necessary, fertile topsoil can be removed to enhance the process. Any slowness or unpre-dictability is more than offset by the low intensity of management required and the high sensitivity to site characteristics. A fine example of a wood rapidly created by natural regeneration following ploughing adjacent to ancient woodland can be seen at Monkswood in Huntingdonshire (see p. 39). The Geescroft and Broadbalk wilderness woods at Rothamsted Experi-mental Station show what can be achieved if one is willing to wait many decades (see Fig. 3.1). There is a natural regeneration grant available from the Forest Authority, it covers 50% of costs but it is rarely taken up. It should be.

There is considerable evidence from North America that ecological suc-cession on disturbed sites can be accelerated by providing bird perches to encourage seed deposition. McClanahan and Wolfe (1992) reported that seed fall beneath perches had a higher diversity of genera, and that seed numbers (at 340 seeds/m^2/year) were 150 times greater than at sites without perches. These converted to 1.4 and 2.0 plants/m^2 at one and two years. McDonnell and Stiles (1983) experimented with different types of perch and recorded the greatest number of seeds associated with real plants, followed by horizontal, pyramidal, arched, and vertical perches. Introducing recruitment foci for bird-dispersed trees and shrubs does not ensure the establishment of the desired species. Robinson and Handel (1992) found that many of the newly arrived species were highly invasive exotic weeds such as *Ailanthus altissima*, *Rosa multiflora*, and *Lonicera japonica*. The conclusion has to be that this is not an alternative, inexpensive method of re-afforesting disturbed land, but should be used in conjunction with the planting of desirable species that have a poor colonizing ability.

Direct seeding

The Forestry Commission has carried out at least 70 experiments on direct sowing since the early 1920s. Direct sowing is defined as the artificial sowing of tree seed onto the final site. It is surface sown, or buried, and frequently preceded by intensive ground preparation and followed by some years of aftercare. The results were extremely variable and the conclusion to this work was that the unpredictable success and irregular stocking made it unsuitable as a method of woodland establishment, except occasionally where it might be combined with hydroseeding on small amenity sites such as roadside embankments (Stevens *et al*. 1990). The Forestry Commision results are disappointing, as the method has intrinsic appeal to conservationists because it can be combined with the collection of local seed. The problems appear to be heavy seed predation and competition from other vegetation. Establishing new woodland by direct seeding is standard practice in North America and parts of continental Europe so it is to be hoped that with further research it can be adapted to British conditions.

Planting

Given the current 'fashion', planting will remain the chief method of woodland establishment. In habitat creation terms, the first requirement is for the creation of a directory of nurseries that can supply local genetic stock or, better still, a proportion could be raised from seed originating from nearby ancient woodlands on soils similar to the planting site. When trees are grown for timber it is normal to select from a range of provenances, so nurseries should be capable of providing the same service for amenity woodland. Ideally, the habitat should be matched as well as the natural area; for example, ash exists as two physiological races, one adapted to dry limestone soils and the other moist fertile ones (Munch and Dieterich 1925).

Little critical work has been carried out on the advantages of using local genetic stock. One of the few studies is by Worrell (1992) who compared European continental and British provenances of some native trees for growth, survival, and stem form. He found considerably reduced growth rates

(>25%) and survival for certain continental provenances. This was most likely to be encountered in species that are relatively fast growing, have a short generation time (pioneers), and have been present in Britain for a long period since the end of the Ice age; for example, Scots pine (*Pinus sylvestris*), birch, alder (*Alnus glutinosa*), and aspen (*Populus tremula*). Conversely, species that have colonized Britain most recently, such as beech (*Fagus sylvatica*) and hornbeam (*Carpinus betulus*), are the least likely to be affected by employing continental seed. So, over long periods of time, local populations appear to have adapted to local conditions, particularly local climatic conditions. This is known as ecotypic variation.

Planting has the advantage that it gives control over open areas; for example, a glade structure that incorporates important existing vegetation and marginal ecotones can be introduced. Rodwell and Patterson (1994) have suggested that a suitable compromise is to plant quick growing pioneer species such as birch, alder and willow while leaving open areas between the clumps where natural regeneration can occur. Much planted amenity woodland would be improved as habitat if substantial areas (20–30%) were left open to allow natural colonization.

Species selection

Every ecologist believes they can design woodland appropriate to their local area by taking the composition of the older woods in the locality as a guide. This approach was adopted at Stansted Airport where 64 ha of woodland planting was based on the composition of nearby ancient woods (Charlton 1990). For people without this confidence, an extensive literature has recently appeared that provides advice on this important matter. Soutar and Peterken (1989) offer lists of trees and shrubs that are suitable for planting within 10 zones covering England, Scotland, and Wales; the zones broadly reflect the natural distribution of the trees. The use of these guidelines, it is suggested, will assist in the maintenance of regional diversity and minimize the degree to which species are planted beyond their natural range. Zone boundaries were selected to give the best fit for the presumed natural distributions of Scots pine, small-leaved lime (*Tilia cordata*), bird cherry (*Prunus padus*), hornbeam, and beech. Tables provide lists of species suitable for each zone.

Their paper includes a timely reminder that planting native trees and shrubs can damage nature conservation interests even if used in the appropriate zone. This applies to species with local forms and those with distributions of scientific interest, for example whitebeam (*Sorbus aria* s. l.) occurs as local races (micro-species), some of which are endemic, and juniper (*Juniperus communis*) has a variety of growth forms. Old woodland indicators should also be planted with care, e.g. small-leaved lime, large-leaved lime (*T. platyphyllos*), wild service-tree (*Sorbus torminalis*), and Midland hawthorn (*Crataegus laevigata*), to help avoid confusion regarding local genetics and past history. Oliver Rackham (1991) expresses it perfectly with respect to the small-leaved lime: 'Its meaning lies in it being a rare and wonderful tree with a mysterious natural distribution. It is devalued by being made a common tree.' The same argument could be applied to the native black poplar (*Populus nigra* subsp. *betulifolia*), yew (*Taxus baccata*), Plymouth pear (*Pyrus cordata*), and box (*Buxus sempervirens*), all of which are vulnerable to loss of meaning through a fashion for excessive planting. Mabey (1996) sees dangers in using the distictiveness-from-rarity argument inflexibly, as many species are rare only because of recent depletion by man. Soutar and Peterken (1989) have concluded that it is most appropriate to encourage common and already widespread species rather than rarer ones, with special attention being given to hazel, holly (*Ilex aquifolium*), and common hawthorn (*Crataegus monogyna*), which are unlikely to be planted for commercial purposes.

A working tool for selecting appropriate planting mixes is the National Vegetation Classification (Rodwell 1991a), particularly its synthesis into Forestry Commission Bulletin 112 *Creating new native woodlands* (Rodwell and Patterson 1994). The NVC recognizes 19 major types of woodland and can predict which might be expected to develop on any site if succession were to proceed unhindered. The Bulletin provides lists of the most ecologically appropriate trees and shrubs to plant in such situations together with information on desired invaders and optimal precursor vegetation. It champions natural colonization but accepts that planting is necessary on sites isolated from seed-parents where the objective is to establish new woods with a full complement of trees and shrubs.

Bulletin 112 recognizes five major woodland planting zones in Britain based on climate and two based on physiographic characteristics (wet woodlands) (Fig. 5.2). Within each zone it is possible to recognize ecological types defined by terrain and soils and from these to predict the trees and shrubs most appropriate for planting. In wet woodland, ground conditions tend to override climatic considerations; Peterken and Hughs (1995) have argued that restoration of the floodplain forests of Britain should be a priority. Figure 5.3 provides lists of trees and shrubs recommended for creating 15 of the 19 NVC woodland types with an indication of the appropriate proportions. Minor species should be used sparingly in a few sites only. Armed with Bulletin 112 it should be possible to identify the appropriate native woodland for any site using information on the local climate, geology, soils, and existing vegetation. It has perhaps been over strict in recommending planting only within the supposed native range of a species. For cultural and landscape reasons it may be permissible to plant species outside their normal range.

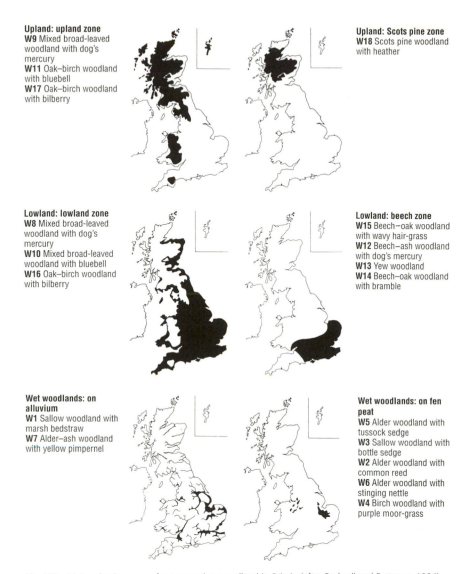

Upland: upland zone
W9 Mixed broad-leaved woodland with dog's mercury
W11 Oak–birch woodland with bluebell
W17 Oak–birch woodland with bilberry

Upland: Scots pine zone
W18 Scots pine woodland with heather

Lowland: lowland zone
W8 Mixed broad-leaved woodland with dog's mercury
W10 Mixed broad-leaved woodland with bluebell
W16 Oak–birch woodland with bilberry

Lowland: beech zone
W15 Beech–oak woodland with wavy hair-grass
W12 Beech–ash woodland with dog's mercury
W13 Yew woodland
W14 Beech–oak woodland with bramble

Wet woodlands: on alluvium
W1 Sallow woodland with marsh bedstraw
W7 Alder–ash woodland with yellow pimpernel

Wet woodlands: on fen peat
W5 Alder woodland with tussock sedge
W3 Sallow woodland with bottle sedge
W2 Alder woodland with common reed
W6 Alder woodland with stinging nettle
W4 Birch woodland with purple moor-grass

Fig. 5.2   Major planting zones for new native woodland in Britain (after Rodwell and Patterson 1994).

Being site specific the above method of species selection is finely tuned to local variations in the environment and ideal when nature conservation is the primary objective. If timber production or general amenity are required a broader approach may be adopted. The Cambridgeshire Landscape

Lowland mixed broadleaved woodland with dog's mercury W8
Upland mixed broadleaved woodland with dog's mercury W9
Lowland mixed broadleaved woodland with bluebell/wild hyacinth W10
Upland oak-birch woodland with bluebell/wild hyacinth W11
Lowland oak-birch woodland with bilberry/blaeberry W16
Upland oak-birch woodland with bilberry/blaeberry W17
Beech-ash woodland with dog's mercury W12
Beech-oak woodland with bramble W14
Beech-oak woodland with wavy hair-grass W15
Scots pine woodland with heather W18
Alder woodland with common reed W2
Alder woodland with stinging nettle W6
Alder-ash woodland with yellow pimpernel W7
Birch woodland with purple moor-grass W4
Alder
Ash
Aspen
Beech
Downy birch
Silver birch
Crab apple
Wych elm
Field maple
Gean
Bird cherry
Holly
Hornbeam
Common oak
Sessile oak
Rowan
Scots pine
Common whitebeam
Crack willow
Goat willow
White willow
Yew

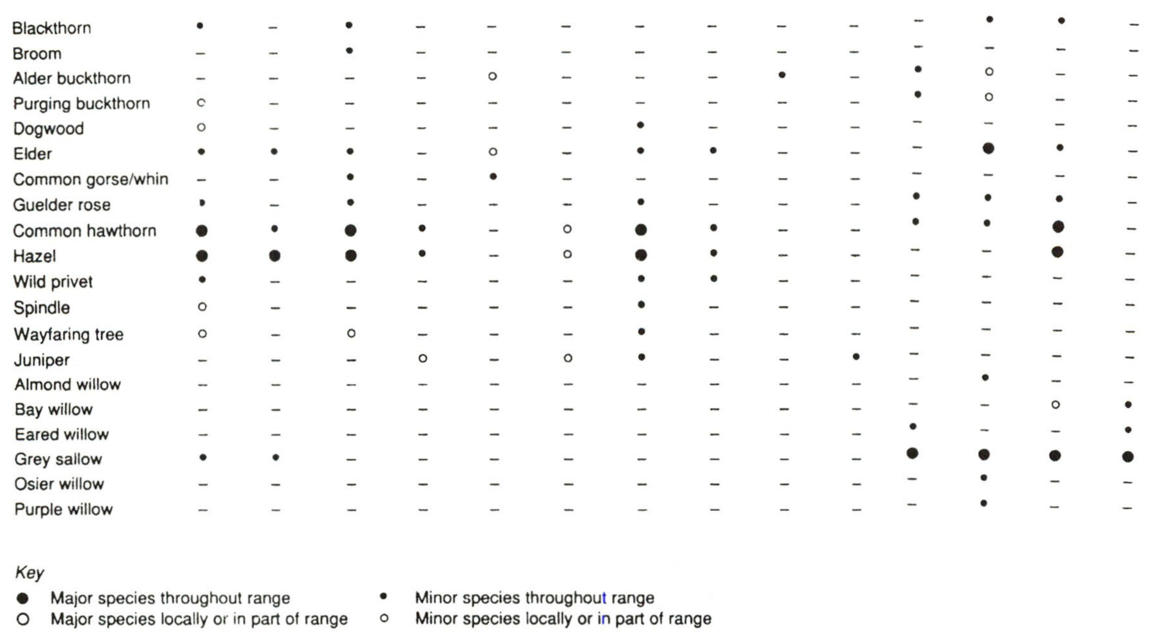

Blackthorn
Broom
Alder buckthorn
Purging buckthorn
Dogwood
Elder
Common gorse/whin
Guelder rose
Common hawthorn
Hazel
Wild privet
Spindle
Wayfaring tree
Juniper
Almond willow
Bay willow
Eared willow
Grey sallow
Osier willow
Purple willow

Key
● Major species throughout range   ● Minor species throughout range
○ Major species locally or in part of range   ○ Minor species locally or in part of range

Fig. 5.3 Major and minor species of trees and shrubs in existing semi-natural woodland (after Rodwell and Patterson 1994).

Guidelines (Cambridgeshire County Council 1991) suggest planting lists for each of the nine areas into which the county has been divided. For the south-east clay hills, the prescription is for new mixed woodland based on oak, ash, and hazel, with subordinate gean, field maple, hawthorn, and elder; recommended hedgerow trees are oak dominant with sub-dominant ash and field maple. By contrast, in the chalklands pure beech woods are recommended on high ground; mixed woodland should contain dominant beech, ash, and hazel with a range of other trees (but no oak) and characteristic shrubs such as wild privet, wayfaring tree, and yew; the recommended hedgerow tree is ash with beech to be used for avenues. The scale of these landscape zones is up to 60 km. If the guidelines were followed slavishly the countryside might become stereotyped and lacking in surprise but in practice this is unlikely to happen. It will not be long before similar prescriptions are formulated for English Nature's Natural Areas, most of which are on an even larger scale. This is planning using ecological principles, and has the potential to re-emphasize local character and re-create a sense of place.

Introduced species

Exotic species have been largely excluded from Bulletin 112 prescriptions as most conservationists feel uneasy about them. However, several are so well established in the UK that it is impossible to prevent them invading planted woods where they can become local dominants. The trees most commonly involved, with their dates of introduction, are sycamore (early 15th century), sweet chestnut (Romans), Norway maple (pre-1683), Turkey oak (1735), holm oak (pre-1600), and, outside their native zones, beech and pine. Many are so well established that there is no way their advance can be halted, urban ecologists have already accepted them as part of the scene.

Sycamore has a secure place in the British countryside and is a component of estate plantations, upland shelter-belts, and several NVC types (W6-W11) on moist fertile soils. Sweet chestnut is a member of W10. Though it would not be popular to hasten the spread of these species, it would be unwise to try to eliminate them if they invade. Arguments in favour of sycamore are provided by Taylor (1985), Gilbert (1989), and Boyd (1992). Nicholson and Hare (1986) have labelled the unquestioning removal of sycamore as the 'John Wayne syndrome', that is, cut down first, ask questions later.

The woodland of holm oak that is colonizing St Boniface Down, Isle of Wight, is developing into a botanically exciting place and illustrates a dilemma that British ecologists are going to have to face as our flora becomes increasingly ingressed by exotic species (Box 5.2). Is it destroying a habitat of even greater value?

**Box 5.2   The holm oak (*Quercus ilex*) wood
on St Boniface Down, Isle of Wight**

This holm oak wood, which covers 16 ha, is considered to have arisen in
the 1920s through the invasion of chalk grassland. The National Trust is
preventing its further expansion by using feral goats (Tutton 1994). It is an
example of the type of woodland that can arise through employing natural
regeneration. Holm oak is dominant, but the wood contains several
additional exotic trees and shrubs such as sycamore (*Acer pseudoplatanus*),
Turkey oak (*Quercus cerris*), *Viburnum tinus*, Norway maple (*Acer
platanoides*), and a single strawberry tree (*Arbutus unedo*), these have
naturalized from gardens. This thoroughly alien wood poses a dilemma for
local naturalists because the potential natural vegetation is beech, but within
the last 20 years, a wide range of scarce wildlife has moved in. The ground
flora includes white helleborine (*Cephalanthera damasonium*), broad-leaved
helleborine (*Epipactis helleborine*), yellow bird's-nest (*Monotropa hypopitys*),
and bird's-nest orchid (*Neottia nidus-avis*). The fungal flora is proving to be
interesting especially for *Amanita* species with the Red Data List species
A. echinocephala recorded, as well as the only permanent British station for
A. ovoidea, and the rare ascomycete *Sarcosphaera coronaria*. The purple
hairstreak butterfly (*Quercusia quercus*) has started to breed on the holm
oak, which is a standard food plant in the Mediterranean.

This wood demonstrates the type of assemblage that may increasingly be
produced by natural regeneration. Holm oak is native as close as Brittany and
appears to have found a permanent home in southern England among our
impoverished woodlands. Should it be welcomed as a new community or
despised as an aggressive alien?

Planting layout

Planting patterns have a major influence on the structure and appearance of
a wood. The planting specification gives the species composition of each area
delimited on the planting plan, their proportion (%) or number, the spacing,
and states whether they are to be distributed singly or in groups. Although far
too much naturalistic and amenity planting is arranged in straight rows, there
has recently been a move to plant in randomly distributed groups of a given
size. For example, oak might be in groups of 25, faster growing birch in groups
of 10, and hazel in randomly distributed groups of 5–25. Instructions might be
given to plant gean mainly at the margins. In this way the fine detail is left to
the contractor and an irregular woodland results. However, this is still far from
the pattern found in a natural wood.

One should aim for a robust pattern that gives every species a chance of
contributing to the mature woodland without relying on future management.

The key to this is wide and variable spacing and natural groupings. It is a common mistake to plant far too many trees and insufficient shrubs. A 40:60 ratio of trees to shrubs is a reasonable goal and allows a good shrub matrix inside the wood, rather than the all too familiar fringe of scrub round the edge. Only if two species are well matched for growth rate (e.g. beech and gean), should mixed groups be specified.

If a mixture of species is at too small a scale and planted too closely, then the faster growing ones will shade out the others and become dominant—unless a lot of respacing and thinning occurs; a well-designed wood should be self-thinning. As the plants increase in size intra-specific competition commences and Watkinson's rule (Watkinson 1986) comes into operation. This rule states that for every increase in plant mass by a factor of 2, there is a corresponding decrease in density by a factor of 3; in other words, the larger the plants the lower their density. By this method, the single-species groups self-thin, with the most competitive individuals becoming dominant and the rest contributing to small diameter dead wood.

Only on the most difficult sites, such as mineral workings, should fast growing nurse species like alder, larch, or pine be employed; in the absence of regular management these species will become the future dominants, rather than the intended species. Even with management it can be difficult to suppress alder, a lesson that was learnt at Warrington New Town.

When it comes to deciding the layout and spacing of amenity/nature conservation woodland, ideas are still heavily influenced by traditional forestry practices aimed at timber production. These require dense planting to promote straight, knot free boles; and for economic reasons the entire site is put under trees. The recommended planting density is usually 2 m spacings (2500 trees/ha); at a spacing of 3 m (1100/ha), canopy closure, which marks the end of the establishment period, is anything up to 10 years. A spacing of 1.5 m (4500/ha) is considered to be wasteful of nursery stock. For timber production an even density across the site is optimal.

The best woodland for nature conservation is irregular, and includes large open areas and a variable density of trees and shrubs. The most radical attempt to develop a different type of layout has been by Rodwell and Patterson (1994) who recommend large clumps up to 50 m in width separated by gaps of between 7 m (which will eventually close over) to 20 m or more. This very open type of woodland favours plant and animal species of wood margins and also provides opportunities for natural colonization. Open areas greater than 25 m are used to provide glades, which are believed to have been a feature of the original wildwood but are often neglected when planning today's over-stocked woods. Tree spacing within clumps should still be at 2 m on average, to promote fast establishment, but in some clumps spacing should be increased to 3–5 m so that there is some bushier growth. An economic reason for employing wide spacing is that fewer plants are required (if local genetic stock is being used there may be a shortage of plants). An occasional group of conifers in deciduous woodland can provide a valuable extra niche for birds.

Establishment

Many choices have to be made at this stage that can make all the difference between success or failure. General texts on woodland establishment are provided by Hibberd (1989), Williamson (1992), and Hodge (1995).

Ground preparation

Ground preparation, such as drainage, will not often be necessary, as the planting mix should have been matched to site conditions (and very wet areas are best left unplanted). The commonest problem, especially on urban sites, will be soil compaction, which causes poor establishment and slow growth. This must be relieved by deep cultivation (0.5–0.7 m) employing a wing-tine ripper, with tines spaced at 1.2 m, mounted behind a tracked dozer, and this activity should be carried out during the summer before planting as soil only shatters satisfactorily when dry. The rip lines do not remain conspicuous for long. The use of fertilizers should be unnecessary if species have been well matched to site. Fertilizer application can be counter productive, with grass (weeds) benefiting more than the trees; the resulting competition can cause reduced tree survival and growth. Fertile soils may also encourage undesirably aggressive species such as rosebay willowherb (*Chamerion angustifolium*), nettles (*Urtica dioica*), and brambles (*Rubus fruticosus*), which delay colonization by less competitive woodland plants. The use of subsoils for woodland establishment, as described in Chapter 2, would avoid these problems.

Planting stock

The planting stock will, in most cases, be that traditionally used in forestry practice, small (40–80 cm high) bare-rooted transplants. These are cheap (20–50 pence) and show good survival and growth. They are also known as '1 + 1' indicating that they have spent one year in the seed bed and one year in a transplant line. The root system may have been trimmed after one year to promote branching and the production of fibrous roots, they are then known as undercuts; these are becoming increasingly popular. Other types of planting stock such as whips, feathers, and container grown material are several times more expensive and remain slow growing. Cell grown stock produced in low-volume containers in one growing season may have a future and are suitable for local tree rearing projects.

Many planting schemes fail due to careless plant handling. It is essential to prevent roots drying out; even on dull, cool days exposure to air can quickly cause irreversible damage. The fine structured root system of birch for example can be killed by 24 hours of exposure to the air (Insley and Buckley 1986). Stock should be bought locally to reduce transit time and transported in sealed, co-extruded polythene bags that are black on the inside and white on the outside. The time trees are out of the ground must be minimized; planting should take place soon after delivery, if this is not possible stock should be temporarily heeled in to ensure the roots are kept moist.

Planting method

On most sites notch planting will be appropriate using a T- or an L-notch. On ripped sites the plants should be sited about 15 cm from the rip line. If the ground is vegetated the notch can be cut in the sward and weed control applied later. Alternatively a square of turf can be cut out first and either removed, with the notch being cut directly in the exposed soil (screef planting), or inverted with the notch being cut through the turf (turf planting). Both methods give a measure of short term weed control. Pit planting is much slower than notch planting but is necessary for larger stock such as whips and feathers. Stock should be planted while dormant, the appropriate planting season extends from early November to late March avoiding frosty periods.

Tree protection

The potential for damage to the newly planted trees from deer, voles, rabbits, hares, and domestic animals is high. There are three options for controlling it, fencing, individual tree protection, or controlling animal numbers. The last option is rarely practicable. Tree protection is costly, so the decision will probably be influenced by financial considerations. A large (>2 ha) regular shaped planting area with straight boundaries can most economically be protected by fencing. Deer/rabbit fencing 1.8 m high costs c. £5/m and rabbit fencing 0.9 m high c. £2.40/m to erect. Hares are slightly more expensive to protect against than rabbits, as a trip wire is required. Good weed control will reduce the risk of vole damage.

Individual protection takes the form of translucent polypropylene tree shelters supported on a stake, which also provide a favourable microclimate around the tree (Fig. 5.4). Their height should be determined by the types of herbivorous mammals present. As well as protecting the trees from mammal damage and greatly increasing survival rates, self-destructing tree shelters will, over their 5-year lives, accelerate early height growth and shield the tree from herbicide damage. The enhanced height growth is thought to be, at least partly, a result of CO_2 build-up within the tube. This can be increased further by

Fig. 5.4   Plastic tree shelters aid the establishment of newly planted young trees but double the cost. It is normal practice to control weeds around their base. The regular dense spacing is not recommended.

pressing the base of the tube into the ground to create a seal and trap the soil respiration.

Spiral guards of loosely coiled plastic can be used to reduce bark stripping by rabbits and hares. However, this form of protection is only suitable for sturdy trees that are taller than 60 cm. All forms of individual tree protection are expensive (particularly with high density planting) and have a negative landscape impact, but tree shelters can double the height increment of many broad-leaved species measured 3 years after planting (Fig. 5.5; Potter 1991).

Weed control

Weed control is the single most important activity during the establishment stage of planted trees. On fertile soils, weeds, particularly grasses, compete aggressively with young trees for water and nutrients, and may also compete for light. Long grass also encourages voles, which damage and kill trees by nibbling the bark. The result of ignoring weed control is slow growing and moribund trees or, sometimes, complete failure (Fig. 5.6a).

If the ground vegetation contains no valuable precursor species it may be possible to start controlling perennial weeds the summer before planting. This can be achieved using a broad spectrum systemic herbicide. Once the trees have been planted, the aim should be to keep a circle of at least 1 m² around

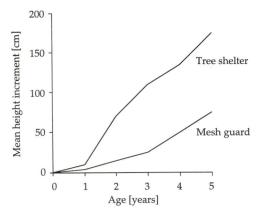

Fig. 5.5 Comparison of early height growth for trees protected by mesh guards or tree shelters (after Potter 1991).

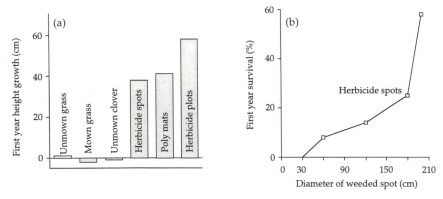

Fig. 5.6 (a) Effect of different forms of weed control on first year height growth of silver maple (*Acer* sp.). (b) Survival of oak (*Quercus* sp.) in relation to area of spot weeding around the young trees (after Hibberd 1989).

each tree free of weeds, or maintain a 1 m weed-free strip along rows of trees; as Fig. 5.6b demonstrates, the bigger the weed-free circle the better the tree growth. Establishment can also be encouraged by adopting a policy of 'bare earth' in the plantations until canopy closure is effected. This can be achieved using glyphosate and simazine; the addition of dye to the spray mix aids placement and allows operatives to prune off branches that receive the spray accidentally (Salter and Darke 1988). Weed control should be carried out once or twice a year (during windless weather) until the canopy has closed (*c*. 3–5 years if the tree spacing is 2 m.). Alternative forms of weed control such as sheet mulches, mulch mats, organic mulches, hoeing, and growth retardants are not appropriate for the establishment of extensive woodland. Particularly inappropriate is mowing or strimming the grass between the trees—this invigorates the sward, thereby increasing soil moisture deficits. In the 1970s this was the main method of weed control used at Rother Valley Country Park. Today the plantations are full of gaps where trees failed; from a distance the hillsides appear to be covered with open scrub.

Management

Thinning is a management operation concerned with producing quality timber and costs £2000–£2500/ha. Thinning should rarely be necessary in well-designed native broad-leaved woodland. Occasionally it may be desirable to remove unwanted exotics, to reduce the cover of prolific species to favour slower growing ones, such as holly and yew, or to maintain designated open habitats, but this is minor restructuring rather than thinning. Following establishment, the only significant management necessary will be connected with developing marginal ecotones, maintaining glades, introducing a field layer, putting in a circulation system, and ensuring the safety of visitors. Maintaining fencing beyond the establishment period may not be necessary—a low level of grazing is beneficial to woodland; in the past, aurochs, red deer, and wild horses played an important part in determining the nature and structure of woodland (Chatters and Sanderson 1994).

Introducing woodland herbs

Work on introducing woodland herbs has been carried out in Milton Keynes (Francis *et al.* 1992; Street and Mond 1992; Francis and Street 1993; Francis 1995), Wolverhampton (Cohn and Packham 1993; Cohn and Millett 1995), Warrington New Town (Tregay 1985), and Wye College (Buckley and Knight 1989). All agree that on most sites it is necessary to wait until the trees and shrubs are well established before starting; by then any herbicide applications will have ceased and a woodland microclimate will be developing. On infertile soils and subsoils, however, carefully selected ground flora species can be introduced from the start (Anderson 1996).

On richer soils, the typical ground flora of newly planted woodland is a rank sward of low species diversity lacking in attractive and interesting plants. This is due partly to the soil conditions, which encourage competitive species, and partly due to their isolation from existing woods to act as sources of colonizing material (Peterken and Game 1984). This means that even in the very long term the developing field layer is likely to remain poor.

In 1980, Milton Keynes Parks Trust decided to enhance their developing plantations by introducing an attractive and diverse ground flora. Preliminary experiments indicated that both direct seeding and planting were options.

These led to large scale trials in 1987 to investigate such basic questions as the timing of introductions, ground pre-treatment, species choice, preferred method of introduction, and the effect of density. By chance, site conditions in the Milton Keynes plantations were ideal for accepting a ground flora as the establishment policy was to maintain a bare earth regime under the trees. Establishment was best where the light level at the ground surface was between 10% and 40% of ambient daylight in summer, conditions that often arise after the first thinning. Seeding was carried out in autumn or winter, to ensure vernalization, at a rate of approximately 3–5 kg/ha (0.3–0.5 g/m²). By 1993, approximately 85 ha of new plantation had been hand-seeded with a labour requirement of 1.4 man days/ha and the seed costing *c*. £600/ha.

The field trials, which were monitored intensively until 1992, identified two suitable growth strategies for woodland herbs and three groups for their introduction purposes (Table 5.1).

1. Woodland edge or marginal species, that can be introduced as seed and that are quick to mature, establish, and spread; e.g. red campion (*Silene dioica*), wood avens (*Geum urbanum*), hedge bedstraw (*Galium mollugo*).

2. Shade-tolerant species that can be introduced as seed, from which they slowly establish; e.g. bluebell (*Hyacinthoides non-scripta*), ramsons (*Allium ursinum*), woodruff (*Galium odoratum*).

3. Shade tolerant species that are most successfully introduced as pot grown plants from which many spread by predominantly vegetative growth; e.g. bugle (*Ajuga reptans*), yellow archangel (*Lamiastrum galeobdolon*), primrose (*Primula vulgaris*).

A different sowing density is recommended for each group with the slower establishing shade-tolerant species requiring the highest density (Table 5.1). The wood edge species are quick to sow themselves back into the community and to establish building populations. It is most satisfactory to introduce the planted species in spring when the ground has warmed up. They should be arranged in single species groups as this simulates the mosaics found in mature woodland. Both techniques are necessary to introduce the full range of woodland ground flora.

In Wolverhampton, the ground flora introductions were made into small (<0.5 ha) urban woods 7–10 years old composed of fast growing, high volume species such as alder, white poplar, and goat willow. The ground flora tended to be grassy with much couch (*Elymus repens*), cock's-foot (*Dactylis glomerata*), Yorkshire-fog (*Holcus lanatus*), nettles, and *Galium aparine*. Mulching with woodbark or woodchip was used to suppress weed growth. Sowings into these woods began in 1989 and were backed-up by trials to investigate the effect of different mulches, mulch depths, and sowing depths within the mulches. The results varied from good to poor, but sowing directly onto or at

Table 5.1
Groups for the introduction of reliable woodland field layer species

Group	Category	Method of introduction	Establishment	Species
1	Woodland edge species	Seed (3 kg/ha)	Rapid	*Alliaria petiolata, Arum maculatum, Bromus racemosus, Brachypodium sylvaticum, Digitalis purpurea, Galium mollugo, Geum urbanum, Hypericum hirsutum, Milium effusum, Silene dioica, Stachys sylvatica, Stellaria holostea, Torillis japonica*
2	Shade tolerant species	Seed (10 kg/ha)	Slower	*Allium ursinum, Conopodium majus, Galium odoratum, Hyacinth. non-scriptus, Primula vulgaris, Viola odorata*
3	Shade tolerant species	Pot plants (3–9/m²)	Slow	*Anemone nemorosa, Ajuga reptans, Circaea lutetiana, Lamiastrum galeobdolon, Mercurialis perennis, Oxalis acetosella, Teucrium scorodonia, Viola riviniana,* most ferns

Source: Francis 1995, and V. J. Cohn, pers. commun.

5 cm depth within a heavy mulch in conditions of partial shade was a guarantee of success for a wide range of species. Mulch type (woodbark, woodchip, leaf litter) was not critical. Appropriate weed control could also be achieved by creating a bare patch using herbicides. The most successful species were false brome (*Brachypodium sylvaticum*), smooth brome (*Bromus racemosus*), nettle-leaved bellflower (*Campanula trachelium*), bluebell; which flowered in 3–7 years, *Geum urbanum*, wood millet (*Milium effusum*), primrose (which was more successful than at Milton Keynes), red campion (which performed better than any other species), hedge woundwort (*Stachys sylvatica*), and greater stitchwort (*Stellaria holostea*). Results with common dog-violet (*Viola riviniana*) and hairy St John's-wort (*Hypericum hirsutum*) were variable, and

Fig. 5.7 Primrose (*Primula vulgaris*) and false brome (*Brachypodium sylvaticum*) established in new woodland by sowing onto wood mulch; Wolverhampton. Photograph by M. Inman.

the performance of both pendulous sedge (*Carex pendula*) and foxglove (*Digitalis purpurea*) was poor.

This method of ground flora introduction can be employed in any wood, not just under those special conditions found in the Milton Keynes plantations. It can be linked to the first thinning, the product of which can be chipped on site to provide a suitable mulch. If the seed mix is sown into a wood as 'buckshot' it will sort itself out into local dominants due to minor variations in site conditions. At one site in Wolverhampton, primrose was dominant in one corner, false brome and *Milium effusum* were well established where there was shade from under-shrubs, while in an area that had been thinned as a result of 'community coppicing' *Geum urbanum* and red campion were doing especially well. It was difficult to believe that the ground flora was only 3–4 years old in that it was so vigorous, seedlings were abundant, and it was distributed in a natural manner. The grasses helped to enhance the appearance of the spring flowers (Fig. 5.7).

The experimental introductions of ground flora at Warrington New Town and Wye used what now appear to be unnecessarily costly techniques. These projects involved intensive weed control and a phased introduction of container grown plants. Buckley and Knight (1989) suggest a cost of around £1000/ha for each container grown species. However, as a one-off operation with a capital cost of less than £1000/ha, the introduction of a woodland ground flora as seed is not expensive in relation to total plantation establishment costs of £10 000–£20 000/ha.

Commercially produced seed of many of the characteristic ground flora species of ancient woodlands (Peterken 1981), is not available. This is no bad thing as, in common with woody plants, restraint should be exercised when dealing with species that have a distinctive ecology; the 'meaning' of moschatel (*Adoxa moschatellina*), wood melick (*Melica uniflora*), herb paris (*Paris quadrifolia*), and greater woodrush (*Luzula sylvatica*) would be lost if they were widely planted in secondary woodland. Most of the seed mixes advertised for shady places are more suitable for woodland openings, edges, or glades (although bluebell, ramsons, and pendulous sedge, which are now generally available, are true shade toleraters). Several seed merchants are still advertising woodland mixes that include meadow grasses and, often, meadow herbs, which are presumably designed to act as a nurse crop. All they do is enhance the competition problem; they are unnecessary and will not survive under a closed canopy.

Fauna

Mammals

Even when bats are excluded, some 32 British mammals are largely associated with or wholly dependent on woodland habitats. New woodland is beneficial to small mammal populations as it is more complex and diverse than the surrounding crops or pastures. There is succession of species till the canopy has closed when wood mice (*Apodemus sylvaticus*), bank vole (*Clethrionomys glareosus*), shrews (*Sorex araneus*, *S. minutus*), and, within their areas of distribution, dormice (*Muscardinus avellanarius*) and yellow-necked mice (*Apodemus flavicollis*) move in. Dormice are largely arboreal, so, if they are expected, special care should be taken to ensure that canopy trees provide occasional 'bridges' over rides.

Large herbivores are being reintroduced into woodland for the role they can play in management and as amenity features. In the Netherlands, between Amsterdam and Lelystad, there is a 5600 ha nature reserve developed on polderland. The site has been allowed to develop as naturally as possible into a mosaic of grassland, wetland, willow groves, and secondary woodland. It supports 300 Heck cattle (recreated Aurochs), 200 Konik horses (descendants of wild tarpanas), and 150 red deer. The grazing of these free ranging herbivores prevents blanket succession and has produced a site far richer and more economic to run than conventional intensive management could ever have done (Whitbread and Jenman 1995). The importance of grazing for maintaining the biodiversity of our woodlands is still largely unrecognized. Chatters and

Sanderson (1994) suggest that around one beef cow or pony per 5–10 ha, left to roam freely, will produce the light, extensive grazing necessary to diversify the woodland structure. In Burnham Beeches, the local authority is experimenting with grazing; a family of Berkshire pigs, 4 cows and several ponies inhabit a 32 ha enclosure. They are popular with the public, and the pigs help control the bracken.

Birds

A great deal is known about the ecology of woodland birds and their preferences. The number of bird species increases with the size of a wood (Moore and Hooper 1975), although the overall density of breeding birds falls off (Ford 1987). Some species, such as nightingale, chiffchaff, marsh tit, and jay, avoid very small woods, which support less stable bird communities than larger woods. The ideal layout, for maximizing bird life, is to have a mixture of small and large woods in the landscape (with some over 5 ha), and to avoid creating small isolated woods. If woods have to be small, cluster them. Rates of predation, by crows for example, may be higher in small woods (Andren and Angelstam 1988).

For attracting birds, the structure of a wood is at least as important as its size and botanical composition, and especially its growth stage and stand structure. Young woods are the optimal habitat for migrants such as turtle dove, tree pipit, and several warblers. Once the canopy has closed the habitat becomes more suitable for nightingale, willow warbler, and garden warbler. Mature woodland is preferred by marsh tits, nuthatchs, tree creepers, willow tits, and woodpeckers. By designing wide rides with shrubby margins it is possible to provide for both groups.

Rides need to be at least as wide, and preferably 1.5 times as wide, as the height of the surrounding trees. So, in mature woodland, a ride will need to be at least 30–45 m wide when measured from the base of the mature trees on either side. Substantial shrub or coppice margins can then be present along the edge without shading the centre of the ride. For breeding birds the marginal shrub belts need to be at least 5 m in width and, ideally, 10–20 m. Many birds that breed in the wood will feed in the rides, sparrow hawks will hunt along them and woodcock use them for their roding display. An alternative to rides are glades; to be interesting to birds these need to be >0.25 ha in size and to include some scrub.

In general, new woods should be planted with a variety of trees and shrubs to promote structural complexity. Different species of tree offer birds different types of food and contrasting types of nest site. Insectivorous birds, for example, find more food on oak, birch, willow, and sycamore than on sweet chestnut, holly, larch, and yew, though the latter may be preferred for roosting. Frugivorous birds also have their partialities. Mixtures of broad-leaved

> **Box 5.3   Nest box study at Bryngwyn
> opencast site, South Wales (Scullion 1994)**
>
> Thirty-nine holed nest boxes were placed in a series of young shelter belts to
> arrest a decline in tit (*Parus* spp.) numbers. These boxes had an occupancy
> rate of 30% in 1991, 41% in 1992, and 52% in 1993. Shelter belts adjacent
> to undisturbed areas had a higher density of breeding tits (10/ha), than more
> centrally located sites (5/ha). Tits nesting in central areas were confined to
> feeding on reinstated land where there was a low number of invertebrates,
> especially during the critical May–June period. This meant that the egg clutch
> size of Bryngwyn great tits (*Parus major*) was low and that chick mortality
> (at 46%) was high in comparison to woodlands elsewhere. Failure levels
> increased with increasing distance from undisturbed land. Clearly a food
> supply problem in the central parts of the reinstated area was limiting the
> population size of great tits and blue tits (*Parus caeruleus*). It was concluded
> that the nest boxes were encouraging birds to attempt to breed in a sub-
> optimal habitat.

and coniferous trees support very rich bird communities that include conifer
specialists such as the coal tit and goldcrest.

When designing a wood, the planting of substantial belts of native shrubs
at the edge (5–10 m wide) or leaving an unplanted zone (20 m wide) to encourage natural regeneration will help create an ecotone that is highly attractive
to song birds, pheasants, and insects, as well as providing roosts for the
thrushes, finches, and buntings that fed on surrounding farmland.

Nest boxes are sometimes introduced into young woodland to encourage
the breeding of hole nesting birds that might otherwise have to wait many
decades for this niche to develop. Though a good idea in theory the outcome
is not always as favourable to the birds as anticipated (Box 5.3).

Invertebrates

Old woodland has the richest invertebrate fauna of any habitat in Britain. This
is due to the former abundance of the habitat, the continuous history of many
individual woods, and its structural complexity. Many of the species involved
have low powers of dispersal, so the creation of new woodland is not likely
to benefit them unless it lies adjacent to an ancient site. New woodland also
offers very little to the important saproxylic (deadwood) fauna, which requires
old trees. Highest priority, therefore, is the conservation and proper management of existing old woods; the creation of new woodland should never be
accepted as mitigation against loss of ancient woodland.

The part of a young wood most valuable to insects are rides and glades. These should be warmed by the sun, sheltered from the wind, and support a rich ground flora. Rides oriented east–west receive more sun during the summer months than those oriented north–south, though this is reversed during the winter. Many woodland butterflies, like birds, prefer very open sunny rides with less than about 20% direct shade. Narrower rides will deteriorate as they become progressively more shaded. In the past, rides were maintained by grazing or cutting for hay. The least beneficial cutting regime is regular mowing from edge to edge as this eliminates all structural variation. Four levels of management have been described by Warren and Fuller (1993) so that design can be matched to available resources. Three of these are illustrated in Fig. 5.8.

Tree, shrub and herb species

Some species of tree support a far larger fauna of foliage-feeding and sap-sucking invertebrates than others (Kennedy and Southwood 1984); the same is true for shrubs and herbs. In general, native species support a richer fauna than introduced ones. The factors that account for this are (in order) host tree abundance in Britain, the length of time the tree has been present in the country, and 'evergreenness'; 74% of the variability in insect numbers is accounted for by these three variables. It would clearly be catastrophic for the dependant invertebrates if an oak–birch–hazel wood was replaced by one composed of sweet chestnut–holm oak–holly. Table 5.2, which shows the number of invertebrates associated with a range of plants, should only be taken as a rough guide when choosing the species composition of a new wood, since it represents only one aspect of invertebrate requirements. For example, a species with an intermediate score like sycamore (43) has, by the end of the summer, developed a very high biomass of aphids that supports a vast food chain of carnivores and parasites. Also, following the death of elms, horse chestnut (9) is now the most important tree for providing permanent sap runs, which are required by some woodland specialists.

Table 5.2 also shows the numbers of Lepidoptera feeding on various woodland ground layer plants. The values of bramble, broad-leaved dock (*Rumex obtusifolius*), golden rod (*Solidago virgaurea*), wild strawberry (*Fragaria vesca*), and nettle should be noted and compared with wood anemone (*Anemone nemorosa*), cuckoo-pint (*Arum maculatum*), and bitter vetch (*Lathyrus montanus*), which have only one or two species each, though in the case of the latter it is the delightful wood white butterfly (*Leptidea sinapis*).

Plants with easily accessible nectar and pollen are important to many woodland invertebrates; their inclusion in new woodland is likely to enhance its amenity value and allow people to observe the insects at close quarters. Open-structured flowers such as umbellifers, composites, and Rosaceae attract more

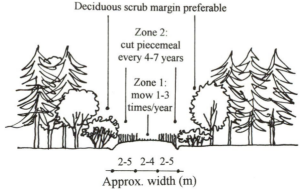

Deciduous scrub margin preferable

Zone 2:
cut piecemeal
every 4-7 years

Zone 1:
mow 1-3
times/year

2-5   2-4   2-5
Approx. width (m)

(a) Simple two-zone system

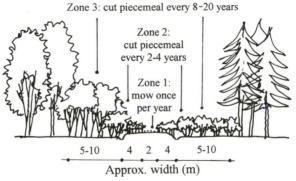

Zone 3: cut piecemeal every 8-20 years

Zone 2:
cut piecemeal
every 2-4 years

Zone 1:
mow once
per year

5-10   4   2   4   5-10
Approx. width (m)

(b) Three-zone system

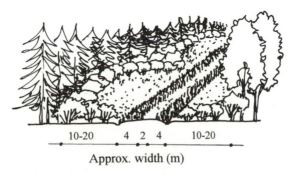

10-20   4   2   4   10-20
Approx. width (m)

(c) Scalloped edges (three-zone system)

Fig. 5.8 Three systems for managing woodland rides to encourage flora and fauna (redrawn by J. Makhzoumi from Warren and Fuller 1993).

Table 5.2
Numbers of phytophagous insects and mites and/or lepidoptera associated with woodland plants. (Kennedy and Southwood 1984; Lepidoptera data from F. Harrison, pers. commun.)

Plant species	Insects and mites	Lepidoptera	Plant species	Insects and mites	Lepidoptera
Trees			Shrubs		
Willows/sallows	450	166	Broom (*Cytisus scoparius*)		39
Native oaks	423	193	Gorse (*Ulex europaeus*)	29	
Birch	334	213	Privet (*Ligustrum vulgare*)	24	
Hawthorn	209	158	Dogwood (*Cornus sanguinea*)		17
Scots pine	172	36	Spindle (*Euonymus europaeus*)		10
Poplar/aspen	153	69	Bird cherry (*Prunus padus*)		9
Blackthorn	153	114	Snowberry (*Symphoricarpus*)		7
Alder	141	71	Gean (*Prunus avium*)	4	
Elm	124	24	Elder (*Sambucus nigra*)		4
Apple	118	76	Box (*Buxus sempervirens*)		1
Hazel	106	68	Herbaceous species		
Beech	98	51	Dock (*Rumex obtusifolius*)		69
Norway Spruce	70	13	Bramble (*Rubus fruticosus*)		63
Ash	68	32	Hedge bedstraw (*Galium mollugo*)		38
Rowan	58	28	Golden-rod (*Solidago virgaurea*)		27
Lime	57	31	Wild strawberry (*Fragaria vesca*)		24
Field maple	51	24	Primrose (*Primula vulgaris*)		23
Hornbeam	51	32	Nettle (*Urtica dioica*)		22
Sycamore	43	17	Wood sage (*Teucrium scorodonia*)		11
Larch	38	15	Red campion (*Silene dioica*)		10
Juniper	32	14	Greater stitchwort (*Stellaria holostea*)		8
Sweet chestnut	11	1	Foxglove (*Digitalis purpurea*)	5	
Holly	10	8	Bluebell (*Hyacinthoides non-scripta*)	4	
Horse chestnut	9	1	Wood avens (*Geum urbanum*)		3
Holm oak	5	4	Wood anemone (*Anemone nemorosa*)	2	
Yew	6	3	Cuckoo-pint (*Arum maculatum*)		1

species than complex flowers, which are only a food source for insects with long tongues. It is a good idea to plan for a succession of flowers; useful early-flowering nectar plants are willows, sallows, and blackthorn, while both species of hawthorn, which bloom in early summer, are particularly valuable. Elder, dogwood, and guelder rose are mid-summer species with readily available nectar. Late summer species are bramble and many herbaceous plants. Ivy is a valuable late nectar source, and also provides hibernating sites for many invertebrates; to strip ivy from a tree is vandalism.

The females of most butterflies take care during egg-laying to place their offspring in situations where they are best able to survive. To attract a given species into a wood it is necessary to present the food plant under optimal conditions. Purging buckthorn (*Rhamnus catharticus*) and alder buckthorn (*Frangula alnus*), the foodplants of the brimstone (*Gonepteryx rhamni*), are frequently planted in the expectation of attracting this handsome nomadic butterfly. However, bushes for egg-laying need to be both in the sun and sheltered from the wind, crowns protruding into sheltered sunshine are particularly favoured. The adults spend much of the day feeding on purple, nectar-rich flowers such as teasel (*Dipsacus fullonum*), purple loosestrife (*Lythrum salicaria*), buddleia (*Buddleia davidii*), and thistles, so these also need to be provided. Clumps of stinging nettles, introduced to encourage small tortoiseshells (*Aglais urticae*) to breed, also need to be presented in a particular way.

Kirby (1992) has provided an overview of the requirements of woodland invertebrates. He is at pains to emphasize the importance of microhabitats in young woodland such as bare ground, churned up ground, sunny stream margins, temporary puddles, and decaying fungi. He suggests that to compensate for the paucity of dead wood, brashings can be used to create a few large litter piles, but points out that if they are gathered together, tied into tight bundles, and then stacked, this a much more valuable habitat as it rarely dries out.

Scrub

There has not been a great deal of interest in creating scrub as a habitat in its own right, which is unfortunate since it has a high potential for birds and invertebrates in particular. This may be because current woodland grants only allow for 10% of shrubby species, and these go either to providing a sparse understory or a scrub margin. The NVC recognizes three types of natural scrub (sub-climax woody vegetation), and two of underscrub (Rodwell 1991a). Their composition is controlled by soil type, available seed sources, condition of the land at time of abandonment, and chance events like mast years and fires. The main type in Britain is *Crataegus monogyna–Hedera helix* scrub, extensive stands of which invade neglected bare ground and abandoned grassland on neutral to base-rich soils. A *Ulex europaeus–Rubus* scrub is found on freely draining acid soils and often contains broom (*Cytisus scoparius*). Most scrub is seral to woodland, but when dense, may remain static for several decades.

Creation

If there are good local seed sources, scrub can be left to develop naturally. Duffey *et al.* (1974) suggested that mature scrub might take 15 years to develop on fertile sites and 30 years in drier, less fertile localities; however, experience shows that the opposite can be true so it is difficult to be predictive. Certain species like bramble and gorse build up seed banks in the soil and can be particularly quick to invade when mowing or grazing ceases. Janzen (1970), working in Central America, studied the distance over which the local influence of woody plant seed parents extended. He considered that the 'seed shadow' fell off with distance, but so did the activity of seed and seedling predators, which were most important near the parent tree. Thus, the probability that a seedling would convert to a mature plant was greater at a distance from the parent. The condition of the ground also determines the rapidity of scrub invasion; much even-aged scrub is the result of a nudation event such as ploughing, a fire, or a sudden relaxation of hard grazing. This was responsible for the great surge of scrub following the myxomatosis epidemic of 1955 and for the patches of birch found on heaths and moors.

Certain types of scrub have been successfully established using direct sowing. This appears to be easiest with gorse and broom, the seed of which is readily available, costing around £70/kg. If it is sown onto cultivated ground, along with a grass seed mix, a good thicket should result. It is best distributed in drifts related to the landform, picking out banks or more acid and well drained patches of soil. There can be a considerable redistribution of seed after it has been sown, so it is best to broadcast it over a smaller area than that designated in the design. Both species have been established successfully by direct sowing on hilltop green space in Sheffield where, in early summer, the splashes of yellow they create are noticeable from 2 km away and are a welcome relief from mown grass.

Planting scrub appears to have been rarely attempted in habitat creation schemes except along wood margins or as hedgerows. However, it would be quite appropriate if the designer was trying to create the feeling of a common, was working in a small scale landscape, or had the space to provide for a variety of habitats. The shrubs should be ordered as bare-rooted forestry size transplants and notch planted employing variable spacing. To obtain maximum effect the planting should be related to site conditions (soil, topography) and will be most attractive to wildlife if it is designed to have a complex three-dimensional structure, with shrubs varying in height, canopy shape,

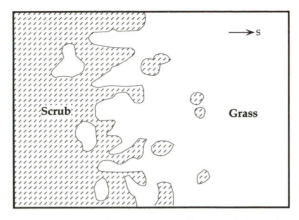

Fig. 5.9 Diagram showing the degree of complexity required in a south-facing scrub margin to maximize its attractiveness to insects.

and spacing. Clearings and sunny glades should be provided to give a high boundary: area ratio (Fig. 5.9). If possible, a marginal zone of tall herbs, where large growth-forms of grassland plants occur, should be incorporated—these are preferred for egg-laying by some invertebrates. Most scrub is species poor, so simple planting mixes guided by the NVC (Rodwell 1991a) are best. If it is not to become 'progressive scrub' and expand to take over large areas, the surrounding grassland/tall herb communities, which may have interest in their own right, will need to be cut or grazed. Since this particular community is very attractive to rabbits they may take over this role. Structural diversity can be maintained by coppicing a proportion of the outer bushes each year.

The benefits of scrub communities are that they provide an additional landscape element when designing with trees and grass. Also, a certain amount of scrub around or within a grassland greatly enhances the invertebrate interest. For example, Waloff (1968) discovered 23 phytophagous species associated with just the seed pods of broom. They were accompanied by 70 parasites and 60 common predatory species. At certain times of year the broom fauna is a valuable food source for birds. Gorse is particularly rich in spiders, while juniper supports a number of uncommon insects.

Breeding birds may be present in scrub in very high numbers. Williamson (1967) found 36 species with about 540 territories on 83 ha of open hawthorn scrub in Buckinghamshire. The most characteristic birds of open scrub are linnet, yellowhammer, willow warbler, grasshopper warbler, dunnock, stonechat, whinchat, meadow pipit, partridge, and cuckoo. As the canopy closes these are replaced by, or joined by, whitethroat, blackcap, wren, garden warbler, and pheasant. The nomadic behaviour of fieldfares and waxwings helps them locate berried scrub in winter. Other species such as wood pigeon, redpoll, brambling, and greenfinch use it for roosting. Further information on the ecology and management of scrub can be found in Crofts and Jefferson (1994) and Hopkins (1996).

Hedgerows

The hedge

Planting new hedgerows is now a commonplace activity and has been stimulated by a range of incentive schemes. A good practical book on their establishment is by McLean (1992). Species composition should be based on existing hedgerows in the area so that local character is reinforced. These patterns have not been identified on a national scale, but it is a matter of common knowledge that Exmoor is typified by beech hedges, Breckland by pine, parts of Staffordshire by holly, South-west Ireland by fuschia, areas of old enclosure such as parts of mid-Wales, Devon and Kent have much hazel, and there are mixed hedges along the Welsh borders. Planted hawthorn hedges predominate in the old open field counties of the east Midlands.

Hawthorn, by far the most popular species for hedgerows, is readily and cheaply available from nurseries. The nurseries will probably have raised them from continental seed, which is often less than half the price of British collected seed. These alien hawthorns can be identified by their habit of early bud-burst, often in February, as they have a phenology poorly adapted to our oceanic climate. Jones and Evans (1994) compared the growth, morphology, and performance of native and commercially obtained continental (Hungarian) hawthorn at an upland site in Wales. Six months after planting, the native plants were 35% taller, 70% more branched, had twice the total stem length, and four times as many thorns as the commercial material. The latter were also more susceptible to powdery mildew. They concluded that there was a good case for using native stock—the alien material had shown poor growth and was consequently swamped by grasses. The latter was also susceptible to die back from both wind scorching and fungal attack.

Most new hedges are planted on farms to provide stock-proof barriers. These can be pure hawthorn or a hawthorn–blackthorn mix in the ratio 4:1. Either mix will quickly grow into a strong thorny hedge. An alternative approach is to create a conservation hedge that will attract and sustain wildlife by using a much wider selection of native species. A composition of proven effectiveness for wildlife consists of the following mix: hawthorn (*Crateagus monogyna*), 50%; field maple (*Acer campestre*), 20%; blackthorn (*Prunus spinosa*) 15%; and 15% of other species, selected from dogwood (*Cornus sanguinea*), wayfaring tree (*Viburnum lantana*), buckthorn (*Rhamnus cathartica*), guelder rose (*Viburnum opulus*), hazel (*Corylus avellana*), spindle (*Euony-*

mous europaeus), dog rose (*Rose canina*), privet (*Ligustrum vulgare*), and holly (*Ilex aquifolium*), depending on soil type and their natural geographical range. Elder (*Sambucus nigra*) and the more vigorous willows such as goat willow (*Salix caprea*) are not included—they tend to dominate their position and suppress other species.

To establish a hedge, ground preparation usually consists of ploughing out and rotovating a 1 m strip to provide a good tilth. A period of fallow is then followed by chemical weed control and planting. An alternative method of weed control is to use a back polythene mulch strip (200 gauge) laid along the planting line and tucked in to hold its position during its life time, which may be 4 years. Notch planting is done through the sheet and can result in spectacularly rapid growth and survival. A cheaper method is to plough out a single furrow, or two parallel furrows if it is to be a double rowed hedge, then line the plants along the furrow wall before replacing the soil and firming them in. If hand planting is chosen this is normally accomplished by notch planting or sometimes by digging out a trench 30 cm deep along the line of the hedge and planting into it. On a big job, many contractors prefer machine planting using a vegetable transplant machine, as it is much faster.

Most Enclosure Act hedges were planted as a single row of young hawthorns spaced at 20–30 cm. Double row hedges consist of two staggered rows of transplants spaced at 30–45 cm, depending on the size of the transplants, with the lines closer together (0.5 m) for a stockproof barrier and wider (0.6–1 m) for a conservation hedge. It is possible to design a two-faced hedge with an inner, closely spaced, thorny stock-proof row and an outer more widely spaced conservation row facing say onto a road or footpath. To maintain local style, it is sometimes desirable to create a hedge bank and plant on top of it. If the young plants are cut back to one third of their height this will promote good bushy growth from low down and produce a better hedge. Group sizes of about two to ten will give a good balance of diversity (Fig. 5.10) but holly, which, at around £2.70 a plant, is several times more expensive than other species (25–50 pence) and is usually used sparingly. Following planting, weed control is necessary for 3–4 years on fertile soils. A well-established hedge will need trimming from about year six. Cutting hedges once every three years can reduce costs by up to 59% in comparison to cutting every year, though there are small additional losses due to shading (Semple *et al.* 1995).

Fencing the hedge against damage by hares, rabbits, and farm stock is expensive and can double establishment costs. Short-term protection can be given by electric sheep netting, but, if it is decided that fencing is necessary, galvanized wire netting 1.05 m high with a further 20 cm buried to deter rabbits from burrowing underneath will be required. A stock-proof fence should be 1.4 m high and constructed using square mesh pig netting plus a trip wire. The fences should be sited at least a metre back from the hedge line (if it is closer

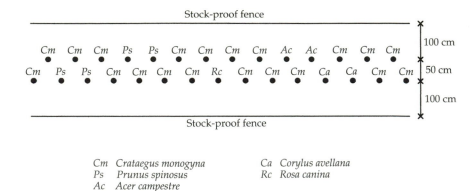

Fig. 5.10 Drawing showing a repeating unit for hedgerow planting. The close spacing will promote fast establishment.

the shrubs will grow through the netting making maintenance difficult). If a badger track crosses the fence line a badger gate should be provided. All aspects of fencing are covered by Brooks (1988).

Hedgerow trees

Hedgerow trees are an essential part of the rich patchwork of our lowland landscapes. Once they would have been an additional source of income to the landowner but are no-longer considered profitable. They provide shade for farm animals but in arable areas create uneven ripening of the crop and are considered a nuisance. They are not compatible with modern, mechanical methods of hedgerow maintenance. Spaced at 50 m intervals they increase costs by about 20% (Semple *et al.* 1995), so their presence has to be justified on general environmental grounds. Their numbers have declined sharply since 1950 and have reached the level at which a deliberate effort is required to reintroduce them. It has been suggested that in today's farmscape they are most appropriate as small corner plantations. However, there is a growing interest in restoring the former beauty of our countryside and all new hedges should include hedgerow trees.

They are best arranged in a random fashion at a mean distance of 40–60 m to avoid an avenue effect. Ash and oak are particularly suitable with lesser amounts of field maple (in the southern half of the country), gean, crab apple, and holly, with alder (*Alnus glutinosa*) and tree willows (*Salix alba, S. fragilis*) in wet areas. The local context is the best guide to species selection. Horse-chestnut, sweet chestnut, and beech are not recommended as they cast a heavy

Fig. 5.11 Hedgerow trees should be established using tree shelters to promote fast growth and make them conspicuous to hedgers.

shade that will suppress the hedgerow. The establishment of trees in a new hedge line is relatively easy. They should be a little larger than the transplants used for the main hedge, say a whip (90–120 cm), pit planted, provided with a mulch mat, and placed in a tree shelter pushed firmly into the soil (Fig. 5.11). This will give them a good start and the tree shelter will help ensure they get noticed when mechanical trimming commences.

Hedge bottom flora

British Coal Opencast have experimented with establishing wild flowers within restored hedgerows (ADAS 1994). The approach taken was to trans-locate hedgerow topsoil to an adjacent newly restored site and assess the extent to which a typical hedge bottom flora developed from seeds and veg-etative fragments. A 30 cm depth of topsoil was taken from the donor site in spring 1989 and formed into a hedgerow ridge approximately 2 m wide and 40 cm deep. The new hedge was planted along the centre of the ridge in December. By 1992, 56 species were present in the hedge bottom, including tufted vetch (*Vicia cracca*), dog's mercury (*Mercurialis perennis*), hedge woundwort, black bryony (*Tamus communis*), and greater stitchwort; abundance data were not given. In another trial, species were introduced either as seeds or pot grown plants. Survival of the pot grown plants (7 cm pots) was disappointing due to competition from the vigorous five-year-old hedgerow shrubs. Sowing a ten species mix onto bare soil adjacent to a newly planted hedge was partially successful; after 5 years, cowslip, wood avens, red campion, perforate St John's-wort (*Hypericum perforatum*), and hedge parsley (*Torilis japonica*) were the most abundant species.

Field margin

The value of a hedge for wildlife can be increased if an uncultivated strip of land, a field margin, is left between it and the crop (Boatman *et al.* 1989). This should be 2–3(–6) m wide, although FWAG (1992) suggest 1 m is an appropriate compromise. Details of how to create a suitable strip can be found in Chapter 9.

Fauna

Mature hedgerows develop their own fauna (Pollard *et al.* 1974; Watt and Buckley 1994). At least 30 species of bird commonly use them for breeding, while they provide food for many more. The whitethroat, yellowhammer, and dunnock have become hedgerow specialists. New hedges may be colonized by ground-nesting birds, such as skylark and pheasant, in their first year; the first shrub nesters colonize in year four. Hedgerows are important for mammals, which will quickly colonize newly planted ones. The chief insectivores are mole, pygmy shrew, water shrew, and common shrew, together with the omnivorous field mouse, wood mouse, bank vole, and short-tailed vole. Harvest mice use them as winter refuges, and radio tracking has shown that specialist predators (particularly weasels and barn owls) concentrate their hunting along them.

To be good for invertebrates a hedge should be over a metre thick, at least 2 m tall, and merge with the surrounding field margin via scrambling vegetation and tall herbs (Kirby 1992). Management on a two or three year rotation should be carried out as late as possible (January or February), adjacent lengths being cut in different years. If this can be achieved, many species of insect, including butterflies, will be found along the hedge, which provides sheltered conditions for flight, nectar sources for the adults, and undisturbed ground for larval food plants.

Hedge planting grants are only available for planting the hedge, not for the creation of a bank to put it on, for the introduction of a basal flora, or for the protection of the new habitat through introducing buffer zones, though these features may be of the greatest importance to their wildlife.

6   Heath and moor

Introduction

Heath and moor are used here in a general sense to embrace all the plant communities, excluding grasslands, that are associated with heathlands and moorlands. In practical terms, the focus is on dwarf-shrub heath, especially heather (*Calluna vulgaris*), because this is where most habitat creation experience lies. In addition, some attention will be paid to the associated plant communities of wet heath, valley bog, and blanket bog. For simplicity, the generic term 'heathland' is used to cover the whole range of such communities in the uplands and lowlands.

The emphasis in the lowlands differs from that in the uplands. In the uplands, there has been less loss of habitat, and more change from dwarf-shrub dominant or co-dominant communities to degraded forms of grassland or other vegetation types, such as cottongrass (*Eriophorum* spp.)-dominated blanket mires (Anderson and Yalden 1981; Bunce 1989). Here the opportunities for habitat creation focus mostly on restoring dwarf-shrub heath, especially heather, to communities in which it was once abundant, or to repairing damage when bare ground is exposed, for example, after the devastating summer fires of 1976 (North York Moors National Park, undated; Phillips *et al.* 1981). By contrast, in the lowlands, the very substantial conversion of heathland to agricultural land, conifer plantation, or other land uses has sharply reduced the extent of heathland (Webb 1990; Gimingham 1992), resulting in a strong emphasis on heathland re-creation on land recently occupied by something quite different.

The uplands

In the uplands, heathland creation has had to grapple with deep, wet peats, which are easily eroded and provide a difficult substrate for vegetation establishment. Physical access for vehicles can be difficult, making the scaling up of plot experiments sometimes impossible. Obtaining seed and spreading it under these conditions has taxed several initiatives, and the upland climate, particularly where acid ran is pronounced, tests everyone.

Probably the most extensive areas where upland heathland creation or restoration techniques have been developed are in the North York Moors and Peak District National Parks. In both, it was the extensive moorland fires, either in 1976 or 1980, that stimulated research into restoration techniques.

In the North York Moors, concern for, and studies of, the heather moorland were initiated in the early 1970s when conversion to agriculture or forestry and bracken (*Pteridium aquilinum*) encroachment had been identified as particular issues. Research into heather burning management had already been initiated by Dr E. Maltby; however, after the devastating fires of 1976, when over 3 km² of moorland was destroyed, new studies (and, in 1982, a fully fledged Moorland Management Programme) were established to investigate ways of restoring damaged ground as well as improving moorland management (North York Moors National Park, undated, 1986, 1991).

In the Peak District National Park, a similar study was initiated after the extensive 1976 fires revealed 33.25 km² of eroding or partly eroding ground, which constituted some 8% of the moorland area (Phillips *et al.* 1981). Furthermore, Phillips *et al.* (1981) concluded that fire, mostly under hot, dry, summer conditions, was responsible for much of the bare ground. Once the vegetation cover is broken and the roots killed, the peat and podsols are then exposed to severe erosive forces. Sheep grazing prevents the return of higher plants, and acid rain precludes the establishment of some bryophytes.

The bare ground occurs in patches, sometimes extending to tens of hectares or more, reflecting the hot patches in a fire. Along gullies, drier vegetation such as crowberry (*Empetrum nigrum*) succumbs, leaving cottongrasses on the wetter peat mounds. In some cases the peat has long gone, with the old fire site 'let into' the hilltop, often with peat pedestals marooned in the middle.

The degree to which this denuded ground presents an opportunity for heathland creation varies depending on accessibility and the feasibility of restoration. In a recent account of the various approaches taken to re-create moorland plant communities, it was concluded that not all damaged areas can, or indeed should, be restored. Action would be appropriate on recently damaged sites, but not necessarily for deep-peat sites dissected by gullies, particularly where these are of scientific importance in their own right, or are simply impossible to restore in practical terms (Anderson *et al.* 1997).

The Environmentally Sensitive Areas (ESAs) and Countryside Stewardship schemes (CSS), provide opportunities for restoring heathland vegetation. However, in the Peak District, uptake is limited to the North Peak ESA. The overall uptake in the moorland environment is shown on Table 6.1. The concentration of moorland re-creation stewardship schemes in the north-west (Carlisle region) is notable, but, compared with the amount of damaged ground, it is not large, although a valuable step forward.

A second focus for moorland restoration is on bare ground adjacent to footpaths where heavy trampling has created multiple tracks. The worst affected areas are where excessive use occurs on material with a low carrying

Table 6.1
Moorland re-creation statistics from MAFF for
Countryside Stewardship agreements up to the end of 1995

MAFF Region	Number of agreements	Area (ha)
Carlisle	13	225.80
Crewe	4	163.98
Exeter/Truro	3	18.07
Northallerton	5	52.80
Nottingham	2	44.09
Reading		
Worcester		
Total	27	505.55

Agreements for 1996 are being finalized and are expected to result in
a 25% increase in total agreements.

capacity—essentially wet peat. For example, the Pennine Way in 1987 had
mean bare ground widths of 7.8 m and trampled zones extending to 100 m.
There is a multimillion pound restoration project in the southern section tackling restoration, much of it to heathland (Porter 1990). In many stretches,
simply concentrating the wear onto a hard surface allows the adjacent
areas to recover naturally; in the worst affected areas, complex habitat creation techniques have been developed (Porter 1990). A similar approach has
been undertaken in many other upland areas, including Snaefell on the
Isle of Man, the Three Peaks in Yorkshire (Yorkshire Dales National Park
1993), and on innumerable paths in the Lake District and Scotland. Bayfield
and Aitken (1992) have reviewed the available restoration techniques and
difficulties.

Other upland heathland creation is geared towards landscaping around or
repairing the damage generated by particular development. Some of the earliest research was carried out on the routes for pipelines (Gillham and
Putwain 1977), and the same principles are being applied to larger schemes
such as opencast coaling in the north and north-west, wind farms in Cumbria,
North Pennines, and Wales, quarries and waste heaps (Putwain and Gillham
1988), masts (Peak District, Isle of Man), reservoirs, and road banks (Environmental Advisory Unit 1988). In many of these situations, where ecologists
are involved at the early stages of project planning, existing vegetation, seed
banks, and soils are being carefully stripped and re-used to assist in the
restoration process. Without such forward planning, restoration can be much
more difficult and expensive.

The lowlands

Even before heathlands were identified in the recent European Habitats Directive as targets for protection, their rapid loss over recent decades, their high nature conservation value, and the need to extend their cover had been taken very seriously. The momentum of re-creation is gathering pace, and there are exciting schemes in many lowland areas. Webb (1994) has developed strategic plans for Dorset Heaths using geographical information systems (GIS) incorporating species and habitat data to construct maps showing the natural potential area. The results indicate that only about 44% of this area is currently occupied by heathland. Such mapping, with species data, for example for the silver-studded blue butterfly (*Plebejus argus*), can assist in decision making that would enhance the species' survival by maximizing opportunities for expansion from fragmented habitat patches.

The primary focus in the lowlands is on reinstating heathland from afforestation where this occupies former heathland. The advantages are that a valuable seed bank tends to have survived in the soil and the soils themselves have not been significantly altered. Once the problems of needle litter and brash have been addressed, heathland restoration is relatively straightforward. Several heathland projects have grasped opportunities to re-create heathland under former pine plantations or infestations (e.g. Heathland Countryside Management Project 1995); Woodrow *et al*. (1996) provide useful information on the costs and machinery that might be involved. English Nature and the Forestry Commission are entering agreements in several areas committing themselves to heathland restoration from commercial forests. For example, Forest Enterprise are converting 140 ha of forest (about 2% of the holding in Dorset) back to heathland over a 5-year period; they are also retaining existing heathland and creating 25 km of heathy rides to strengthen links between heathland patches in Dorset. Similarly, they are also extending heathy rides and clearings in parts of Thetford Forest in the Brecks to cater for the woodlark (*Lullula arborea*) and nightjar (*Caprimulgus europaeus*) populations that favour the forest–heather boundary (Currie 1994).

A second approach is to re-establish dwarf-shrub heath on agricultural land that was formerly occupied by heathland. This poses more problems as significant changes in soils (including increased nutrient and pH levels) render them less suitable, or totally unsuited, to heathland re-creation. These issues have been addressed by, among others, Smith *et al*. (1991) on abandoned agricultural land in Dorset, and Marrs (1985) and Owen *et al*. (1996) in Suffolk.

As in the uplands, the ESAs and CSS schemes are providing valuable opportunities for heathland re-creation in the lowlands (Table 6.2). The most significant hectarage is in the South-West and East Anglia, with the Berkshire area following close behind.

Table 6.2
Heathland re-creation statistics from MAFF for
Countryside Stewardship agreements up to end of 1995

MAFF region	Number of agreements	Area (ha)
Bristol	9	215.90
Cambridge	9	130.95
Carlisle	2	7.20
Crewe	4	21.38
Exeter/Truro	8	24.47
Northallerton	3	42.02
Nottingham	1	6.96
Reading	10	97.40
Worcester	2	5.60
Total	48	551.88

Agreements for 1996 are being finalized and are expected to result in
a 25% increase in total agreements.

Heathland is also a valuable after-use of gravel workings and quarries. It
has developed naturally on many coal waste tips in the Midlands (Telford and
Stoke-on-Trent areas, for example) where it is now recognized as being of
value and is less often converted to amenity grass with planted trees. Several
gravel extraction sites, for example, in Dorset (Parker 1995), are being actively
restored, with appropriate planning conditions, to heathland swards. The same
principle is being applied to road banks; one near Bracknell was seeded with
heather (although it has had to compete with a sweet chestnut (*Castanea
sativa*) invasion; J. Davey, Berkshire County Council, pers. commun.), and
various roads in South Dorset (e.g. the Ferndown Bypass; Parker 1995) have
developed a heathery or heather–gorse (*Ulex* spp.) cover.

Ecological issues

Soils

Table 6.3 gives soil characteristics from a number of heathland and moorland
communities. The essential qualities are a low pH (mostly between about 3.5
and 5.5; Environmental Advisory Unit 1988) coupled with equally low nutrient levels. Available phosphorus and nitrogen are particularly low, the latter
due to low rates of mineralization. Soils are essentially podsols or peaty ones,
with low calcium levels. Compare these with sites where heathland restoration has been, or is being, attempted (Table 6.4); it is clear that there are sometimes significant differences, particularly of calcium, pH, and phosphorus, a

Table 6.3
Soil nutrient levels on a variety of heathland sites

Site	Units	Ca	Mg	K	P	N	Type of moorland	pH	Soil depth (mm)
Blanchland Moor, Hexham[a]	kg/ha	111*	61*	238*	432†	6396*	2 years since burning		
Blanchland Moor, Hexham[a]	kg/ha	66*	19*	127†	334†	1991†	>10 years since burning		
Cairn o' Mount, Kincardineshire[a]	kg/ha	605†	376†	189†	207†	5794†	3 years since burning		
Cairn o' Mount, Kincardineshire[a]	kg/ha	591†	3321†	178†	166†	5394†	>15 years since burning		
Polworth Moss, SE Scotland[a]	kg/ha	86*	70*	112†	623†	5083†	Young heather		
Polworth Moss, SE Scotland[a]	kg/ha	89*	68*	86*	496†	4259†	Old heather		
Listonshiels SE Scotland[a]	kg/ha	33*	81*	223†	437†	5814†	Young heather		
Listonshiels SE Scotland[a]	kg/ha	31*	70*	163†	406†	5415†	Old heather		
Poole Basin, Dorset[b]	kg/ha	229†	236†	288†	37†	2210†			
Hartland Moor, Dorset[c]	ppm	1119.0*	517.1*	508.8*	19.1*	29.2†		3.86	0–20
Stoborough Heath[c]	ppm	668.0*	278.6*	263.1*	19.2*	10.9†		4.06	0–20
Arne Heath[c]	ppm	1012.0*	566.7*	356.0*	20.8*	06.8†		3.70	0–20
Hartland Moor Dorset[d]	ppm	555.0*	297.3*	264.9*	5.2*	14.0†		3.80	0–40
Minsmere[e]	ppm	<150*			<5*			3.8–4.2	
Shap, Cumbria[f]	ppm	252†		688†	789†	1.1†		3.05	0–20
Muggleswick Common, Durham[f]	ppm	270†		467†	528†	0.89†		3.12	0–20
Lazonby Fell, Cumbria[g]	ppm	68–97.0*		38.9–66.3	6.2–8.2*	0.2–0.5*		3.4–3.7	0–100
Crosby Fell, Cumbria[g]	ppm	116.0–156.0*		31.04–64.97*	1.8–3.55*	1.33–11.1†		3.72–4.24	0–100

* Extractable nutrients.
† Total nutrients.
Sources: [a]Robertson and Davies (1965); [b]Chapman (1967); [c]Pywell et al. (1994); [d]Pywell et al. (1995); [e]Evans (1992); [f]Environmental Advisory Unit (1988); [g]Aberdeen Centre for Land Use (1990).

Table 6.4
Soil analysis at a range of restoration sites

Site	Unit	pH	Phosphorus*	Potassium*	Magnesium*	Calcium*	Nitrogen[†]
Upland							
Great Dun Fell, Cumbria[a]	mg/l	4.6	9	147	61		
Little Dun Fell, Cumbria[a]	mg/l	4.4	20	173	89		
Snaefell, Isle of Man[a]	mg/l	5.3	9	95	94		
Whalley Copy, Lancashire[a]	mg/l	4.1	14	146	59		
Conistone Moor, Yorkshire[a]	mg/l	4.4	15	147	61		
BBC Holme Moss, Peak District[b]	mg/l	3.3–3.8	2–12	11–45	28–133		
Geojute, Holme Moss, Peak District[b]	ppm	3.4	2	11	136		
Featherbed Moss Peak District[c]	ppm	3.5	3	15	50		
Devil's Dike Peak District[c]	ppm	3.3	3	31	61		
Lowland							
Middlebere, Dorset[d]	ppm	4.93	5.2	35.1	102.4	748.5	0.26
Three Barrows, Dorset A[d]	ppm	4.78	4	83	135.6	584.3	0.27
Three Barrows, Dorset B[d]	ppm	5.9	6.3	93.6	205.3	2284.8	0.56
Crighton's, Dorset[e]	ppm	4.98	4.8	75.4	224.2	1492	0.65
Minsmere, Suffolk[e]	ppm	6–7.2	7–15			500–1100	

* Extractable nutrients.
[†] Total nutrients.
Sources: [a] Unpublished data collected by Penny Anderson Associates; [b] Anderson et al. (1997); [c] Bayfield (1988); [d] Pywell et al. (1994); [e] Evans (1992).

finding that was strongly corroborated by Pywell *et al.* (1994) and that influences the success of the project.

Although there is no definitive guidance available on the range of soils suited to heathland creation, common sense suggests that it should be within the range of nearby heathland sites. This may necessitate amelioration of some kind. On ex-agricultural land, this usually involves reducing the pH and nutrient content, whereas in the uplands, especially where acid rain is having a significant impact, the addition of lime and nutrients are more likely to be needed.

These contrasting requirements are exemplified by a variety of projects. In Dorset, Smith *et al.* (1991) found that rotovation of ex-agricultural land with added heath material and turf stripping favoured individual heathland species, increasing their frequency and richness. In this case, a history of leaching and low nutrient applications favoured natural regeneration. In contrast, Marrs (1985) reduced nutrient loadings on Roper's Heath, Suffolk, by harvesting a cereal rye crop (see Chapter 2); the burning of the stubble (no longer allowed) was considered to remove further nutrients. The addition of inorganic nitrogen, to help remove more phosphorus, could work for some crops; however, on Roper's Heath, the cropping did not reduce extractable phosphorus sufficiently (from 65 ppm to 48 ppm), and Marrs (1985) concluded that topsoil stripping to a 20 cm depth would have had distinct advantages. Aerts *et al.* (1995), in comparing both abandoned sandy arable land and an equivalent site stripped of its topsoil with heathland, came to a similar conclusion; extractable phosphorus levels in the arable topsoil in this case were much higher.

Parker (1995) has updated progress on Roper's Heath where a bent–fescue–sand sedge (*Agrostis capillaris–Festuca ovina–Carex arenaria*) sward has developed through natural colonization since 1981 after three arable crops were taken. Heather is spreading in from the surrounding heathland but, so far, only around the edges. This is a site where inoculation using heathland seed or litter might have been advantageous.

However, the sward has now developed into a valuable Breckland grassland, with lichen patches, valuable for invertebrates and birds like stone curlew (*Burhinus oedicnemus*) and woodlark (Welch and Wright 1996). A heather dominated sward should not always be the expected or desirable end product of heathland re-creation schemes—grass–heath mixtures or grass-dominated heaths are equally valuable in particular sites, especially in the Brecklands.

Major experiments are under way in areas of Suffolk in an effort to acidify and reduce nutrient levels on ex-arable soils. The Royal Society for the Protection of Birds (RSPB) purchased a farm at Minsmere with the specific objective of creating heathland to link together two existing areas. The 158 ha of farmland had been cropped regularly and this had resulted in enhanced nutrient and pH levels (see Table 6.4). Five years of cropping by adding nitrogen to increase the uptake of other nutrients successfully depleted phosphorus to levels close to those typical of heathland, but the pH and exchangeable calcium levels showed little sign of depletion (Evans 1992; Welch and Wright 1996). Experiments on the site to reduce pH used applications of pine chippings, bracken mulch, or elemental sulphur (Owen *et al.* 1996). A 10 cm layer of bracken mulch reduced the pH from 6.7 to 4.7 over a 29-month period, but 1–2 tonnes of sulphur/ha was more effective over a shorter time span (Welch and Wright 1996). Chambers and Cross (1996) found sulphur at 3 tonnes/ha equally effective on Breckland soils, reducing pH in the topsoil from 5.7 to 2.9 in 2 months. However, Davey *et al.* (1992), experimenting with adding buried peat from Sizewell to arable soil, reduced the pH quickly to about 2.5 and generated unwanted sulphuric acid as the peat oxidized. They point out the potential of careful mixing of such peat with arable soils to reduce nutrients and available calcium, and to act as a mulch to reduce weed growth. Care, however, would need to be taken with any sulphur application not to contaminate the ground water or nearby streams and ditches.

In contrast, in a 4.5 ha moorland re-creation scheme around a new communications mast at 530 m in the Peak District, the peat was so acid that lime needed to be applied to increase its pH from 3.3 to 3.8, which is the minimum required for the growth of common cottongrass (*Eriophorum angustifolium*) (Richards *et al.* 1995); nutrients were also added (Anderson *et al.* 1997). The same approach, adding lime and fertilizer, has been used at several other moorland sites, for example, by the National Trust on the west face of Kinder Scout in the Peak District (see Anderson *et al.* 1997) and in the Pennine Way restoration work (Porter 1990).

In general, site selection for heathland creation should be focused on soils that are already within the normal range for heathland communities. It is much more difficult, as the RSPB are experiencing at Minsmere, to alter soils that are too rich and limey. On the other hand, many soils in habitat creation schemes are suited to heathland vegetation but fail to be recognized and are lost by adding lime, etc., so they can support grass or trees.

Plant growth and competition

Closely linked to soils is the issue of plant growth and competition. Heathland vegetation is essentially stress-tolerant *sensu* Grime (1979) and Grime *et al.* (1988). Although there is considerable variation between species, the growth of most dwarf-shrubs tends to be slow, more so in the most stressed environments (such as at high altitude, at the lowest nutrient levels, or in drought conditions). In addition, heather, and probably many of the other heathland species, require light for germination and establishment (Gimingham 1972, 1992). In the lowlands, colonization gaps only need to persist for a

Fig. 6.1 Spreading lime and fertilizer on blanket peat from a helicopter on Kinder Scout, Peak District (National Trust). Photo: Peter Kay (National Trust).

year or so to ensure good establishment (although not all seed germinates at once, and a prolonged establishment phase is advantageous). Under more exposed or stressed conditions, seedlings grow very slowly and 2–3 years is needed for establishment.

This has several implications. Colonization gaps need to be kept open long enough for the desirable species to establish. However, this often has the effect of allowing unwanted, competitive species to colonize at the same time. Experiments in East Anglia on ex-arable soils found weed growth to be a particular problem that tended to swamp growth of heather seedlings (Chambers and Cross 1996; Owen *et al.* 1996), and the same results were found on an ex-arable trial site in Scotland (Williams *et al.* 1996). This problem can be avoided by paying special attention to the seed bank's potential (removing it where necessary) and to the choice of sites. Soils that are too fertile, or have too high a pH and that are not modified in any way, are most likely to produce problems. This was exemplified by a small scheme in Derbyshire where various horticultural varieties of heather were planted on a restored tip but were eventually overtopped and outcompeted by a vigorous growth of grasses such as Yorkshire fog (*Holcus lanatus*) and cock's-foot (*Dactylis glomerata*), and of thistles (*Cirsium vulgare* and *C. arvense*). In this example, the lack of management did not help, but it would have been difficult to control the problem, which could have been resolved by better choice of soils.

Seed and plant source

Many of the plants of heath and moor are stress-tolerators (see Grime's model Chapter 2). This has implications for habitat creation since many, as a consequence, produce few viable seeds, and so are not available commercially on any significant scale. Fortunately, heather is a prolific seed producer, the seeds are viable with no complicated dormancy, and eminently collectable, since heather often grows in extensive patches. This combination means that heather seed is widely used in heathland creation schemes. Other species producing viable seed include bell-heather (*Erica cinerea*), the different gorses, and cross-leaved heath (*E. tetralix*). Putwain (1992) and Putwain and Gillham (1990), for example, have grown both of the *Erica* species successfully from a seed bank, although neither equalled their relative abundance in the vegetation above. Nearly all the accompanying grasses produce prolific crops of seeds, although few have been collected in quantity for heathland creation.

The more difficult species, which give real character to different heathland communities, such as bilberry (*Vaccinium myrtillus*) and cowberry (*V. vitisidaea*), crowberry, cottongrasses, and most of the mire species, either seldom establish by seed, or are difficult to collect in seed form and germinate. For example, in upland heathland restoration projects in the Peak District, bilberry has very rarely been found to establish from seed, although crowberry can appear slowly. This is corroborated by Putwain and Gillham (1990) who did not record bilberry seedlings in their seed bank tests from a variety of sites where it was present in the vegetation. It is reputed that the berries normally have to pass through the gut of a grouse, or similar animal, before they will germinate (Ritchie 1956; Bell and Tallis 1973). Similarly, the cottongrasses do not establish readily, although hare's-tail conttongrass (*Eriophorum vaginatum*) has gradually colonized a bare plot in the Peak District (Anderson *et al.* 1997). This may be more a product of the difficult conditions for establishment rather than seed viability, since seed from the same area grew readily on its indigenous peat in the protected environment of a windowsill (PA, personal observation).

Rather than using seed, some species have been introduced as plant plugs derived from cuttings from local stock in an effort to diversify the establishing sward. Bilberry has not been found to take readily from cuttings, but crowberry and cross-leaved heath worked well (Anderson *et al.* 1997). Planting rhizomes is probably the best means of establishing common cottongrass, since it will spread out subsequently in the same way as marram (*Ammophila arenaria*) on a sand-dune (Richards *et al.* 1995; Anderson *et al.*

Fig. 6.2 Bilberry, crowberry, and cross-leaved heath. Plants grown from local cuttings ready for planting out on Holme Moss, Peak District.

1997). These, or divots, may also prove to be useful for introducing some of the mire species such as sedges (*Carex* spp.), bog asphodel (*Narthecium ossifragum*) and others into a new community. Bayfield (1991) successfully planted out divots of various blanket bog species including mat-grass (*Nardus stricta*), crowberry, and hare's-tail cottongrass in some early experiments on the Pennine Way.

A further source of propagules could be derived from turf cutting on nearby heathland areas. This management technique is used to remove unwanted vegetation and mineral nutrients but, in turn, provides a rich source of seed and vegetative fragments that can regenerate quickly (Pywell *et al.* 1995). Shallow stripping (to a depth of 50 mm—the seed bank is concentrated in this layer; Putwain and Gillham 1990) by rotovation to shred the sward, and respreading of the topsoil and plant fragments, ideally in autumn, onto over-burden or exposed mineral ground, can produce a better mixture of characteristic plants than the alternative methods of inoculation.

Seed collection

Various techniques have been developed for collecting seed from existing heath and moor. The options are either to collect directly from plants or to remove the semi-rich litter layer below. Both have their advantages and disadvantages. Seed collection from the vegetation has been undertaken using forage harvesters or a brush collecting mechanism.

Heather seed ripens in October–November, with little observable variation across the country. Ripening can be identified by examining a fresh capsule with a hand lens. When the seed turns from pale straw or brown to dark brown, it is ripe and the capsule will detach more readily from the stem. It should be noted that more viable seed has been found to develop at lower than higher altitudes; an important consideration when choosing a donor site for high-altitude projects. Investigations in the Yorkshire Dales (PA, personal observation) revealed an average of 6.88 seeds per capsule at the end of November, while in Hampshire (PA, personal observation) 13.5 seeds per capsule were recorded in mid-October. In both cases, the numbers of seeds per capsule declined as the season progressed. This mirrors the results of other studies (Barclay-Estrup and Gimingham 1975) and is highly pertinent since it sets the optimum seed-collecting season, although this varies from year to year.

A major drawback to harvesting heather seed in autumn is the scarcity of other ripe and collectable species at the same time. Western gorse (*Ulex gallii*), an important component of some heathland communities, may be a valuable exception; however, most of the grasses, bell-heather, and cross-leaved heath all disperse their seeds earlier (Bannister 1965, 1966). Nevertheless, Pywell *et al.* (1995) did find minor quantities of both *Erica* species in material harvested in early December. A second disadvantage of this seed source is that freshly collected heather seed does not always germinate immediately; it seems to need a period of after ripening before it will establish. Thus, seed collected in autumn one year mostly does not germinate until the following autumn; indeed, in restoration work on the Suffolk Sandlings, seed did not germinate

---

Box 6.1   Seed bank tests

To conduct seed bank tests, collect several subsamples from the top 1–3 cm below any undecomposed litter, or from the bare soil or soil heap, as appropriate. Spread out thinly onto sterile acidic compost (peat free, of course) in a seed tray. Label with date of collection and location; water and place inside a polythene bag (to maintain humidity and prevent contamination). Place on a sunny windowsill but do not allow to dry out. Heather seedlings can establish within weeks depending on the time of year. If seedlings are pulled out once they are identifiable, and the soil disturbed, more will establish. All can be counted over a given period (e.g. 3 months), and an idea of the range and relative abundance of species gained.

for 18 months after an autumn sowing (Fitzgerald 1992). Experience in Scotland has shown this period can extend to as long as 2–3 years (Scottish Agricultural Colleges, personal communication). Only on a few southern heathland sites, in suitable weather conditions, has seed established in the spring after spreading (PA, personal observation).

Collecting seed from the litter layer has the benefit of potentially holding a greater range of species, but there is also the prospect of including tree seed, especially birch (*Betula* spp.), on some heathland sites, and its control in any subsequent heathland creation project could be onerous without sensitive grazing. Conducting a seed bank test on potential donor sites would obviously be a fruitful exercise (see Box 6.1 and Putwain and Gillham 1990).

The choice of collection technique depends on the availability of machines, what seed is required, the accessibility of the site, and whether a mulch is also needed. Double-chop and precision chop forage harvesters (the first producing cut material averaging about 7–10 cm long, and the second about 15–20 cm) combined with silage trailers have been used on various projects, and were first developed for restoration purposes by the North York Moors National Park (1986). Old machines are best used, but care still needs to be taken to avoid obscured rocks, holes, and wet areas.

The forage harvester can be set at different heights to take just the current year's growth (plus capsules) or more of the plant. The former can expose the rest of the plant to frost damage in exposed areas, so some site managers prefer to burn the cut stems. The whole plant should be taken where a mulch is required, for example, on bare mineral ground to provide a suitable microclimate for seed establishment, or on deep peat in an attempt to stabilize it. The material will need to be spread by hand on inaccessible sites, but can be dispersed from a (clean) agricultural muck spreader elsewhere (Anderson *et al.* 1997) or even hydroseeded dry, as onto a major bank on the Crowthorne–Sandhurst Bypass, Berkshire (J. Davy, Berkshire County Council, pers. commun.).

Seed can also be collected from *in situ* plants by running a brush over the canopy. This was first developed in Scotland by the Heather Trust (Phillips 1990) and has since been used widely in the Peak District, Countryside Stewardship, and ESA restoration schemes. It consists of a polypropylene brush, with a 'Heath Robinson' collecting box on the back. The seed can subsequently be mixed with sawdust for marking and diluting its coverage; however, when wet this sticks and hinders spreading. There is also some suggestion that if stored ready mixed with the sawdust, the seed loses its viability (S. Ward, pers. commun.). Seed is also collected from existing plants by a number of commercial seed suppliers using a variety of equipment from modified combine harvesters to specially developed suction or brushing machines. Care needs to be taken to avoid collecting significant numbers of invertebrates at the same time (as described in Chapter 4).

Fig. 6.3 A seed collecting brush and box mounted on the back of a tractor. The brush can be set at the height of the heather flowers (Katharine Longden).

Animals

Heathland is generally created to provide a new or restored habitat, and it is anticipated that the characteristic animals will follow provided there are populations close enough. However, creating specific conditions for selected animals may be desirable. Target species are most likely to be those needing special measures to conserve and enhance populations, such as the sand lizard (*Lacerta agilis*) or nightjar, or those that are too often neglected, such as most invertebrates. Heathland re-establishment after conifer clearance is being pursued for sand lizards in parts of the New Forest, for example, where litter has been windrowed and bare sand created on suitably warm slopes for egg-laying. Heathland re-establishment by the Forestry Authority in Thetford (Norfolk) is specifically designed to support the increasing populations of woodlark and nightjar (Currie 1994).

Bare, warm, sandy sites are important for a wide range of insects such as burrowing bees and wasps, crickets, grasshoppers, and ground beetles, many of which are specialist heathland species (Kirby 1992). It is important, in any scheme, to assess the chances of various animals colonizing and attempting to create the requisite bare ground, gorse bushes, sunny basking banks, or other requirements, as appropriate.

Heathland creation techniques

Based on the principles outlined above, a range of techniques are available for heathland creation. Since complex techniques are the most costly, it is important to assess a site carefully to avoid wasting effort and resources. Such an assessment should include the nature of the seed bank, the soil, existing vegetation, potential erosion problems, the general environmental conditions, and any other site-specific features.

Seed bank tests need not be expensive or 'scientific' to provide useful information (see Box 6.1). They are equally important whether starting with bare ground or whether converting an existing non-heathland vegetation, such as grassland or conifer plantation. There is an obvious advantage if there are desirable species in the seed bank, and the quantities do not need to be large to ensure the development of a dwarf-shrub community. Table 6.5 shows the numbers of seeds that have been estimated in various existing and restoration sites. It is pertinent to note that, although the heathland seed bank more closely matches the above ground community than in other habitats (Miles 1973), the predominance of species does not necessarily match their abundance in the existing swards. Heather, bell-heather, and cross-leaved heath, various grasses, especially fescues, bents, purple moor-grass (*Molinia caerulea*), and some of the acid grassland/moorland species in the uplands, such as tormentil (*Potentilla erecta*), heath rush (*Juncus squarrosus*), and woodrushes (*Luzula campestris* and *L. multiflora* in particular) feature in most seed banks. Other dwarf-shrubs like bilberry, crowberry, and cowberry are notable for their absence.

In soils where rushes have been (or are) present, there can be a substantial

Table 6.5
Results of seed bank trials

Site	Thousands of germinated seeds/m^2			
	Ericoids	Rushes	Dicots	Grasses
Lazonby Fell, Cumbria[1]	28–138	2–5	5–18	14
Crosby Ravenworth, Cumbria[1]	2–154	9–508	7–115	2
Wet heaths, Cumbria[1]	>20	<30	14–28	2–9
Moel Fammau, Clwyd[2]	5.3			
Denbigh Moors, Clwyd[2]	5.2			
Burbage Moor, Peak District[2]	5.3			
Fellhouse Fell, Northumberland[2]	2.5			
Lee Moor, Cornwall[2]	4.42	0.02	0.05	1.08
Fair Isle, Scotland[3]	1.4–20			

Sources: [1] Aberdeen Centre for Land Use (1990); [2] Putwain and Gillham (1990); [3] Nolan, *et al.* (Undated).

seed bank, especially of soft and conglomerate rushes (*Juncus effusus* and *J. conglomeratus*), which can be a problem, particularly where soils are regraded as part of a restoration scheme.

Starting from bare ground

The ground may be bare through inappropriate activity such as fire, vehicle damage, or trampling, which has destroyed the vegetation cover, or it may be part of a restoration scheme in which a new ground surface has been created.

Why not do nothing?

The first step is to decide why bare ground has not revegetated naturally with the desired species. This could be due to several factors—erosion or sedimentation may be producing an unstable substrate, grazing or trampling may be removing plants, seeds may not be present, or the pH and soil nutrient levels could be inappropriate. Having found that there is an adequate seed bank of desirable species in the soil, or that the adjacent vegetation can provide a sufficient input, it may only be necessary to fence out grazing animals or people for the site to revegetate.

If erosion is a key factor, for example on steep slopes damaged by vehicles or trampling, restoration work to stabilize slopes and reduce run-off may be needed before revegetation can commence. Compaction of the ground may be an issue in certain locations, but heathland restoration on the coast in Jersey after cars were confined to new car parks has progressed slowly once rabbits were excluded (PA, personal observation).

On sites where heathland creation is on restored ground, it is very important to separate and re-use any seed bank and upper soil layers separately from the lower horizons. The availability of a useful restorative resource for re-use will depend on whether vegetation was translocated prior to the development (the rights and wrongs of which are not covered within this book), or whether the upper soil layer was scraped off and stored. On the other hand, all the topsoil (to an engineer this probably means all the soil) may have been stripped off and stockpiled, thus mixing and diluting the seed bank.

Bearing in mind that the majority of the seed bank in heathland and moorland soils is restricted to the top 5 cm (Gillham and Putwain 1977; Putwain and Gillham 1990), preserving this for later re-use is essential. However, even diluted stockpiles have produced promising embryonic heathland communities in Dorset when re-spread over quarrying sites following storage for a significant period (PA, personal observation). Testing the seed bank in such soils will determine whether supplementary seed application would be desirable or not. On sites where a seed bank is present, simply leaving the site to develop naturally may be the best option.

Fig. 6.4 The effect of fencing a heathland plot.

Fencing

Where sheep or rabbits are having a significant effect on heathland creation attempts, fencing to exclude them is critical. The need for this cannot be judged solely from a knowledge of the numbers involved, since sheep in particular graze selectively on areas of short or newly establishing vegetation of preferred species. This has been confirmed on many moorland restoration sites in the Peak District, where significant differences in the rate of revegetation of bare ground have been recorded (Anderson *et al.* 1997). For example, on one lower moor (at 420 m altitude), a fenced, seeded area had developed an average heather cover of 40% after 2 years fenced from sheep (Tallis & Yalden 1983); in an adjacent seeded but unfenced area, only a 71% average higher plant cover (54% of which was heather) had established after 16 years (Anderson *et al.* 1997).

On lowland heaths, where growing conditions are generally not so exacting, the establishment of vegetation exposed to grazing may be more rapid. However, in plots in the New Forest, established after a fire in 1989, the dwarf-shrub heath cover was more continuous and dense after 6 years in fenced areas. In this case the grazing animals are ponies and deer rather than sheep (National Heathland Conference 1996).

Rabbits can be equally unwelcome, often sitting on top of 'topiaried' vegetation to graze what would otherwise be out of reach. Trials to re-establish dune heathland after the removal of gorse (*Ulex europaeus*) in Jersey failed because of the intensity of rabbit grazing, yet, if fenced out totally, acid grassland species outcompeted any dwarf-shrub heath seedlings (Anderson 1994*b*). Rabbit grazing in this case would be very difficult to manipulate constructively.

Changing soils

Where soils are unsuited to heathland, but the objective is still to establish it, for example to link fragmented patches, then ameliorative techniques need to be adopted, as described earlier and by Pywell *et al.* (1994). However, having altered the pH and reduced the nutrient levels as far as possible, successful heathland creation still depends on managing the residual weed flora (a problem faced on several sites; e.g. Owen *et al.* 1996; Rees 1992). If this weed flora is undesirable, it will need to be herbicided and, if necessary, left fallow for a season and herbicided again before it seeds, with the heathland inoculation taking place in the following autumn, preferably without further soil disturbance.

Adding dwarf-shrub seed or plants

Where the seed bank is absent or inadequate, suitable seed or plants have to be added. This may also be advisable where the establishing heathland species are in competition with others, or where colonization gaps are likely to close quickly.

The quantity of seed to add is difficult to determine—the conversion of the quantities used in small scale experiments to those needed in field situations is not a straightforward task, especially when cut material varies so much in weight and seed content. A general rule of thumb that has been applied in a number of restoration projects has been to spread double-chopped forage harvested material over twice the area from which it was cut (Fitzgerald 1992; Anderson *et al.* 1997). The efficacy of this, however, will depend on the ratio of seeding material to older growth. However, on the fire site already described in the New Forest, forage harvested material with seed was spread over three and six times the area from which it was collected; no visual differences in these treatments could be distinguished compared with the untreated control, which still contained significant areas of bare ground after 6 years (National Heathland Conference 1996; PA, personal observation).

Gimingham (1992) generally recommends 6000–10000 kg/ha of fresh cut material, and this reflects the ranges of trials on a number of upland and lowland sites. Heather litter applications can be much lower (1000–1500 kg/ha).

The density of potted plants, turves, or rhizomes added to diversify a developing community will depend on the circumstances and objectives. For example, on Holme Moss in the Peak District, potted plants grown from locally collected cuttings were added (after heather seed had been spread) at a density of 1 plant per $4\,m^2$, on the premise that the species (crowberry, bilberry, and cross-leaved heath) would spread vegetatively over time. The spacing was also restricted due to cost and the area being treated (4.5 ha). The need to add them was based on a high sheep grazing density—crowberry and cross-leaved heath are generally unpalatable and should survive once the fence is removed. At the same site, spade sized turves of common cottongrass were cut and successfully used in concentrated (but not contiguous) patches to block run-off channels that were beginning to develop (Anderson *et al.* 1997).

Very limited attention has been given to creating mires associated with heath or moor, although a number of projects building on or enhancing existing communities are in place, such as the Somerset Trust for Nature Conservation work at Westhay Nature Reserve (Parker 1995). Most examples have involved very small-scale projects and have added plants rather than seeds to the sites. For example, the British Trust for Conservation Volunteers (BTCV) created a miniature bog at the Stoke City National Garden Festival; also, Merridale School, Wolverhampton, have successfully established an artificial *Sphagnum* bog in their school grounds (Parker 1995).

Nurse species

In most situations a companion or nurse grass is unnecessary and, indeed, could compete too successfully with the dwarf-shrub heath species. However, there are occasions when a grass nurse is essential to stabilize soils long enough for the slow-growing heathland species to establish. Most such sites are in the uplands or on steep slopes in the lowlands. There is some debate about the most appropriate species, owing to the difficulty in obtaining native species in quantity. In many sites, sheep's fescue (*Festuca ovina*), wavy hairgrass (*Deschampsia flexuosa*), or common bent (*Agrostis capillaris*) would be most suited to stabilizing the ground. However, none of these is available regularly, in quantity from native wild plants. Unless you can collect your own seed, alternatives will usually be needed. For example, on Cannock Chase, a small restored slope was successfully sown with locally collected wavy hair-grass.

One of the most useful nurse species is highland bent (*Agrostis castellana*), a non-vigorous variety from Oregon, USA, which is very similar to common bent (Hubbard 1984). This has been sown with various mixtures of sheep's fescue, blue fescue (*Festuca longifolia*), and wavy hair-grass (native species, but foreign seed) on the restoration site on Holme Moss in the Peak District; the highland bent and wavy hair-grass were the only ones to persist long enough to be useful. Indeed, the highland bent was a perfect nurse grass,

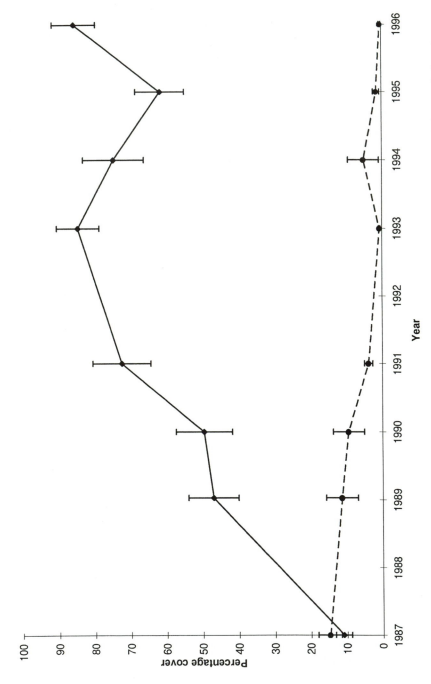

Fig. 6.5 The changes in heather (solid line) and the bent-grass (broken line) nurse in re-vegetation trials on Holme Moss, Peak District (including Standard Error).

providing a thin but widespread sward for 4 years before gradually dis-appearing (Fig. 6.5). A similar approach was followed by the National Trust on the Kinder Scout restoration work (Anderson *et al.* 1997).

On sites where nature conservation values are high, the desirability of intro-ducing species such as the above may be questionable. On the Pennine Way restoration work, for example, it was decided not to risk using non-native or closely related bents, fescues, or wavy hair-grass, but to sow a lowland meadow mixture instead that would completely disappear within a few years (Porter 1990). However, in this instance, this approach required significant nutrient and lime additions on very acidic infertile upland peats.

The quantity of grass seed to be sown is difficult to gauge. The objective is to establish enough cover to aid the establishment of the heathland species, but not so much that colonization gaps are lost or the slower growing species swamped. The quantity needed will, therefore, relate to the demands of the site, including its vulnerability to erosion and the extremes of its climate. In addition, the seed size of many of the grasses available varies significantly. Bent grass, for example, has 15 000 seeds/g, while sheep's fescue weighs in at 1000 seeds/g. Furthermore, bent grass is reputed to establish more successfully in a mid-season sowing, while fescues do better in spring; wavy hair-grass does best as freshly collected seed in late summer. The quantities used of the various seeds need to be modified accordingly, with the chances of establish-ment taken into consideration at the same time.

Because of these considerations, but also due to the experimental nature of much of the work, the quantities of companion grasses used in various pro-jects have varied, as shown in Table 6.6.

Fertilizer and lime

A similar cautionary note applies to the application of fertilizers and lime. Table 6.7 shows the range and variation of quantities used. It is essential to establish the need for fertilizers or lime by analysing the soils. Lime applica-tion is only needed to ameliorate markedly acidic soils. For example, Richards *et al.* (1995) have shown that the pH of blanket peat needs to be increased from 3.2–3.4 to 3.7 in order to support common cottongrass; Anderson *et al.* (1997) raised the pH of blanket peat from 3.2–3.3 to 3.6–3.7 by adding 1000 kg/ha of lime in order to establish a bent nurse crop and heathland species.

These examples are of the use of soil ameliorants in particularly stressed and extreme conditions. In general, the application of lime and/or fertilizer is most likely to be needed only where soils are particularly acidic (a pH of 2.8 has now been recorded from acid rain affected peats in the Peak District), and where nutrients are so low that the adequate growth of a nurse and the desired heathland species is in doubt.

Table 6.6
Nurse crop quantities

Site	Grasses	Percentage by weight	Sowing rate (kg/ha)
BBC Holme Moss, Peak District 1986[a]	Highland bent	20	
	Wavy hair-grass	20	
	Sheep's fescue	30	
	Blue fescue	30	90
BBC Holme Moss, Peak District 1984[a]	Red fescue	60	
	Highland bent	30	
	Sheep's fescue	10	90
Geojute Holme Moss and Kinderlow, Peak District[a]	Sheep's fescue	60	
	Wavy hair-grass	20	
	Highland bent	20	90
Caesars Camp, Berkshire[b]	Sheep's fescue	60	
	Wavy hair-grass	20	
	Highland bent	20	60
Farnborough, Hampshire[c]	Bent-grass	40	
	Red fescue	45	
	Wavy hair-grass	10	90–100
	Blue fescue	5	
Lee Moor, Cornwall[d]	Perennial rye grass	N/A	50
	Highland bent	N/A	15
	Fine-leaved sheep's fescue	N/A	3
Pennine Way, Peak District[e]	Common bent-grass	75%	
	Red fescue ⎫ Sheep's fescue ⎭	25%	350

Sources: [a] Anderson *et al.* (1997); [b] Penny Anderson Associates, unpublished; [c] Parker and McNeilly (1991); [d] Putwain (1992); [e] M. Rhodes, Pennine Way Project Officer, personal communication.

Stabilizers

When faced with unstable peat or steep eroding slopes, some form of stabilizer may be beneficial. The problem of bare blanket peat, in particular, relates to its expansion and contraction in freeze–thaw cycles. The expanded peat puffs up then collapses back, usually downslope, and is subsequently washed around or blown away. This acute instability, often combined with high acidity and low nutrient levels, renders such sites difficult, if not impossible, to vegetate on a large scale, particularly if access for vehicles is a problem.

Various techniques have been explored in an attempt to stabilize bare peat long enough for a protective vegetation cover to develop. Tallis and Yalden (1983) experimented with a bitumen spray and larch brashings but found that

Table 6.7

Rates of fertilizer and lime added to restoration sites

Site	Rate of application of fertilizer (kg/ha)	Fertilizer type	Rate of application of lime (kg/ha)	Rate of application of alginate (litres/ha)
Holme Moss 1984, Peak District[a]	150	15:22:15 NPK	1000	12
Holme Moss 1986, Peak District[a]	200	15:22:15 NPK	1000	12
Holme Moss Geojute, Peak District[a] (Three trial plots)	125	17:17:17 NPK	2000	
	200	Grasphos	2000	
	130	Triple-super phosphate	2000	
Kinderlow, Peak District[a]	517		1034	
Shaugh Moor, Cornwall[b] (Three trial plots)	100	NPK		
	300	NPK		
	150	Enmag		
Pennine Way Project, Peak District[c]	75	NPK	1000	

Sources: [a] Anderson et al. (1997); [b] Putwain (1992); [c] M. Rhodes, personal communication.

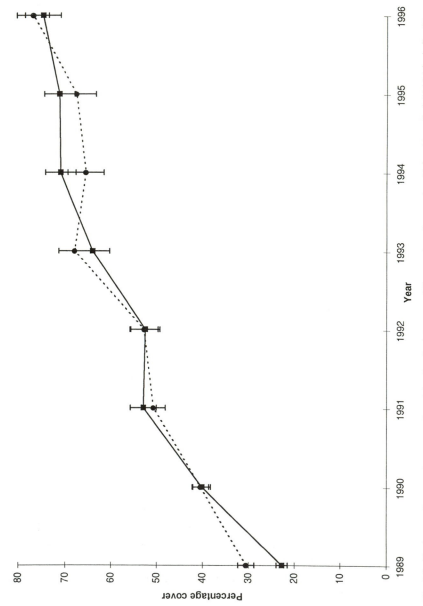

Fig. 6.6 Total vegetation cover in re-vegetation trials using Geojute as a stabilizer on deep, bare peat on Holme Moss, Peak District (including Standard Error). Solid line represents a 100% cover of Geojute; broken line represents a 50% cover.

neither helped significantly. The latter was used on a larger scale (about 0.2 ha) at Holme Moss to cover cut heather; however, it tended to blow away and its usefulness proved patchy (Anderson *et al.* 1997). A sisal mesh netting (Geojute) has proved much more successful (Anderson *et al.* 1997). When wet it is heavy enough to hold the peat down physically while plants establish between the cross fibres. Although it is supposed to break down in 2–3 years in the lowlands, it took 5 years to begin to disintegrate substantially in the uplands; even after 7 years it had not completely disappeared. Figure 6.6 shows that Geojute applied on deep peat at an altitude of 530 m as a 100% cover had no significant advantages over a 50% cover.

Economic heathland establishment

The range of techniques described and the examples given of their application demonstrate that the easiest sites on which to establish dwarf-shrub heath are those where the conditions are not too extreme, a seed source is present or locally available, and neither deep peat nor erosion is an issue. In such circumstances, extensive areas of new heathland, whether in the uplands or lowlands can be and are being developed. Where environmental conditions are more extreme, greater effort and resources are required to achieve an equivalent result. In the most difficult situations, heathland creation may not be cost effective.

Where particular patterns of peat erosion are of scientific interest, as in much of the Pennines, these should not be the subject of restoration attempts. There is a cogent argument for this approach in the Peak District moorlands (Anderson *et al.* 1997), where Ratcliffe (1977) was among the first to identify a natural component to gully erosion and identify its scientific and nature conservation interest.

However, a further aspect of heathland creation needs to be addressed. Careful analysis of existing heaths and moors reveals a mixture of communities, some with abrupt, others with merging boundaries; these boundaries tend to reflect small-scale changes in soil depth, wetness, management (past or present), or other environmental factors. Except in the more impoverished sites, there tends to be a considerable diversity of plant species across these communities. Many are not dominated by heather; in some, heather does not even feature. Yet the dwarf-shrub heath habitat creation and restoration projects have, perforce, focused on heather establishment. Few examples of other heathland community projects have been found. There is a danger of creating 'heatherland', rather than the varied communities of heath and moor; this limitation, compared to long-established communities needs to be kept in mind. On the other hand, when placed adjacent to existing heathland, opportunities are provided for colonization by some of this wider range of plants and by characteristic animals. Only time will tell whether the rather bland attempts at heathland creation will develop into something more akin to existing communities.

Heath and moor creation for animals

Little research effort seems to have been directed at finding out whether a characteristic fauna can colonize re-created heathland. One of the few exceptions to this is the National Trust's work on Kinder Scout (Anderson *et al.* 1997). Here, the steady increase in the grouse population showed a positive relationship with the expansion of heather on the lower slopes (Anderson and Radford 1994), but changes in some invertebrates were more variable. Total carabids showed a strong decline, which might be expected since they are principally species of open ground. This is exemplified by the species *Patrobus assimilis* and *Pterostichus adstrictus*. Some, but not all, staphylinids showed similar trends, including two notable north-western species, *Arpedium brachypterum* and *Othius angustus*. In contrast, a number of species showed no trends, but significant variations, with rarities appearing irregularly, and some species, as might be expected, expanded with the increasing vegetation cover, such as the spiders *Walckenaeria incisa* and *Dicymbium tibiale*.

Adding dwarf shrubs to existing vegetation

Adding dwarf shrubs to an existing vegetation can be more difficult than creating heathland on bare ground. The key is to create colonization gaps that will last long enough for heather and other dwarf shrubs to establish and compete successfully with the other species. Swards in which dwarf shrubs might be introduced are those dominated by bracken, fine leaved grasses on acid soils (wavy hair-grass, fescues, mat-grass or bents), and purple moor-grass or cottongrasses. The most suitable swards are those where dwarf shrubs were known to have been present in the past, and where the soils still fall within the normal pH range for dwarf-shrub heaths (see Table 6.1). There may be vestiges of tenacious species such as bilberry, which can survive in the most overgrazed acid grassland for many years. Other desirable species may be present in the seed bank.

The first decision is whether the existing vegetation should be removed completely or not. It is customary to dispatch invasive rhododendron, woodland, scrub, and bracken with the help of appropriate herbicides. In many situations, however, a thick litter layer then prevents, or significantly slows down, establishment of dwarf-shrub seedlings; this will need to be removed. Windrowing the litter on accessible flat surfaces may be possible so that strips of vegetation can re-establish and then gradually spread. This has been tried after bracken clearance in the Yorkshire Dales and in the New Forest after the removal of conifers. On Caesar's Camp, an Iron Age fort near Bracknell, the conifer litter was carefully scraped off without damaging the archaeological interest and heather seed sown. The heather cover developed much faster after such treatment compared with uncleared areas (Fig. 6.7). Woodrow *et al.* (1996) give advice on machines useful for clearing litter to facilitate heathland re-establishment. The same problem of litter arises on *Molinia*-covered ground, particularly if the vegetation has not been burnt for some years. It may be possible, in the right weather conditions, to burn off bracken and *Molinia* litter before spraying it.

There are dangers involved in removing all of the existing vegetation prior to seeding—erosion may become a problem, and the subsequent growth of the seed bank may need to be controlled. On a moor near Macclesfield (Cheshire), for example, *Molinia* was herbicided, which led to a prolific establishment and growth of wavy hair-grass that competed with the small heather plants and presented a difficult management problem (Anderson *et al.* 1997).

The alternative approach is to retain the existing sward, but create colonization gaps. This has been successfully achieved by the Heather Trust in Scotland using a Forestry Screefing TTS 10 machine (Phillips 1990). The blades can be set to turn a row of turf over at the required depth; a metre of undisturbed land is left in between. The simple adaptation of an old fertilizer spreader box and some drain pipes can allow heather seed (collected in the brush collector) to be dropped into the screefed line at the same time. Provided the furrows do not flood, heather can be established effectively using this method (Anderson *et al.* 1997). Various shallow ploughs and cultivators have also been tried, for example on Countryside Stewardship Heathland Restoration Schemes in Lancashire, Yorkshire, and Derbyshire. However, where the screefed or disturbed vegetation closes within a year, heather seed rarely has a chance to establish.

Post-establishment management

Management priorities during the post-establishment period will largely centre on ensuring the dwarf-shrub heath or other desirable communities survive and grow. The establishment period may be only 1–2 years, but can be as long as 5, or possibly up to 10, years in the most extreme conditions.

Management may be needed either to control competition, usually from grasses, or to nurture slow-growing plants suffering from extreme environmental conditions. Competition can be controlled by judicious manipulation of grazing, if it is available. By concentrating animals, preferably sheep since they are selective grazers, in spring and summer when grasses begin to grow

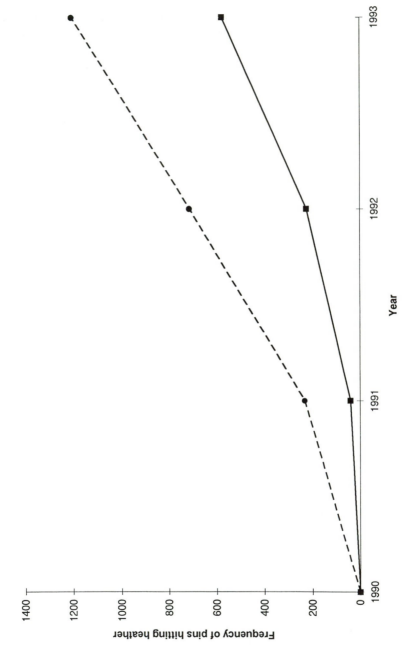

Fig. 6.7 The frequency of heather on heathland creation plots, raked (broken line) and unraked (solid line) to remove conifer litter, on Caesar's Camp, Berkshire.

more prolifically, these grasses can be controlled. Some heather will also be taken if it is intimately mixed with the grasses, but this is preferable to it being swamped by competition.

Another problem is birch and pine (*Pinus* spp.) invasion. A sea of birch seedlings among the newly establishing heather can be a depressing sight. Again, this is best controlled by grazing, as demonstrated in the Surrey Heaths Project (Heathland Countryside Management Report 1995), but the use of an appropriate herbicide on a weed wipe bar may be possible if the birch grows taller than the desirable species. Bacon (1994) has been developing a weed wipe for use on thistles and other problem species in flower-rich grassland; it may be possible to modify this device.

In extreme situations, where inadequate growth rather than competition is the issue, further applications of lime and fertilizer may be needed to provide the desired boost to growth. Soil analysis will be needed first to decide whether this would assist and, if so, the amount required.

Once established and providing a near complete vegetation cover, traditional management can be applied, whether it be upland grazing and grouse moor management or a lowland heathland programme. Gimingham (1992) gives detailed advice on management, and further assistance is available in several of the heathland project reports from Dorset, Surrey, Hampshire, and the Sandlings (e.g. Woodrow *et al.* 1996), and in the Heather Trust reports on the various restoration work being conducted in the uplands.

Critical to all initiatives to create and restore heathland and moorland is the need to monitor the results over a long time period, not just by looking or taking photographs, but preferably by collecting quantitative data on plants and various animal groups. Manipulation of management and of future projects to reflect the results is good practice, as exemplified by the RSPB's Dorset heathland project (Woodrow *et al.* 1996).

7 Montane and submontane habitats

Introduction

This section deals with habitat creation where high altitude or latitude, shallow infertile soils, and the severity of the climate render the communities vulnerable to both natural and human damage. The main threats are the development of ski facilities, damage from trampling, and localized construction or mining projects. On the scale of change in montane and submontane areas, none of these are large or extensive compared with the degradation of communities as a result of overgrazing by sheep and deer (Thompson *et al.* 1987). Reversal of these effects is more the subject of habitat restoration than habitat creation or repair. Although not at the same elevation, there is a considerable and relevant North American literature relating to the repair of tundra damaged by oil related development or strip mining.

Organized skiing began in Scotland around 1950; by 1962 chair-lifts had been opened at Cairnwell and Cairn Gorm. There are now five main ski developments and others are planned. Ski developments encourage the year-round use of mountains and are associated with new roads, dirt tracks, car parks, chair-lifts, tows, cafes, constructed pistes, and extensive footpath development. Damage to vegetation is particularly severe during the construction period when pistes are gouged out of the hillside. This creates large areas of bare, raw soil that may be extended by gully erosion and slumping, which leads to the burial of vegetation under gravel fans up to a metre deep. Recovery from burial depths of over 7 cm is negligible (Bayfield 1974). Further destruction is caused by skis cutting up the vegetation; this is worst on convex slopes and around tows. Damage reached a peak of 14 ha of bare ground in the Cairngorms around 1970, of which 2.8 ha was erosion fans, and although contractors are now more careful, ski-lift companies still need to carry out regular habitat creation and repair work Fig. 7.1.

In contrast, damage in the mountains from footpath trampling produces a relatively narrow but often fairly continuous strip of vegetation loss, sometimes accompanied by erosion and gullying. Recreation in the countryside has been encouraged by the provision of long-distance footpaths, tracks, and trails, but this has not, in general, been backed with funds for maintenance work. Path widths are largely related to levels of use, but where they cross boggy,

Fig. 7.1 A bulldozed and re-seeded piste on the Cairngorm Plateau.

rough, or steep ground they are especially prone to wear and may eventually become 25 m wide strips of bare, poached peat or eroding mineral soil visible from up to 5 km away. This is an increasing problem; Watson (1984) reported that between 1961 and 1980, footpath length on the Cairngorm Plateau increased from 1.3 to 17.1 km.

A number of methods have evolved to help deal with the problem. Where the traffic of feet, mountain bikes, or horses is particularly high, path construction using surface aggregates, stone pitching, board walks, or stone slabs has been used. Other techniques vary from re-routing paths, to controlling surface erosion with geotextiles, soil stabilizers, or stepped surface moulding. Experience has shown that vegetation is far superior to any artificial surface in breaking the impact of rain drops, trapping water borne sediment, stabilizing the upper layers of the soil, increasing surface permeability, and reducing the velocity of surface run-off. A comprehensive, up-to-date review of restoration and management techniques has been prepared by Bayfield and Aitken (1992).

In the past it was acceptable to provide almost any kind of vegetation cover to minimize erosion and visual intrusion; however, countryside managers have recently begun to demand higher standards of revegetation involving the use of native species and the creation of vegetation patterns similar to those of intact ground. Often several approaches need to be employed to suit the

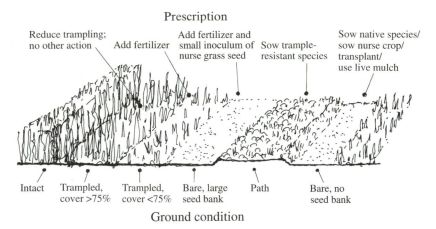

Fig. 7.2 Revegetation tactics along footpaths should depend on site conditions and levels of damage. Details of individual techniques can be found in the text (redrawn from Bayfield and Aitken 1992).

severity of damage and site conditions. An example of how appropriate revegetation tactics depend on ground conditions and level of use is illustrated in Fig. 7.2.

Very few developments, apart from skiing, impose threats to high-altitude habitats, but one where associated vegetation repair and habitat creation have been needed is with the instilation of radar stations and their associated communications facilities. These tend to be placed on exposed situations on the tops of hills, such as those on Great Dun Fell (Cumbria), Snaefell (Isle of Man), and several hills near Glasgow and Dundee (Scotland). The nature of the repair work associated with such installations depends on when a restoration ecologist becomes involved. It is much better to re-use existing vegetation and to organize this prior to any site works than it is to be faced with a mixed heap of topsoil and subsoil and incipient gully erosion once the engineering project has been completed.

Repair and creation techniques: seed bank, turfing, transplants

The approach in the high-altitude environment is similar to that in the more exacting examples of moorland sites (Chapter 6). An equivalent range of techniques has been tested in different situations, sometimes with partially conflicting results.

Soil seed banks

Most soils contain a reservoir of buried viable seed. This can be a valuable source of native plant material. Seed bank statistics for a wide range of upland habitats have been prepared; these reveal that the largest numbers of seeds are contributed by rushes and heathers, followed by dicotyledons, with grasses and sedges less important (see Table 6.5). Seed bank composition varies widely from community to community and site to site, but seed numbers are staggeringly high—often being over $20000/m^2$ and sometimes reaching more than half a million (Miller and Bayfield 1989).

The seed bank can be stimulated to germinate by the addition of compound fertilizer, which also improves establishment and early growth. Miller *et al.* (1991) found that the number of plants produced from the seed bank of peat soils increased with the rate of fertilizer application. The heaviest rate ($86 g/m^2$ of $7:7:7$ NPK) was the most effective. After three growing seasons, cover was almost complete on fertilized plots but less than 40% on unfertilized ones. Scarifying the surface or adding lime was of little benefit. A few words of warning are required, the vegetation cover produced is likely to be patchy, dry, and high-altitude sites respond less well to this approach. Also there is the danger of enriching the soils too much so that a competitive sward develops and slower growing species succumb; the issue of high fertilizer application levels (particularly of inorganic material in semi-natural areas) needs to be addressed.

Turfing

If there is a suitable source of material then this is a rapid and successful means of revegetating damaged ground. Hand-cut turves are laid to form either a complete (close turfing) or a discontinuous (spot turfing) cover. Turfing has been used on a small scale in footpath repair work (Bayfield and Aitken 1992), and on a larger scale on the top of Snaefell where acid grassland from a site about to be afforested was used to restore disturbed ground around a new communications mast.

Bare root transplants

Tussocks of species such as mat-grass (*Nardus stricta*), tufted hair-grass (*Deschampsia cespitosa*), and soft rush (*Juncus effusus*), or creeping species like common cottongrass (*Eriophorum angustifolium*), can be dug up and pulled apart to form a large number of rooted fragments or divots for transplanting. Provided they are not allowed to dry out, the transplants have high survival rates and are a good way of generating mosaics of patterned vegetation. Of course, care is needed to avoid damaging the donor site. Substituting pot grown transplants is costly and establishment can be disappointing. Nevertheless, this is possible with careful selection of individual plants or by restricting turves to the size of spades; the technique has been used successfully to introduce soft rush into a seasonally ponded area in the restoration work around the new radar dome on top of Great Dun Fell and greater woodrush (*Luzula sylvatica*) and bilberry (*Vaccinium myrtillus*) onto the top of Snaefell around a new mast; also, cottongrasses and other upland species have been successfully introduced into restored ground beside footpaths (Bayfield and Aitken 1992).

Potted plants

Where divots and turves are unavailable or unsuitable, but particularly characteristic species of the area are unlikely to colonize naturally, the introduction of potted plants, as described in Chapter 6, can be appropriate. On Great Dun Fell, the surrounding hillside was surveyed to identify the key species that had not successfully colonized the areas that had previously been disturbed. Three were regarded as important to the hilltop—bilberry, stiff sedge (*Carex bigelowii*), and heath bedstraw (*Galium saxatile*). These species were subsequently added to the restoration scheme as potted plants grown from locally collected cuttings to match the genetic stock in this World Biosphere Reserve. Monitoring the survival rate of the plants subsequently proved difficult as the surrounding vegetation developed, but the heath bedstraw and stiff sedge spread well vegetatively and establishment was good. Using pot grown transplants is not cheap (Chapter 4), but the cost of raising them has to be compared with the cost of labour and machines for collecting and planting divots or handling turves.

Repair and creation techniques: seeding

Scotland

This is probably the most widely employed method in high-altitude situations, with examples available from the restoration of trampling on paths, and damage from ski developments as well as other construction projects. Methods have been developed and improved with time. Initially, damaged areas, such as those associated with ski facilities, were treated with a mixture of fast-growing agricultural grasses, sometimes including a clover (*Trifolium* spp.), and fertilizer; the whole lot was then held in place by a bitumen spray.

An example of this method has been monitored by Bayfield (1971, 1974, 1980, 1996) who was interested mainly in the rate of recruitment of native taxa into the sown sward. He recorded changes on three bulldozed pistes

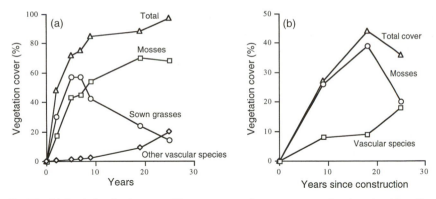

Fig. 7.3 (a) Graph showing how, over 25 years, a cover of sown grasses was largely replaced by native vascular plants and mosses at 1080 m in the Cairngorms, Scotland. (b) Graph showing how, over 25 years, native vascular plants and mosses colonized and built up a 40% cover on an unseeded site at 1000 m in the Cairngorms (from Bayfield 1996).

between altitudes of 1000 and 1080 m on Cairn Gorm over 25 years. Two had been treated at the time of construction and the third left unsown. The surrounding intact vegetation is open *Juncus trifidus–Racomitrium lanuginosum* rush heath (NVC U9; Rodwell 1992) growing on gritty granite gravel with a pH of 4.5. The bare areas were first hand-raked and dressed with 7.5 tonnes/ha of ground limestone and 1.2 tonnes/ha of basic slag. The ground was then hand sown with the following mixture: *Phleum pratense* 'Canadian', 11 kg/ha; *Phleum pratense* 'S50', 11 kg/ha; *Cynosurus cristatus*, 9 kg/ha; *Festuca rubra* 'Creeping', 22 kg/ha; and *Poa pratensis*, 9 kg/ha; compound fertilizer was added at 500 kg/ha. This mixture was raked in and the surface sprayed with a bitumen emulsion (Bitumuls 55) to bind it. During the first ten years occasional dressings of fertilizer were given to the sward when the sown grass looked sickly.

Total cover rose steeply to over 70% during the first five years, with smaller increases thereafter until at 25 years it was 89% (Fig. 7.3). For the first seven years, mosses and sown grasses contributed in almost equal amounts; after this the sown grasses declined rapidly, probably in response to lime and fertilizer being leached out of the soil. This opened up the sward and moss cover continued to increase slightly; the proportion of local angiosperms increased substantially, attaining over 20% cover after 25 years. The main invaders, in decreasing order of abundance, were dwarf cudweed (*Gnaphalium supinum*), dwarf willow (*Salix herbacea*), three-leaved rush (*Juncus trifidus*), alpine lady's-mantle (*Alchemilla alpina*), mat-grass, spiked woodrush (*Luzula spicata*), and crowberry (*Empetrum nigrum*), together with the mosses *Polytrichum* spp., *Racomitrium heterostichum*, *R. lanuginosum*, and *Oligotrichum hercynicum*, and a low cover of lichens (*Cetraria islandica*, *C. deliseii*,

Cladonia spp., and *Steinia geophana*). *Festuca rubra* was easily the most persistent of the sown grasses with *Poa pratensis* a poor second; the other species declined to insignificance.

At the unseeded site, left entirely to natural colonization, the build-up of total plant cover was much slower. Initially it was composed almost entirely of mosses, which peaked at 35% after eighteen years; vascular plants continued to rise so that total cover after 25 years was around 40% (Fig. 7.3). Viviparous sheep's-fescue (*Festuca vivipara*) and three-leaved rush were recruited preferentially into the unsown areas; nevertheless, at the end of the monitoring period these unsown plots had less that half the biodiversity or cover of the seeded plots. It is evident that, over the first 25 years, the seeded areas were superior to those left to nature in restoring bare ground.

On seeded ground below 750 m, sown grasses were almost entirely replaced by self-sown heather (*Calluna vulgaris*) after eight years (Bayfield 1980); at higher levels, no native species displayed sufficient seed production or establishment efficiency to become rapidly dominant (three-leaved rush came the nearest). For this reason, it has been predicted that at sites over 900 m the sown species are likely to persist for at least another 15 years (Bayfield 1996).

Today, the seeded pistes blend well with the surrounding ground and fairly close inspection is needed to reveal differences in species composition from adjacent undisturbed areas. Local vascular plants provide more cover than the sown grasses and have a suitably patchy distribution. In contrast, the unseeded areas still have a raw, largely bare appearance, though these are coming to resemble open rush heath (NVC U9). The main conclusion of this impressive monitoring is that grass seeding substantially enhances colonization by native species.

Currently, Cairngorm Sports Development Ltd is advised on re-seeding by the seed merchants Rigby Taylor who have recently designed mixes of highly bred cultivars resistant to cold and tolerant of temperature fluctuations (Table 7.1). The mixtures are sown at a rate of 170 kg/ha by a hydroseeding machine, during the period June–August, together with gypsum (which flocculates fine material) at 25 kg/ha, 'Seanure' (to help microbial activity) at 25 kg/ha, a compound fertilizer at 25 kg/ha, and bitumen. The thinking behind species selection is that the fast germinating rye-grass provides short term nurse cover, which then dies out giving way to the medium term *Festuca rubra* cultivars, which are themselves eventually replaced by the fine fescues and bents, and, in the long term (60–80 years), by the native flora.

Pennines and the Isle of Man

A similar application of grass seed has been used successfully to provide a cover into which native plants can colonize on damaged mountain tops in the

Table 7.1
Mixes of highly bred cultivars resistant to cold and tolerant of temperature
fluctuations designed for sowing on the Cairngorm Plateau, Scotland

Mix	Species	Strain	Proportion within mix (%)
1	Chewing's fescue *Festuca rubra* spp. *commutata*	Bingo	5
	Hard fescue *Festuca longifolia*	Crystal	15
	Brown-top bent *Agrostis capillaris*	Highland	7.5
	Slender creeping red fescue *F. rubra* spp. *littoralis*	Suzette	20
	Fine-leaved sheep's fescue *F. filiformis*	Bornito	20
	Perennial rye-grass *Lolium perenne*	Surf	20
	Creeping bent *Agrostis stolonifera*	Prominent	2.5
	Strong creeping red fescue *F. rubra*	Boreal	10
2	Perennial rye-grass *L. perenne*	Superstar	45
	Hard fescue *F. longifolia*	Triana	30
	Brown-top bent *A. capillaris*	Highland	10
	Slender creeping red fescue *F. rubra* spp. *littoralis*	Recent	10
	Creeping fescue *F. rubra*	Lustre	5

Pennines and Isle of Man, and for footpath repair work in the uplands in
various locations. Heavily used areas need trample-resistant species (Table
7.2), while little-used ones can be seeded with a wider range of native plants,
if they are available. A seeding rate of 5–10 g/m² is sufficient, with forbs making
up no more than 20% by weight. The seed is normally broadcast by hand on
small sites, perhaps mixed with sand or sawdust to help ensure an even distribution. On larger, accessible sites, hydroseeding is successful. Nurse species
are sometimes included in mixtures to provide quick cover, and shelter for
slower growing plants. Rye-grass (*Lolium perenne*), which does not persist on
infertile soils, and Yorkshire fog (*Holcus lanatus*), which is not very frost resistant, are suitable nurse species for use in the uplands (but not at lower altitudes where they could be too competitive). Trials in the Three Peaks area of
north-west Yorkshire concluded that although a nurse of Yorkshire fog gave
a slight boost to total cover in the first year, there was a generally lower total
cover in the second and third year than on plots without a nurse species
(Bayfield *et al.* 1991).

A similar approach was also used on Great Dun Fell, which, at 850 m, is one

Table 7.2
The trampling resistance of a range of commercially available grasses

Trampling resistance	Species
Very tolerant	Perennial rye-grass (*Lolium perenne*) Annual meadow-grass (*Poa annua*)
Tolerant	Smooth-stalked meadow-grass (*Poa pratensis*) Chewing's red fescue (*Festuca rubra* ssp. *commutata*) Timothy (*Phleum pratense*)
Fair	Sheep's fescue (*Festuca ovina*) Crested dog's-tail (*Cynosurus cristatus*) Common bent (*Agrostis capillaris*) Creeping red fescue (*Festuca rubra* ssp. *rubra*)
Poor	Rough-stalked meadow-grass (*Poa trivialis*) Creeping bent (*Agrostis stolonifera*)

of the highest points of the Pennines. This site is of particular interest in revealing details of patterns of succession, while, at the same time, providing pertinent lessons for restoration planning. A new radar dome was constructed on the fell in the early 1990s; the 2.8 ha of damaged ground was completely bare when revegetation work began in 1986–1988. This ground had a rough surface and abundant rock material in a mixed top/subsoil cover. The pH of the subsoil material was 7.4 and was significantly higher than the adjacent undamaged topsoil (pH 4.6); nutrient levels were very low. The habitat re-creation specification was based on the character of the surrounding subalpine grassland. A seed mix was hydroseeded, supplemented with a slow-release fertilizer (Palmers No. 10 Bio-organic) at 20 g/m². Establishment conditions were so severe that part of the area had to be re-seeded and fertilized in 1989. As described earlier, selected species were introduced as potted plants.

Monitoring showed that after 4–6 years, sown grasses provided most of the cover, and bare ground had declined to 6.6–25.1%. The sward diversity increased in the first few years but then stablized as the sward became denser. Grazing will be needed to control the more vigorous grasses and permit further spread of more locally native species.

The range of species that have colonized is of interest. It includes plants characteristic of a number of local habitats, widespread common but usually lowland species, those more typical of the immediate high altitude surroundings, and a number (about a quarter) that have not been recorded elsewhere on the reserve (Rawes 1981). Species found at low altitudes and in meadows include soft brome (*Bromus hordeaceus*), lady's mantle (*Alchemilla xanthochlora*), meadow foxtail (*Alopecurus pratensis*), and red campion (*Silene dioica*). Harebell (*Campanula rotundifolia*) and crested dog's-tail (*Cynosurus cristatus*) had colonized the fell above their normal altitudinal range. Of particular interest was the number of species normally found in springs and flushes or beside streams that appeared. These included yellow sedge (*Carex demissa*), marsh foxtail (*Alopecurus geniculatus*), greater bird's-foot trefoil (*Lotus uliginosus*), and blinks (*Montia fontana*). On the other hand, there were many species in the surrounding communities that had not appeared on the restored summit. This was probably partly due to the high grazing pressure and consequent lack of seed.

This case study serves to illustrate the considerable range of species that can establish on new sites, provided colonization gaps persist. This is dependent on the careful selection of appropriate grass species, balancing the need to generate a skeletal cover, by assisting only as necessary through the addition of nutrients. Only time will tell if the decisions made were the right ones to maximize the diversity of the new communities. However, research in the North American tundra has shown that when the wrong decisions are made, colonization by native plants is restricted.

North America

Habitat creation work to repair the damage from 50 years of oil exploration and extraction has found that there is now plenty of evidence that sowing well-adapted grass cultivars onto fertilized substrata decreases the rate and alters the pattern of succession by preventing or inhibiting the establishment and growth of many native species (Densmore 1992; Younkin and Martens 1987). Northern varieties of commercial grasses specially selected for survival under arctic or boreal conditions include creeping red fescue ('Arctared') and Kentucky bluegrass (*Poa pratensis* 'Nugget') (Elliott *et al.* 1987; Younkin and Martens 1987). Other cultivars such as timothy ('Engmo' and 'Climax'), reed canary-grass (*Phalaris arundinacea* 'Frontier'), and spring-rye (*Secale cereale* 'Prolific') provide rapid first year cover but are killed over winter (Younkin 1972).

Members of the flora that are particularly constrained in this persistent grass cover include most forbs and small seeded shrubs such as sage (*Artemisia tilesii*), grey-leaf willow (*Salix glauca*), and felt-leaf willow (*S. alaxensis*). This effect is thought to be the result of the live canopy of planted grasses, their dense shallow root system, and the high moss cover that develops in sown swards. These factors combine to reduce both the number of available germination sites and the resource level in the soil; in other words, competitive exclusion. Chemical inhibition by the grass root system is also a possible controlling factor; root leachates from *Festuca rubra* have been shown to inhibit shoot and root growth in shrubs (Fales and Wakefield 1981).

A seeding experiment on an abandoned oil exploration site in the Caribou Hills of northern Canada, which was monitored for over 12 years (Younkin

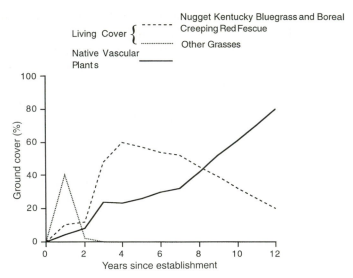

Fig. 7.4 Graph showing how, over 12 years, native vascular plants (solid line) invaded a sown grass sward at a turndra site in northern Canada. The grass mix included both well adapted species ('Nugget' Kentucky blue-grass and 'Boreal' creeping red fescue; broken line) and nurse species (dotted line) (redrawn from Younkin and Martens 1987).

and Martens 1987), confirmed that well-adapted cultivars such as 'Nugget' and 'Arctared' curtailed incursion by native species to less than 15% cover after 12 years through their competitive ability. On the other hand, seed mixtures containing the above taxa plus a substantial proportion of poorly adapted 'nurse' cultivars, such as *Phleum pratense*, reed canary-grass, and spring-rye (Younkin 1972), provided a high first year cover (45%) that died back and opened up considerably during the winter (Fig. 7.4). Invasion of native species into this plot was consistently higher than into other seeded plots, reaching 80% after 12 years; this equalled that of unseeded and unfertilized control areas in terms of species composition, vascular plant cover, and growth rates. So, in areas where rainfall is not a problem, the detrimental effects of grass seeding may outweigh the benefits.

A novel approach to revegetation has been devised by Chapin and Chapin (1980) who worked on a damaged organic hare's-tail cottongrass (*Eriophorum vaginatum*) tundra soil in the Alaskan interior. After 10 years of monitoring a range of fertilized and control plots sown with adapted grass cultivars, it became clear that none of the species were suited to the organic soil. Within five years of sowing, the exotic grasses had disappeared from all but one unfertilized plot; however, total vegetation cover had increased to 50–100% through the natural invasion of the cottongrass and stiff sedge. The abundance of these two species was unrelated to fertilizer levels. The origin of the sedge was predominantly dormant buried seed, while the cottongrass established from seed blown in from the surrounding tundra. So, at this site, the sowing of exotic grasses and the use of fertilizers served little purpose. Dependable commercial seed sources of the two successful native species are not available, but it was discovered that fertilizing the surrounding tundra with phosphorus and potassium increased inflorescence density 25-fold, resulting in a greatly enhanced seed fall. Revegetation using this method is cheaper than a programme of sowing and avoids the potential danger of introducing exotic species.

This technique has also been used by on restoration sites along the Pennine Way in England in an effort to disperse grazing away from the path revegetation work. A single application of 70g/m^2 of the slow release fertilizer ENMAG was successful on a cottongrass community, though the species stimulated—sheep's fescue (*Festuca ovina*), soft rush, common sedge (*Carex nigra*), and bryophytes—did not include cottongrass. In other trials, grassland dominated by heath rush (*Juncus squarrosus*) showed a moderate response, while no apparent benefit was gained by fertilizing a mat-grass community (Bayfield *et al.* 1990). Further work is needed to identify which types of site can benefit most from this form of treatment.

Vegetation and soil reinforcement

In heavily used and particularly exposed locations, expensive durable geotextiles may be incorporated into the surface. These vary from stone mosaics to plastic grids. Soil reinforcement using netting placed just below the surface helps to spread the pressure exerted by foot traffic. The netting should be relatively inelastic, fairly strong, and with a mesh size of over a centimetre (Bayfield and Aitken 1992). An example on Arthur's Seat, Edinburgh, has been in place since 1980, with the vigour of the grass maintained by dressings of fertilizer.

A recent innovation in geotextile engineering is soil strengthening by the inclusion of small pieces of plastic mesh. These interlock simulating the strengthening action of roots. The mesh elements are typically about 2.5×2.5 cm with openings of 1×1 cm. They are mixed at a density of 0.1–0.2% of soil volume into the surface layers, where they considerably improve the load-bearing and wear-resisting properties (Andrawes *et al.* 1986).

Geojute, a jute mesh, has been used at high altitudes, as in the experimental plots on blanket peat described in Chapter 6. On Snaefell summit in the Isle of Man, Geojute was used in small areas where frost heave and the resultant mobility of the peaty soil was a particular problem. The important feature of any geotextile is the contours of the surface, even on a small scale, so that water cannot run below it and erode a gully. Most such textiles are held in

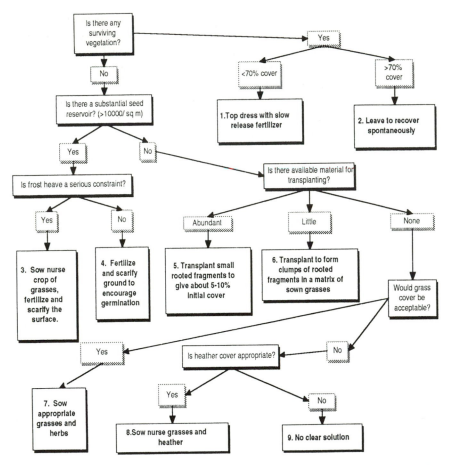

Fig. 7.5 A 'decision guide' for selecting appropriate revegetation techniques at sites on the Pennine Way (Bayfield and Aitken 1992).

place with metal pins. These will need to be re-set regularly as frost heave at high altitude or latitude can push the pins out of the ground within a few years. The most suitable materials to use in semi-natural environments are biodegradable, so that no long-term pollution is caused. It takes much longer in extreme climates for degradation to occur, during which time vegetation can re-established.

Conclusion

In time, some bare soil in mountainous areas will become revegetated by natural colonization. Studies of bulldozed roads in the Cairngorms have shown that even at 1000 m their margins have developed an almost continuous cover after 30 years (Bayfield *et al.* 1984). This, however, is unacceptably slow for most sites, where damaged surfaces need to be reinstated fast to minimize both erosion and visual intrusion. Deciding which techniques to use requires careful site evaluation, which should include an assessment of types and levels of use by humans, stock, and wild herbivores, the nature of the soils, seed bank, and vegetation, together with an appraisal of constraints among which accessibility and cost will probably figure prominently. Special problems of montane environments are the extreme climate. The 'decision guide' produced for the southern end of the Pennine Way (Fig. 7.5) provides a useful starting point and is equally pertinent for non-footpath projects. Several approaches may need to be employed at any site.

It is important not to over-design or over-resource habitat creation and repair in arctic and mountain environments. Although erosion control has been a major objective, questions are increasingly being raised concerning the influence of adapted grass cultivars on the rate of return of the native flora and the re-establishment of natural communities. Where erosion is a concern, it is generally accepted that protection of the soil base is of prime importance. However, where it is not an issue, areas can be left to revegetate naturally, perhaps helped by fertilizing the surrounding vegetation to increase seed fall onto the disturbed site. A compromise would be to use a seed mix containing nurse species that opens up to provide germination gaps after the first year or two. Concern has been expressed over the potential danger of introducing any exotic species into arctic and alpine areas (Chapin and Chapin 1980). Elsewhere in the world, graminoid-dominated communities have been greatly altered by the unintentional introducition of exotic species (Billings 1974), and, although this phenomenon has not yet been observed in the arctic tundra, two species of *Poa* are the most successful vascular plant introductions in Antarctica (Longton 1966). Whatever method is employed, it has been estimated that the time required to re-establish natural communities in the tundra or the Scottish Highlands may be of the order of 60–80 years.

8 The coast

In a major habitat creation initiative English Nature has committed itself to trying to reverse the recent substantial and the predicted future loss of coastal habitats. As part of this strategy, a goal has been set to maintain coastal habitats equivalent to their distribution and total area in 1992 (English Nature 1992). This crisis is the consequence of centuries of 'coastal squeeze', which results from a combination of development or intensive agriculture pushing seawards (land claim) and the landward movement of the high-water mark due to erosion or rising sea level. Coastal protection schemes employing static structures (e.g. sea walls, groynes) also contribute to coastal squeeze by disrupting natural processes (e.g. longshore drift). Eight major coastal habitats can be recognized (Pye and French 1993) and, for each, estimates of recent rates of loss have been made together with projected trends over the next 20 years. From these, target figures for habitat creation needs, on a 'no net loss scenario', have been made (Table 8.1).

Information on recent habitat loss is patchy, but a comparison of aerial photographs has shown that estuaries in south-east England experienced a 10–44% loss of saltmarsh between 1973 and 1988; these losses were mainly due to erosion (Burd 1992). There have also been significant losses of saltmarsh in the Severn Estuary and along the south coast. The reduction of other habitats has been on a smaller scale and, in general, has been related to human activities, such as development, waste tipping, and aggregate extraction. Projected losses are tied up with a possible accelerated sea-level rise of between 40 and 100 mm over the next 20 years as a result of global climate change, and an expected increase in the frequency and severity of storms. These storms are likely to cause widespread erosion along the coast, especially of intertidal sediments (Tubbs 1995).

Habitat creation schemes are being favoured by the recent preference for 'soft' coastal engineering methods and by the growing awareness of the importance of the coastal zone for recreation and conservation. Despite this, all coastal habitats are predicted to experience losses. The techniques available for their reinstatement include the following: (1) 'managed retreat', which involves the setting back or removal of sea defences; (2) 'managed advance' in areas where natural accretion is taking place or where erosion is being reversed by the construction of breakwaters; and (3) 'managed stability',

Table 8.1
The extent, in England, of each major coastal habitat and minimum targets for
re-creation to replace likely losses over the next 20 years

Habitat	Extent (ha)	Re-creation target (ha)
Sand dunes	11 897	240
Saltmarsh	32 462	2750
Intertidal flats	233 361	10 000
Shingle	12 376	200
Saline lagoons	1215	120
Coastal heath	462	50
Maritime cliff grassland	1895	150
Unprotected soft cliffs	256*	10*

* Units: kilometres.
Source: Pye and French (1993).

which uses techniques such as foreshore recharge and sediment recycling.
Encouragingly, the last two decades have seen an increase in statutory protection and a tightening of planning regulations in the coastal zone. These
changes are helping to ensure that much of what we have is safeguarded—
techniques for its re-creation and repair are still perfunctory. All eight habitats are listed among the 38 key habitats recognized by the Government as
requiring special attention and the production of action plans (UK Biodiversity Steering Group 1995).

Sand dunes

These include all areas of coastal wind-blown sand. They are widespread in
the UK except along the south-eastern and southern coasts of England, with
71% of the national resource being in Scotland (Doody 1985). Dunes are
among the most natural habitats in the country and are valued for their specialized flora and fauna, recreational opportunities, and the important role
they play in sea defence.

Natural threats are principally associated with coastal erosion of the frontal
dunes, but the situation is complicated as losses on one beach are often compensated for by gains on an adjacent one. Total net loss of dunes as a result
of erosion in England over the last 20 years is estimated to be less than 1%
(120 ha). Losses due to human activity in the form of cultivation, forestry, sand
mining, golf courses, and urban development have steadily declined (except
in the Outer Hebrides) over the last 20 years.

So, in comparison with most other coastal habitats, sand dunes remain
relatively abundant and are no longer seriously threatened. Net losses over

the next 20 years in England are not expected to exceed 240 ha (or 2%); this is the target for habitat creation (Pye and French 1993). Most dunes respond to coastal erosion by moving inland. When backed by residential development, stabilization measures in the form of beach feeding are preferable to the construction of hard defences.

One of the best documented examples of sand dune creation comes from Koge Bay Seaside Park on the Baltic coast of Denmark (Vestergaard and Hansen 1992). Here, an artificial dune 8 km long and 300 m wide was established from dredged sand in 1977–78. The morphology of this artificial dune, which comprises a sandy beach *c.* 50 m wide, a dune, and a grassland area behind (Fig. 8.1), was modelled on a natural barrier system further south. In 1978 the dune top and outer dune slope were planted with marram grass (*Ammophila arenaria*). Figure 8.1 shows the changing relief of the structure

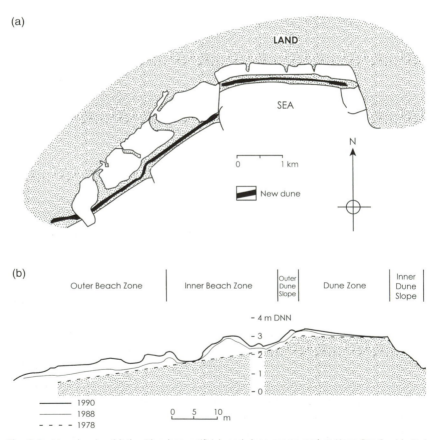

Fig. 8.1 Map showing (a) the 8 km long artificial sand dune constructed at Koge Bay Seaside Park, Denmark, and (b) the changes in relief of the beach and dune between 1978 and 1990 (redrawn from Vestergaard and Hansen 1992).

over the next 12 years. It can be seen that the inner dune slope remained fairly constant, but over the rest of the system a considerable net accumulation of wind-blown sand was recorded. Accumulation rates were especially high during the first five years. On the inner beach, a new dune ridge formed parallel to the constructed dune, eventually spreading over it. The source of this dune was *Ammophila* that had spread naturally from the original plantings and, to a lesser extent, lyme-grass (*Leymus arenarius*), sand couch (*Elytrigia juncea*), and *Ammophila baltica*.

The new dunes that arose on the upper part of the beach were the result of invasion by rhizomatous dune-building grasses, their rapid establishment being due in part to the planted source of propagules on the adjacent constructed dune. The new fore-dunes starved the constructed dune of fresh sand. As a consequence, the planted marram grass, which for the first few years had formed a dense sward, gradually degenerated and was replaced by creeping red fescue (*Festuca rubra*) that had been sown onto the dune hinterland. In the future, shrubs such as Japanese rose (*Rosa rugosa*) and sea-buckthorn (*Hippophae rhamnoides*) may play an increasing role in this dune grassland. Over the first 12 years the newly created habitat was spontaneously invaded by a wide range of dune species, including sea rocket (*Cakile maritima*), sea pea (*Lathyrus japonicus*), sea sandwort (*Honkenya peploides*), and saltwort (*Salsola kali*).

A different approach to dune habitat creation and repair has been taken at several sites in the Netherlands where the aim was to reverse the stagnation of natural processes, reduce eutrophication of the normally nutrient deficient soils, and recreate dune slacks (Van Bohemen and Meesters 1992). The basic principle was to complement natural processes, that is, to work with the sand rather than using hard construction materials. At these problem sites, sand replenishment was instigated either in front of, on, or behind the fore-dunes (Fig. 8.2). For example, the 8 km stretch of dunes between 's-Gravenzande and Kijkduin were reinforced in 1988 using 1.4 million m³ of coarse, desalinated, shell-rich sand deposited on top of and behind the fore-dunes. The sand sculpting followed, as far as possible, the natural contours of the dune system, with slopes as steep as possible (1 in 3). Marram grass was planted and fed with a slow-release fertilizer to stimulate its growth. Two years after completion, the extent of marram grass cover (25%) was relatively low and the vegetation contained a high number of species not typical of dunes, but these are thought to be decreasing. The restricted degree of sand drift was reducing colonization by the specialist flora (which is favoured by disturbance). Dutch ecologists now consider that beach or foreshore replenishment is more successful at countering erosion than dune reinforcement.

One of the largest, and certainly the most expensive dune restoration projects in Britain is in Suffolk, at the site of Sizewell B Power Station. Here, restoration of 800 m of species-rich sand dune was preceded by eight years of

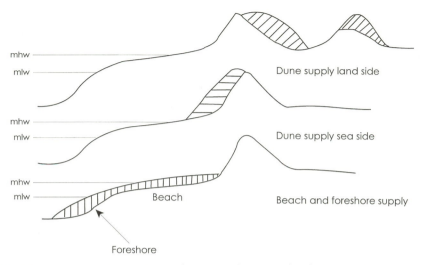

mhw
mlw

Dune supply land side

mhw
mlw

Dune supply sea side

mhw
mlw   Beach

Beach and foreshore supply

Foreshore

Fig. 8.2 Cross sections showing dune reinforcement techniques used in the Netherlands; mhw, mean high-water; mlw, mean low-water (redrawn from Van Bohemen and Meesters 1992).

research, which included the collecting of seed of local genetic stock, investigating its storage and germination requirements, propagating species in a holding nursery, and carrying out establishment trials (Walmsley 1994). Over 70 000 container grown plants or vegetative shoots of 36 species were planted onto the reshaped dunes. Marram grass and sand sedge (*Carex arenaria*) established well and showed rapid growth (Fig. 8.3) as did wild flowers such as sea-holly (*Eryngium maritimum*), rest-harrow (*Ononis repens*), and the dune annual, sea mouse-ear (*Cerastium diffusum*). It is unusual to establish more than a matrix of grasses then leave the site to nature, so the subsequent development of the vegetation will be followed with interest. It is anticipated that weed control may be the most important maintenance task in the future.

After two years, a comparison of the planted dunes with adjacent undisturbed ones showed them to be comparable with regard to higher plants; however, the older dunes were characterized by a high cover of moss and lichen, for which transplant techniques have not yet been developed. The planted marram, which was set out in lines, still looks somewhat unnatural (see also Fig. 11.1). One way to help overcome this is to use fertilizer. About half the fore-dunes were fertilized, which resulted in a much greater growth of marram but poorer establishment of the other species, particularly dune annuals.

An alternative method of introducing species has been tried on Les

Fig. 8.3 A recently created sand dune planted with marram grass (*Ammophila arenaria*) two years previously; Sizewell B Power Station (photograph by Nuclear Electric).

Blanches Banques dunes in Jersey (Channel Islands), where spade-sized turves of species-rich vegetation from the grey dunes were inserted into an open marram grass sward planted in an area impoverished by trampling and erosion. Some of the species, particularly autumn hawkbit (*Leontodon autumnalis*), colonized outside the turves, but, unfortunately, birds pulled up the turves and cut short the experiment, (PA, pers. obs.). This appears to be a hazard of turf transplants; at a site in Derbyshire rabbits either dug them up or damaged them by defecation.

Dune slack creation is not always welcome, at Gibraltar Point, Lincolnshire, it has been criticized for being carried out at the expense of semi-natural dune vegetation (Radley 1994). However, the slacks there have been created for a specific purpose—the reintroduction of natterjack toads (*Bufo calamita*). This amphibian requires specialized conditions—ponds that dry out in late summer, as this helps to reduce aquatic plants and invertebrates, and discourages other amphibia (Hawke and Wilson 1994), as, due to its late breeding, the natterjack is sensitive to interspecific competition.

Saltmarshes

These occupy the upper levels of the intertidal zone and are covered with halophytic vegetation; they lie approximately between mean high-water neap tides and mean high-water spring tides. In England the 32 462 ha of saltmarsh (Burd 1989) is well distributed, with the most extensive tracts occurring along estuaries in Essex, North Kent, Lancashire, Lincolnshire, and Hampshire. They are valued as roosting sites for birds of international importance, for their specialized vegetation, and as sea defences.

The principal natural threat is erosion. While saltmarshes in the north and the south-west have experienced stability or accretion over the last 20 years, a high proportion of those in the south have suffered net erosion. Burd (1992) reported that between 1973 and 1988 20% of the marsh area was lost in Suffolk, Essex, and North Kent, with a staggering 44% in the Stour (Essex) estuary. Losses caused by human activity are minor by comparison; such losses result from agricultural land claim, marina and dock development, and tipping. The target for habitat creation over the next 20 years has been set at 2750 ha, with the majority to take place in the south-east (Pye and French 1993).

Techniques available for saltmarsh creation involve both (1) managed advance by encouraging extension seawards through the construction of off-shore breakwaters, the raising of foreshore levels by sediment nourishing, and the artificial transplanting of pioneer marsh vegetation, and (2) managed retreat through the breaching of sea defences. The latter is the preferred option, particularly where there is a secondary line of sea defences—it is relatively cheap and does not have an adverse affect on any associated intertidal mudflats. A combination of 'set back' and beach feeding with dredged spoil speeds the conversion to saltmarsh. A further option, still in its infancy, is to modify the hydraulic behaviour of entire estuaries through soft engineering; however, small scale piecemeal measures have so far met with only limited success.

Since the mid 1970s Anglia Water/National Rivers Authority (NRA) have been investigating ways of restoring the saltmarsh sea defences of Essex, principally by adapting methods in use elsewhere in Europe. Holder and Burd (1990) produced a summary of these experimental sites and methods; following this report, a modified version of the Schleswig-Holstein method is now favoured. This process involves building brushwood fences or groynes on the foreshore by driving in a double row of stakes at 60 cm intervals and 30 cm apart, the gap between the stakes is filled with pine brashings lashed with wire. These reduce wave action. The sedimentation field thus enclosed is up to 400 m^2 and situated on the mudflats in front of the saltmarsh. The enclosures are then trenched (gripped), the role of the ditches being to collect and consolidate sediment. The trenches are traditionally 100 m long, 40–50 cm wide

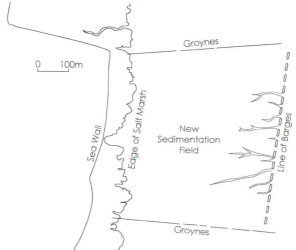

Fig. 8.4 Map and photograph of the Marsh House wave break of sunken barges forming the seaward boundary of a polder enclosed by groynes. The structure protects 720 m of sea wall threatened by erosion of the salt marsh visible in the foreground of the photograph.

and 25–40 cm deep, with 5–6 m between grips, though they may be wider and deeper on the lower shore. In Schleswig-Holstein, grips are dug during calm weather at the end of the summer, which minimizes disruption and enables the large autumn sediment loads to be caught. To be successful, management is required in the form of repairing the groynes and re-gripping late each summer or, if sedimentation rates are high, in spring as well. Once a sedimentation field has been established it will be many years before any advantages are felt. In Schleswig-Holstein, seven years was the shortest period before vegetation became established (the usual period is nine years) and full development to saltmarsh may take 30–40 years (Wagret 1968).

At the 16 sites in Essex where saltmarsh restoration works have been installed, accretion has been reported at 11 and erosion at one, while at 3 sediment is merely being recycled, and 2 have been abandoned. A traditional style Schleswig-Holstein polder was established at Deal Hall in 1980; since then there have been marked and increasing rates of accretion of up to 330 mm a year, accompanied by the establishment of cord-grasses (*Spartina*), glassworts (*Salicornia*), and eelgrasses (*Zostera*). Another successful scheme is at Marsh House where the wave break at the seaward edge of the polder is composed of 16 sunken, silt-filled barges spaced a barge length apart in a line 500 m offshore (Fig. 8.4); lateral groynes were also constructed and *Spartina* transplanted. Mean annual accretion is 11 mm. The barges attract large numbers of mullet, bass, and eels, the mudflats are used by wildfowl and waders, including avocet (*Avocetta recurvirostra*), while foxes (*Vulpes vulpes*) regularly use the cover provided by the groynes to prey on birds. Although at Marsh House the *Spartina* survived, this is not always the case; at other sites where it has been planted into freshly won sediment it has failed to establish due to being planted too early in the year (April) or into mud that did not satisfy its high nutrient demands.

The Government has recently adopted the view that, in most areas natural coastal processes should be allowed to take their course. In response to this, since 1993, MAFF has been reluctant to provide grants for coastal defence work (Tubbs 1995). With saltmarsh this means favouring managed retreat (set back) or even unmanaged retreat, although this creates a conflict in that the retreat is frequently over habitats that are already nature reserves or SSSIs. In the UK two managed retreat schemes have been implemented. The first, dating from 1991 involved just 0.8 ha of National Trust land at Northey Island on the Blackwater Estuary, Essex. The change from typical semi-improved coastal grassland dominated by red fescue and creeping bent (*Agrostis stolonifera*) has been spectacular (Turner and Dagley 1993). Within a year these grasses had been killed off by the sea water and saltmarsh plants had started to invade. After two years, glassworts and annual seablite (*Suaeda maritima*) were widespread, together with 17 other species. Pioneer saltmarsh communities clearly establish themselves very readily. By summer 1996, higher plant cover was comparable with adjacent marshes and there was pan and creek formation; only sea lavender (*Limonium*) was missing.

At Tollesbury Fleet, also on the Blackwater Estuary, 21 ha of farmland was flooded in 1995 by deliberately breaching the sea wall to allow free tidal flow. There is a saltmarsh option in the set-a-side programme under which farmers can receive payment for allowing land to revert to marsh in this fashion.

Following the flooding at Tollesbury, saltmarsh birds and marine creatures moved in rapidly (Reid 1996).

There is still much to learn about managed retreat, for example, how do different widths of breach affect the establishment of saltmarsh? With regard to levels, many sites appear too low for immediate saltmarsh creation and will require a period of 'warping up'.

Intertidal sand and mudflats

These are areas of generally bare or algal covered sediment, between the high- and low-water marks. In England there is 233 360 ha of intertidal sand and mudflats, which is chiefly associated with the gently sloping shores of estuaries such as the Humber, Wash, Outer Thames, Medway, and Severn. Those in the south tend to be mud dominated, while sand flats, which are twice as extensive, occur along the east coast and in the north. Mudflats support the higher density of invertebrates and are consequently the more important feeding grounds for birds. Intertidal flats also serve a valuable coastal defence role by dissipating wave energy.

The principal natural threat is erosion. In Essex, 50% of intertidal flats appear to have been lost over the last 30 years; this is probably related to sea-level rise, which has caused a steepening of the intertidal profile and the low-water mark to move landwards. Human induced losses are associated with land claim for industrial and port developments and, in the long term, tidal barrages and pollution. Estuaries such as the Tyne and Tees have lost almost all their intertidal habitat due to urban development over the last hundred years.

It is estimated that the landward movement of the low-water mark over the next 20 years might be in the region of 10 m (Pye and French 1993), which would lead to a loss of 8000–10 000 ha of intertidal habitat. This will need to be recreated through (1) managed retreat; (2) foreshore recharge using material dredged from navigation channels offshore; (3) allowing the sacrificial erosion of soft cliffs; and (4) the construction of groynes and breakwaters.

For years, dredged silt in the UK has been dumped far out to sea; instead, as in the Netherlands, it could be deposited close to the shore where tidal action and water flow should carry it onto existing mudflats and saltmarshes. This 'trickle charging concept' is controversial—some port authorities believe that the silt will be washed back into the estuary from where it originated, which will consequently increase the frequency of dredging. An experiment commencing in the Medway Estuary in 1996 should help resolve this. An orange tracer is being incorporated into the dredged silt so that its pattern of deposition can be mapped. At Horsey Island, Essex, material dredged from

Harwich Harbour is augmenting a line of sunken barges and helping to recharge the eroding foreshore.

Shingle structures

These are beaches, spits, or forelands composed of pebbles in the size range 2–64(–200) mm. They may be active or relict, and frequently occur in combination with other coastal habitats. The extent of shingle features in England is 12 376 ha; they are concentrated in the south-east and southern England, with 60% in Kent and Sussex. Most result from the reworking of material deposited on the continental shelf by the Pleistocene ice sheets, with a small contribution from the erosion of coastal cliffs and littoral drift. They support specialized communities of plants, lichens, insects, spiders, and breeding birds, and are, in addition, important natural sea defences. Threats include coastal defence works, which are starving some shingle structures of sedimentary material, aggregate extraction, housing development, industry, and recreation.

Where shingle structures are being managed as sea defences foreshore recharge is becoming popular. This involves replenishing the beach with marine or land-derived material. Consequently, many shingle structures on developed coasts are being fixed and not allowed to deteriorate. Losses due to natural processes over the next 20 years are not expected to be great; instead, losses will be due mostly to human activities and have been estimated at around 200 ha (Pye and French 1993). The creation of compensatory, totally new shingle structures on a large scale will be difficult and expensive due to the scarcity of suitably large volumes of sedimentary material and competition from the aggregate industry. Surveys are urgently needed to identify offshore sources of shingle. As always, the best option is greater protection of the existing resource; existing resources contain local coastal history in their structure, a feature that cannot be re-created.

When designing new shingle structures it should be borne in mind that coarse shingle is a poor substrate for plant establishment; coarse shingle is drought prone and allows seeds to get washed too deep down the profile for successful germination. Vegetated shingle always has at least 10% of fine material (<10 mm in diameter); if there is less, then the shingle will remain bare (Fuller and Randall 1988). The leading pioneer shingle species is sea campion (*Silene uniflora*), which often shapes the overall vegetation pattern; other species include sea-kale (*Crambe maritima*), yellow horned-poppy (*Glaucium flavum*), sea pea, English stonecrop (*Sedum anglicum*), lichens, mosses, and a range of annual ruderal species. None of these is available in commercial quantities.

Major shingle structures often contain marshy hollows. The large steep-sided pits that result from modern aggregate extraction are unsuitable alternatives to these. It is better to provide a series of small (25 × 20 m) wetlands delimited by shingle bars in which the winter water depth is 0.5–1.5 m (Ferry and Waters 1988). Since shingle provides a mildly acid environment, it is important to avoid calcareous infill materials such as concrete or builders' rubble.

Experience in creating shingle beach vegetation is limited, but best exemplified by the project at the Sizewell B power station. Here the shingle beach vegetation was extensively damaged during the construction of the station. This has now been repaired following an eight year investigation into restoration methods carried out by the University of East Anglia (Walmsley and Davy 1997*a,b,c*), who studied the germination and establishment biology of six key species: sea-kale, sea pea, yellow horned-poppy, sea-holly, sea sandwort, and curled dock (*Rumex crispus*), using seed collected from the site. All but the dock possessed innate seed dormancy that could be broken by stratification or scarification. Directly sowing the seed onto the beach into pure shingle, organic-matter treated plots, and sandy plots, produced erratic results and cannot be recommended (except for annual or monocarpic species, such as the yellow horned-poppy, which rapidly produced self-sustaining populations and is now making quite a show). Seedling establishment can be relatively rare in this habitat compared with establishment from vegetative fragments.

Planting container-grown plants of the six species raised in polythene tunnels from stored seed was far more successful than sowing seed directly. Neither organic matter nor fertilizer additions affected survival, but location on the beach influenced establishment—establishment was best in seaward plots where the shingle was coarsest. In the main restoration, which was a major engineering and ecological exercise and has won an award for its success, 10 815 container grown plants of 11 species were planted onto the reshaped shingle area (Fig. 8.5).

Saline lagoons

These are defined as bodies of salt water, varying from brackish to hyperhaline, that are partially separated from the adjacent sea by barriers of sand or other sediment. They may be natural or formed artificially by excavation. In Britain this scarce habitat is found mainly along the eastern and southern coasts of England, where around 130 saline lagoon and lagoon-like features are known (Smith and Laffoley 1992). Saline lagoons contain specialist species with highly localized distributions, such as the foxtail stonewort (*Lamprothamnium papulosum*), the lagoon sand-shrimp (*Gammarus insensibilis*), the starlet sea-anemone (*Nematostella vectensis*), and the trembling sea-mat (*Victorella pavida*)—their conservation is of the highest importance. They are

Fig. 8.5 Pot-grown plants of sea pea (*Lathyrus japonicus*) introduced onto the beach at Sizewell B Power Station. This is a rare plant, its seeds will only germinate if the dormancy is first broken. (Photograph by A. C. Walmlsey).

a priority habitat under the EC Habitats Directive, and most are SSSIs. Their biology is well described by Barnes (1980) and Bamber *et al.* (1992).

Major saline lagoons are generally threatened by sea-level rise and coastal retreat (Tubbs 1995); smaller lagoons, which usually have little statutory protection, are also threatened by drainage, waste tipping, the dumping of industrial spoil, and water sports.

The Joint Nature Conservation Committee (1996*b*) has provided guidelines for the selection of saline lagoon Sites of Special Scientific Interest (SSSIs) that are also helpful in directing their creation. Large lagoons are best, being more stable in character than small ones, which encourages species richness, especially of the specialist fauna. Shape and complexity are also important; for example, a long narrow shape encourages a longitudinal salinity gradient and localized variation in the habitat. So, large lagoons with a complex shape are preferable to small simple ones. If they can be structured so that there is a series of interconnecting basins along a salinity gradient providing different conditions of oxygenation and summer warming of surface layers, then a wide range of communities will be encouraged. Particularly noteworthy assemblages occur if beds of tassleweed (*Ruppia*), eelgrass, or stoneworts (*Chara*) are introduced. An artificial origin need not be a negative factor. Indeed, some of the best examples of lagoon creation for nature conservation are those established by the Royal Society for the Protection of Birds (RSPB). Mins-mere, for example, is an entirely man-made brackish lagoon in which salinity is carefully controlled to produce a gradient that determines the vegetation pattern.

A minimum target of 120 ha of newly created saline lagoon is considered desirable over the next 20 years (Pye and French 1993). Creation could be linked to proposals for sand and gravel extraction. An alternative approach would be to lower artificially part of a ridge crest to enhance overtopping by tidal waters. Further research is needed to define the environmental require-ments of many lagoon species.

Maritime cliff grassland

This refers to unimproved grasslands on cliff tops that are markedly influ-enced by sea spray and contain a high proportion of maritime species (NVC MC 8–12) (Rodwell 1997). Creeping red-fescue is usually abundant together with sea pink (*Armeria maritima*), sea campion and buck's-horn plantain (*Plantago coronopus*). These grasslands form a belt from a few metres to a few hundreds of metres wide. Their extent in England is thought to be 1895 ha, 50% of which is in Cornwall.

In soft-rock areas they are threatened by coastal squeeze, but the main risk is from human activities such as pasture improvement, conversion to arable, or use as caravaning/camping grounds. Heavy grazing is not harmful, though its abandonment is, as it may lead to the expansion of scrub or scrub wood-land. A realistic target for the creation of maritime cliff grassland over the next 20 years is a total of 150 ha (Pye and French 1993).

The National Trust are recreating maritime grassland in Cornwall on a large scale. At Predannack, on the Lizard Peninsula, a group of cliff top fields, which were formerly under full agricultural tenancy, were either left to revert natu-rally or after first being sown down to *Festuca rubra* 'Dawsons' in 1988. Figure 8.6 shows the National Trust's plan for the area. A wide cliff and cliff-top belt of semi-natural grassland was composed of a seaward strip of natural com-munities supplemented by a landward strip of reverted agricultural land; both are grazed by cattle and Shetland ponies to control scrub invasion; no fertil-izers are applied. Behind this is a buffer zone where certain agricultural activ-ities are controlled; for example, there is no herbicide or pesticide use, no drainage work, and only one application of fertilizer per year. Set well back from the sea cliffs, intensive farming starts. The 'reversion' fields have recently been resurveyed (A. Cameron, pers. commun.). It was discovered that the rate of entry of desirable species into the sward was governed by soil type, aspect (which controlled salt blast), the nature of local seed sources, and to a lesser extent, by management.

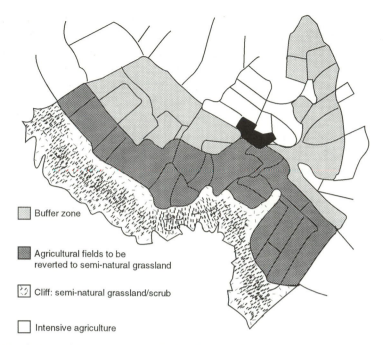

Buffer zone

Agricultural fields to be
reverted to semi-natural grassland

Cliff: semi-natural grassland/scrub

Intensive agriculture

Fig. 8.6 The National Trust's scheme for extending the cliff-top belt of maritime grassland at Predannack, Lizard, Cornwall. Site of the farm shown in black.

In another reversion, this time at Lizard Point, the National Trust bought a group of cliff-top fields that were being double cropped with cauliflowers and new potatoes under polythene. For landscape and ecological reasons these have now been sown down to red fescue and are used for cattle grazing and hay. Preliminary investigations had shown that the depth of topsoil (>1 m) was too great to be stripped off the 20 ha site, so this is regarded as habitat creation on a long time-scale. An initial assessment of the 'Cauliflower Fields' reversion is that it has not been too successful, the red fescue is growing so densely on the fertile soil that few desirable species have invaded. However, these are early days, a good salt storm could open the sward up almost overnight; it is unrealistic to expect instant results.

Coastal heaths

Coastal heaths are defined as climax heath communities that occur close to the shore, and may or may not be influenced by salt spray. Transitional communities to inland heath are usually present. Of the 462 ha present in England, the largest area is found in Cornwall, followed by Devon, Norfolk, and Dorset;

one eighth of the total is on the Lizard Peninsula. Maritime heath is represented by the *Calluna vulgaris–Scilla verna* community (NVC H7; Rodwell
1991*b*); it is characterized by wind-pruned and salt-scorched ericaceous sub-
shrubs together with grass and herb species, and is found on exposed cliff tops.
The other types of coastal heath are as follows: *Erica vagans–Schoenus nigri-
cans* heath (H5) on wet, base-rich soils; *Erica vagans–Ulex europaeus* heath
(H6) on dry, base-rich soils; and *Calluna vulgaris–Ulex gallii* heath (H8) on
acidic soils in areas only slightly influenced by salt spray.

The main threat to these heaths is from agricultural improvement, which
leads to them being ploughed out and replaced by grass/clover swards. As a
working objective, Pye and French (1993) suggest a target of creating a
minimum of 50 ha of new maritime heath over the next 20 years. This can
probably best be achieved by allowing reversion of improved pasture back to
heath. A number of techniques for reducing soil fertility are discussed in
Chapters 2 and 6.

Trials set up to re-establish Cornish heath (*Erica vagans*) in ley pasture on
the Lizard Peninsula have demonstrated the difficulties of working with a
species of poorly known ecology (P. A. Dyke, unpublished report). Seed-rich
litter and vacuum-collected seed capsules were sown into fenced plots that
had been stripped of their topsoil to remove residual nutrients. Three years
later no plants of Cornish heath had appeared despite the heavy sowing rate
($200–3000$ seeds/m^2), yet parallel cold frame experiments had shown both seed
sources germinating and establishing well after four weeks. The lack of success
was attributed to unfavourable conditions for germination. Greater success
was achieved at Bournemouth, Dorset, where turves of heather were used to
clad a precipitous eroding cliff face. The turves were rescued from a site due
to be lost; in their re-use they stabilized the cliff and provided a long-term
vegetation cover that has subsequently been colonized by sand lizards
(*Lacerta agilis*).

Unprotected soft cliffs

This habitat includes all cliffs of soft, poorly consolidated material that are
unprotected by a wall, revetments, or gabions at their base; groynes are permissible. They may be formed of glacial till, outwash deposits, friable sand,
clays, or shales; chalk and Mesozoic limestones are excluded. It is thought that
the extent of this habitat in England is 256 km, with Yorkshire, Hampshire, the
Isle of Wight, Norfolk, and Suffolk having the greatest lengths. Their importance is as a source of sediment for beaches in areas downdrift, in providing
fresh exposures for geological teaching and research, and as features of geomorphological interest.

Loss of this habitat is related primarily to protection works that isolate the cliff from the action of the sea. However change is in the air; a philosophy of abandoning coastal defences is increasingly being adopted by local authorities. Instead, they no longer allow the siting of permanent structures within a 100–300 m buffer zone adjacent to eroding cliff edges.

Habitat creation can take the form of removing coastal defences from the base of cliffs or replacing hard defences with breakwaters that limit rather than prevent erosion (Powell 1992). These techniques are best practised at sites where there is only limited existing development close to the cliff edge, where benefits to other coastal features can be demonstrated, and where current protection consists of wooden revetments and groyne systems that will shortly require replacement. Pye and French (1993) suggest that a mimimum of 10 km of soft cliff should be released from protection over the next 20 years if the habitat is to be maintained at 1992 levels.

Summary

Centuries of coastal defence work involving hard engineering have resulted in a stagnation of natural geomorphological processes, which has caused great harm to many coastal habitats. The policy of preserving the *status quo* is now being challenged by an alternative approach that places reliance on the dynamic character of the coast. This new willingness to accept change and instability is providing exciting opportunities for coastal habitat creation that doubles as low cost sea defence work. Due to the natural instability of the coast, many of the organisms involved posses preadapted mobility—they can invade newly constructed habitats rapidly. This is most satisfactory when compared to the effort and time-scales involved in creating, for example, woodland. Rising sea-levels and the realization that we have surplus agricultural land have also stimulated the present high degree of interest in coastal habitat creation.

9 Farmland

Changes in lowland farming since 1945

The 1945 Agriculture Act, driven by a perceived need for agricultural self-sufficiency in the wake of the Second World War, set the scene for agricultural intensification and marked a watershed for farmland as a habitat for wildlife (Dodds *et al.* 1995; Stoate 1996). With subsidies available, huge areas of un-improved grassland were replaced either with arable or carefully managed swards composed of cultivated varieties of rye-grass (*Lolium perenne*) and white clover (*Trifolium repens*). This grassland took the form of short-term leys within a rotation, and longer-term grazed pastures. These productive alternatives meant that it was no longer economic to manage water meadows, and most old unimproved pastures were ploughed out or, with the help of large amounts of inorganic nitrogenous fertilizer, converted to productive, species-poor swards. During the 1970s silage started to replace hay as winter feed (Fig. 9.1); this involved two or three cuts a year starting in mid-May and even higher levels of fertilizer application. This intensification of grassland management, with its concomitant disturbance and trampling, had a considerable impact on wader nesting success (Smith 1983), in addition to eliminating any botanical or entomological interest.

Meanwhile, parallel developments were taking place in cereal growing with the introduction of new short-stalked, early-ripening, disease-resistant varieties capable of responding to the increased use of nitrogen. During the 1980s, autumn sown cereals became profitable and this caused a substantial decline in the area of weedy winter stubbles. This, combined with improved harvesting efficiency, resulted in a greatly reduced winter food supply for seed-eating birds such as finches and buntings. In addition, earlier ripening and harvesting in July rather than September, caused large numbers of abandoned nests for late breeders such as corn buntings (*Miliaria calandra*) (Donald and Evans 1994). The loss of spring tillage is considered to be one of the main causes of the decline in the lapwing (*Vanellus vanellus*).

An increase of over 600% in the use of nitrogenous fertilizer in the post-war period, coupled with the expansion of autumn cultivation from the early 1980s, resulted in a greater leaching of nitrates from the soil in winter and consequent eutrophication of watercourses. Soil erosion from ploughed fields

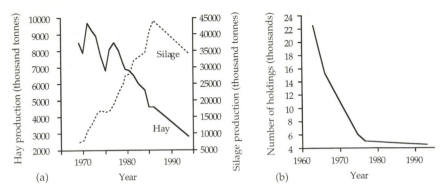

Fig. 9.1 (a) The switch from hay to silage in Britain since the late 1960s. (b) The loss of general mixed farms in England and Wales since the mid-1960s (after Dodds *et al.* 1995).

caused increased siltation of streams, leading (along with eutrophication) to a general deterioration of riparian habitats. Large-scale drainage of valley bottoms and the canalization of rivers were undertaken so cereals could be grown on land previously only suitable for summer grazing.

Economies of scale saw massive hedgerow destruction to accommodate larger machinery, and the abandonment of mixed farming (Fig. 9.1) in favour of arable meant that in the east hedges were no-longer needed. The decline in crop diversity had an adverse effect on species such as grey partridge (*Perdix perdix*), hares (*Lepus europeaus*), and lapwing. Until banned, the use of organochlorine pesticides caused a decline in birds of prey and carnivorous mammals, while herbicides all but eliminated previously common arable weeds such as corn buttercup (*Ranunculus arvensis*) and shepherd's needle (*Scandix pecten-veneris*), which have been replaced by a range of troublesome grasses including black-grass (*Alopecurus myosuroides*), barren brome (*Anisantha sterilis*), and wild oat (*Avena fatua*).

In 1973 Britain entered the EEC. This led to further intensification of the high-yielding autumn sown cereals and new crops such as oilseed rape started to appear. The use of agrochemicals reached a peak with many non-target species being severely affected. Agricultural production increased to embarrassing levels costing vast amounts in subsidies and storage. It was this, rather than the ecological deterioration of farmland, that led to European-wide agricultural reform in the form of set-aside in 1988.

The opportunites

Although not all the available schemes aimed at reversing the decline of wildlife associated with farmland have habitat creation as a main objective, most provide at least limited opportunities. A voluntary set-aside programme for arable farming was introduced by the EEC in 1988, with the aim of removing land from agricultural production while keeping it in a sound condition. Take up was low, but reform of the Common Agricultural Policy in 1992 dramatically increased its role. There are two main options under the scheme, rotational and non-rotational set-aside. The latter requires a commitment to set-aside the same plots of land for at least five years and so provides the best opportunity for habitat creation. A proportion of the land, originally 15% but now 5%, must be withdrawn from production and managed specifically as field margin, grassland, for natural succession, wild bird cover, non-food crop, biofuel, or some other option proposed by the farmer. Most establish a green cover to minimize nitrate leaching and cut it annually to keep down weeds. Set-aside is usually seen as whole field blocks but can be distributed around field margins (minimum: 0.3 ha and 20 m width). The rules vary from year to year.

Following growing concern in Britain about the deterioration of farmland as a habitat for wildlife, a number of schemes have been introduced that rely on the principle of on-going compensation payments to farmers for taking land out of intensive agriculture. About 10% of agricultural land in Britain falls under the Environmentally Sensitive Areas Scheme (ESAs). Farmers in these areas participate voluntarily and receive annual payments per hectare for managing their land to enhance the character of the area in which the ESA lies, such as in maintaining high water levels or converting arable to grassland.

The Countryside Stewardship Scheme was launched by the Countryside Commission (now transferred to MAFF) in 1990 and was followed by a parallel scheme, 'Tir Cymen', in parts of Wales. These provide incentives for a range of conservation measures in specific landscape and habitat types such as 'Old Meadow and Pasture', 'Upland Landscapes', and 'Waterside Landscapes'. Uptake in Wales over the first four years was 39% of the eligible land. A more satisfactory whole-farm scheme, the 'Countryside Premium Scheme', is being developed in Scotland.

In 1994, MAFF announced details of a pilot 'Water Fringe Management Scheme' involving three river Sites of Special Scientific Interest (SSSIs) and two lake SSSIs. Under the scheme, farmers with land bordering the water will be able to receive payment for removing land from agricultural production (for 20 years) or for extensifying current farming practices. The objectives are to create wildlife habitat and to reduce watercourse pollution from agriculture.

There are also a number of grants available from National Park Authorities, Local Authorities, and other public agencies for the planting of hedgerows, the construction of ponds, and the introduction of woodland to farms. All these schemes are encouraging the shift back towards lower-intensity, high-biodiversity farming. Public funds are now helping to produce

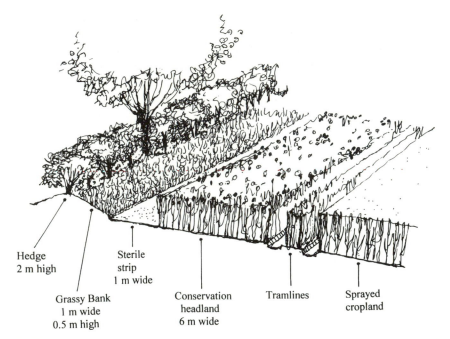

Hedge
2 m high

Sterile
strip
1 m wide

Grassy Bank
1 m wide
0.5 m high

Conservation
headland
6 m wide

Tramlines

Sprayed
cropland

Fig. 9.2 A field margin designed to encourage the nesting and feeding of wild birds (including game) and the conservation of arable weeds and to prevent the spread of troublesome grasses into the crop. (Redrawn by J. Makhzoumi from Game Conservancy Trust 1995*b*).

a more attractive and varied countryside, rather than contributing to food surpluses.

Arable land

Field margins and birds

A field margin designed to be sympathetic towards wildlife, and to aid pest and weed control (Fig. 9.2), is being promoted by the Game Conservancy Trust (1995*b*) and the Royal Society for the Protection of Birds (RSPB) (Andrews and Rebane 1994). It comprises the field boundary (hedge, fence, etc), a grassy bank/nesting strip, a sterile strip (cultivated area between the grassy bank and the crop), and a conservation headland (the outer 5–8 metres of the crop, depending on boom width). The conservation headland is introduced to encourage the growth of broad-leaved weed species in the crop, together with their associated insects (thus providing food for insectivorous and seed eating birds). Insecticides must not be used in this zone after 15 March and herbicides that control dicotyledons must be avoided altogether; fungicides are allowed. In a square 16 ha field, a 6 m wide headland all the way round would occupy 6% of the land. When dealing with smaller or irregular fields only a proportion of the margin needs to be managed as headland. In a square 4 ha field, for example, margins only half the width would provide the same 6% headland. Headlands should avoid areas where there are difficult weeds, such as barren brome or cleavers (*Galium aparine*), and are best sited next to good nesting habitat. Apart from the reduction in spraying, headlands are cultivated in the normal way.

The boundary or sterile strip is purely for good husbandry, to prevent the invasion of the crop by weeds. It is created by rotovation in early spring and must be at least a metre wide. The grassy bank/nesting strip, as well as providing nesting sites for ground nesting birds, is an overwintering habitat for beneficial insects. If should also be at least a metre wide, preferably sited on a bank, and support non-weedy perennial grasses and herbs. A build up of dead material should be allowed and the vegetation topped every few years to avoid scrub encroachment. It must be kept free of pesticides and fertilizers. The hedge needs to be trimmed every other year in sections to permit fruiting (or a few important hedges could be managed on a longer cycle of 10–20 years). If possible, free-growth should be allowed at hedge junctions, which are sites favoured by song birds (Lack 1988).

Field margins and arable weeds

In 1986 a survey was initiated to investigate the status of 25 of Britain's less common arable weeds. The results were alarming (Smith 1986). Formerly abundant species such as shepherd's needle, corn buttercup, cornflower (*Centaurea cyanus*), red hemp-nettle (*Galeopsis angustifolia*), mouse-tail (*Myosurus minimus*), pheasant's eye (*Adonis annua*), and corn cleavers (*Galium tricornutum*) had become extremely rare. In addition, widespread species, such as common poppy (*Papaver rhoeas*) and charlock (*Sinapis arvensis*), have also declined in the face of blanket herbicide applications. Today, most of these arable weeds have retreated to chalky sites in the south and east where they are confined to narrow strips within approximately 4 m of the edge of the field (Marshall 1989; Wilson 1989).

Other agricultural developments that have played a part in the decline of these species include more-efficient seed cleaning, nitrogen inputs that render crop plants more competitive, and changes in the crop growing cycle. The general trend towards sowing in early autumn has mitigated against spring germinating species, such as corn marigold (*Chrysanthemum segetum*), night-flowering catchfly (*Silene noctiflora*), and weasel's snout (*Misopates oronitum*), and is even too early for many autumn germinating species (Wilson 1992).

Recommended conservation measures take advantage of the fact that, in

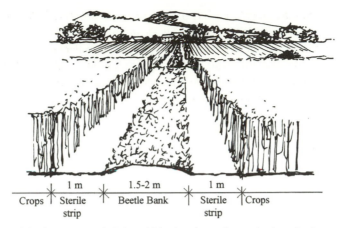

Crops | Sterile strip | 1 m | Beetle Bank | 1.5-2 m | Sterile strip | 1 m | Crops

Fig. 9.3 Beetle banks are narrow (1.5–2 m wide) strips of tussocky grassland crossing large arable fields. They support insect predators of crop pests and are favoured by the grey partridge (*Perdix perdix*). (Redrawn by J. Makhzoumi from Game Conservancy Trust 1995a).

most cases, the area in which the richest weed floras are present are within 4 m of the field edge—the part that is most difficult to farm and the least productive for crops. The Game Conservancy Trust's 'Conservation Headland' (Fig. 9.2) for increasing the numbers of wild game birds avoids the use of herbicides on 6 m strips at the edge of fields (Game Conservancy Trust 1995b). This has proved popular with farmers and has helped increase weed populations (as food for the birds). Work in Gloucestershire has shown that a cessation of herbicide applications really does allow previously scarce cornfield weeds to return. In Breckland, rare annual speedwells (*Veronica praecox*, *V. triphyllos*, and *V. verna*) have been fostered in this way for many years as part of SSSI agreements, under which farmers are compensated for inconvenience and loss of earnings. The set-aside option of sowing broad grass strips around the edge of fields is very harmful to the survival of our uncommon weeds.

Grass baulks or 'beetle banks'

In very large fields, where the centre of the field is over 200 m from the edge, 'beetle banks' are being promoted (Game Conservancy Trust 1995a) as mid-field refuges for predatory insects and a habitat for other wildlife, including ground-nesting birds. After a few years, abundant populations of ground beetles, rove beetles, and spiders may develop at densities of over 1500/m². A 'beetle bank' is just an uncultivated, unsprayed, grassy strip running across the field, like a hedge bank but without the woody shrubs. It is created by ploughing to make a ridge 0.2–0.4 m high and 1.5–2 m wide. It should be drilled or hand sown with tussock and mat-forming grasses such as 50:50 cock's-foot

(*Dactylis glomerata*) and Yorkshire fog (*Holcus lanatus*) at $3 g/m^2$. A sterile strip may be needed to facilitate weed control (Fig. 9.3).

A 20 ha field with good boundaries needs one ridge across its centre, with poor boundaries it would require a second ridge, while fields of 30–50 ha ideally need three or four to get an even distribution of predators moving into the crop. Care must be taken to avoid insecticide spray drift into the strip, but the main idea is that the banks, which cost less than £80 per 400 m to create (including £30 for loss of crop), will render pesticide use unnecessary. For further information see Andrews and Rebane (1994) and The Game Conservancy Trust (1995*a*).

Rotational set-aside for birds

Any benefits to wildlife from set-aside are incidental to its main aim, which is to reduce the cost of price support for food production. Set-aside may disappear as rapidly as it arrived or industrial cropping for non-food purposes may take over. For the time being, however, naturally regenerating stubbles provide nesting and feeding opportunities for many birds and some invertebrate and plant species. The winter stubbles associated with rotational set-aside are helping to reverse the decline of species such as cirl bunting (*Emberiza cirlus*) and corn bunting, while skylark (*Alauda arvensis*) and lapwing often nest in arable crops but feed on nearby grassland. Set-aside escapes the annual application of insecticide, so provides insects for birds such as grey partridge chicks.

The RSPB recently assessed the numbers of wintering birds using 15 matched pairs of fields in south Devon; in each pair, one field was a winter cereal field and the other was managed under rotational set-aside. The results showed that among the 46 species recorded 11 were found significantly more frequently (and 13 in significantly greater numbers) on set-aside than on winter cereals. Only the black-headed gull (*Larus ridibundus*) was recorded more frequently on winter cereal (Table 9.1). There was also a significant positive correlation between the number of seed-eating birds found on a field and its weediness.

Evidence is accumulating that set-aside benefits many birds during the breeding season—for example, skylark, grey partridge, corncrake (*Crex crex*), pheasant (*Phasianus colchicus*), and lapwing. Work in Sweden showed that the abundance of linnets (*Carduelis cannabina*), whitethroats (*Sylvia communis*), and whinchats (*Saxicola rubetra*) was higher in field margins around set-aside than around cereal fields (Berg and Part 1994). Set-aside also represents patches of high prey availability for raptors such as barn owl (*Tyto alba*), sparrowhawk (*Accipiter nisus*), and kestrel (*Falco tinnunculus*). It is not yet possible to compare the benefits of rotational and non-rotational set-aside, or field margin set-aside as against whole-field set-aside. However, Table 9.2

Table 9.1
Bird species for which there was a significant difference between
their occurrence in winter cereal fields and cereal stubbles in rotational set-aside

Species	Significant difference in frequency	Significant difference in number
Sparrowhawk	S	S
Pheasant		S
Snipe	S	S
Black-headed gull	C	
Wood-pigeon	S	S
Skylark	S	S
Meadow pipit	S	S
Redwing	S	S
Blue tit		S
Carrion crow	S	S
Linnet	S	S
Yellowhammer	S	S
Cirl bunting	S	S
Reed bunting	S	S

Source: Wilson *et al.* (1995).
C, significantly more observed in winter cereal fields; S, significantly more observed in rotational set-aside stubble.

Table 9.2
Mean territory density, nest density, and fledgling success of skylarks
(*Alauda arvensis*) on winter cereal and set-aside in Suffolk and Oxfordshire, 1993–94

	Territories/ha	Nests/ha	Chicks fledged per pair
Conventional winter wheat (175 ha)	0.05	0.02	0.26
Conventional winter barley (115 ha)	0.10	0.09	0.29
Set-aside; grass sown, managed by cutting (77 ha)	0.25	0.17	1.30
Set-aside; naturally regenerating, managed by cutting or herbicide (68 ha)	0.36	0.25	1.67

Areas are summed over both study sites and years.
Source: Wilson *et al.* (1995).

compares the breeding success of skylarks on two types of winter cereal and two types of set-aside. The message is that skylarks are very sensitive to land use, any management should be delayed as long as possible (until mid-July/August) to allow chicks to become independent.

Non-rotational set-aside and birds

This option can benefit grey partridge, corn bunting, and barn owl. It can be employed on a field-by-field basis or as 20 m strips around fields. The vegetation cover can be naturally regenerated or sown, preferably as tussocky grasses. It should be cut as late as possible if it is to provide seeds, insects, and nest sites. After the first year a part might be replaced with wild bird cover, which should be an unharvestable mix of at least two crops, such as cereal and brassicas. Grey partridge numbers benefit enormously from this option.

At Courtyard Farm, North Norfolk, areas of wheat with cornflowers and other arable 'weeds' were sown (first in spring 1994) in the central areas of three set-aside fields. The seed, 500 kg of wheat and 10 kg of cornflower mix, were sown separately onto a total of 6 ha of disced land at a cost of £300. Patches of thistles were herbicided, and the fields left until the following March before being disced and sown again. It is expected that only the wheat will need to be sown in future years. Not only does the mixture look extremely attractive but it has attracted large flocks of yellowhammers (*Emberiza citrinella*), chaffinches (*Fringilla coelebs*), and reed buntings (*Emberiza schoeniclus*), with even a few lapland buntings (*Calcarius lapponicus*) and linnets. Corn buntings and grey partridges were also present in good numbers (Lord Melchett, pers. commun.).

Pastures and meadows

Incentives are now available (through the Countryside Stewardship Scheme and ESAs) to allow arable land to revert and to improve leys to permanent grassland to be managed for wildlife and landscape benefits. These are usually created on fields with a high nutrient status and little in the way of a seed bank. For this reason it is best to choose reversion sites adjacent to existing unimproved grassland and on the poorer soils to improve the rate of colonization. There are several establishment options: natural regeneration of the sward; sowing a weak mix of slow-growing grasses that remains open to invasion; sowing a tussocky grass mix; sowing a wild flower mix; hay strewing; or ley grassland can be slot seeded or pot planted with appropriate wild flowers. Further details of these techniques can be found in Chapter 4. On highly fertile sites, topsoil striping should be considered.

Before starting a grassland habitat creation project, the wildlife objectives must be set and the long-term management needs considered within the constraints of the geographical location and soil type. For butterflies and other invertebrates a low-fertility, herb-rich sward should be the aim, with grasses not too dominant. Larval food plants of grassland butterflies need to be

Table 9.3
Some commoner grassland butterflies and their larval food plants

Species	Larval food plant	Distribution
Common blue	Bird's-foot trefoil, rest-harrow	UK
Dingy skipper	Bird's-foot trefoil	UK
Essex skipper	Mainly cock's-foot grass	South and central England
Gatekeeper	Fine and medium leaved grasses	England, Wales
Grayling	Fine and medium leaved grasses	UK
Large skipper	Coarse grasses, especially cock's-foot	England, Wales
Marbled white	Fescue grasses	Southern England, Wales
Meadow brown	Fescues and meadow grasses	UK
Orange-tip	Crucifers, e.g. *Cardamine*, *Alliaria*	UK
Ringlet	Tussocks of coarse grass	UK
Small copper	Common sorrel, sheep's sorrel	UK
Small heath	Fine-leaved grasses	UK
Small skipper	Chiefly Yorkshire fog	England, Wales
Wall brown	Coarse grasses	UK

included (Table 9.3), together with good nectar sources. Moderate grazing is the ideal management; alternatively, half of the field can be cut each winter to provide short and tall swards and good cover for hibernation. For small mammals, and hunting barn owls and kestrel, a species-poor tussocky grass sward on fertile soil is suitable. This may be the only economically feasible wildlife option on some nutrient-rich soils and will suit harvest mice (*Micromys minutus*), which have taken to nesting in tussocks of cock's-foot grass (Clinging and Whiteley 1980).

A breeding pair of barn owls requires approximately 1.5 ha of rough grassland within 2 km of the nest as a hunting ground; the species composition of the grassland is not critical. Vegetation structure is more important than composition for ground-nesting birds also; for example, lapwing prefer a short sward less than 15 cm high, while redshank (*Tringa totanus*) require a medium height of 12–25 cm with taller growth for nesting. Farmers may receive grant-aid payments for creating goose pastures to accommodate the increasing numbers of wintering geese (see Chapter 4).

Some imaginative examples of farm grassland habitat creation have been carried out by the National Trust (Hearn 1994). On the south side of Ivinghoe Beacon, Hertfordshire (and also elsewhere on the chalk) extensive areas of arable land have been restored to permanent pasture to extend the area of nationally important calcareous grassland. A cauliflower farm on the Lizard cliffs in Cornwall is being restored to grazed maritime grassland (see Chapter 8), while a series of disused water meadows on the Sherbourne Estate in Gloucestershire has been recreated (as described in Chapter 10). A length of the River Cole in Oxfordshire is being restored to its former winding course with attendant flood meadows. The National Trust has so much faith in habitat creation that it is specifically acquiring misused properties for restoration.

Heathland/scrub creation on rough grazing

If the soil conditions are suitably acidic, then the creation of heathland is particularly worthwhile. It is particularly valuable if the site links two existing heaths or extends an existing but small one that is of wildlife value. Technical details for establishing ericaceous plants are provided in Chapter 6. If the land is adjacent to a wood then this may cause long-term management problems of succession unless regular grazing, cutting, or burning takes place. Alternatively, the site could be seeded with heathland grasses, such as mat-grass (*Nardus stricta*), common bent (*Agrostis capillaris*), sheep's-fescue (*Festuca ovina*), and wavy hair-grass (*Deschampsia flexuosa*), which can be collected from an existing heath using a forage harvester. To increase diversity, banks can be created and hand sown or planted with gorse and broom. Small bare patches, which can be important for invertebrates and reptiles, should be left unsown.

New farm woodland

There is a considerable literature on establishing farm woodland (Hibberd 1988; Insley 1988; Williamson 1992; Andrews and Rebane 1994). In the past, the reason for having woodland on a farm was usually to improve its value for shooting or fox hunting, with timber production and shelter secondary considerations. Today, wildlife habitat and visual amenity are more likely to be important objectives. Farmers are not usually in the forestry business, so new farm woods tend to be small (<5ha), and despite the availability of several grants their uptake has been disappointing. This may not always be the case as timber is one of the few crops not in surplus, with only around 12% being home grown.

Where possible, new farm woodland should adjoin existing woods and be sympathetic to land-form and enclosure pattern. If attention is paid to designing good 'wildlife/game bird edges', then the centre of the wood can be given over to timber production if required, but would benefit wildlife if it was designed more with nature conservation in mind. Existing sites of wildlife interest should never be planted up, but might be incorporated at the edge to create a habitat mosaic (Fig. 9.4). Guidance on species selection, establishment, and early management for nature conservation can be found in Chapter 5. For most purposes, the larger the small wood the better. Not too much

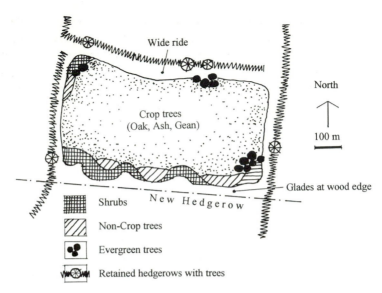

Fig. 9.4 Conservation features of a new farm wood.

should be expected of small secondary woodlands in the way of amenity, it will be several generations before they start to develop the fascination of mature woodland.

New hedgerows and farm trees

The primary role of hedgerows is to provide a stock-proof barrier; if there is no stock on a farm, it is economically difficult to justify hedgerows unless there are problems of soil blow or a need to harbour pollinators and predators. In pastoral and mixed farming countryside, however, hedgerows are a common feature of the landscape and provide a valuable habitat. As habitat, new hedges are most beneficial if they link existing, isolated, semi-natural sites such as woodland, scrub, stream corridor, and rough grassland. Ground-nesting birds will benefit if the hedge is placed on a bank of soil 0.4 m high and 1 m wide. Up to five species of locally native shrub should be used planted in small groups to aid survival. Avoid barberry (*Berberis vulgaris*) and buckthorn (*Rhamnus cathartica*), which carry cereal rusts, and spindle (*Euonymus europaeus*), which is an overwintering host of the black bean aphid. Trees such as crab apple (*Malus sylvestris*) and ash (*Fraxinus excelsior*) should be included at intervals. When encouraging trees in existing hedgerows, favouring self-sown saplings is cheaper and usually more successful than using planted stock.

The value of a hedge for wildlife depends to a great extent on its size and structure. Large complex hedges that include dead wood are easily the best. For example, hedges that are remnant, recently laid, mechanically cut, or dense and trimmed, support on average less than 10 pairs of breeding birds of 10 species per km; in contrast, bushy hedges with outgrowths of blackthorn average 34 nests of 19 species per km (Pollard *et al.* 1974). The value of a hedge can also be increased by managing the adjacent field margin in a sympathetic manner. Detailed information on establishing hedgerows can be found in Chapter 5.

The farm conservation plan

If conservation is to come out of the field corners and have a real impact on farm practice it needs to be integrated within the agricultural side of the business in a whole farm plan. Straightforward decisions, such as introducing conservation headlands, do not need a detailed plan; however, to take account of all the opportunities that exist to look after wildlife, a whole farm conservation plan covering management and habitat creation is helpful. After making an audit of what is present already and what could reasonably be expected to colonize or be created, the following points should be considered:

1. How much of the farm to include?
2. How much advice to seek from bodies such as FWAG and the Game Conservancy?
3. Will the work be eligible for grant aid?
4. What survey work is necessary?
5. Decide on priorities and rank sites.
6. Weigh up the practicalities.
7. Prepare a marked up plan, work programme, and budget.

A worked example of a farm conservation plan can be found in Andrews and Rebane (1994), while the 'Silsoe Exercise' (Barber 1970), though dated, is a stimulating discussion of alternative approaches to farming 200 ha in Bedfordshire. The conclusion of the 'Silsoe Exercise' was that just as a nature reserve can also produce mutton, one would hope that an efficiently managed farmscape can also provide for public amenity, wildlife conservation, and the retention of pockets of high scientific interest.

10 Wetlands

Ponds, lakes, rivers, and streams have long been valued for their recreational and amenity values. But wetlands also include other habitats, such as swamps, marshes, fens, reed-beds, bogs, and mires, that may be less 'attractive' or 'romantic' but still evoke a particular sense in that they represent areas in which water plays a key role. Defined in simple terms, wetlands should be considered as representing those habitats that occupy the transitional zones between true terrestrial (dry) areas and fully aquatic (wet) environments.

The issues

The impetus behind the creation of new wetlands is largely a product of extensive and successive environmental damage and habitat loss. Ponds have been filled in or silted up, marshes and reed-beds drained, rivers cannelized, and fens dried out (Table 10.1). There has been an attempt to balance the rate of wetland loss through habitat creation in Europe and North America. However, as Zedler and Weller (1990) observed, most freshwater wetland creation projects tend to be aesthetically pleasing with visible wildlife values rather than replacing the habitats that continue to be lost. Ponds, reservoirs, and lakes in former extraction workings are the main new habitats being created rather than complex and mature marshes, fens, and bogs. Although new wetlands can readily acquire wildlife value, as demonstrated by the internationally important winter bird numbers using sites like Abberton Reservoir, Essex, and Rutland Water, Rutland, it is important to remember that these are new in character and do not replace those that are still being lost. This view is emphasized by experience in the United States, where there is a legal requirement to restore, enhance, or create wetlands to offset unavoidable adverse impacts wherever practicable. Zedler and Weller (1990) have pointed out that although new wetlands can look like natural ones, there is little evidence that they behave and function like them. Often wetlands that are lost are at a late stage in ecological succession and therefore (typically) biologically diverse, whereas newly created wetlands are at an early stage in ecological succession and are correspondingly relatively simple and subject to large fluctuations in numbers of species and individuals.

Table 10.1
Examples of wetland losses

Location	Habitat type	Loss	Source
East Anglia	Fens	90% (to 10 km²) since 1934, 3380 km² in 1637	English Nature 1997
Britain	Ponds	75% this century	English Nature 1997
Cheshire	Ponds	59% between 1970 and 1985	Hull et al. 1992
England and Wales	Rivers	90% of samples in river habitat survey structurally modified	English Nature 1977
North Kent	Grazing marsh	48% lost between 1935 and 1982	Williams and Bowers 1987
East Essex	Grazing marsh	82% lost between 1938 and 1981	Williams and Bowers 1987
Britain	Wet ground	20 000 km² drained with government grants 1940–81	Smith 1983; Williams and Bowers 1987
USA	All wetlands	450 000 acres (182 110 ha) lost each year; less than half since European settlement now remain	Kusler and Kentula 1990

There are so many habitat creation objectives for wetlands, and this brief chapter cannot do justice to them all. There are already various excellent documents providing sound advice and guidance on pitfalls and the execution of plans. These will be highlighted to assist the practitioner. What is important here is to give a flavour of the range of wetland creation that might be considered. Historically, there has been too much emphasis on open water and not enough on other wetland types. The following can help redress this balance.

Wetlands are the habitat type to consider for the lowest-lying, dampest part of a site. However, a failure to recognize the existing value of rushy fields and marshes means that many have been lost to new wetlands, often to rather poorly designed new ponds. It is essential, therefore, that the existing nature conservation value of the proposed wetland site is first assessed by an experienced ecologist before a new wetland option is pursued.

The design and construction of wetlands

Some general principles

Habitat creation principles, such as the setting of appropriate objectives and site context, apply across the whole spectrum of wetland types and are expounded in Chapter 2. Other principles, such as defining the vegetation and hydrology, will vary depending on the required specifications for individual wetland types.

Hydrology

The hydrological component of a wetland is central in influencing characteristics such as species composition, nutrient cycling, and overall productivity. Inappropriate hydrological design can result in failure.

Water sources and the wetland water balance

To be considered a wetland, the created habitat must be inundated or saturated with water for a period that is of sufficient duration to allow hydrophytic vegetation to prosper. There is a variety of potential water sources for wetland creation, but not all may be available in every situation. Variations in meteorological conditions must be identified on regional and local scales to ensure that precipitation and evapotranspiration are sustainable and appropriate for the habitat design. In the UK, the Meteorological Office has developed a nationwide data-base on a 40 km grid of weather stations to provide information on precipitation and evaporation (known as the 'MORECS' scheme). Temporal fluctuations can be identified by investigating detailed climatic records or, more simply, through liaison with local landowners, farmers, and gardeners.

Groundwater sources can be utilized through the direct inflow of water emerging from springs and seepages, or by excavating to below the depth of the local water-table. Seasonal groundwater levels may vary, possibly causing drying out. This may be desirable for some wetlands, such as ponds created to support breeding amphibians rather than fish populations. Groundwater can also be pumped from boreholes either directly, or via ditches, into a wetland. However, the costs and long-term sustainability of such an approach may be prohibitive and the chemical quality of the water needs careful evaluation.

Surface water can be routed from rivers, ditches, or lakes via pipes or drains to the desired habitat creation location. Depending on the hydrology of the source water body, relatively constant inflows can be maintained through the use of dams, sluices, and weirs. The legal implications must be taken into account. For example, in the UK, the Land Drainage Act 1991 and the Water Resources Act 1991 require consultation between the statutory body and any other party that wishes to undertake river engineering works (such as the diversion of surface flows into a created wetland) prior to manipulating surface waters for wetland habitat creation.

An alternative to diverting surface water is to utilize or reinstate historic flooding regimes. Wet meadows, ponds and associated habitats occupying areas within floodplains may currently or previously have been subjected to inundation from overbank flood waters. Where flooding currently occurs, this water source can be managed, diverted, and controlled to provide a water source for a wetland creation scheme. In some situations, the river channel may have been subjected to flood impoundment to prevent inundation of adjacent land, in which case it will be necessary to alter the flood control structures. Alterations can range from the introduction of sluices to allow controlled inputs of water from the impounded channel to the created wetland area, to the total removal of flood control embankments and a reinstatement of 'natural' flooding conditions.

A simplified understanding of groundwater inflows and outflows is potentially difficult to achieve, unless hydrological connection with groundwater is absent, as in the case of small, lined ponds, or areas underlain by impermeable clay. Where wetland habitats are to be created on permeable deposits with high hydraulic conductivities and high water-tables, (such as sands and gravels), groundwater may act as a water source. This is often the case for the wetland habitats created around the margins of the former gravel pits in areas such as the lower Thames Valley, UK. However, in areas of similar geology and substrate but with the water-table characteristically at depth, the rates of groundwater recharge and outflow may preclude the successful establishment of wetland habitats.

Frequency, depth and duration of waterlogging

The variations in the depth, duration, and frequency of waterlogging within a created wetland can be utilized to create a diverse range of habitats that can vary from permanent open water to seasonally or occasionally inundated areas. Each has a separate ecological identity and is potentially equally valuable for wildlife. Thus, a shallow, nutrient-poor pond that dries out seasonally may cater for the increasingly rare plants characteristic of a well-grazed drawdown zone, while winter flood meadows and washland on a large scale can attract nationally important numbers of wildfowl. In contrast, well vegetated, permanent, unpolluted water over 1–2 m in depth can foster valuable fish communities, with shallow margins catering for marsh or reed-bed communities or with steep sandy banks attracting breeding kingfishers (*Alcedo atthis*) or sand martins (*Riparia riparia*) (Fig. 10.1).

Construction methods

Usually, construction methods will include engineering solutions such as the following: blocking surface and sub-surface drains to increase the degree of waterlogging; creating or re-creating areas of relatively low elevation or depressions that can be flooded and can retain water; excavating to the depth of the seasonal water-table; physically diverting surface waters through ditches, drains, or pipes; or using pumps, weirs, or sluices to move water from

Fig. 10.1 Sand martins (*Riparia riparia*) nesting in an artificially created steep sand bank.

its original source into the created wetland. If an existing sub-surface drainage system is destroyed, increased wetness 'upstream' can result. Whether this matters or carries liabilities needs to be considered. The reinstatement of natural conditions of flooding, through the removal of riverine flood defences, such as flood embankments, can be utilized to re-create wetland habitats in re-flooded environments. Generally, the manipulation of 'natural' hydrological flows should be seen as being more sustainable and favourable than solutions requiring extensive engineering, pumping, or maintenance.

Water quality

Irrespective of the wetland types to be created, the use of water of the appropriate quality is of paramount importance (see Chapter 2). It is imperative that information on the nutrient levels, suspended sediments, and contaminants present in the water source is available and understood. In England and Wales these data can sometimes be obtained from the Environment Agency.

Nutrients

Water entering a wetland will inevitably bring chemicals with it. These will affect the functioning of the system and dictate the nature of the created habitats. Heathwaite *et al.* (1993) categorized wetlands based on their water

Table 10.2
Wetland types and water chemistry

Category	Water chemistry	Examples
Eutrophic	High nutrient and calcium content	Lowland lakes, canals, and rivers on limestone and chalk
Mesotrophic	Medium nutrient and calcium content	Lowland ponds, lakes, and rivers on mixed geologies
Oligotrophic	Low nutrient and calcium content	Upland turns and streams on acidic geologies
Dystrophic	High humic acid content	Upland bog ponds

Source: Heathwaite *et al.* (1993).

chemistry as eutrophic, mesotrophic, oligotrophic, and dystrophic (Table 10.2).

As with soils, if the desired objective is to develop a diverse community, low nutrient loads, especially of nitrogen and phosphorus, are essential. If, instead, high productivity is required with its associated narrow range of species (but often very large populations; for example, invertebrates in organic muds to attract feeding waders), a eutrophic water source is required. However, defining the exact chemical limits for nutrient loads associated with distinct vegetation communities is problematic (Ross 1995). This is further complicated by the ability of wetlands to cycle, retain, and export nutrients from incoming waters. Various wetland biological, chemical, biochemical, and physical processes can immobilize, transform, and fix nutrients. For example, large amounts of phosphorus can be retained through the sedimentation of suspended solids (Hupp *et al.* 1993) and soluble phosphorus can be adsorbed onto wetland soils and sediments (Russell and Maltby 1995). Similarly the retention and removal of nitrogen by wetlands through processes such as plant uptake, assimilation, and denitrification is widely reported (Peterjohn and Correll 1984; Haycock and Burt 1993; Baker and Maltby 1995).

It follows from this that the nutrient load of waters entering a wetland will not necessarily be the same as that of water leaving the system. Changes in water chemistry from the point of entry to the point of exit can be utilized and manipulated to establish a range or complex of wetland habitats across the site. For example, mesotrophic or eutrophic water entering a created wetland could initially be passed through an area dominated by common reed (*Phragmites australis*), which may be succeeded by a fen community comprising, for example, reed sweet-grass (*Glyceria maxima*), reed canary-grass (*Phalaris arundinacea*), or lesser pond sedge (*Carex acutiformis*). This may give way to more mesotrophic habitats dominated by, for example, soft rush (*Juncus effusus*) communities.

Sediments and contaminants

Other than nutrients, the water supply to a created wetland may be contaminated by a range of substances that greatly reduce the potential for successful habitat creation. Where waters carry excess heavy metals, sensitive plants and animals will be affected. The toxicity of plant species to individual or combinations of heavy metals varies with organic matter, oxygen, and temperature levels. Acute toxicity by metals in freshwaters is less common, and therefore less important than chronic toxicity, that is, long-continued sublethal levels (Haslam 1992). Prior to creating wetland habitats, it is important that the concentrations of heavy metals (copper, lead, zinc, etc.) are known, and that levels are appropriate for a healthy ecosystem. The EC Directive on the quality of freshwaters needing protecting or improvement in order to support fish life (78/659/EEC) provides guideline and imperative values for heavy metal concentrations.

All surface water sources contain suspended solids that can reduce light penetration thereby lowering plant productivity. Rates of deposition depend on the sediment load, particle size, and flow velocities. Excessive deposition of suspended sediments can lead to the silting up of salmon spawning gravels, suffocation of gill-breathing invertebrates, damage to shallow-rooted plants, and, over time, the infilling of ponds (Fig. 10.2). Often there is a close correlation between sediments and both phosphorus and heavy metals, owing to their tendency to be particulate-bound.

Other contaminants that may influence the water source and frustrate the successful creation of sustainable wetland habitats include the following: pesticides, polychlorinated biphenyls (PCBs), detergents, surfactants, salinity, chlorides, and thermal pollution. Assessment of the levels of all of these in the water supply would greatly increase the potential success of a wetland habitat creation scheme. In England and Wales, the Environment Agency may be able to advise on the likelihood of contamination.

Soil and substrate

Soils are important to the overall function of a created wetland and are the primary medium for plant rooting. Consideration should be given to their texture, their capability to retain water, their chemical and nutrient status (pH, N:P ratios), and organic matter levels. Often, wetlands can be established on subsoil or the underlying recent geological material, but if the water supply is also nutrient deficient, the development of the plant and animal community will be impeded. In many cases this will be advantageous, but to accelerate succession where the waterlogged substrate is devoid of organic material and water nutrient levels are low, various ameliorants can be added. Street (1984) demonstrated that in lakes straw bales form instant habitats for invertebrates

Fig. 10.2 Foaming caused by eutrophic water passing over a weir. The inappropriate use of eutrophic waters can undermine successful wetland habitat creation.

as well as supplementing the organic material. They are relatively low in nutrients, and need to be thoroughly wetted or weighed down so that the water surface is not covered in loose straw. Merritt (1994) lists other organic materials and their nutrient contents, and along with Street (1989) provides useful advice on the subject. Contrary to some published advice, eutrophic topsoils may not be suitable substrates for wetland creation as they can encourage algal growth or the development of monocultures of aggressive species such as reed-mace (*Typha latifolia*) or reed sweet-grass.

Waterproofing

Although it is preferable to use the natural water-holding capacity of a site, there will be occasions when a liner is needed. Merritt (1994) and BTCV (1981) give useful advice on these. Puddling clay is the traditional material, the finer the particles the more effective it is, but it can be costly to obtain and transport. Where periodic drying occurs at the edges, the clay needs to be covered with at least 300 mm soil to avoid cracking and leakages. Butyl liners are suitable for small ponds, but also need to be covered to protect them from ultraviolet light; edge slopes have to be shallow so the cover does not slip off. The various bentonite sandwiches that can be rolled out onto the prepared surface avoid this problem, but still need to be covered with at least 150 mm of subsoil material. Small ponds are often lined with old carpets or newspapers before the liner is put into place—this prevents sharp stones from causing punctures. A layer of sand or fines from quarries is equally functional.

Design principles

General guidance on placing new habitats in the ecological landscape is provided in Chapter 2. Wetlands need to be designed in the wider context more carefully than other habitats, owing to the considerable number of species that depend on the non-wetland areas for part of their life-cycle. Amphibians, for example, need walls, scrub, woodland, tussocky grassland, or specially constructed refugia for hibernation and cover, while dragonflies benefit from light scrub, herbaceous vegetation, and clearings (glades) open to direct sunlight but shielded from the wind where they can hawk for invertebrate prey. Ponds are best placed close to others to facilitate colonization. Amphibia will not reach a new pond if it is further than 1 km away from existing haunts (Merritt 1994); but a distance of 500 m between ponds would ensure more rapid colonization provided there are not major barriers such as a river or motorway between.

There are a number of design principles that apply to most wetland types. In general, the larger the better (Street 1989), but clusters of ponds of varying design are better than one large one for diversity of species. A second general principle is to create as diverse a structure as possible, in keeping with the scale and habitat type. This includes small scale variations in horizontal and vertical profiles, variation in slopes (from steep banks for breeding kingfisher and sand martin to shallow marshy ones), deep and shallow water, and variation in the use of materials. The latter is illustrated by the use of organic-rich materials and muds to create wader habitat and the use of gravels for breeding terns and plovers, often on the same site. The same principle applies to other species. Different fish, invertebrates and plants favour different substrates—gravels, sands, silt, clay, and peat (Merritt 1994)—and different flow regimes across them, which influences fluvial dynamics, sediment load, and oxygen levels.

In all new wetlands, being able to control the water levels is highly desirable as it facilitates future management. To this end, most large wetlands, such as reed-beds (Hawke and José 1996), are usually designed as a cluster of units with controllable water levels in each allowing for draw-down in one without affecting others. The same principle has been incorporated into Rutland Water with a bund across the inlet end so water levels can be controlled in the nature reserve zone independently of the widely fluctuating levels in the rest of the reservoir.

Vegetation

The appropriate vegetation to introduce into a created wetland will depend on the type of habitat required, the geographical and climatic region, and the hydrological, hydrochemical, and topographic constraints. Attention should be paid to whether the desired plants are likely to colonize the site naturally (see Chapter 3), or whether a planting programme will be needed; in the latter case, attention should also be paid to whether the desired species are available commercially at an affordable price, and whether seeds, plugs, container-grown plants, or bare-rooted material will be used. There are several methods of establishing new vegetation in a created wetland (Barber 1992), and the same principles will prevail of creating locally native communities that match the environmental conditions as described in Chapter 2.

Where water flows into a new wetland from a well vegetated source, or where previous wetlands on the site are likely to provide desirable species, natural colonization may be adequate. However, where sources of propagules are distant, introductions will be necessary. In water, these will nearly always be in the form of plants rather than seed, although removing excess vegetation from one site (with the landowner's permission) for inoculation of another of similar character is a sound approach. Additional advantages of the latter method are the sediments, invertebrates, and micro-organisms that are introduced at the same time.

On damp or wet soils, seeding is usually most cost effective. If the areas are to be flooded in winter, then spring seeding rather than autumn seeding is more likely to succeed (see Chapter 4). However, as in other habitats, some characteristic species, such as marsh pennywort (*Hydrocotyle vulgaris*) and bugle (*Ajuga reptans*), do not establish readily from seed and are better introduced as plants.

Animals

Perhaps more than any other habitat, wetland design often incorporates specific features to attract animals. Birds have been the main beneficiary, but ponds, in particular, have also been designed to entice dragonflies and other invertebrates as well as amphibians. Raw and Pilkington (1988), for example, describe pond creation specifically for natterjack toads (*Bufo calamita*). There are, of course, many ponds created for fishing, but these are not always also designed for other wildlife. In Britain, wetland design for birds has been developed by the Wildfowl and Wetlands Trust (WWT), the Game Conservancy

Trust, and the Royal Society for the Protection of Birds (RSPB) in particular, whilst the British Dragonfly Society has published booklets offering guidance on wetland habitat creation. Similar opportunities have been incorporated into some new reservoir designs, with Rutland Water in England standing out in this respect. The extensive research and practical experience in habitat creation for waders and wildfowl and their presentation to the public is being put into practice at Barn Elms, London, where WWT are converting four redundant reservoirs into a complex of lagoons, grazing marshes, mudflats, and shingle islands designed to attract wildfowl and waders in particular (Fig. 10.3). In order to develop the optimum invertebrate populations for waders, sewage sludge is being mixed with the mineral soils to provide a high fertility habitat in which elevated densities of organic mud-dwelling invertebrates will attract waders. At the same time, micro-profiling to create small-scale variation in edges and slopes will provide maximum shore-line and pool complexes at different water levels. Shingle beaches and islands are being placed for breeding terns (*Sterna* spp.), ringed plovers (*Charadrius hiaticula*), and little ringed plovers (*C. dubius*), while extensive grazing marshes are being sown using seed collected from the same habitat type on a WWT reserve. Systematic monitoring and research are being built into the design and management programme (Wilson 1997).

The principles behind the Barn Elms scheme are common to all schemes, being based on the ecological needs of the different species at all stages of their life cycle and in different seasons; there is also an appreciation of competitive interactions and exclusions and community dynamics of the plants and animals involved and, in particular, knowledge of the functioning of a wetland ecosystem in terms of bio-chemical cycles, nutrient turnover, and interactions with different water regimes. As Zedler and Weller (1990) point out, there is insufficient understanding and dearth of relevant research on the functioning aspects of new wetlands, which is why monitoring is so important. However, practical advice on habitat requirements for different species is available in Merritt (1994), BTCV (1981), Street (1989), and Kirby (1992), among others, covering plants, amphibians, dragonflies, other invertebrates, fish, and, of course, birds.

Ponds and lakes

There is no agreed definition that separates ponds from lakes, although some authors adopt 1 ha as a cut-off size. However, 1 ha would be a large pond; most are much smaller. Small lakes or ponds are often incorporated into landscape schemes (Bickmore and Larard 1989), such as in Stockley Park near London's Heathrow Airport. Larger lakes may be created as reservoirs or may result from mineral extraction. The principles involved in creating a valuable wildlife

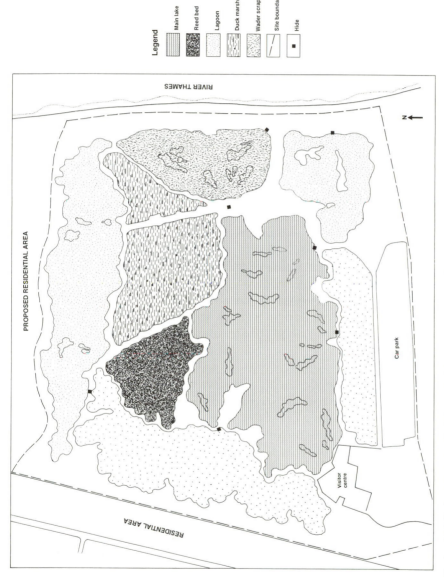

Fig. 10.3 Wildfowl and Wetlands Trust reserve at Barn Elms, London. A complex of created lagoons, grazing marsh, mudflats, shingle islands, and water bodies.

resource are similar, but particular advice on gravel pit restoration is provided by Andrews (1991) and Andrews and Kinsman (1991).

Pond and lake design

In general, attention is paid to the external features of ponds and lakes at the expense of the sub-surface ones. In addition, there are many stereotyped designs that fail to cater for the potential variation in pond and lake type.

Shape and character, particularly of ponds, should complement local patterns. Thus, in Cheshire, where clusters of marl-pit ponds are common historic features in the agricultural landscape, it would be appropriate to create similar ones (see Fig. 10.4). This is not so easy with larger ponds, lakes, and reservoirs, but attention to land-form, and attempts to integrate new waterbodies into the local topography would give them the semblance of being natural.

Water depth and profiles are important aspects of design. Ponds are usually less than 3 m, (and often only 1–2 m) deep. This protects hibernating or vulnerable animals in the coldest winters, but shallower ponds, even those that dry out in dry summers, are equally valuable, especially to prevent the build-up of stickleback (*Gasterosteus* spp.) and other predators that feed on amphibian tadpoles. Lakes and gravel pits are likely to be deeper than ponds; however, aquatic plants will rarely grow in depths greater than 3 m. In creating deeper water an understanding of temperature inversions and associated changes in aquatic functions (geochemical cycling etc.) with depth is important. Water deep enough to provide for wintering fish, and to attract diving birds is beneficial, but extensive areas of deeper water are of little value. Merritt (1994) provides the optimum depths for a wide variety of plants and animals.

Required size, depth, and the space available often dictate the shore profiles of small water bodies. However, attention needs to be given to the marginal and marsh zones. The marsh occupies the permanently or seasonally wet soil as water levels rise in winter. It is a zone that is often neglected, yet marshes support a wide variety of animals, making them of high conservation value, and there are a considerable number of marsh plants available commercially. The manipulation of water levels and creation of small-scale topographical variation in a broad marshy zone around at least part of a pond or lake is highly beneficial.

Similarly, an extended shallow edge to the pond or lake will also cater for the many emergent plant species as well as providing warm shallows for amphibians, fish, invertebrates, and a safe place for duckling broods to feed away from predators such as pike (*Esox lucius*) (Street 1984). Many marginal plants tolerate only shallow water depths (down to about 30 cm), but others such as reed, reed mace, and reed canary-grass will grow in water up to 1–2 m deep. In small ponds, it is best not to introduce the more vigorous

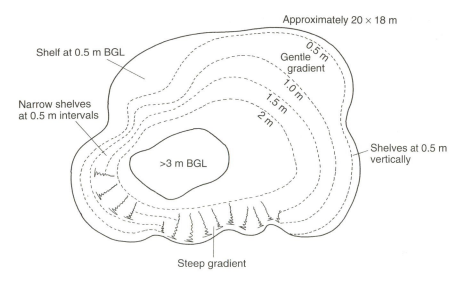

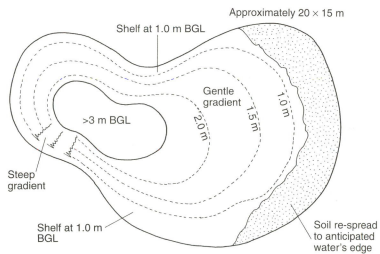

Fig. 10.4 The design features of ponds created in Cheshire. The design incorporates features that re-create ponds that are similar to the ones that have been lost locally. BGL, below ground level.

invaders, including the last three species, since they can quickly fill in the open water. On the other hand, a few ponds dominated, for example by reed-mace, cater for the specialist invertebrates of this habitat, which include hoverfly genera such as *Anasimyia* and *Parheliophilus*.

In large waterbodies, deep water channels can be used to restrict the spread of some of the more aggressive species (Merritt 1994; Hawke and José 1996). Steep banks also have their own value. Where banks are made of suitably

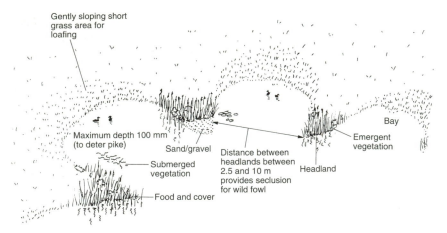

Gently sloping short grass area for loafing

Maximum depth 100 mm (to deter pike)

Sand/gravel

Submerged vegetation

Food and cover

Distance between headlands between 2.5 and 10 m provides seclusion for wild fowl

Headland

Emergent vegetation

Bay

Fig. 10.5 Ecological advantages associated with creating sinuous edges to water bodies: greater seclusion is offered to wildfowl and greater ecological diversity is provided, which is especially important for invertebrates such as dragonflies.

soft material, breeding kingfisher and sand martins can burrow into them. Andrews and Rebane (1994) describe how to attract these species. Margins are also important elements of the design. There is little room for variation in a small pond, but larger waterbodies can incorporate sinuous edges. On a small scale, these will hold larger numbers of territorial dragonflies, while on a larger scale, more duck territories can fit in if neighbouring birds are screened from each other along an indented margin (Fig. 10.5). The creation of small islands, with gently sloping banks offer ground-nesting birds protection from many predators.

There are differing views on whether to add plants to ponds and lakes, or wait for natural colonization. In a survey of farm ponds in Wales, Gee *et al.* (1994) found no relation between plant species richness, whether there had been planting, or age, and Williams *et al.* (1997) advocate a policy of natural colonization in most cases. In contrast, Galatowitsh and Van der Valk (1995) found that prairie potholes in the USA that were re-flooded, only acquired a representative flora if there were retained ditches to act as refugia. Without these, only about half the species colonized that were present in comparable natural wetlands. However, marginal draw-down and sedge meadow species failed to colonize altogether. The decision whether to add species must be based on an evaluation of which species are likely to colonize and how fast (in relation to nutrient levels) they are likely to spread. Water bodies with a surface water inflow are likely to be colonized rapidly by species within the wider drainage system; more-isolated wetlands may not be. Two ponds established recently by one of us (PA) in Staffordshire were colonized only by marsh foxtail (*Alopecurus geniculatus*), creeping bent (*Agrostis stolonifera*), and Canadian pondweed (*Elodea canadensis*) in the first two years, even though there was a small river nearby and other ponds in the vicinity. These plants would have taken over rapidly had they not been controlled. This experience is shared by other pond creators. In mesotrophic or eutrophic waters, introducing a few individuals of the desired range of species is usually beneficial.

The submerged flora is too often neglected in favour of the more visually attractive marginal species. Submerged plants are essential in providing the habitat structure for the animals and supply food and much of the oxygen. Great care is needed in obtaining a desirable range of plants. Specialist aquatic nurseries should be used to ensure native stock and to avoid the introduction of undesirable alien species like the New Zealand pygmyweed (*Crassula helmsii*). This invasive plant colonized, or was introduced, into 530 water bodies in England between 1980 and 1995 (English Nature 1997) and could become a notifiable weed.

The introduction of fish is a controversial subject. Water bodies connected to the drainage system will be colonized naturally, and sticklebacks at least are likely to reach many ponds. However, if conservation of amphibians is a principal objective for a pond, it is best not to introduce fish, since the predatory species feed on the tadpoles. Too many fish in any water body reduces the habitat richness and increases water turbidity, possibly to the extent that submerged plants die from lack of light. Fish that prey on invertebrates, such as carp (*Cyprinus carpio*) and tench (*Tinca tinca*), are also best avoided in eutrophicated waters where algal blooms are liable to occur. Without fish, zooplankton that feed on algae can multiply and algal blooms can be contained (Moss *et al.* 1996). An alternative method of controlling algae, either 'blanket weed' or unicellular species, is to place bales of barley straw in the pond—these release a powerful algicide (Gibson *et al.* 1990). However, further research at the Open University (Milton Keynes) suggests that rotting wood in water has similar algicidal properties.

To attract more birds and provide a safe refuge from mammalian predation, islands and rafts can be added to larger ponds or lakes. Although the basic principles are well tested and widely applied, there are still too many steep-sided islands that make access difficult for ducks, which like to walk out of the water to breeding, loafing, and roosting sites. Many such islands are also clothed with totally inappropriate vegetation. If the guidance provided by Andrews and Rebane (1994) on island shape and design, rafts and nest boxes, and by Burgess and Becker (1989) on the creation and management of islands and rafts is followed, more useful habitats for terns, wildfowl, and some waders would results. Merritt (1994) gives examples and plans of sites where the principles have been applied, such as at St Aidans in the Aire Valley, West Yorkshire.

Fig. 10.6 Reed-bed growth after cessation of peat cutting on the Somerset Levels. (Photograph by Peter Worrall).

Reed-beds

Reeds commonly colonize lake edges or larger wet areas naturally (Fig. 10.6). The RSPB reserve at Minsmere (Suffolk), for example, was invaded by common reed after the area was flooded as an anti-invasion measure during the Second World War (Everett 1989). Reeds can grow under several different environmental conditions. Some reed-beds are short-lived and disappear through succession, for example in new clay pits. Others can occur in sheltered bays along lake margins, but these are rare, as are the eutrophic lakes in which they grow. Reed-beds also grow on the tidal reaches of rivers, often in brackish conditions, as at the RSPB's reserve at Blacktoft Sands on the Humber and along the floodplains of the coast and lowland rivers (Everett 1989).

The creation of new reed-beds is seen by many as a priority habitat needed to support the bittern (*Botaurus stellaris*) and other specialist species, some of which are the subject of species recovery programmes, such as marsh harrier (*Circus aeruginosus*). Experience has shown that a minimum area of 20 ha is needed to support breeding bittern, marsh harrier, bearded tit (*Panurus biarmicus*), and Savi's warbler (*Locustella luscinioides*) (Bibby and Lunn 1982). However, even small reed-beds only a few metres in size will attract breeding reed warblers (*Acrocephalus scirpaceus*). The reed-bed is only part of the habitat. Open water in the form of meres amongst the reeds, and dykes between beds, carr, and fen vegetation, are all an integral part of the habitat (Everett 1989). Large and complex reed-beds are being developed in the UK by the RSPB on the Somerset Levels. Others have been planted in Norfolk, on reclaimed opencast coalmining sites in Northumberland, and in Montgomery (Hawke and José 1996). The basic requirements are a reliable, adequate, and controllable water supply capable of maintaining a 30 cm depth in summer, land with a level or shallow gradient, a source of reed, and access for management. Hawke and José (1996) and Tyler (1994) provide comprehensive guidance on how to design and construct new reed-beds, especially for birds, while Burgess and Evans (1989) describe best practice management operations.

The cheapest way to establish a new reed-bed is to flood land where reed already exists and wait for it to spread (Tyler 1994). Reed spreads most readily from rhizomes, but recent investigations by, among others, the WWT have found ways of germinating seed so that locally native sources can be grown on a large scale for planting (Hawke and José 1996). The most common opportunities for creating new reed-beds are associated with disused industrial, arable, or pasture land and disused mine or gravel workings. By using the sand washings to fill in a deep gravel pit, for example, an extensive reed-bed has established at Attenborough, Nottinghamshire, UK. All these opportunities need to be grasped if the 1040 ha of reed-bed needed to meet the target of 100 booming bitterns by 2020 is to be reached (Hawke and José 1996).

Wet grassland and duck marsh

There seem to be very few examples of the creation of wet grassland for wildlife, although advice on its establishment is available from Merrit (1994) and Andrews and Rebane (1994). The main focus has been on creating wet grassland for birds, although many other species can also benefit. For birds, there are two basic kinds of wet grassland: one in which the water-table is kept high in the breeding season to attract waders, and a second, often referred to as a duck marsh, which is generally wetter (Fig. 10.7).

For wet grasslands, areas of over 2 ha, and ideally more than 5 ha, are required. A minimal edge to core ratio assists in reducing disturbance and predation. Open, safe areas are needed without trees or shrubs that can affect sight-lines and provide perches for predators. There must be a source of water (preferably unpolluted) and a means of controlling it in ditches round and through the site. The ditches also provide excellent habitats in their own right. Ideal conditions for breeding waders such as redshank (*Tringa totanus*), snipe (*Gallinago gallinago*), and lapwing (*Vanellus vanellus*) are created by retaining a high water-table throughout March to June so that the surface remains

Fig. 10.7 Enhancement of wet grasslands for waders and wildfowl on the Ouse Washes, Cambridgeshire.

wet. Lowering the water-table from July to October enables grazing and other management to be conducted. Wintering wildfowl can also be attracted to these wet grasslands by shallow flooding of the hollows to 0.3 m depth from November to February. Self *et al.* (1994) and Evans *et al.* (1995) provide water management advice.

For breeding waders, the surface needs to be irregular, possibly created in a ridge and furrow pattern, or contoured to establish drier areas and small pools where water depths are only 50–100 mm. The same principles of nutrient- and plant-species selection apply as for dry grasslands (see Chapter 4). However, birds like redshank and snipe need tussocky grasses or rushes, while lapwing prefer short vegetation. The seed mix needs to take this into account. In addition, abundant soil invertebrate prey and a soft soil texture to facilitate feeding is needed to attract breeding waders. This is best achieved through enhanced organic matter, either by adding suitable materials, by using topsoils, or by choosing peaty sites (so long as they are not already of ecological value) for wet grassland creation. In such circumstances, the soils will often be nutrient rich and a low plant diversity is inevitable. High growth rates, however, will result, and seasonal grazing, preferably by cattle, will be essential.

A duck marsh differs from wet grassland by having higher April–May water levels to attract passage waders and some waterfowl. Rather than a grass community, reduced water levels in late May and June expose damp mud which then colonizes with annuals. These die and the seeds and invertebrates on them are released when the areas are flooded again in September to 50–100 mm, which provides food for the autumn passage of migrants and wintering wildfowl. The winter water levels are then maintained at 300–400 mm. This kind of habitat creation depends on natural colonization rather than sowing of plants. Creating wader scrapes with extensive organic muds are often estab-lished in a similar fashion. Such duck marshes can be created as part of wider wetland complexes with wet grassland, open water, and reed-beds if there is space.

Rivers and floodplains

In recent years there has been a strong shift away from traditionally engi-neered river management characterized by canalization, drainage, flood embankments, and the discharge of pollutants. As interest in the restoration of the river channel and its wider riparian and floodplain environment has gained momentum, many opportunities for wetland habitat creation have arisen.

Petts and Amoros (1996) have identified important reasons for creating new wet habitats within the river corridor. River and floodplain habitats possess high biological diversity, high productivity, contain refuge habitats, can include refugia from pre-industrial disturbance, and are routes for species dispersal. For example, a study by Knopf et al. (1988) showed that although riparian habitats occupy less than 1% of the western North American landscape, they provide a home for more species of bird than all other habitats combined.

In England and Wales the former National Rivers Authority (NRA) iden-tified the improvement of degraded river corridors and other channel features as a key issue for research and development (National Rivers Authority, 1993). Implicit in this is the creation of wet habitats at the aquatic–terrestrial interface, including wet berms adjacent to the channel, pool–riffle sequences within the channel, and wet grasslands on the adjacent floodplain (Fig. 10.8). These newly created wetland habitats may not truly represent the restoration of a former pristine system, due to the degree of anthropogenic alteration, but the resultant habitat creation has the potential to restore functional aspects to the wider river system.

Before embarking on a wetland habitat creation project within a river or floodplain environment it is important that some fundamental guidelines are followed. Clear objectives should be set that respect the wider practical, leg-islative, economic, and environmental issues. Any habitat creation objectives must take into account the fact that rivers are dynamic in space and time. Iso-lated habitat creation projects must be placed in the context of a wider river

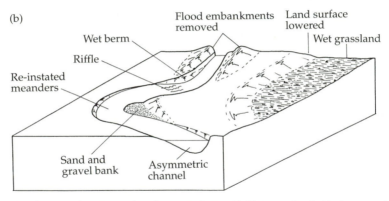

Fig. 10.8 Diagrammatic representation of a range of created habitats associated with the restoration of a river channel and flood plain; (a) before habitat creation; (b) after habitat creation.

continuum, and an understanding of the ecological implications of matter and water exchange is vital to ensure the success of the project.

Setting objectives

The restoration or creation of habitats that 'totally duplicate' a naturally occurring wetland is impossible (Kusler and Kentula 1990). This is due to the complexity and variation that occurs in both natural and created systems, and the subtle relationships that exist between hydrology, soils, vegetation, and animal life. However, with clearly defined objectives, the chances of long-term success can be increased greatly, as can the ability to evaluate the success of

Table 10.3
Some objectives for river and floodplain wetland creation (after Hansen 1996)

Objective
Creating better physical conditions in the watercourse.
Enhancing the self-purification capacity within the watercourse and encouraging greater denitrification potential in adjacent wet habitats.
Development of a more varied and diverse landscape.
Production of a greater number of more varied habitats for (threatened and rare) plants and animals.
Increasing the variety and number of dispersal corridors for plants and animals.
Protection of groundwater resources.
Enrichment of recreational and amenity aspects, including fishing, swimming, and bird watching.
Compliance with international (and national) obligations on the protection of wetlands.
Implementation of riparian buffer zones to retain and remove nutrients and contaminants, thus improving in-stream water quality.
Creation and enhancement of species specific habitats, such as de-silting salmon (*Salmo* spp.) spawning gravels or building bank-side otter (*Lutra lutra*) holts.
Mitigation for loss or alteration to rivers and floodplain habitats.

the scheme. The objectives and long-term goals should be used to assist in project design, the choice of methods and techniques, and in setting up future management and monitoring programmes (Table 10.3).

Practicalities and constraints

Apart from the acknowledged uncertainties and gaps that exist in the scientific knowledge base (Brookes and Sear 1996), there are a number of practical and technical constraints that need to be considered when setting project objectives and design criteria (Table 10.4). The constraints may be at the site of habitat creation or restoration, or they may be external constraints beyond the control of the wetland creation project. Many floodplain and river habitat creation schemes depend on effective integration with existing landscape planning systems. The majority of floodplains in industrialized nations have been developed and may currently be under the ownership of various private individuals and organizations. Potential constraints may exist if a habitat creation or river restoration project impinges on multiple landowners, especially if land purchase is necessary. Another possible problem is the potential of a scheme to impact adjoining land that may be under separate ownership, for example, through increased flooding.

Land ownership and availability differ between urban and rural situations. In the urban environment less land is generally available for habitat restoration or creation, thus, objectives may have to be more limited. Small-scale

Table 10.4
Practical and technical constraints on river and floodplain habitat creation and restoration

Practical constraints	Technical constraints
Land ownership	Hydrological and hydraulic considerations
Availability of land	Geomorphological considerations
Legal framework	Catchment scale influences
Cost implications	Water quality
Construction problems	Information from analogous projects
Scale considerations	

habitat creation can often be the only viable option, due also to constraints provided by the positioning of underground services and roads. A successful example of habitat creation within such restraints is provided by the River Wandle at Carshalton, South London. The objective of the scheme was to enhance the habitat value of a 65 m stretch of steel-piled river bank, which abutted against an industrial estate, and to lessen the contrast with the other bank, which formed part of a nature reserve. A semi-natural toe habitat was created alongside the steel-piled bank using dredged silt, and this was planted by hand with yellow flag (*Iris pseudacorus*), sedge (*Carex* spp.), and reedmace. Within five years the vegetation on the terrace, which averaged less than 3 m wide, had developed to such an extent that the piling had been totally screened; other plants, such as gipsywort (*Lycopus europaeus*) and purple loosestrife (*Lythrum salicaria*), had also colonized, and nesting moorhens (*Gallinula chloropus*) were present (Ward *et al.* 1994).

Within the rural environment, land is often more freely available. In the UK, schemes aimed at reducing production and increasing the conservation value of agricultural land, such as the Countryside Stewardship Scheme and the Environmentally Sensitive Areas (ESA) scheme (see Chapter 9), are providing opportunities for river and floodplain habitat creation. Such schemes provide incentives for landowners to raise water levels, increase flooding, and to restore and create habitats on riparian land. A limitation that may be encountered is the lack of continuity between areas of land that are available to be taken out of production. Often projects concentrate on the restoration and creation of a series of patches of floodplain and riparian habitats on areas that are of low agricultural value and prone to flooding and waterlogging. These areas are not necessarily linked although it is beneficial if they are.

Often when planning a river or floodplain habitat creation scheme an overriding constraint will be cost. This may include land purchase, landowner compensation, downstream mitigation, design and construction, and subsequent maintenance and management. The practical and cost constraints associated

Table 10.5
Examples of practical constraints on river restoration projects

Practical constraint
What do you do to control flow in the channel during construction?
Should you build the project working upstream or downstream?
What do you do with the excavated material?
What should you do for erosion and sediment control during construction?
What do you do when you encounter rock outcrops?
What permits do you need and where do you obtain them?
How do stream restoration projects fit within the framework of local land use (i.e. zoning) restrictions?
How do you decide to move an existing bridge or culvert rather than routing the new channel through them?
What if the channel is underlain by karst areas or abandoned mines (how can you keep the entire stream from going underground)?
What are the keys to constructing waterfalls, drop structures, or rapids?
What do you do about the utility crossings and water supply intakes that must be moved?
How much money should be budgeted for project maintenance?

Source: modified from Brookes and Shields (1996).

with the construction phase of river restoration projects can often preclude success at planning application stage, or subsequently cause major problems at the implementation stage (see Table 10.5).

Any floodplain or river restoration project must take cognizance of the hydrological and geomorphological implications of altering the established regimes. Protection from increased flooding, altered flow velocities, and undesirable sedimentation, erosion, and pollution must be ensured. Hydraulic modelling will be necessary to determine the extent, duration, depth, and return of flood events, as well as to ensure that the appropriate hydrological conditions are provided for any created habitats. Hydrological considerations must extend upstream and downstream to embrace the river continuum concept. Habitat creation in floodplain and riverine environments has the potential to affect flood pattern and sediment budgets downstream, which, if not fully understood, can produce effects that may extend over several decades, or even longer in some cases.

In some cases, such as in the design and implementation of riparian buffer zones, the objective may be to create a habitat that can improve water quality. It is important to understand the quality of the incoming water and to set objectives for the quality of the water to be discharged. To set water quality objectives will involve an understanding of the hydrological and biogeochemical processes that will be operating in the created buffer zone.

Table 10.6
Examples of methods and techniques employed in river
restoration and associated creation of diverse wetland habitats

Channel and floodplain restoration	In-channel restoration
Alterations to the course of the river, recreation of former landform features and creation of large-scale habitats.	Changes to the in-channel and channel bank structures, recreation of diverse habitats and reinstatement of hydrological diversity of flow. All of the common methods listed below can potentially be utilized in conjunction with the methods listed for channel and floodplain restoration.
Methods and techniques: • re-meandering the watercourse • re-installation of two-stage or multiple channels • creation of on-stream and off-stream ponds and back-waters • lowering the floodplain surface • removal of flood embankments to reinstate inundation of the floodplain • raising the floodplain ground-water levels • creating riparian buffer zones • re-profiling river banks to include wet and dry berms	Methods and techniques: • planting of emergent vegetation • insertion of boulders on the channel bed • insertion of a diverse and variable substrate • creation of pools and riffles • formation of fish hiding places • construction of otter (*Lutra lutra*) holts • insertion of flow deflectors or current concentrators • removal of revetments or concrete channel bed and walls • re-opening of culverts

In many cases the identification of practical or technical constraints will ultimately set the objectives of a habitat creation scheme. Even though there is an inherent uncertainty in most aspects of river and floodplain habitat creation, an evaluation of these constraints will benefit long-term project success.

Methods and techniques

Many different methods can be employed for the creation of wetland habitats within the river and floodplain environment (Ward *et al.* 1994; Eiseltová and Biggs 1995; Brookes *et al.* 1996; Hansen 1996) (Table 10.6). It is worth noting that all but the application of the most minor of techniques affect natural river processes; a thorough understanding of any induced change is therefore vital. A brief review of the application of a range of the available techniques is provided by the following series of European case studies.

River Brede, Denmark

Despite earlier attempts at improvement, prior to 1989 the ecological quality of the Brede catchment was low—most streams had been regulated and wetland habitats were almost non-existent. To restore the streams a number of projects were initiated, which considered a multitude of potential problems and ultimately produced one of the most impressive examples of river restoration in Europe. The scheme involved a series of sub-projects that evolved throughout the 1990s. Funding for the work was principally from the EU-Life project, the Danish Ministry of the Environment, and the County of Jutland (Nielsen 1995, 1996; Hansen 1996).

The majority of the projects commenced between 1990 and 1995. Initially, the work involved flooding and re-creating a former 1.2 ha lake and adjacent wetland areas. Following this, almost 10 km of the main corridor of the River Brede was restored by re-meandering former straightened and channelized reaches, removing concrete weirs and replacing them with riffles capable of supporting salmonid spawning areas, creating on- and off-stream ponds, elevating ground-water levels across the floodplain to encourage the establishment of wet grasslands, and re-profiling the channel to produce wet riparian berms.

The large scale re-creation of meanders represented the most radical aspect of the programme. Planning the re-created meanders involved investigations of historical maps, aerial photographs and existing data on the local geology and stream hydrography. After a survey of the levels of the stream and its surrounding areas, the hydraulic consequences of different restoration variables, such as channel depth and meander sinuosity, were modelled using computer-based hydraulic simulation models. Attempts were made to simulate natural riffle–pool sequences, where the length of a riffle is usually 2 to 3 times the channel width, re-occuring at intervals of between 5 and 7 times the channel width. When the hydraulic engineers were satisfied with the meander design, the plans were taken into the field. Coloured, wooden pegs were used to map out the new meandering river course, acting as guides for the excavation operator. The degree of precision was kept to within a few centimetres. Careful profiling of the river banks and the emplacement of different river bed substrates ensured the creation of a diversity of habitats.

After re-vegetation and flooding, it has been possible to evaluate the impact of the restoration projects. The in-stream and bankside vegetation has become more diverse, and there is now a higher frequency of environmentally beneficial species such as water starwort (*Callictriche platycarpa*) and large-flowering water crowfoot (*Batrachium peltatum*). The variety of river bed substrates has encouraged a greater number of benthic macro-invertebrate species, and electro-fishing has shown that numerous large sea trout (*Salmo trutta*) now migrate up the river.

Several lessons have been learnt from this 'flagship' European project. It involved 10 local landowners as well as the local municipality, and demonstrated, through regular information exchange, how to ensure that there was mutual benefit for both local landowners and wider environmental concerns. The restoration demonstrated that the re-meandering helped to mitigate flooding downstream, and improved water quality, even during the construction phase. But possibly the most important aspect of the River Brede project is the demonstration that, with a good deal of effort, it is possible to marry nature conservation, ecosystem benefits, and societal need democratically across a wide catchment.

Romaubach Stream, Austria

This is a much smaller example of river restoration and associated wetland habitat creation. During the 1960s, a 1.5 km reach was straightened, channelized, and concrete lined to improve its flood defence potential. However, over the years, the channel silted up and the efficiency of the land drains feeding the stream were greatly reduced (Schlott 1995). Consent for the restoration had to be achieved via a compromise between riparian landowners and local government. The land made available constrained the restoration objectives to a strip of land only 15 m wide. Within this narrow strip meadows were to be reinstated, the banks re-profiled, and the natural functioning of the stream improved.

Unlike the detailed hydraulic modelling and geomorphological analysis associated with the River Brede programme, no detailed plans of the stream bed were prepared prior to construction. The excavator driver was simply instructed to create a new channel with a wide diversity of slopes, depths, and curvature of bends (Schlott 1995). The banks were stabilized using excavated concrete from the former channelized stream, packed with dredged sediment, and covered with grass turf. Slope gradients were all reduced from 1:3 to 1:10, and in some sections 1:15.

Within three years the channel had stabilized, and the banks and channel had been successfully recolonized by a wide variety of marginal, emergent and aquatic plants. Trees (mainly alder (*Alnus glutinosa*), but some grey alder (*A. incana*)), were planted at regular intervals along the restored reach. However, due to a lack of hydrological and soil analysis, most failed. Three years later, using information gained from analysis of the soil types associated with different assemblages of re-colonizing vegetation, five tree species (alder, sallow (*Salix cinerea*), bird cherry (*Prunus padus*), guelder rose (*Viburnum opulus*), and silver birch (*Betula pendula*)) were planted in groups. This planting was far more successful.

Even with the use of simple techniques and low levels of technology, the restoration of the Romaubach Stream has produced environmental benefits. The increased sinuosity of the channel, even without a detailed design, has increased the water retention time and improved flood protection. The re-profiling of the banks has created diverse riparian habitats. The planting of trees has produced patchy shading in the channel, reducing the growth of submerged macrophytes, and increasing the diversity of the overall scheme.

Maghull Brook, UK

Maghull Brook is situated at Lydiate, within Merseyside District, in a pre-dominantly urban catchment with some local areas of high-grade agricultural land. In 1970 the channel was culverted to prevent lateral scour and erosion from undermining a local road. A 1.2 m diameter concrete culvert was con-structed over a 250 m reach and fitted with a debris screen to prevent block-age. Despite clearing and maintenance, the culvert regularly became blocked with debris, causing flooding to the surrounding farmland, buildings, and road. Although the culvert was designed to carry 1-in-50-year flood flows, the problem of flooding was being greatly exacerbated by the clogging of the debris screen. The solution adopted involved the construction of an open channel 400 m long through the agricultural land adjacent to the existing culvert. The existing debris screen was removed and the concrete culvert bypassed and decommissioned (Rowlands 1997).

The new open channel was designed to accommodate a 1-in-50-year flood event, with the principal dimensions being similar to the existing upstream and downstream channel reaches. A meandering channel with sloping banks was constructed. Low level berms, which also met the flood defence require-ments, were created adjacent to the channel to encourage plants and animals. Trees and shrubs planted at the site perimeter acted as 'screens' during construction, and also provide a diversity of habitat. Bed-check weirs were installed within the channels to reduce the gradient of the stream bed by intro-ducing a series of small (less than 300 mm) steps and to provide environmen-tal benefits. Above the weirs higher water levels attract plants and animals that favour ponded conditions with fine sediment substrates. At the weir struc-ture itself, the rapid velocity and smooth surface provides a habitat for algal and moss growth, while, downstream of the weir, the coarse substrate creates a habitat for water-milfoil (*Myriophyllum* spp.) and invertebrates such as blackflies and stoneflies. The weirs also help to oxygenate the water, improv-ing the overall environmental quality of the water. The adjacent areas were landscaped using the excavated material, and planted with trees and shrubs to provide improved wildlife corridors.

Post-project appraisal has, correctly, been an important component of this scheme. The decommissioning of the culvert and the creation of an open watercourse has significantly enhanced the environmental quality of the area. The channel is developing varied geomorphological features, marginal and emergent plants have naturally colonized the new reach, and the numbers of routine and emergency maintenance visits has greatly reduced. Overall, the scheme has been an environmental success.

The examples detailed above show that, with clearly defined objectives, knowledge of the practical constraints, and the incorporation of a range of methods and techniques, a wide variety of wetland habitats can be created in

Fig. 10.9 Planting of a constructed wetland to treat domestic waste water, Castle Espie, Northern Ireland. (Peter Worrall).

river and floodplain environments. With careful post-project appraisal and management, even the most simple schemes can produce long-term ecological benefits.

Constructed wetlands

Wetlands can act as sinks, stores, and transformers of contaminants and pollutants. Worldwide there are currently over a thousand natural or constructed wetlands receiving and treating municipal, industrial, agricultural, and urban run-off waste waters (Kadlec and Knight 1996). The size of these systems ranges between $200\,m^2$ to over $4000\,ha$. The one structural attribute that all constructed wetlands have in common with natural wetlands is the presence of emergent plants. Some systems are characterized by monocultures of single species, such as common reed or reed-mace, while others possess a wide variety of plant species in relatively natural, diverse assemblages (Fig. 10.9).

Since the mid-1980s in Europe, constructed wetlands have been utilized increasingly to treat waste waters. Each newly constructed wetland treatment system is an additional wetland habitat, and other than simply acting as waste water treatment works, newly created constructed wetlands can provide additional direct or indirect environmental benefits, including the provision of habitats for birds and invertebrates, offering flood storage potential, and providing amenity, recreational, or scientific study opportunities. Often these additional environmental benefits are incidental, and not specifically targeted. However, as treatment wetland design formulae diversify and hybrid treatment wetland systems proliferate, constructed wetlands often integrate features to enhance wildlife conservation; increasingly, constructed wetlands are being installed to protect or provide water resources for adjacent sensitive and diverse aquatic habitats (Worrall *et al.* 1996).

Design criteria

Traditionally, within the waste water industry, constructed wetlands have been designed primarily to treat effluent with high levels of biological oxygen demand (BOD) and suspended solids (SS). Often designs based on a one- or two-function approach have proved to be inefficient at treating other parameters such as ammonia, ortho-phosphate, total-nitrogen, or total-phosphorus. Increasingly, the design of constructed wetlands for waste water treatment is taking into account the notion that the biological reduction of the key water quality parameters operates in a sequential fashion. From a survey of 285 temperate wetland systems, Haycock and Worrall (1996) conclude that once BOD has been reduced by at least 80%, ammonia reduction will occur at rates in excess of 80%, and total-nitrogen reduces more quickly once BOD and ammonium concentrations have been reduced. Total-phosphorus reduction also seems to be influenced by the degree to which BOD levels have been attenuated. The acceptance of this theory has resulted in the growing development of hybrid constructed wetland systems and a return to the basic principles of sequential wastewater treatment (Hiley 1995). The appreciation of the need to design for differential processes has resulted in a variety of designs to address a range of specific stage of treatments.

A dilemma that faces the designers of wetlands constructed as both multi-functional effluent treatment systems and wildlife habitat refuges is the moral question of whether attracting animals to sites that are inherently polluted is an appropriate action. At present this question remains largely unresolved and requires a much greater understanding of the bioaccumulation rates of toxins and their subsequent redistribution throughout the environment and associated food webs. Careful consideration needs to be applied in situations where it is known that effluents treated and retained by constructed wetlands can have detrimental impacts on wildlife. In such cases, it may transpire that constructed wetlands are not an appropriate option.

Designing constructed wetlands to address particular water quality issues takes experience and should only be attempted by experts in the field of constructed wetlands—otherwise the risk of failure may be high. Despite this, through sympathetic awareness of the nature conservation opportunities that can exist, increased environmental benefits can become part of the design criteria.

Nature conservation value of constructed wetlands

The extent to which constructed wetlands can play a significant role in nature conservation is debatable. The following factors will constrain any wildlife objectives associated with the development of a constructed wetland:

1. The size of the constructed wetland.
2. The structural diversity of the wetland as a habitat.
3. The biological stresses imposed by the nature of the influent.
4. The design features of the wetland, especially surface versus sub-surface flow.

Constructed wetlands vary greatly in terms of their size. Large-scale constructed wetlands have the potential to offer opportunities for habitat creation as well as improving the treatment efficiency for some contaminants such as phosphorus. This dual approach of large-scale habitat creation and pollutant removal is being pursued by the RSPB and other supporting agencies in the Ham Wall project in Somerset, England. A large (140 ha) wetland has been constructed that will demonstrate the capacity of a more 'natural' constructed wetland both to remove nutrients from contaminated influents and to provide an important habitat for wildlife of a high conservation value, such as bittern and marsh harrier (Hawke and José 1996).

The majority of constructed wetlands in Great Britain are smaller than 0.25 ha and characteristically support a monoculture of common reed. However, even these small areas can provide habitats for a range of species (Table 10.7), even if they are not those of recognized conservation concern.

Table 10.7
Wildlife that may be supported by a constructed dry reedbed of 0.25 ha

Wildlife
Up to 4 pairs of breeding reed warblers (*Acrocephalus scirpaceus*)
1 or 2 pairs of breeding reed buntings (*Emberiza schoeniclus*)
1 pair of breeding sedge warblers (*A. schoenobaenus*)
1 pair of breeding wrens (*Troglodytes troglodytes*)
1 feeding, possibly nesting pair of moorhens (*Gallinula chloropus*)
Feeding bearded tits (*Panurus biarmicus*) in winter
Breeding harvest mice (*Micromys minutus*)
Feeding, possible breeding short-tailed voles (*Microtus agrestis*)
A range of invertebrates (vital to support most of the above; some uncommon species may colonize if populations nearby)

Source: Hawke and José (1996).

Irrespective of the size of the constructed wetlands, it has been shown that by increasing the structural diversity it is possible to retain, and sometimes improve, their ability to remove pollutants and, at the same time, to extend opportunities for wildlife (Merritt 1994). For example, by constructing open water ditches at right angles to the flow direction across a reed-bed, or by increasing the irregularity of the open water–reed margin mosaic, waterfowl and invertebrates such as dragonflies may be encouraged. Whether large or small, constructed wetlands, when placed in the context of catchment planning, can contribute positively to biodiversity.

Summary

Wetlands are often neglected and threatened habitats. Traditionally they have been drained, degraded, and lost. However, through a combination of the application of simple techniques and an awareness of the potential opportunities that exist, a wide range of wetland habitats can be re-created. The creation and enhancement of ponds, wet grasslands, reed-beds, rivers and streams, floodplains, and constructed wetlands, either in isolation or as components of larger projects, results in habitats that possess high conservation values as well as aesthetic, amenity, and economic benefits to society. By combining scientific research with monitoring of these new wetlands, a greater understanding of the processes and functioning will be gained.

11 Getting it right

We have constantly emphasized that habitat creation should never be regarded as a substitute for preserving the better semi-natural habitats. Its role is to improve our environment by helping to offset losses that have already occurred due to agriculture, urbanization, construction, and other destructive land uses. Despite criticism (Sutherland and Gibson 1988) habitat creation is an approach that is here to stay. Already it is central to government policies such as the Natural Areas Programme, Countryside Steward-ship, Tir Cymen, Environmentally Sensitive Areas, and long-term set-aside, as well as being practised regularly by Local Authorities and landscaping firms. The new approaches to coastal protection rely heavily on habitat creation as an alternative to expensive engineering solutions, while inland it is helping to reduce the isolation and fragmentation of existing semi-natural habitats. Worryingly, it is also being used to justify habitat losses associated with new roads, quarries, and various other forms of development; this is where it is most controversial.

If we are not careful, techniques developed to compensate for serious habitat loss will be used as an excuse to destroy further habitat (Hopkins 1989). What cannot be achieved by habitat creation is the subtlety, complexity, and biodiversity of an ecosystem that has evolved over time.

Project planning and design

The success of habitat creation can be increased by paying attention to project planning and design. Having reviewed 104 case studies, Parker (1995) concluded that, to be successful, schemes should not be too ambitious, should be in harmony with the surrounding habitats and land use, and should be costed within the constraints of available finance. Capital expenditure should be separated from that required for long-term management. Designer habitats, where there is full intervention and management, are still the most popular, but are also the most demanding technically.

The hardest aspect to achieve is a high degree of naturalness, especially initially (Fig. 11.1), but this should not bother ecologists who take a long view. In woodland, naturalness derives from a range of subtle features, such as the

Fig. 11.1 Recently planted marram grass (*Ammophila arenaria*) illustrates the difficulties of achieving a natural appearance in the early years; Sizewell B Nuclear Power Station, Suffolk.

age class structure, openings, edges, the presence of dead wood, local combinations of trees, shrubs, and ground flora, and processes such as disturbance and succession. Variety needs to be built in from the start as little management may occur unless a financial return is expected. Variety does not mean planting everything everywhere.

When Jones (1990) carried out a questionnaire survey of >150 terrestrial habitat creation projects, the approach of promoting the natural succession was the least popular, despite being cheap and leading to a high level of naturalness. To be successful, all sites benefit from being adjacent to species-rich vegetation, so that genetically adapted flora and fauna can invade. In practice it is often best to employ several design approaches on a site to produce habitat mosaics. Where a site is large, simply fencing part of it and leaving it to develop naturally should always be considered.

An ecologist, whether in-house or from an external agency, must be involved in the pre-planning stages, and always before any planning application is submitted. Even the most simple decisions, if taken before a site is properly surveyed, can cause untold problems as Kerslake and Fraser (1995) have related. They were involved with a long derelict site at Ruddington, Nottinghamshire, which was earmarked for development as a country park. No detailed ecological survey had been carried out before the decision was made to raze it and start again. Ecologists were then called in to advise on habitat creation. It was conceded that a very small area of grassland containing bee orchids (*Ophrys apifera*) could be retained, but most of the country park was to be acres of sown wild flower meadow, a large lake, and tree planting. As work progressed a colony of bats was disturbed when the building they were hibernating in was demolished, and it was learnt that a recently levelled pond had contained a colony of great crested newts (*Triturus cristatus*). Four years on, parts of the site were judged a success, but the vast areas of featureless, barren amenity grassland were a poor substitute for the pre-existing butterfly-rich communities. The lessons learnt were that ecologists must be involved at the outset, they need to spend a lot of their time supervising contractors, the temptation to raze a site and start again must be resisted, and you must get the public behind any scheme. Some of these points are elaborated on later. An example of what can go wrong, even when four ecologists were involved from the outset, is given in Box 11.1 and Fig. 11.2.

It is important to have a project plan with clear objectives so that the project can later be assessed against it. Monitoring and long-term management must be essential features of the plan.

The importance of using local genetic stock

This aspect of habitat creation is frequently discussed, but apart from the work of Lines (1987), Worrell (1992), and Jones and Evans (1994) there is lack of hard data to back up the theory. Currently, there is considerable concern about the millions of foreign oak seedlings that are being bought in to stock the present wave of new woodland planting. The reason for their popularity is that they are around 35% cheaper than native material. The oaks of eastern and central Europe have been isolated from British oaks for up to four million years and, consequently, the species that live on them have evolved separately. When we use these trees we expect our wildlife to move in, but it may well not do so or be less successful than anticipated. For example, the foreign oaks leaf two weeks later than British oaks and, as a result, birds that rely on caterpillars that eat bursting oak buds to feed their young could face starvation. Other delicate food chains may also suffer. Scientists suspect that the bark, wood, leaves, and acorns of these alien trees have a chemistry that makes their nutritional status and palatability different. If these new forests are intended to recreate what has been lost, then it is essential that locally native trees are used.

Despite the increasing desire to use local provenances, the supply is often inadequate or completely unavailable—few nurseries stock a range of reliably sourced material. Ideally, woodland planting schemes should start with seed collected from a matched site type, which is then grown to contract. However,

Box 11.1 Tinsley park Opencast habitat creation scheme

Thirty-two hectares of an opencast coal site on the edge of Sheffield was redesigned as amenity public open space using habitat creation techniques to produce a landscape of small woods in a wild flower grassland–scrub setting with heathland on the high ground and a chain of ponds (Fig. 11.2). Four ecologists working for different agencies were involved in the design. The grass sward was sown in autumn 1991 before the wild flower seed had arrived, as the engineers required some cover during the winter to prevent possible erosion. This cover had to be sprayed out the following autumn, using glyphosate, and re-sown with the correct grass–wild flower mixes. The meadows appear never to have received the late summer cut that was recommended. Establishment of the wild flowers has been patchy, though a tall non-native cultivar of bird's-foot trefoil (*Lotus corniculatus*) is doing well. A native provenance for all grass and wild flora had been specified and funded!

In the planting season of 1992–93, the woodland went into fenced plots that had been sown with a grass–wild flower mix. As subsequent maintenance (specified as a 1 m diameter weed-free area round each plant) was not carried out, many specimens failed due to competition from the *Festuca rubra*-dominated sward. The best survivor in the mid-slope woodland has been alder (*Alnus glutinosa*), which was not specified for these blocks. Woodland wild flora was specified to be sown into grass-free patches covering a third of each block, at 3 g/m^2. Whether this was done is not known—none of the nine species have appeared.

Patches of gorse (*Ulex europaeus*) and broom (*Cytisus scoparius*) were hand sown into the mid-slope grassland to occupy 30% of the community. These, especially the gorse, established well and now occupy far more than 30% of the grassland. There must have been considerable redistribution of the seed by natural agencies following sowing—it is now threatening to take over the site, but may encourage breeding stonechat (*Saxicola torquata*) and whinchat (*S. rubetra*). Aquatic planting, using pot-grown material, around and in the ponds has been successful with all 26 species establishing fast and starting to spread. Reed-mace (*Typha latifolia*), which colonized naturally, is already a problem, but the nearby airport company is happy as it disapproves of open water that could attract large birds.

The heathland, established using 'turf transplants' and through the spreading of heather litter (10 g/m^2) into an acid grassland sown at a rate of 2 g/m^2, was a complete failure. With hindsight the ground preparation and soil conditions were incorrect. Four years later the remains of the failed heathland were destroyed as the upper parts of the site had to be regraded to match airport regulations.

Despite these set-backs, the scheme is regarded by planning officers of the local authority, from a landscape and amenity point of view, as a success; the land-forms are very satisfying, the area has a natural feel, and the ponds are eye-catching features. The ecologists involved are disappointed.

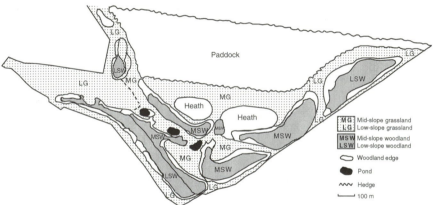

Fig. 11.2 Plan and photograph of the Tinsley Park Opencast habitat creation scheme, Sheffield. For further details see Box 11.1.

this will add to the cost and there are unhelpful EEC regulations to be overcome. Nevertheless, a move is required away from the 'cheapest is best' philosophy of the 1980s to a more sustainable approach. The success of the Native Pinewood Scheme in Scotland shows what is possible. This scheme has encouraged many Scottish nurseries to grow locally sourced trees and shrubs, through only grant-aiding those schemes that use local genetic stock. However, it should be noted that natural regeneration is strongly preferred

Fig. 11.3 Native pine woodland being extended by natural regeneration in Rothiemurchus, Speyside; this option is greatly preferred to planting.

to planting as a way of extending native pine woods (Fig. 11.3); planting is only approved for grant support if natural regeneration has been unsuccessful over at least five years.

Control of the contractor

Habitat creation schemes can be expertly designed and specified on paper, but if the contractor takes short cuts or misinterprets instructions the end result can be a disaster. Practitioners can pay more attention to their plant assemblages rather than simply ensuring that ground preparation is adequate, but both are equally critical for success. Soil depths and fertility levels are time-consuming and sometimes costly to check, with the result that sites are often left in too fertile a condition; also, problems of soil compaction are frequently poorly addressed. Conveying details to the drivers of large machines can be difficult—they have spent a lifetime creating angular, engineered finishes and equate any irregular land-forms requested with bad workmanship. At the opposite end of the scale is the problem of contractors who do not use their judgement but slavishly follow the contract conditions, even when the unanticipated arises. For such reasons it is important to ensure adequate on-site supervision at all stages in the contract.

When dealing with plants there can be problems over the substitution of material and with genuine error. When a fescue-based grass seed mix is specified, rye-grass with fescue may be sown because the contractor has some bags of rye-grass (*Lolium perenne*) left in his store from a previous contract. Worse is the substitution of a carefully selected species for one with a similar name because the intended one proves difficult to locate. An example from Sheffield was the sowing of tall fescue (*Festuca arundinacea*) instead of reed canary-grass (*Phalaris arundinacea*) in a wetland nature reserve. At Stansted Airport, purging buckthorn (*Rhamnus cathartica*) was replaced with alder buckthorn (*Frangula alnus*), which was totally unsuited to the soils and not locally native. This kind of duplicity is annoying as it may mean spraying the sward out or uprooting young trees and starting again, thereby delaying completion. Deliberate substitution is easy to detect so is not often attempted.

Errors in ordering or supplying material can be equally bothersome. Native beech (*Fagus sylvatica*) was specified for the north side of the Humber Bridge; instead, copper beech was delivered and hundreds of trees had to be replaced, though a few remain to commemorate the incident. In certain compartments of the naturalistic planting on the ash mound at Drax Power Station the native elder (*Sambucus nigra*) proved to be c.v. 'Aurea' and the English oak (*Quercus robur*) was c.v. 'Variagata' with creamy white margins; neither was replaced—they are treated as landscape features. It is not uncommon for *Quercus robur* to be misread as *Quercus rubra* (red oak) and vice versa. These mistakes would not be tolerated in a habitat creation scheme.

More difficult is determining the provenance of plant material if local genotypes have been specified. Due to competitive tendering, contractors may deviate from recommended suppliers, perhaps for the benefits of discount bulk buying or quick delivery, and there is no accreditation system for hardwoods. The answer is to buy in the material for the contractor to plant. With cloned material it is impossible to obtain genetically varied batches. The Wild Flower Seeds Working Group is so concerned about this that they are examining ways of introducing an accreditation system for native seed (Akeroyd 1994).

Establishment techniques for woody species are now the exact opposite of nature's way. A few specimens are planted and carefully tended so they grow into perfect trees. Nature's method is to produce a self-thinning regeneration core in which most individuals are crooked or otherwise imperfect. Contractors cannot imitate this. When it comes to planting they do not usually understand the concept of randomness, equating it with 'equal distribution'. If random spacing at an average of 2 m is requested they will probably lay the material out in rows 2 m apart with 2 m between each plant, whereas, in true randomness, the spacing would vary from around 20 cm to 3–4 m. Another reason for contractors preferring rows is that the trees are easier to count and to maintain through the liability period.

Management, monitoring, and interpretation

Management beyond the contract liability period is necessary for the success of most schemes, unless the soil is highly infertile. Many species rely on grazing, hay making, coppicing, or trimming for their survival. This is the stage at which many under-funded projects fail or become forgotten and give habitat creation a bad name. If money is limited, a scheme that is based largely on natural colonization should be considered, and the price of a long period before the desired communities develop must be accepted.

Monitoring is important to ensure the project achieves the aims stated in the project plan, to help fine-tune management operations, and to add to the sum of knowledge on the state of the art. There is a lack of scientific information and documented examples, particularly of schemes that have failed; more of the results need to be made public so we can all learn. Monitoring need only take a day a year, and after a while only a day every two or three years. It is rewarding to return to a site, relocate the transect line or permanent plots and monitor change over the years. It can alter ones perspective of a scheme. For example, after monitoring a wild flower meadow for four years, the sown species had reached an all time low and an article was written entitled '*A wild flower mix with a short life*' (Gilbert 1985). However, by year ten, *Sanguisorba minor* ssp. *muricata*, about the only sown species remaining, had increased to a 30% cover producing an attractive and singular meadow in a school grounds; it could no longer be called a failure. Monitoring on the same site revealed how an accidental application of the herbicide Kerb, targeted on grasses, altered the balance of competition and turned round a failing wild flower meadow so it was a riot of colour.

Part of the subsequent management of any scheme should involve interpretation, explaining the significance of the site to those who visit it, and perhaps why it looks untidy and the reasons behind any restrictions on access. During the restoration of the dunes at Sizewell B Nuclear Power Station, 800 m of the dune ridge were fenced off to allow the newly planted vegetation to establish. This meant that the public were restricted to a narrow path. Notices explaining why this was necessary provided brief details of the habitat creation scheme. This helped to prevent vandalism and curbed resentment (Fig. 11.4). The same approach has been taken by Cairngorm Sports Development Ltd with their erosion control work on the summit of Cairn Gorm. When taking this approach it is important to convey the message quickly and clearly.

Fig. 11.4 Good interpretation helps prevent vandalism through curbing resentment; Sizewell B Nuclear Power Station, Suffolk.

Whole environment management

Much of the advice given in this book is based on a piecemeal, individual site approach, even though some of the schemes described have been extensive. The National Trust is examining a new style where-by whole estates and whole catchment areas are assessed for their habitat creation and management needs to prevent damage to both local and global natural resources—soil, water, air, fauna and flora (Hearn 1994). The idea is that valuable habitats will no longer be islands, but part of a sympathetically managed landscape. It is hoped that, eventually, agricultural funding will be directed into realizing this ideal. In practical terms it means that land capability surveys will match farming, stocking, and cropping to the geology, soils, topography, and hydrology. If the whole area is experiencing hypertrophication from fertilizer input and slurry, a change from mixed farming to an extensive sheep and beef enterprise might be considered. The benefits would be cleaner water in springs, streams, and lakes, and the extent of semi-natural grassland would be greatly increased (through allowing natural colonization from surviving small relics). Woodland, instead of being bordered by nettles, would be allowed to develop a wide scrub margin through natural regeneration and there would also be a move towards minimal intervention. In this system habitat creation is seen as part of the tool kit for reversing 50 years of agricultural intensification.

The benefits of habitat creation

Habitat creation brings with it a wide range of benefits. At the personal level it provides contact with nature for a public that enjoys wildlife and, who not being professional ecologists, do not have their pleasure spoilt if, in the early years, it is a facsimile rather than the real thing. When, in the 1970s, the Nature Conservancy Council started their work on creating wild flower meadows at Monks Wood (Wells *et al.* 1981) the objective was simply to provide attractive grassland in public places; this is still a valuable goal.

The state of the art has now moved on. As confidence with more natural techniques grows, habitat creation is increasingly being used as a tool by conservationists who wish to reverse habitat loss. In the Natural Areas Programme it is being used to link-up habitats that have become fragmented and to benefit wide-ranging species that have suffered through the isolation of sites within a hostile landscape. Opportunities are endless; in the Lake District, habitat creation is being used to re-establish the altitudinal succession from lake shore to mountain top, to extend broad-leaved woodland through natural regeneration, and to restore heather moorland. On the Stiperstones, Shropshire, substantial expansion of the heathland and the re-creation of flower-rich meadows are being planned. Certain local authorities see substantial environmental benefits in expanding the area of semi-natural habitat in their district, both for reasons of general amenity and to strengthen local character. They regard the visual appearance of such habitats as an additional asset.

It is likely that the very reasonable cost both of creating and maintaining semi-natural habitats will turn out to be an irresistible attraction. Through working with nature, having long time-scales rather than expecting instant landscapes, and by employing flexible designs, the degree of soil amelioration, level of planting, and need for complex maintenance measures are all greatly reduced.

Problems still to be resolved include biological, non-biological, and philosophical aspects of the practice (Jordan *et al.* 1987*a*). For example, will it ever be possible for habitat creation to play a significant role in the conservation of rare and endangered species and of biodiversity in general? Can authentic communities with a complete complement of plants and animals ever be a feasible goal? It is also affected by abiding conflicts between short- and long-term planning, local economics, and politics. To help resolve these conflicts, there needs to be a full investigation of the capital and on-going management costs compared with other methods of land restoration. At a philosophical level, the widespread adoption of habitat creation might help industrial societies resolve the problem of their relationship with nature.

References

Aberdeen Centre for Land Use (1990). *Northwest ethylene pipeline: phase II ecological survey*. Aberdeen Centre for Land Use, Aberdeen.

ADAS (Agricultural Development and Advisory Service) (1994). *A review of ADAS research and development for British Coal Opencast*. ADAS, Mansfield.

ADAS (1996). *Botanical monitoring of grassland in the South Downs ESA 1987–1995. Environmentally Sensitive Areas Scheme*. ADAS Report to the Ministry of Agriculture, Fisheries and Food, London.

Aerts, R., Huiszoon, A., Van Oostrum, J. H. A., Van de Vijver, C. A. D. M. and Willems, J. H. (1995). The potential for heathland restoration on formerly arable land at a site in Drenthe, The Netherlands. *Journal of Applied Ecology*, **32**, 827–35.

Akeroyd, J. (1994). *Seeds of destruction? Non-native wildflower seed and British floral diversity*. Plantlife, Natural History Museum, London.

Anderson, P. (1994*a*). Flower-rich grassland creation. *Enact*, **2**, 21–2.

Anderson, P. (1994*b*). *Ouaisné Common. Plot A monitoring results*. Unpublished report to Jersey Island Development Commitee.

Anderson, P. (1995). Ecological restoration and creation: A review. *Biological Journal of the Linnean Society*, **56** (Suppl.), 187–211.

Anderson, P. (1996). The wrong trees and what about the shrubs? *Enact*, **4**, 20–2.

Anderson, P. and Yalden, D. A. (1981). Increased sheep numbers and loss of heather moorland in the Peak District, England. *Biological Conservation*, **20**, 195–213.

Anderson, P. and Radford, E. (1994). Changes in vegetation following reduction in grazing pressure on the National Trust's Kinder Estate, Peak District, Derbyshire, England. *Biological Conservation*, **69**, 55–63.

Anderson, P., Tallis, J. H. and Yalden, D. (1997). *Moorland management project, Phase III*. English Nature/Peak Park Joint Planning Board, Bakewell.

Andrawes, K. Z., McGown, A., Hytiris, N., Mercer, F. B. and Sweetland, D. B. (1986). *The use of mesh elements to alter the stress–strain behaviour of granular soils*. pp. 839–44. Third International Conference on Geotextiles, 21986, Vienna.

Andren, H. and Angelstam, P. (1988). Elevated predation rates as an edge effect in habitat islands: experimental evidence. *Ecology*, **69**, 544–7.

Andrews, J. (1991). Restoration of gravel pits for wildlife. In *RSPB Conservation Review 5*, (ed. J. C. Cadbury), pp. 78–81. Royal Society for the Protection of Birds, Sandy, Bedfordshire.

Andrews, J. and Kinsman, D. (1991). *Gravel pit restoration for wildlife*. Royal Society for the Protection of Birds, Sandy Bedfordshire.

Andrews, J. and Rebane, M. (1994). *Farming and wildlife. A practical management handbook*. Royal Society for the Protection of Birds, Sandy, Bedfordshire.

Andrews, M. (1989). *In search of the picturesque*. Scolar Press, Aldershot.

Ash, H. J., Bennett, R. and Scott R. (1992). *Flowers in the grass. Creating and managing grasslands with wildflowers*. Nature Conservancy Council, Peterborough.

Ash, H. J., Gemmell, R. P. and Bradshaw, A. D. (1994). The introduction of native plant species on industrial waste heaps: a test of immigration and other factors affecting primary succession. *Journal of Applied Ecology*, **31**, 74–84.

Atkinson, M. D., Trueman, I. C., Millett, P., Jones, G. H. and Besenyei, L. (1995). The use of hay strewing to create species-rich grasslands. (ii) Monitoring the seed bank. *Land Contamination and Reclamation*, **3**, 108–10.

Bacon, J. (1994). A prickly problem. *Enact*, **2**, 12–15.

Baines, J. C. (1989). Choices in habitat recreation. In *Biological habitat reconstruction*, (ed. G. P. Buckley), pp. 5–8. Belhaven Press, London.

Baker, C. J. and Maltby, E. (1995). Nitrate removal by river marginal wetlands: factors affecting the provision of a suitable denitrification environment. In *Hydrology and hydrochemistry of British wetlands*, (ed. J. M. R. Hughes and A. L. Heathwaite), pp. 291–313. John Wiley, Chichester.

Bamber, R. N., Batten, S. D., Sheader, M. and Bridgwater, N. D. (1992). On the ecology of brackishwater lagoons in Great Britain. *Aquatic Conservation: Marine and Freshwater Ecoystems*, **2**, 65–94.

Bannister, P. (1965). Biological Flora of the British Isles: *Erica cinerea* L. *Journal of Ecology*, **53**, 527–42.

Bannister, P. (1966). Biological Flora of the British Isles: *Erica tetralix* L. *Journal of Ecology*, **54**, 795–814.

Barber, D. (ed) (1970). *Farming and wildlife: A study in compromise*. Royal Society for the Protection of Birds, Sandy, Bedfordshire.

Barber, R. J. (1992). *Restoring and creating wetlands. A planning guide for the Central States Region, Iowa, Kansas, Missouri, and Nebraska*. US Environmental Protection Agency, Region 7, Kansas.

Barclay-Estrup, P. and Gimingham, C. H. (1975). Seed-shedding in heather (*Calluna vulgaris* L. Hull). *Transactions of the Botanical Society of Edinburgh*, **42**, 275–8.

Barnes, R. S. K. (1980). *Coastal lagoons: the natural History of a neglected habitat*. Cambridge University Press, Cambridge.

Bayfield, N. G. (1971). Ecological effects of recreation on Cairngorm. *Nature Conservancy Range Ecology Group Progress Report*, **1**, 47–55.

Bayfield, N. G. (1974). Burial of vegetation by erosion debris near ski lifts on Cairngorm, Scotland. *Biological Conservation*, **6**, 246–51.

Bayfield, N. G. (1980). Replacement of vegetation on disturbed ground near ski lifts in the Cairngorm Mountains, Scotland. *Journal of Biogeography*, **7**, 249–60.

Bayfield, N. G. (1988). *The potential for revegetation at four problem sections of the Southern Pennine Way*. Institute of Terrestrial Ecology, Banchory.

Bayfield, N. G. (1991). *1990 Progress report: Snake Pass revegetation and fertilizer trials*. Institute of Terrestrial Ecology, Banchory.

Bayfield, N. G. (1996). Long-term changes in colonization of bulldozed pistes at Cairn Gorm, Scotland. *Journal of Applied Ecology*, **33**, 1359–65.

Bayfield, N. G. and Aitken, R. (1992). *Managing the impacts of recreation on vegetation and soils. A review of techniques*. Institute of Terrestrial Ecology, Banchory.

Bayfield, N. G., McGowan, G. M. and Patterson, I. S. (1991). *Monitoring of seeding trials in the Three Peaks 1991*. ITE Report No. 12 to Yorkshire Dales National Park, pp. 20. Institute of Terrestrial Ecology, Banchory.

Bayfield, N. G., Mills, D., McGowan, G. and Patterson, I. S. (1990). *Vegetation reinforcement trials: 1986–90*. Report No. 7 to Yorkshire Dales National Park, pp. 26. Institute of Terrestrial Ecology, Banchory.

Bayfield, N. G., Urquhart, U. H. and Rothery, P. (1984). Colonisation of bulldozed track verges in the Cairngorm Mountains, Scotland. *Journal of Applied Ecology*, **21**, 343–54.

Bell, J. N. B. and Tallis, J. H. (1973). Biological Flora of the British Isles: *Empetrum nigrum* L. *Journal of Ecology*, **61**, 289–305.

Berg, A. and Part, T. (1994). Abundance of breeding farmland birds on arable and set-aside fields at forest edges. *Ecography*, **17**, 147–52.

Bibby, C. J. and Lunn, J. (1982). Conservation of reed beds and their avifauna in England and Wales. *Biological Conservation*, **23**, 167–86.

Bickmore, C. J. and Larard, P. J. (1989). Reconstructing freshwater habitats in development schemes. In *Biological Habitat Reconstruction*, (ed. G. P. Buckley), pp. 189–200. Belhaven Press, London.

Billings, W. D. (1974). Environment, concept and reality. In *Handbook of vegetation science. Part 6. Vegetation and environment*, (ed. B. R. Strain and W. D. Billings), pp. 9–35. Dr W. Junk, The Hague.

Bisgrove, R. and Dixie, G. (1994). Wild flowers: plugging the gap. *Enact*, **2**, 18–20.

Boatman, N. D., Dover, J. W., Wilson, P. J., Thomas, M. B. and Cowgill, S. E. (1989). Modification of farming practice at field margins to encourage wildlife. In *Biological habitat reconstruction*, (ed. G. P. Buckley), pp. 299–311. Belhaven Press, London.

Boyce, D. (1994). Survival and spread of pot-grown flowers inserted into a perennial rye-grass ley. In *Grassland management and nature conservation*, (ed. R. J. Haggar and S. Peel), pp. 238–9. *British Grassland Society Occasional Symposium No. 28*.

Boyd, J. M. (1992). Sycamore—a review of its status in conservation in Great Britain. *Biologist*, **39**, 29–31.

Bradshaw, A. D. (1983). The reconstruction of ecosystems. *Journal of Applied Ecology*, **20**, 1–17.

Bradshaw, A. D. (1984). Land restoration, now and in the future. *Proceedings of the Royal Society Series B*, **223**, 1–23.

Bradshaw, A. D. and Chadwick, M. J. (1980). *The restoration of land: the ecology and reclamation of derelict and degraded land*. (Studies in Ecology, Vol. 6.) Blackwell Scientific Publications, Oxford.

Brenchley, W. E. and Adam, H. (1915). Recolonisation of cultivated land allowed to revert to natural conditions. *Journal of Ecology*, **3**, 193–210.

Brookes, A. and Sear, D. A. (1996). Geomorphological principles for restoring channels. In *River channel restoration: Principles for sustainable projects*, (ed. A. Brookes and F. D. Shields, Jr), pp. 75–101. John Wiley, Chichester.

Brookes, A. and Shields, F. D. Jr (1996). Towards an approach to sustainable river restoration. In *River channel restoration: Principles for sustainable projects*, (ed. A. Brookes and F. D. Shields, Jr), pp. 385–402. John Wiley, Chichester.

Brookes, A., Knight, S. S. and Shields, F. D., Jr (1996). Habitat enhancement. In *River channel restoration: principles for sustainable projects*, (ed. A. Brookes and F. D. Shields, Jr), pp. 103–26. John Wiley, Chichester.

Brooks, A. (1988). *Hedging: a practical conservation handbook*. British Trust for Conservation Volunteers, Wallingford.

Brown, R. J. (1989). Wild flower seed mixtures: supply and demand in the horticultural indurstry. In *Biological habitat reconstruction*, (ed. G. P. Buckley), pp. 201–14. Belhaven Press, London.

Brown, V. K. and Gibson, C. W. D. (1993). Re-creation of species-rich calcicolous grassland communities. In *Grassland management and nature conservation*, (ed. R. J. Haggar and S. Peel), pp. 125–36. BGS Occasional Symposium, No. 28.

Brown, V. K., Gibson, C. W. D. and Sterling, P. H. (1990). The mechanisms controlling insect diversity in calcareous grasslands. In *Calcareous grasslands ecology and management*, (ed. S. H. Hillier, D. W. H. Walton and D. A. Wells), pp. 79–87. Proceedings of the British Ecological Society/Nature Conservancy Council symposium.

BTCV (1981). *Waterways and wetlands, a practical handbook*. British Trust for Conservation Volunteers, Easton Press Ltd, Reading.

Buckley, G. P. (1989). *Biological habitat reconstruction*. Belhaven Press, London.

Buckley, G. P. and Knight, D. G. (1989). The feasability of woodland reconstruction. In *Biological habitat reconstruction*, (ed. G. P. Buckley), pp. 171–88. Belhaven Press, London.

Buckley, G. P. and Insley, H. (1984). Sward control strategies for young amenity trees. *Aspects of Applied Biology*, **5**, 97–107.

Bunce, R. G. H. (ed) (1989). *Heather in England and Wales*. ITE Research publication No. 3, HMSO, London.

Burd, F. (1989). *The saltmarsh survey of Great Britain*. Research and Survey in Nature Conservation No. 17, Nature Conservancy Council, Peterborough.

Burd, F. (1992). *Erosion and vegetation change on the saltmarshes of Essex and North Kent between 1973 and 1988*. Research and Survey in Nature Conservation No. 42, Nature Conservancy Council, Peterborough.

Burgess, N. D. and Becker, D. B. (1989). *The creation and management of islands and rafts on RSPB reserves*. Royal Society for the Protection of Birds, Sandy, Bedfordshire.

Burgess, N. D. and Evans, E. (1989). Management of reedbeds. In *RSPB Conservation Review 3*, (ed. J. C. Cadbury and M. Everett), pp. 20–4. Royal Society for the Protection of Birds, Sandy, Bedfordshire.

Butcher, G. S., Niering, W. A., Barry, W. J. and Goodwin, R. H. (1981). Equilibrium biogeography and the size of nature reserves: and avian case study. *Oecologia*, **49**, 29–37.

Byrne, S. (1990). *Habitat transplantation in England. A review of the extent and nature of the practice and the techniques employed*. Nature Conservancy Council England Field Unit, Report No. 104, Peterborough.

Cambridgeshire County Council (1991). *Cambridgeshire landscape guidelines. A manual for management and change in the rural landscape*. Cambridgeshire County Council and Granta Editions, Cambridge.

Chambers, B. J. and Cross, R. B. (1996). Recreating lowland heath on exarable land in the Breckland Environmentally Sensitive Area. Vegetation in forestry, amenity and conservation areas. *Aspects of Applied Biology*, **44**, 393–400.

Chapin, F. S. and Chapin, M. C. (1980). Revegetation of an arctic disturbed site by native tundra species. *Journal of Applied Ecology*, **17**, 449–56.

Chapman, S. B. (1967). Nutrient budgets for a dry heath ecosystem in the South of England. *Journal of Ecology*, **55**, 677–89.

Charlton, P. (1990). An airport in the countryside. *Landscape Design*, **190**, 24–7.

Chatters, C. and Sanderson, N. (1994). Grazing lowland pasture woods. *British Wildlife*, **6**, 78–88.

Clear Hill, B. H. and Silvertown, J. (1994). The effect of slugs, sward conditions and sheep grazing on seedling emergence. In *Grassland management and nature conservation*, (ed. R. J. Haggar and S. Peel), pp. 252–3. British Grassland Society Occasional Symposium No. 28.

Clements, F. E. (1916). *Plant succession. An analysis of the development of vegetation*. Carnegie Institute, Washington.

Clinging, V. and Whitely, D. (1980). Mammals of the Sheffield Area. *Sorby Record Special Series*, **3**, 1–48.

Cohn, E. V. J. and Millett, P. (1995). Problems of the implementation and management of urban woodland habitat creation schemes. *Land Contamination and Reclamation*, **3**, 89–92.

Cohn, E. V. J. and Packham, J. R. (1993). The introduction and manipulation of woodland field layers: seeds, plants, timing and economics. *Arboricultural Journal*, **17**, 69–83.

Cole, L. (1986). Urban opportunities for a more natural approach. In *Ecology and design in landscape*, (ed. A. D. Bradshaw, D. A. Goode and E. Thorpe), pp. 417–32. British Ecological Society 24th Symposium.

Cousens, J. E. (1963). Variation of some diagnostic characters of the sessile and pedunculate oaks and their hybrids in Scotland. *Watsonia*, **5**, 273–86.

Crofts, A. and Jefferson, R. G. (1994). *The lowland grassland management handbook*. English Nature/Wildlife Trusts.

Currie, F. (1994). *Lowland Heaths and Forestry*. Forestry Commission. HMSO, London.

Darwin, C. (1859). *On the origin of species by natural selection*. John Murray, London.

Davey, A., Dunford, S. and Free, A. (1992). Feasibility studies for heathland creation on arable land in the Suffolk Sandlings. In *Proceedings of the Seminar on Heathland Habitat Creation*, (ed. A. Free and M. T. Kitson). Suffolk Wildlife Trust, Ipswich.

Davis, B. N. K. (1982). Regional variation in quarries. In *Ecology of quarries*, (ed. B. N. K. Davis), pp. 12–19. Institute of Terrestrial Ecology, Cambridge.

Davis, B. N. K. (1989). Habitat creation for butterflies on a landfill site. *The Entomologist*, **108**, 109–22.

Davis, B. N. K. and Coppeard, R. P. (1989). Soil conditions and grassland establishment for amenity and wildlife on a restored landfill site. In *Biological habitat reconstruction*, (ed. G. P. Buckley), pp. 221–34. Belhaven Press, London.

Davis, B. N. K., Lakhani, M. C. and Park, D. G. (1985). Early seral communities in a limestone quarry: an experimental study of treatment effects on cover and richness of vegetation. *Journal of Applied Ecology*, **22**, 473–95.

Densmore, R. V. (1992). Succession on an Alaskan tundra: disturbance with and without assisted revegetation with grass. *Arctic and Alpine Research*, **24**, 238–43.

Department of the Environment (1993). *Countryside survey 1990: main report.* HMSO, London.

Department of the Environment (1994). *The reclamation and management of metalliferous mining sites.* HMSO, London.

Derek Lovejoy Partnership and Penny Anderson Associates (In preparation). *A55 North Wales coast road ecological study and enhancement programme.* Technical Report. Welsh office, Highways Directorate.

Dodds, G. W., Appleby, M. J. and Evans, A. D. (1995). *A management guide to birds of lowland farmland.* Royal Society for the Protection of Birds, Sandy, Bedfordshire.

Donald, P. F. and Evans, A. D. (1994). Habitat selection by corn buntings *Miliaria calandra. Bird Study,* **41**, 199–210.

Doody, J. (1985). The conservation of sand dunes in Great Britain—a review. In *Sand dunes and their management,* (ed. J. Doody), pp. 43–53. Focus on Nature Conservation No. 13, Nature Conservancy Council, Peterborough.

Duffey, E., Morris, M. G., Sheail, J., Ward, L. K., Wells, D. A. and Wells, T. C. E. (1974). *Grassland ecology and wildlife management.* Chapman & Hall, London.

Eiseltová, M. and Biggs, J. (eds.) (1995). *Restoration of stream ecosystems—an integrated catchment approach.* IWRB Publication 37, International Waterfowl and Wetlands Research Bureau.

Elliot, R. (1995). *Environmental ethics.* Oxford University Press, Oxford.

Elliott, C. L., McKendrick, J. D. and Helm, D. (1987). Plant biomass, cover, and survival of species used for stripmine reclamation in south-central Alaska, U.S.A. *Arctic and Alpine Research,* **19**, 572–7.

Emery, M. (1986). *Promoting nature in cities and towns, a practical guide.* Croom Helm, London.

English Nature (1992). *Campaign for a living coast. Coastal zone conservation— English Nature's rationale, objectives and practical recommendations.* English Nature, Peterborough.

English Nature (1993). *Strategy for the 1990s: Natural areas.* Peterborough.

English Nature (1997). *Wildlife and fresh water—an agenda for sustainable management.* English Nature, Peterborough.

English Nature (undated). *The Stiperstones upland. A conservation and restoration strategy.* English Nature, Peterborough.

Environmental Advisory Unit (University of Liverpool) (1988). *Heathland restoration: A handbook of techniques.* British Gas, Southampton.

Evans, C. (1992). Heathland Recreation on Arable Land at Minsmere. In *Proceedings of the seminar on heathland habitat creation,* (ed. A. Free and M. T. Kitson). Suffolk Wildlife Trust, Ipswich.

Evans, C. *et al.* (1995). Water and sward management for nature conservation: a case study of the RSPB's West Sedgemoor Reserve. In *RSPB Conservation Review 9,* (ed. J. C. Cadbury), pp. 60–72. Royal Society for the Protection of Birds, Sandy, Bedfordshire.

Everett, M. J. (1989). Reedbeds—a scarce habitat. In *RSPB Conservation Review 3,* (ed. J. C. Cadbury and M. Everett), pp. 14–19. Royal Society for the Protection of Birds, Sandy, Bedfordshire.

Eyre, M. D. and Luff, M. L. (1995). Coleoptera on post-industrial land: a conservation problem? *Land Contamination and Reclamation,* **3**, 132–4.

Fairbrother, N. (1970). *New lives, new landscapes.* The Architectural Press, London.

Fales, S. L. and Wakefield, R. C. (1981). Effects of turf grass on the establishment of woody plants. *Agronomy Journal*, **73**, 605–10.

Ferry, B. W. and Waters, S. J. P. (1988). Natural wetlands on shingle at Dungeness, Kent, England. *Biological Conservation*, **43**, 27–41.

Fitzgerald, C. (1992). Heathland Restoration: Some experience from the Suffolk Sandlings. In *Proceedings of the Seminar on Heathland Habitat Creation*, (ed. A. Free and M. T. Kitson). Suffolk Wildlife Trust, Ipswich.

Ford, G. (1984). Local authority experience. In *Creating Attractive Grasslands. Workshop Report No. 5*, (ed. G. Taylor), pp. 20–4. National Turfgrass Council, Bingley, West Yorkshire.

Ford, H. A. (1987). Bird communities on habitat islands in England. *Bird Study*, **34**, 205–18.

Francis, J. L. (1995). The enhancement of young plantations and new woodlands. *Land Contamination and Reclamation*, **3**, 93–5.

Francis, J. L. and Street, M. (1993). The establishment of woodland herbs in new plantations. *Urban Nature*, **1**, 107–10.

Francis, J. L., Morton, A. J. and Boorman, L. A. (1992). The establishment of ground flora in recently planted woodland. *Aspects of Applied Biology*, **29**, 171–8.

Friends of the Earth (1994). *Losing interest. A survey of threats to sites of Special Scientific Interest in England and Wales*. Friends of the Earth, London.

Fry, R. and Lonsdale, S. D. (1991). *Habitat conservation for insects—a neglected green issue*. Amateur Entomologists Society, Middlesex.

Fuller, R. M. and Randall, R. E. (1988). The Orford shingles, Suffolk, U. K.—classic conflicts in coastline management. *Biological Conservation*, **46**, 95–114.

FWAG (Farming and Wildlife Advisory Group) (1992). *Farming and field margins*. National Agricultural Centre, Stoneleigh, Kenilworth.

Gagen, P. J. and Gunn J. (1988). A geomorphological approach to limestone quarry reclamation. In *Geomorphical and Public Policy*, (ed. J. Hooke), pp. 121–42. J. Wiley, London.

Galatowitsch, S. M. and Van der Valk, A. G. (1995). Natural revegetation during restoration of wetlands in the Southern Prairie Pothole region of North America. In *Restoration of temperate wetlands*, (ed. B. D. Wheeler, S. C. Shaw, W. J. Fojt and R. A. Robertson), pp. 129–42. J. Wiley, London.

Game Conservancy Trust (1995a). *Beetle banks—helping nature to control pests*. (Pamphlet.) Fordingbridge, Hants.

Game Conservancy Trust (1995b). *Guidelines for the management of field margins: Fact sheet 2*. Fordingbridge, Hants.

Gee, J. H. R., Lee, K. and Griffiths, S. W. (1994). *The conservation and amenity value of farm ponds*. Contract Science Report, No. 44, Countryside Council for Wales.

Gemmell, R. P. (1982). The origin and botanical importance of industrial habitats. In *Urban Ecology* (ed. R. Bornkamm, A. Lee and M. R. D. Seaward), pp. 33–9. Blackwell, Oxford.

Gibson, C. W. D. (1995). *Chalk grasslands on former arable land: a review*. Bioscan Report No. EO491R2, Bioscan (UK) Ltd, Oxford.

Gibson, C. W. D. and Brown, V. K. (1992). Grazing and vegetation change: deflected or modified succession? *Journal of Applied Ecology*, **29**, 120–31.

Gibson, C. W. D., Watt, T. A. and Brown, V. K. (1987). The use of sheep grazing to recreate species-rich grassland from abandoned arable land. *Biological Conservation*, **42**, 165–83.

Gibson, M. T., Welch, I. M., Barrett, P. R. F. and Ridge, I. (1990). Barley straw as an inhibitor of algal growth II: laboratory studies. *Journal of Applied Phycology*, **2**, 241–8.

Gibson, C. W. D., Hambler, C. and Brown V. K. (1992). Changes in spider (Aranae) assemblages in relation to succession and grazing management. *Journal of Applied Ecology*, **29**, 132.

Gilbert, O. L. (1983*a*). Chatsworth, the Capability Brown lawn and its management. *Landscape Design*, **146**, 8.

Gilbert, O. L. (1983*b*). The ancient lawns of Chatsworth, Derbyshire. *Journal of the Royal Horticultural Society*, **108**, 471–4.

Gilbert, O. L. (1985). A wild flower mix with a short life. *Landscape Design*, **157**, 47–9.

Gilbert, O. L. (1989). *The ecology of urban habitats*. Chapman & Hall, London.

Gilbert, O. L. (1991). Diversification of an established sward using native herbs; the first nineteen years. *Landscape Design*, **200**, 15–16.

Gilbert, O. L. (1995). Urban commons: colourful alternatives. *Enact*, **3(4)**, 10–11.

Gilbert, O. L. and Wathern, P. (1980). The creation of flower-rich swards on mineral workings. *Reclamation Review*, **3**, 217–21.

Gillham, D. A. and Putwain, P. D. (1977). Restoring moorland disturbed by pipeline installation. *Landscape Design*, **119**, 34–6.

Gimingham, C. H. (1972). *Ecology of heathlands*. Chapman & Hall, London.

Gimingham, C. H. (1992). *The lowland heathland management handbook*. English Nature Science No. 8, English Nature, Peterborough.

Gough, M. W. and Marrs, R. H. (1990). A comparison of soil fertility between semi-natural and agricultural plant communities: implications for the creation of species-rich grassland on abandoned agricultural land. *Biological Conservation*, **5**, 83–6.

Greenwood, E. F. and Gemmell, R. P. (1978). Derelict land as a habitat for rare plants in South Lancashire and West Lancashire. *Watsonia*, **12**, 33–40.

Greig-Smith, P. (1983). *Quantitative plant ecology*, 3rd edn. Blackwell, Oxford.

Griffith, G. H. (ed.) (1995). *Landscape ecology: theory and application*. Proceedings of the fourth annual IALE (UK) conference, The University of Reading 19–20th September 1995. IALE (UK).

Grime, J. P. (1979). *Plant strategies and vegetation processes*. John Wiley, Chichister.

Grime, J. P., Hodgson, J. G. and Hunt, R. (1988). *Comparative plant ecology: a functional approach to common British species*. Unwin Hyman, London.

Hall, A. D. (1905). On the accumulation of fertility by land allowed to run wild. *Journal of Agricultural Science*, **1**, 241–9.

Hall, M. L. (1987). *Butterfly Monitoring Scheme: instructions for independent recorders*. Institute of Terrestrial Ecology, Cambridge.

Hansen, H. O. (ed.) (1996). *River restoration—Danish experience and examples*. National Environmental Research Institute, Denmark.

Haslam, S. M. (1992). *River pollution: an ecological perspective*. Bellhaven Press, London.

Hawke, C. and José, P. (1996). *Reedbed management for commercial and wildlife interests*. Royal Society for the Protection of Birds, Sandy, Bedfordshire.

Hawke, C. and Wilson, K. (1994). Designing for natterjacks. *Enact*, **4(2)**, 19–22.

Haycock, N. E. and Burt, T. P. (1993). Bole of floodplain sediments in reducing the nitrate concentrations of subsurface runoff: a case study in the Cotswolds, UK. *Hydrological Processes*, **7**, 287–95.

Haycock, N. E. and Worrall, P. (1996). Constructed wetlands—can they cope? *Enact*, **4(3)**, 17–20.

Hearn, K. (1994). The 'Natural Aspect' of the National Trust. *British Wildlife*, **5**, 367–78.

Heathland Countryside Management Project (1995). *Annual report April 1994 to March 1995*. Heathland Countryside Management Project, Godalming.

Heathwaite, A. L., Eggelsmann, R. and Göttlich, K. H. (1993). Ecohydrology, mire drainage and mire conservation. In *Mires: Process, exploitations conservation*, (ed. A. L. Heathwaite and K. H. Göttlich), pp. 417–84. John Wiley, Chichester.

Helliwell, D. R. (1996). *Case studies in vegetation change, habitat transference and habitat creation*. Reading Agricultural Consultants, Reading.

Hibberd, B. G. (1988). *Farm woodland practice*. Forestry Commission Handbook No. 3, HMSO, London.

Hibberd, B. G. (1989). *Urban forestry practice*. Forestry Commission Handbook No. 5, HMSO, London.

Highways Agency (1993). The wildflower handbook. In *Design manual for roads and bridges 10(1)*. Department of Transport, Scottish Office Industry Department, The Welsh Office & Department of the Environment for N. Ireland.

Hiley, P. (1995). The reality of sewage treatment using wetlands. *Water Science and Technology*, **32**, 329–38.

Hodge, S. J. (1995). *Creating and managing woodland around towns*. Forestry Commission Handbook No. 11, HMSO, London.

Hodge, S. J. and Harmer, R. (1995). The creation of woodland habitats in urban and post-industrial environments. *Land Contamination and Reclamation*, **3**, 86–8.

Hodgson, J. G. (1982). The botanical interest and value of quarries. In *Ecology of quarries*, (ed. B. N. K. Davis), pp. 3–11, Institute of Terrestrial Ecology, Cambridge.

Holder, C. L. and Burd, F. (1990). *Overview of saltmarsh restoration sites in Essex*. Contract Surveys No. 83, Nature Conservancy Council, Peterborough.

Hopkins, J. J. (1989). Prospects for habitat creation. *Landscape Design*, **179**, 19–22.

Hopkins, J. J. (1996). Scrub ecology and conservation. *British Wildlife*, **8**, 28–36.

Hubbard, J. C. E. (1984). *Grasses: A guide to their structure, identification, uses and distribution in the British Isles*, (3rd edn). Penguin Books, Middlesex.

Hughes, J. and Heathwaite, L. (1995). *Hydrology and hydrochemistry of British wetlands*. John Wiley, Chichester.

Hull, A. P., Boothby, J., Jeffreys, D. A. and Small, R. W. (1992). *Farm ponds in North West England: A disappearing wetland resource*. Paper presented to the Columbus 1992 Wetlands Conference, Ohio State University, Columbus, USA.

Humphries, R. N. (1982). The establishment of vegetation on quarry materials: physical and chemical restraints. In *Ecology of quarries*, (ed. B. N. K. Davis), pp. 55–61. Institute of Terrestrial Ecolcogy, Cambridge.

Hupp, C. R., Woodside, M. D. and Yanosky, T. M. (1993). Sediment and trace element trapping in a forested wetland, Chickahominy River, Virginia. *Wetlands*, **13**, 95–104.

Insley, H. (1988). *Farm woodland planning*. Forestry Commission Bulletin No. 80, HMSO, London.

Insley, H. and Buckley, G. P. (1986). Causes and prevention of establishment failure in amenity trees. In *Ecology and design in the landscape*, (ed. A. D. Bradshaw, D. A. Goode and E. H. P. Thorpe), pp. 127–41. Blackwell, London.

Janzen, D. H. (1970). Herbivores and the number of tree species in tropical forests. *American Naturalist*, **104**, 501–28.

Jarvis, M. S. (1960). *The influence of climatic factors on the distribution of some Derbyshire plants*. PhD Thesis, University of Sheffield.

Joint Nature Conservation Committee (1996a). *Birds of conservation concern*. Press Release, 31/5/96. JNCC.

Joint Nature Conservation Committee (1996b). *Guidelines for selection of biological SSSIs: intertidal marine habitats and saline lagoons*. JNCC, Peterborough.

Jones, A. T. and Evans, P. R. (1994). A comparison of the growth and morphology of native and commercially obtained continental European *Crataegus monogyna* Jacq. (Hawthorn) at an upland site. *Watsonia*, **20**, 97–103.

Jones, D. and Haggar, R. J. (1994). Field margins as sources of wildflower propagules in grassland extensification for diversity. In *Grassland management and nature conservation*, (ed. R. J. Haggar and S. Peel). BGS Occasional Symposium No. 28.

Jones, G. H. (1990). Learning from experience. *Landscape Design*, **193**, 40–4.

Jones, G. H., Trueman, I. C. and Millett, P. (1995). The use of hay strewing to create species-rich grasslands. (1) General principles and hay strewing versus seed mixes. *Land Contamination and Reclamation*, **3**, 104–7.

Jordan, W. R. III and Packard, S. (1989). Just a few oddball species: restoration practice and ecological theory. In *Biological habitat reconstruction*, (ed. G. P. Buckley), pp. 18–26. Belhaven Press, London.

Jordan, W. R. III, Gilpin, M. E. and Aber, J. D. (1987a). Restoration ecology: ecological restoration as a technique for basic research. In *Restoration ecology*, (ed. W. R. Jordan, M. E. Gilpin and J. D. Aber), pp. 1–21. Cambridge University Press, Cambridge.

Jordan, W. R. III, Gilpin, M. E. and Aber, J. D. (1987b). *Restoration ecology*. Cambridge University Press, Cambridge.

Kadlec, R. H. and Knight, R. L. (1996). *Treatment wetlands*. Lewis Publishers.

Kennedy, C. E. J. and Southwood, T. R. E. (1984). The number of species of insects associated with British trees: a re-analysis. *Journal of Animal Ecology*, **53**, 455–78.

Kerslake, L. J. and Fraser, A. (1995). The role of ecologists in derelict land reclamation—case studies from Nottinghamshire. *Land Contamination and Reclamation*, **3**, 130–1.

Kirby, P. (1992). *Habitat management for invertebrates: a practical handbook*. Joint Nature Conservation Committee, Peterborough.

Knopf, F. L., Johnson, R. R. and Rich, T. (1988). Conservation of riparian ecosystems in the United States. *Wilson Bulletin*, **100**, 272–84.

Kusler, J. A. and Kentula, M. E. (eds.) (1990). *Wetland creation and restoration—The status of the science*. Island Press, Washington DC.

Lack, P. C. (1988). Hedge intersections and breeding bird distribution in farmland. *Bird Study*, **35**, 133–6.

Land Use Consultants and Wardell Armstrong (1996). *Reclamation of damaged land for nature conservation*. HMSO, London.

Lawes, J. B. (1884). In the sweat of thy face shalt thou eat bread. *Country Gentleman*, 18 September.

Lawes, J. B. (1895). Upon some properties of soils. *Agricultural Studies Gazette*, **7**, 65–72.

Lines, R. (1987). *Choice of seed origins for the main forest species in Britain.* Forestry Commission Bulletin No. 66, HMSO, London.

Lloyd, P. S., Grime, J. P. and Rorison, I. H. (1971). The grassland vegetation of the Sheffield region. 1. General features. *Journal of Ecology*, **59**, 863–86.

Longton, R. E. (1966). Alien vascular plants on Deception Island, South Shetland Islands. *British Antarctic Survey Bulletin*, **9**, 55–60.

Lott, D. and Daws, J. (1995). The conservation value of urban demolition sites in Leicester for beetles. *Land Contamination and Reclamation*, **3**, 79–81.

Lunn, J. and Wild, M. (1995). The wildlife interest of abandoned collieries and spoil heaps in Yorkshire. *Land Contamination and Reclamation*, **3**, 135–7.

Luscombe, G. and Scott, R. (1994). *Wildflowers work—a technical guide to creating and maintaining wildflower landscapes.* Landlife, Liverpool.

Mabey, R. (1996). The native black poplar: a species in the ghetto? *British Wildlife*, **8**, 1–6.

MacDonald, A. W. (1992). Succession in a three year old flood-meadow near Oxford. In *Vegetation management in forestry amenity and conservation areas. Aspects of Applied Biology*, **29**, 345–52.

MacDonald, A. W. (1994). The role of aftermath grazing in a flood-meadow community. In *Grassland management and nature conservation*, (ed. R. J. Haggar and S. Peel), pp. 308–9. British Grassland Society Occasional Symposium No. 28.

McLean, M. (1992). *New hedges for the countryside.* Farming Press Books, Ipswich.

MAFF (1993). *Code of good agricultural practice for the protection of soil.* Ministry of Agriculture, Fisheries and Food, Welsh Office, Agriculture Department, MAFF publications.

Marrs, R. H. (1985). Techniques for reducing soil fertility for nature conservation purposes: a review in relation to research at Ropers Heath, Suffolk, England. *Biological Conservation*, **34**, 307–32.

Marrs, R. H. (1993). Soil fertility and nature conservation in Europe: Theoretical considerations and practical management solutions. *Advances in Ecological Research*, **24**, 241–300.

Marrs, R. H., Roberts, R. D., Skeffington, R. A. and Bradshaw, A. D. (1983). *Nitrogen and the development of ecosystems.* In 22nd Symposium of The British Ecological Society, (ed. J. A. Lee, S. McNeill and I. H. Rorison), pp. 113–36. Blackwell, Oxford.

Marshall, E. J. P. (1989). Distribution patterns of plants associated with arable field edges. *Journal of Applied Ecology*, **26**, 247–58.

Mason, C. F. (1991). *Biology of freshwater pollution.* Longman, London.

McClanahan, T. R. and Wolfe, R. W. (1993). Accelerating forest succession in a fragmented landscape: the role of birds and perches. *Conservation Biology*, **7**, 279–88.

McDonnell, M. J. and Stiles, E. W. (1983). The structural complexity of old field vegetation and the recruitment of bird dispersed plant species. *Oecologia*, **56**, 109–16.

Mellanby, K. (1968). The effect of some mammals and birds on regeneration of oak. *Journal of Applied Ecology*, **5**, 359–66.

Merritt, A. (1994). The wildlife value and potential of wetlands on industrial land. In *Wetland management. Proceedings of the international conference organized by the institution of civil engineers and held in London on 2–3 June 1994*, (ed. R. A. Falconer and P. Goodwin), pp. 226–31. Thomas Telford, London.

Miles, J. (1973). Natural recolonisation of experimentally bared soil in Callunetum in North East Scotland. *Journal of Ecology*, **61**, 399–412.

Miles, J. (1979). *Vegetation dynamics*. Chapman & Hall, London.

Miller, G. R. and Bayfield, N. G. (1989). *Seed banks of organic soils at the Three Peaks*. ITE Report No. 5 to the Yorkshire Dales National Park, Institute of Terrestrial Ecology, Banchory.

Miller, G. R., Bayfield, N. G., Paterson, I. S. and McGowan, G. M. (1991). *Restoration of natural vegetation on organic soils from buried viable seeds*. ITE Report No. 10 to the Yorkshire Dales National Park, Institute of Terrestrial Ecology, Banchory.

Mills, J., Box, J. and Coppin, N. (1995). Natural legacies. *Landscape Design*, **238**, 23–5.

Moore, N. W. and Hooper, M. D. (1975). On the number of bird species in British woods. *Biological Conservation*, **8**, 239–50.

Morris, M. G. (1990*a*). The hemiptera of two sown calcareous grasslands. 1. Colonization and early succession. *Journal of Applied Ecology*, **27**, 367–78.

Morris, M. G. (1990*b*). The hemiptera of two sown calcareous grasslands. 2. Differences between treatments. *Journal of Applied Ecology*, **27**, 379–93.

Morris, M. G. (1990*c*). The hemiptera of two sown calcareous grasslands. 3. Comparisons with the Auchenorhyncha faunas of other grasslands. *Journal of Applied Ecology*, **27**, 394–409.

Moss, B., Madgewick, J. and Phillips, G. (1996). *A guide to the restoration of nutrient-enriched shallow lakes*. W. W. Hawes, Suffolk.

Munch, E. and Dieterich, J. (1925). Kalkeschen und wassereschen. *Forstlliche Wochenschrift Silva*, **13**, 129–35.

National Heathland Conference (1996). *Conference Proceedings 18th–20th September 1996*, Forestry Commission, Hampshire.

National Rivers Authority (1993). *NRA R&D Strategy*. National Rivers Authority Head Office, Bristol.

Nature Conservancy Council (1984). *Nature conservation in Great Britain*. Nature Conservancy Council, Peterborough.

Nicholson, B. and Hare, A. (1986). The management of urban woodland. *Ecos*, **7**, 38–43.

Nielsen, B. (1995). Restoration of streams and their riparian zones—South Jutland, Denmark. In *Restoration of stream ecosystems—an intergrated catchment approach*. IWRB Publication 37. (ed. M. Eiseltová and J. Biggs), pp. 30–44. International Waterfowl and Wetlands Research Bureau, Slimbridge, Gloucestershire.

Nielsen, M. B. (1996). Lowland stream restoration in Denmark. In *River channel restoration: principles for sustainable projects*. (ed. A. Brookes and F. D. Shields Jr), pp. 129–289. John Wiley, Chichester.

Nolan, A. J., Hulme, P. D. and Wheeler, D (Undated). The status of *Calluna Vulgaris* (L.) Hull on Fair Isle. *Botanical Journal of Scotland*, **47**, 1–16.

North York Moors National Park (1986). *Moorland management*. North York Moors National Park, Helmsley.

North York Moors National Park (1991). *Moorland management programme 1985–1990*. North York Moors National Park, Helmsley.

North York Moors National Park (Undated). *Moorland research 1977–79*. North York Moors National Park, Helmsley.

OECD (1982). *Eutrophication of waters. Monitoring, assessment and control.* Organisation for Economic Co-operation and Development, Paris.

Oldham, R. S. (1994). Habitat assessment and population ecology. In *Conservation and management of great crested newts*. Proceedings of a symposium held on 11th January 1994 at Kew Gardens, Surrey. English Nature Science Report No. 20. English Nature, Peterborough.

Oldham, R. S. and Nicholson, M. (1986). *Status and ecology of the warty newt* Triturus cristatus. CSD Report No. 72. Report by Leicester Polytechnic to Nature Conservancy Council, Peterborough.

Opdam, P. (1993). Population responses to landscape fragmentation. In *Landscape ecology of a stressed environment* (ed. C. C. Vos and P. Opdam), pp. 147–71. Chapman & Hall, London.

Owen, K. M., Marrs, R. H. and Snow, C. S. R. (1996). Soil acidification and heathland establishment on former arable land. *Aspects of Applied Biology*, **44**, 385–92.

Park, D. G. (1982). Seedling demography in quarry habitats. In *Ecology of quarries*, (ed. B. N. K. Davis), pp. 32–40. Institute of Terrestrial Ecology, Cambridge.

Parker, D. M. (1995). *Habitat creation—a critical guide*. English Nature Series No. 21, English Nature, Peterborough.

Parker, D. M. and McNeilly, T. (1991). Re-creation of dry *Calluna* heathland within a nationally important heathland/mire complex. In *Terrestrial and aquatic ecosystems: perturbation and recovery*, (ed. O. Ravera) pp. 434–43. Ellis Horwood, Chichester.

Peel, S., Swash, G. and McKenzie, S. (1994). Seed mixtures for chalk downland. In *Grassland management and nature conservation*, (ed. R. J. Haggar and S. Peel), pp. 310–2. British Grassland Society Occasional Symposium No. 28.

Penny Anderson Associates (1993). *Entomological survey of the M42/M6 motorways intersection*. Unpublished, Highways Agency.

Peterborough Environment City Trust (1995). *The Peterborough natural environmental audit: consultation document*. Peterborough Environment City Trust, Peterborough.

Peterjohn, W. T. and Correll, D. L. (1984). Nutrient dynamics in an agricultural watershed: observations on the role of a riparian forest. *Ecology*, **65**, 1466–75.

Peterken, G. F. (1981). *Woodland conservation and management*. Chapman & Hall, London.

Peterken, G. F. (1995). An overview of native woodland creation. In *The ecology of woodland creation*, (ed. R. Ferris-Kaan), pp. ix–xviii. Wiley, Chichester.

Peterken, G. F. and Game, M. (1984). Historical factors affecting the number and distribution of vascular plant species in woodlands of central Lincolnshire. *Journal of Ecology*, **72**, 155–82.

Peterken, G. F. and Hughs, F. M. R. (1995). Restoration of floodplain forests in Britain. *Forestry*, **68**, 187–99.

Petts, G. E. and Amoros, C. (ed.) (1996). *Fluvial hydrosystems*. Chapman & Hall, London.

Phillips, J. (1990). The problems of 'white' moorland. In *Sixth Annual Report. Joseph Nickerson Reconciliation Project, May 1990*. pp. 40–2.

Phillips, J., Tallis, J. and Yalden, D. (1981). *Peak District moorland erosion study: phase 1 report*. Peak Park Joint Planning Board, Bakewell.

Piggott, C. D. (1974). The response of plants to climate and climatic change. In *The flora of a changing Britain*, (ed. F. Perring), pp. 32–44. E. W. Casey, Farringdon, Berks.

Pollard, E., Hooper, M. D. and Moore, N. W. (1974). *Hedges*. Collins, London.

Porter, K. (1994). Seed harvesting—a hay meadow dilemma. *Enact*, **2 (1)**, 4–5.

Porter, M. (1990). *Pennine Way management project. Final Report*. Peak National Park/Countryside Commission.

Potter, M. J. (1991). *Tree shelters*. Forestry Commission Handbook No. 7, HMSO, London.

Powell, K. A. (1992). Engineering with conservation issues in mind. In *Coastal zone planning and management*, pp. 237–49. Thomas Telford, London.

Putwain, P. D. (1992). The creation of heathland vegetation: theory and practice. *Aspects of Applied Biology*, **29**, 33–40.

Putwain, P. D. and Gillham, D. A. (1988). Restoration of heather moorland. *Landscape Design*, **172**, 51–56.

Putwain, P. D. and Gillham, D. A. (1990). The significance of the dormant viable seed bank in the restoration of heathlands. *Biological Conservation*, **52**, 1–16.

Pye, K. and French, P. W. (1993). *Targets for coastal habitat re-creation*. English Nature Science No. 13, English Nature, Peterborough.

Pywell, R. F., Webb, N. R. and Putwain, P. D. (1994). Soil fertility and its implications for the restoration of heathland on farmland in southern Britain. *Biological Conservation*, **70**, 169–81.

Pywell, R. F., Webb, N. R. and Putwain, P. D. (1995). A comparison of techniques for restoring heathland on abandoned farmland. *Journal of Applied Ecology*, **32**, 400–11.

Rackham, O. (1986). *The history of the countryside*. J. M. Dent & Sons, London.

Rackham, O. (1991). Landscape and the conservation of meaning. Reflection Riding Memorial Lecture. *Royal Society of Arts Journal*, **139**, 903–15.

Radley, G. P. (1994). *Sand dune suvey of Great Britain: a national inventory. Part 1: England*. English Nature, Peterborough.

Ratcliffe, D. A. (1974). Ecological effects of mineral exploitation in the United Kingdom and their significance to nature conservation. *Proceedings of the Royal Society London Series A*, **339**, 355–72.

Ratcliffe, D. A. (1977). *A nature conservation review*. Cambridge University Press, Cambridge.

Raw, K. and Pilkington, G. (1988). Bringing back the natterjack toad. In *RSPB Conservation Review 2*, (ed. J. C. Cadbury and M. Everett), pp. 81–4. Royal Society for Protection of Birds, Sandy, Bedfordshire.

Rawes, M. (1981). Aspects of the ecology of the North Pennines. Occasional Papers No. 12, Moor House.

Rees, S. (1992). Moorland restoration and reinstatement in the North York Moors. In *Proceedings of the seminar on heathland habitat creation*, (ed. A Free and M. T. Kitson), pp. 61–5. Suffolk Wildlife Trust, Ipswich.

Reid, C. (1996). Breach gives birth to bird bonanza. *Enact*, **2 (5)**, 10–11.

Richards, J. R. A., Wheeler, B. D. and Willis, A. J. (1995). The growth and value of *Eriophorum angustifolium* Honck. in relation to the revegetation of eroding blanket peat. In *Restoration of temperate wetlands*, (ed. B. D. Wheeler, S. C. Shear, W. J. Fojt and R. A. Robertson). J. Wiley, Chichester.

Ritchie, J. C. (1956). Biological Flora of the British Isles: *Vaccinium myrtillus* L. *Journal of Ecology*, **11**, 291–9.

Robertson, R. A. and Davies, G. E. (1965). Quantities of plant nutrients in heather ecosystems. *Journal of Applied Ecology*, **2**, 211–19.

Robinson, G. R. and Handel, S. N. (1993). Forest restoration on a closed landfill: rapid addition of new species by bird dispersal. *Conservation Biology*, **7**, 271–8.

Rodwell, J. S. (ed.) (1991*a*). *British plant communities, vol. 1: Woodlands and scrub*. Cambridge University Press, Cambridge.

Rodwell, J. S. (ed.) (1991*b*). *British plant communities, vol. 2: Mires and heaths*. Cambridge University Press, Cambridge.

Rodwell, J. S. (ed.) (1992). *British plant communities, vol. 3: Grasslands and montane communities*. Cambridge University Press, Cambridge.

Rodwell, J. S. (ed.) (in press). *British plant communities, vol. 5: Maritime and weed communities*. Cambridge University Press, Cambridge.

Rodwell, J. and Patterson, G. (1994). *Creating new native woodlands*. Forestry Commission Bulletin 112, HMSO, London.

Rogers-Martinez, D. (1992). The Sinkyone intertribal park project. *Restoration and Management Notes*, **10 (summer)**, 64–9.

Ross, S. M. (1995). Overview of the hydrochemistry and solute processes in British wetlands. In *Hydrology and hydrochemistry of British wetlands*, (ed. J. M. R. Hughes and A. L. Heathwaite), pp. 133–81. John Wiley, Chichester.

Rowlands, I. (1997). *Engineering the creation of wildlife habitats in the River Alt and Maghull Brook*. CIWEM & Coastal Group/Environment Group Winter Meeting, London, 31 January 1997.

Russell, M. A. and Maltby, E. (1995). The role of hydrologic regime on phosphorus dynamics in a seasonally waterlogged soil. In *Hydrology and hydrochemistry of British wetlands*, (ed. J. M. R. Hughes and A. L. Heathwaite), pp. 245–60. John Wiley, Chichester.

Salter, B. R. and Darke, R. F. (1988). Use of herbicides in the establishment of amenity plantings in Milton Keynes. *Aspects of Applied Biology*, **16**, 347–50.

Schlott, G. (1995). Case studies from Central and Eastern Europe. In *Restoration of stream ecosystems—an integrated catchment approach*. IWRB Publication 37, (ed. M. Eiseltová and J. Biggs), pp. 113–25. International Waterfowl and Wetlands Research Bureau, Slimbridge, Gloucestershire.

Scott, R. (1995). A case for creative conservation. In *Land contamination and reclamation special issue*, pp. 84–5. Proceedings of the British Ecologial Society Conference: Recent Advances in Urban Ecology.

Scullion, J. (1994). *Restoring farmland after coal: The Bryngwyn project*. British Coal Opencast, University of Wales, Aberystwyth.

Self, M., O'Brien, M. and Hirons, G. (1994). Hydrological management for waterfowl on RSPB lowland wet grassland reserves. In *RSPB Conservation Review 8*, (ed. J. C. Cadbury), pp. 45–56. Royal Society for the Protection of Birds, Sandy, Bedfordshire.

Semple, D., Bishop, C. and Morris, J. (1995). *The economics of sustainable hedge cutting*. Silsoe College, Bedfordshire.

Shaw, P. (1994). Orchid woods and floating islands—the ecology of fly ash. *British Wildlife*, **5**, 149–57.

Sheffield Development Corporation (1994). *Landscape and nature conservation strategy for the Lower Don Valley*. Sheffield Development Corporation, Sheffield.

Skaller, P. (1977). *Plant colonisation and soil development in the Jamesville Quarry*. PhD thesis, State University, Syracuse, New York.

Smith, A. (1986). *Endangered species of disturbed habitats*. Nature Conservancy Council, Peterborough.

Smith, K. W. (1983). The status and distribution of waders breeding on wet grasslands in England and Wales. *Bird Study*, **30**, 177–92.

Smith, B. P. and Laffoley, D. (1992). *Saline lagoons and lagoon-like habitats0*. Draft Report, Marine Section, English Nature, Peterborough.

Smith, R. S. and Rushton, S. P. (1994). The effects of grazing management on mesotrophic (meadow) grassland in Northern England. *Journal of Applied Ecology*, **31**, 13–24.

Smith, R. E. N., Webb, N. R. and Clarke, R. T. (1991). The Establishment of Heathland on old Fields in Dorset, England. *Biological Conservation*, **57**, 221–34.

Soutar, R. G. and Peterken, G. F. (1989). Regional lists of native trees and shrubs for use in afforestation schemes. *Arboricultural Journal*, **13**, 33–43.

Spellerberg, I. F. (1995). Biogeography and woodland design. In *The ecology of woodland creation*, (ed. R. Ferris-Kaan), pp. 49–62. Wiley, Chichister.

Stevens, F. R. W., Thompson, D. A. and Gosling, P. G. (1990). *Research experience in direct sowing for lowland plantation establishment*. Forestry Commission Research Information Note 184, Forestry Commission, Edinburgh.

Stevenson, M. J., Bullock, J. M. and Ward, L. K. (1995). Recreating semi-natural communities: Effect of sowing rate on establishment of calcareous grassland. *Restoration Ecology*, **3**, 279–89.

Stoate, C. (1996). The changing face of lowland farming and wildlife. Part 2. 1945–1995. *British Wildlife*, **7**, 162–72.

Stromberg, M. R. and Kephart, P. (1996). Restoring native grasslands in California old fields. *Restoration Management Notes*, **14**, 102–11.

Street, M. (1984). *The restoration of gravel pits for wildfowl*. ARC, Chipping Sodbury.

Street, M. (1989). *Ponds and lakes for wildfowl*. The Game Conservancy, Fordingbridge.

Street, M. and Mond, J. R. (1992). Management practices for urban woodlands in Milton Keynes. *Aspects of Applied Biology*, **29**, 389–94.

Sutherland, W. J. and Gibson, C. (1988). Habitats to order. *New Scientist*, **1597**, 70.

Sutherland, W. J. and Hill, D. A. (ed.) (1995). *Managing habitats for conservation*. Cambridge University Press: Cambridge.

Tallis, J. H. and Yalden, D. W. (1983). *Peak District moorland restoration project, Phase 2 Report: Re-vegetation trials*. Peak Park Joint Planning Board, Bakewell.

Taylor, N. W. (1985). *The sycamore in Britain—its natural history and value to wildlife*. Discussion Papers in Nature Conservation 42, University College, London.

Thompson, D. B. A., Galbraith, H. and Horsfield, D. (1987). Ecology and resources of Britains mountain plateaux: land use conflicts and impacts. In *Agriculture and conservation in the hills and uplands*, (ed. M. Bell and R. G. H. Bunce), pp. 22–31. Institute of Terrestrial Ecology Symposium No. 23, ITE, Grange-over-Sands.

Thurston, J. M. (1958). Geescroft wilderness. *Report of Rothamsted Experimental Station for 1957*, pp. 94.

Tilman, D., Dodd, M. E., Silvertown, J., Poulton, P. R., Johnston, A. E. and Crawley, M. J. (1994). The Park Grass experiment: insights from the most long-term ecological study. In *Long-term experiments in agricultural and ecological sciences*. CAB International.

Tregay, R. (1985). A sense of nature. *Landscape Design*, **156**, 34–8.

Trueman, I. C., Millett, P., Jones, G. H. and Besenyei, L. (1991). *Factors controling vegetational change in habitat creation Schemes*. BES Conference, Nottinghamshire.

Tubbs, C. R. (1995). Sea level change and estuaries. *British Wildlife*, **6**, 168–76.

Turner, K. M. and Dagley, J. (1993). What price sea walls? *Enact*, **1**, 8–9.

Tutton, T. (1994). Goats versus holm oak. *Enact*, **2**, 8–9.

Tyler, G. (1994). Management of reedbeds for bitterns and opportunities for reedbed creation. In *RSPB conservation review 8*, (ed. J. C. Cadbury), pp. 57–62. Royal Society for the Protection of Birds, Sandy, Bedfordshire.

UK Biodiversity Steering Group (1995). *Volume 1: Meeting the Rio challenge*. HMSO, London.

Van Bohemen, H. D. and Meesters, H. J. N. (1992). Ecological engineering and coastal defence. In *Coastal dunes*, (ed. R. W. G. Carter, T. G. F. Curtis and M. J. Sheehy-Skeffington), pp. 369–78. Balkema, Rotterdam.

Vestergaard, P. and Hansen, K. (1992). Changes in morphology and vegetation of a man-made beach-dune system by natural processes. In *Coastal dunes*, (ed. R. W. G. Carter, T. G. F. Curtis and M. J. Sheehy-Skeffington), pp. 165–76. Balkema, Rotterdam.

Vickery, J. A., Sutherland, W. J. and Lane, S. J. (1994). The management of grass pastures for brent geese. *Journal of Applied Ecology*, **31**, 282–90.

Vos, C. C. and Opdam, P. (ed.) (1993). *Landscape ecology of a stressed environment*. Chapman & Hall, London.

Wagret, P. (1968). *Polderlands*. Methuen, London.

Walmsley, C. A. (1994). *Sizewell 'B' Power Station vegetation restoration project*. Unpublished report to Nuclear Electric plc.

Walmsley, C. A. and Davy, A. J. (1997a). Germination characteristics of shingle-beach species, effects of seed aging and their implications for vegetation restoration. *Journal of Applied Ecology*, **34**, 131–42.

Walmsley, C. A. and Davy, A. J. (1997b). The restoration of coastal shingle vegetation: effects of substrate composition on the establishment of seedlings. *Journal of Applied Ecology*, **34**, 143–53.

Walmsley, C. A. and Davy, A. J. (1997c). The restoration of coastal shingle vegetation: effects of substrate composition on the establishment of container-grown plants. *Journal of Applied Ecology*, **34**, 154–65.

Waloff, N. (1968). Studies on the insect fauna of scotch broom. *Advances in Ecological Research*, **5**, 87–208.

Ward, D., Holmes, N. and José, P. (ed.) (1994). *The new rivers and wildlife handbook*. Royal Society for the Protection of Birds, Sandy, Bedfordshire.

Waring, P. (1990). Observations on invertebrates collected up during wildflower seed harvesting in a hay meadow with particular reference to the butterflies and moths. *British Journal of Entomology and Natural History*, **3**, 143–52.

Warren, M. S. and Stephens, D. E. A. (1989). Habitat design and management for butterflies. *The Entomologist*, **108**, 123–34.

Warren, M. S. and Fuller, R. J. (1993). *Woodland rides and glades: Their management for wildlife*. (2nd edn) Joint Nature Conservancy Committee, Peterborough.

Wathern, P. (1976). *The ecology of development sites*. PhD thesis, Sheffield University.

Wathern, P. and Gilbert, O. L. (1979). The production of grassland on subsoil. *Journal of Environmental Management*, **8**, 269–75.

Watkinson, A. R. (1986). Plant population dynamics. In *Plant ecology*, (ed. M. J. Crawley). Blackwell, Oxford.

Watson, A. (1984). Paths and people in the Cairngorms. *Scottish Geographical Magazine*, **100**, 151–60.

Watt, T. A. and Buckley, G. P. (1994). *Hedgerow management and nature conservation*. Wye College Press, Ashford.

Webb, N. R. (1990). Changes in the heathlands of Dorset, England, between 1978 and 1987. *Biological Conservation*, **51**, 273–86.

Webb, N. R. (1994). The habitat, the biotope and the landscape. In *Proceedings of the third annual IALE (UK) conference, held at Myerscough College, Preston, 13–14th September 1994*. IALE (UK).

Webb, N. R. and Hopkins, P. J. (1984). Invertebrate diversity on fragmented *Calluna* heathland. *Journal of Applied Ecology*, **21**, 921–33.

Welch, G. and Wright, M. (1996). Arable to heath: a progress report. *Enact*, **4 (2)**, 10–11. English Nature, Peterborough.

Wells, T. C. E. (1984). An ecologists view of floristic possibilities—a scene setting review. In *Creating attractive grasslands. Workshop report No. 5*. pp. 8–19. The National Turfgrass Council, Bingley, West Yorkshire.

Wells, T. C. E. (1987). Establishing chalk grassland on previously arable land using seed mixtures. In *Calcareous grasslands—ecology and management*, (ed. S. H. Hillier, D. W. H. Walton and D. A. Wells), pp. 169–70. Proceedings of a joint British Ecological Society/Nature Conservancy Council symposium. Bluntisham Books, Bluntisham, Huntingdon.

Wells, T. C. E. (1990). Establishing chalk grassland on previously arable land using seed mixtures. In *Calcareous grasslands—ecology and management*, (ed. S. H. Hillier, D. W. H. Walton and D. A. Wells), pp. 169–70. Bluntisham Books, Huntingdon.

Wells, T. C. E. (1991). Restoring and re-creating species-rich lowland dry grassland. In *The conservation of lowland and dry grassland birds in Europe*, (ed. P. D. Goriup, L. A. Batten and J. A. Norton), pp. 125–32. JNCC, Peterborough.

Wells, T. C. E., Bell, S. and Frost, A. (1981). *Creating attractive grasslands using native plant species*. Nature Conservancy Council, Peterborough.

Wells, T. C. E., Bell, S. and Frost, A. (1986). *Wild flower grasslands from crop-grown seed and hay bales*. Nature Conservancy Council, Peterborough.

Wells, T. C. E., Cox R. and Frost, R. (1989). *The establishment and management of wildflower meadows*. Nature Conservancy Council, Peterborough.

Wheater, C. P. and Cullen, W. R. (1997). The flora and invertebrate fauna of abandoned limestone quarries in Derbyshire, United Kingdom. *Restoration Ecology*, **5**, 1–9.

Whitbread, A. and Jenman, W. (1995). A natural method of conserving biodiversity in Britain. *British Wildlife*, **7**, 84–93.

Williams, C. M., Ford, M. A. and Lawson, C. S. (1996). The transformation of surplus farmland into semi-natural habitat. II. On the conversion of arable land to heathland. In Vegetation management in forestry, amenity and conservation areas: managing for multiple objectives. *Aspects of Applied Biology*, **44**, 185–92.

Williams, G. and Bowers, J. K. (1987). Land drainage and birds in England and Wales. In *RSPB Conservation Review 1*, (ed. J. C. Cadbury and M. Everett), pp. 25–30. Royal Society for the Protection of Birds, Sandy, Bedfordshire.

Williams, P., Biggs, J., Corfield, A., Fox, G., Walker, D. and Whitfield, M. (1997). Designing new ponds for wildlife. *British Wildlife*, **8**, 137–50.

Williamson, D. R. (1992). *Establishing farm woodlands*. Forestry Commission Handbook No. 8, HMSO, London.

Williamson, K. (1967). Some aspects of the scientific interest and management of scrub in nature reserves. In *The biotic effects of public pressure on the environment*, (ed. E. Duffey), pp. 94–100. Monks Wood Experimental Station Symposium No. 3, The Nature Conservancy, Council, Monks Wood.

Wilson, J., Evans, A., Grynderup-Poulsen, J. and Evans, J. (1995). Wasteland or oasis? The use of set-aside by breeding and wintering birds. *British Wildlife*, **6**, 214–23.

Wilson, M. (1997). Win/win in Barnes. *Urban Wildlife News*, **13 (1)**, 3.

Wilson, P. J. (1989). The distribution of arable weed seed banks and the implications for conservation of endangered species and communities. *Brighton Crop Protection Conference—Weeds*, pp. 1081–6.

Wilson, P. J. (1992). Britain's arable weeds. *British Wildlife*, **3**, 149–61.

Witts, K. J. (1964). Broadbalk wilderness: flora. *Report of Rothamsted Experimental Station for 1964*, pp. 219–22.

Woodrow, W., Symes, N. and Auld, M. (1996). *RSPB Dorset heathland project 1989–1995: A management case study*. Royal Society for the Protection of Birds, Sandy, Bedfordshire.

Worrall, P., Peberdy, K. J. and Millett, M. C. (1996). Constructed wetlands and nature conservation. *5th International Conference on Wetland Systems for Water Pollution Control, Vienna 1996*.

Worrell, R. (1992). A comparison between European continental and British provenances of some British native trees: growth, survival and stem form. *Forestry*, **65**, 253–80.

Yorkshire Dales National Park (1993). *Three Peaks Project*. Yorkshire Dales National Park, Grassington, North Yorkshire.

Younkin, W. E. (1972). Revegetation studies of disturbance in the Mackenzie Delta Region. In *Botanical studies of natural and man-modified habitats in the eastern Mackenzie Delta Region and the arctic islands*. (eds L. C. Bliss and R. W. Wein). pp. 175–229. ALUR 1971–72. Department of Indian Affairs and Northern Development, Ottawa, Canada.

Younkin, W. E. (ed.) (1976). Revegetation studies in the northern Mackenzie Valley region. *Arctic Gas Biological Report Series*, **38**, 1–122.

Younkin, W. E. and Martens, H. E. (1987). Long-term success of seeded species and their influence on native species invasion at an abandoned rig site A-01 Caribou Hills, N.W.T., Canada. *Arctic and Alpine Research*, **19**, 566–71.

Zedler, J. B. and Weller, M. W. (1990). Overview and future directions. In *Wetland creation and restoration—The status of the science*, (ed. J. A. Kusler and M. E. Kentula), pp. 405–13. Island Press, Washington DC.

Glossary

ADAS Agricultural Development and Advisory Service.

Arisings Cut material.

Bentonite An aluminium silicate clay with the ability to swell and become impermeable on contact with water. Used as a liner to ponds.

Bio-accumulation The long-term accumulation of pollutants within living tissues.

Biogeochemical processes Biological or chemical processes operating in the soil.

BTCV British Trust for Conservation Volunteers. A group of (mainly) volunteers who carry out conservation tasks as a hobby.

Buffer zone A vegetated zone established, usually adjacent to a high-quality habitat, that has the ability to trap nutrients.

C horizon In soils, a mineral horizon generally unaffected by biological activity.

CSS Countryside Stewardship Scheme. Scheme in England covering landscape, archaeological, and nature conservation enhancement funded by MAFF.

Dune slack A flat-bottomed hollow within a sand-dune system that is close to the permanent water table and supports a marshy flora.

Ecotone A narrow and fairly sharply defined transition zone between two communities. Such edge communities are typically species rich.

ESA Environmentally Sensitive Area. Areas of high landscape, nature conservation, and, often, archaeological value where landowners or occupiers can enter into voluntary agreements to manage and enhance the landscape in return for payments.

Eutrophic Applied to freshwater bodies or mires that are rich in plant nutrients and therefore highly productive.

Eutrophication Artificial enrichment of water or soil with nutrients.

Forb A non-grassy herbaceous species.

FWAG Farming and Wildlife Advisory Group. A largely county-based organization in Britain providing advice on nature conservation to farmers.

Graminicides Selective herbicides affecting only grasses.

Habitat creation The creation of habitats on sites that are either bare or have a very low wildlife value.

Habitat restoration The improvement of degraded habitats; frequently achieved by altering the management regime.

Halophytic A term used to describe an organism that lives in an environment containing a high concentration of salt.

Hydraulic conductivity HCS. An expression of the ease with which water can flow through rocks or soil. High HCS represents a relatively quick passage.

Hydroseeding The use of a machine to spray a mixture of seed and soil ameliorants onto steep or otherwise inaccessible sites.

Long-term set-aside Land for which a farmer is paid a subsidy to take out of agricultural production for a minimum of five years.

MAFF Ministry of Agriculture, Fisheries and Food. The government body responsible for controlling agriculture in Britain.

Mesotrophic Applied to freshwater bodies or soils which contain moderate amounts of plant nutrients and are therefore moderately productive.

Natural A relative term used to describe communities that have been little influenced by the activities of man.

NVC National Vegetation Classification. A comprehensive description of all types of British vegetation using a standardized system.

Oligotrophic Applied to freshwater bodies or mires which are poor in plant nutrients and therefore unproductive.

Plugs Very small container-grown plants.

Propagule A structure, sexual or vegetative, that becomes separated from the parent plant and serves as a means of propagation.

Ripping The aeration of compacted ground.

RSPB Royal Society for the Protection of Birds. Britain's leading bird conservation pressure group.

Ruderal Used to describe plants or animals that are adapted to living under disturbed conditions.

Secchi disc A circular disc used to measure the transparency of water bodies. It is lowered into the water and the depth at which it disappears is recorded as the depth of transparency.

SDC Sheffield Development Corporation A government funded organization responsible for regenerating a run-down industrial area in Sheffield.

Semi-natural A relative term used to describe communities that have a natural aspect but are under human influence through management (e.g. grazing, mowing, coppicing, etc.).

Seral A stage in the sequential development of a climax community.

Set-aside Land for which the farmer is paid a subsidy to take out of agricultural production.

SSSI Site of Special Scientific Interest. A site designated by a government agency because of the particular interest of its flora, fauna, geology, or physiographic features. Owners require special permission before undertaking operations that could damage them.

Stone picking   The removal by hand, or machine, of the larger stones from recently cultivated soil.

Tyned machine   A machine with heavy duty prongs used for ripping and aerating compacted ground.

Wild flower grassland   Used in the text to denote grassland established by sowing a wild flower grassland seed mix.

Windrow   The mounding of material into long rows as in hay making.

Index

acid soils, natural succession 42
acidification 29
afforestation, reinstating heathland
    from 133
agricultural land, *see* farmland
alder (*Alnus glutinosa*) 9, 95, 99,
    120, 126, 230, 239
    buckthorn (*Frangula alnus*) 121,
    242
algae 219
alkaline wastes 42
alkalinization, *see* liming
alpine habitats, *see* montane habitats
anemone, wood (*Anemone
    nemorosa*) 118, 120
animals/fauna 11–13
    in heath/moorland 144
    created for animals 156
    in hedgerows 128–9
    in scrub 123–4
    in wetland 213–14, 219, 220,
    221–3, 234
    in woodland 115–21
    see also specific (types of) animals
apple 120
    crab (*Malus sylvestris*) 95, 126,
    202
    orchard (*Malus domestica*) 9
aquatic systems, nutrient content 26;
    see also specific systems
arable land 194–9; *see also* fields
arctic habitats, *see*
    montane/submontane
    habitats

ash (*Fraxinus excelsior*) 34, 39, 95,
    97, 104, 120, 126, 202
aspen (*Populus tremula*) 99, 120
asphodel, bog (*Narthecium
    ossifragum*) 141
Auchenorryncha 80, 82
Austria, Romaulbach Stream 230
avocet (*Avocetta recurvirostra*) 182

banks
    'beetle' 196–7
    seed, *see* seed bank
    wetland 207, 208
        ponds/lakes 217–18
        river, buffer zone 227
barberry (*Berberis vulgaris*) 202
bark stripping, rabbits/hares 109
Barn Elms 214, 215
baulks, grass 196–7
beaches, *see* sand; sand dunes;
        shingle
bedstraw
    heath (*Galium saxatile*) 42, 164
    hedge (*G. odoratum*) 112, 120
    lady's (*G. verum*) 60
    limestone (*G. sterneri*) 45–6
    slender (*G. pumilum*) 42
beech (*Fagus sylvatica*) 99, 104, 120,
    126, 242
Beech House Farm Wood 95
'beetle banks' 196–7
bellflower
    clustered (*Campanula glomerata*)
        71, 90

nettle-leaved (*C. trachelium*) 113
bell-heather (*Erica cinerea*) 140,
    142, 145
benefits of habitat creation 245
bent (*Agrostis* spp.) 71, 137, 145,
    151, 152, 167–8
    common (*A. capillaris*) 60, 149,
        201
    creeping (*A. stolonifera*) 182,
        219
    highland (*A. castellana*) 149–51
betony (*Betonica officinalis*) 95
bilberry (*Vaccinium myrtillus*) 140,
    145, 156, 164
biological oxygen demand, effluent
    with high levels of 233
birch (*Betula* spp.) 97, 99, 120, 143,
    230
    invading heather 159
bird(s)
    farmland
        field margins 194–5
        set-aside *see* set-aside
    hedgerow 128
    scrub 123–4
    wetland 213–14, 219, 220, 221–3
    woodland 94, 116–17
        seed dispersal and 97–8
bird's-foot trefoil (*Lotus
    corniculatus*) 10, 36, 60, 90,
    239
    greater (*L. uliginosus*) 169
bittern (*Botaurus stellaris*) 220
black-grass (*Alopecurus
    myosuroides*) 192
blackthorn (*Prunus spinosa*) 124
Blackwater Estuary 182–3
bluebell (*Hyacinthoides non-scripta*)
    39, 112, 113, 120
box (*Buxus sempervirens*) 100, 120
bracken (*Pteridium aquilinum*) 131
bramble (*Rubus fruticosus*) 49, 107,
    118, 120, 121

Brecklands 137
Brede, River 228–30
Broadbalk Wilderness 38–9
brome
    barren (*Anisantha sterilis*) 192,
        195
    false (*Brachypodium sylvaticum*)
        113, 114
    smooth (*Bromus racemosus*) 113
    soft (*B. hordaceaus*) 168
    upright (*B. erecta*) 60
brooklime (*Veronica beccabunga*)
    52
broom (*Cytisys scoparius*) 120, 122,
    123, 239
brush, seed collecting 76, 142–4
bryony, black (*Tamus communis*)
    128
buckthorn
    purging (*Rhamnus cathartica*)
        121, 124, 202, 242
    sea (*Hippophae rhamnoides*) 177
buddleia (*Buddleia davidii*) 9, 42,
    121
buffer zone, riparian 227
bugle (*Ajuga reptans*) 91, 112, 213
bunting
    cirl (*Emberiza cirlus*) 197
    corn (*Milaria calandra*) 191, 199
    Lapland (*E. lapponicus*) 199
    reed (*E. schoeniclus*) 199, 234
burdock, greater (*Arcticum lappa*)
    49
burnet (*Sanguisorba minor*) 11, 41,
    46, 60, 243
bur-reed (*Sparganium erectum*) 28
buttercup (*Ranunculus acris*) 70, 90,
    91
    bulbous (*R. bulbosus*) 89
    corn (*R. arvensis*) 192, 195
butterflies 11–12
    brimstone (*Gonepteryx rhamni*)
        121

brown hairstreak (*Thecla betulae*) 83

common blue (*Polyommatus icarus*) 36, 84, 200

dingy skipper (*Erynnis tages*) 200

Essex skipper (*Thymelicus lineolus*) 12, 84, 200

farmland 200–1

gatekeeper (*Pyronia tithonus*) 200

grassland for 11–12, 83, 84, 85

grayling (*Hipparchia semele*) 200

green-veined white (*Pieris napi*) 84

hedge brown (*Pyronia tithonus*) 84

holly blue (*Celastrina argiolus*) 84

large skipper (*Ochlodes venata*) 84, 200

large white (*Pieris brassicae*) 84

marbled white (*Melanargia galatea*) 200

marsh fritillary (*Euphydryas aurinia*) 83

meadow brown (*Maniola jurtina*) 84, 87, 200

orange tip (*Anthocharis cardamines*) 84, 200

painted lady (*Cynthia cardui*) 84

peacock (*Inachis io*) 84

purple hairstreak (*Quercusia quercus*) 105

red admiral (*Vanessa atalanta*) 84

ringlet (*Aphantopus hyperantus*) 200

silver-spotted skipper (*Hesperia comma*) 4

silver-studded blue (*Plebejus argus*) 133

small copper (*Lycaena phlaeas*) 84, 200

small heath (*Coenonympha pamphilus*) 84, 200

small skipper (*Thymelicus sylvestris*) 84, 200

small tortoiseshell (*Aglais urticae*) 121

small white (*Pieris rapae*) 84

species supporting 118, 120, 121

wall brown (*Lasiommata megera*) 84, 200

wood white (*Leptidea sinapis*) 118

woodland 118

Cairngorms 160, 161, 164–6

calcareous spoil 41

Cambridgeshire
    Ouse Washes 222
    woodland 93, 101–4

campion
    red (*Silene dioica*) 49, 112, 113, 114, 120, 128, 168
    sea (*S. uniflora*) 184, 187

Canada, Caribou Hill 169–70

candytuft, wild (*Iberis amara*) 4

Castle Espie 232

catchfly, night-flowering (*Silene noctiflora*) 195

cauliflower field (*Lizard*) 188, 200

Central Forest Park 54

cereal, winter, birds on 197, 198

chaffinch (*Fringilla coelebs*) 199

chalk grassland, seeding 59, 60

charlock (*Sinapis arvensis*) 195

cherry, bird (*Prunus padus*) 34, 35, 99, 120, 230

Cheshire, ponds 216, 217

chestnut
    horse (*Aesculus hippocastanum*) 120, 126
    sweet (*Castanea sativa*) 104, 120, 126, 134

chickweed (*Stellaria media*) 49

chiffchaff (*Phylloscopus collybita*) 94, 116

clay mixes, seed ratios in 72, 73
cleavers (*Galium aparine*) 49, 195
cliffs, maritime 187–8, 189–90
    grassland 52, 187–8
    unprotected soft 189–90
climate, local 21, 21–2
clover
    red (*Trifolium pratense* var.
        sativum) 10, 78, 90
    suffocated (*T. suffocatum*) 52
    white (*T. repens*) 11, 52, 59, 90,
        191
coal mine, opencast 239
    natural succession 53
coast 174–90
    cliffs, *see* cliffs
    defences, restoring
        saltmarshes 180–2
        hingle structures 184
    defences, setting back/removal
        174
        saltmarshes 180, 182–3
cock's-foot grass (*Dactylis
    glomerata*) 41, 49, 112, 139,
        196–7, 200
cold-tolerant cultivars 167
Coleoptera 79–80
colonization, natural, *see* natural
        colonization
communication facilities, high-
        altitude 162, 168
competition (and competitors) 22,
        23
    in heathland 138–40
        controlling 157–9
    in natural succession 43–4
conservation measures
    farms 195–6, 203
    in habitat design 16–18
conservation value, constructed
        wetlands 234–5
conservationists' views 1–2

contaminants, wetland water source
        210
context analysis, site 18–20
contractor, control of 241–3
cord-grass (*Spartina* spp.) 182
corncrake (*Crex crex*) 197
cornflower (*Centaurea cyanus*) 195
cost, economic
    cutting grassland 86
    establishing heathland 155–6
    seed for grassland 56
cotoneaster (*Cotoneaster* spp.) 9,
        42
cottongrass (*Eriophorum* spp.) 130,
        140, 141, 151, 163, 170–1
couch (*Elymus repens*) 112
    sand (*Elytrigia juncea*) 177
Countryside Commission
    Character Area project 33
Countryside Stewardship Schemes
        (CSS) 56
    farmland 193, 199
    heaths 131, 132, 133, 134
    rivers/floodplains 226
Courtyard Farm 199
Cow Green Reservoir 47–8
cowberry (*Vaccinium vitis-idaea*)
        140, 145
cowslip (*Primula veris*) 60, 70, 78,
        91, 128
creating new native woodlands 100
crop, field margin between hedge
        and, *see* field
cropping, depletion 29
    grassland 63
    heathland 137
crowberry (*Empetrum nigrum*) 53,
        131, 140, 141, 145, 149, 165
crowfoot, water (*Batracthium
        peltatum*) 229
cuckoo-pint (*Arum maculatum*)
        118, 120

cudweed, dwarf (*Gnaphalium supinum*) 165
curlew, stone (*Burhinus oedicnemus*) 137
cutting, grassland 84–7
  'spring'/'summer' meadows 90

daisy (*Bellis perennis*) 47, 52
dandelion (*Taraxacum officinale*) 41, 47, 52, 67
Denmark
  River Brede 228–30
  sand dunes 176–7
depletion cropping, *see* cropping
designer habitats 6
designing new habitats, planning and 16–37, 236–8
  grassland 239
  heathland 239
  process 17
  setting objectives, *see* objectives
  wetland 205–14, 233–4
    ponds/lakes 216–19
    principles 212–13
  woodland 93–5, 239
Diptera 79–80
dispersal in woodland
  birds and 97–8
  ground flora, poor ability 49
diversity, species 22, 23
  of existing dull grassland, increasing 87–9
  Shannon Weiner index of 49–50
  species richness vs. 24
  succession and 49–50
dock 120
  broad-leaved (*Rumex obtusifolius*) 118
  curled (*R. crispus*) 185
dog's mercury (*Mercurialis perennis*) 128

dog's-tail, crested (*Cynosurus cristatus*) 60, 168–9
dogwood (*Cornus sanguinea*) 34, 40, 120, 121
dormouse (*Muscardinus avellanarius*) 115
dragonfly 212–14, 218
dredged silt dumped on saltmarshes/mudflats 183–4
duck marsh 221–3
dunes, sand 175–9
dwarf-shrubs in heathland
  adding 148–9, 156–7
  to existing vegetation 156–7
  lowland 133
dystrophic water 209

ecologists involved in planning and design 237–8, 239
ecology
  heath and moor 134–45
  landscape surrounding new site, *see* landscape
economics, *see* cost
eelgrass (*Zostera* spp.) 182, 186
effluent, wetlands used to treat 232–3
elder (*Sambucus nigra*) 104, 120, 121, 125, 242
enchanter's nightshade (*Circaea lutetiana*) 39
English Nature
  coastal policies 174
  Natural Areas, *see* Natural Areas
environment, management of whole 244
Environmentally Sensitive Areas (ESAs) 5, 16, 56, 59, 199
  farmland 193
  heaths 131, 133
  rivers/floodplains 226

erosion
  heathland 146
  peat 155
  montane/submontane areas, *see*
    montane/submontane
    habitats
establishment 42–3
  grassland 78–9
  heathland 145–55
  economic 155–6
  hedgerow 125
  woodland 107–11
    options 95–9
ethics 1–2
European and North American
    concepts of habitat
    creation/restoration
    compared 3
eutrophic water 209
exotic species, *see* non-native species
eye-bright (*Euphrasia nemorosa*)
    44, 45, 78

farmland (lowland) 191–203
  changes since 1945 191–2
  opportunities 192–4
  see also fields
fauna, *see* animals
fencing
  heathland 146
  hedges 125–6
  trees 108
fern (*Dryopteris* spp.) 49
fertility, *see* nutrients
fertilizer 244
  butterflies and 12
  coastal areas 178
  farmland 191
  grassland 46
  heathland 138, 139, 151, 152
  montane areas 163, 165, 170–1
  woodland 107
fescue (*Festuca* spp.) 45, 46, 60, 71,

137, 145, 151, 152, 167–8, 242
  blue (*F. longifolia*) 149
  creeping red (*F. rubra*) 41, 52,
    155–6, 169, 177, 182, 187,
    239
  sheep's (*F. ovina*) 149, 166, 171,
    201
fields
  hay, seed mixes 76–7
  margin (between hedge and crop)
    128, 194–6
    birds and 194–5
    weeds and 195–6
  see also meadows; pastures
fig, wild (*ficus carica*) 9
fish 219
  carp (*Cyprinus carpio*) 219
  pike (*Esox lucius*) 216
  sea trout (*Salmo trutta*) 229
  stickleback (*Gasterosteus* spp.)
    216
  tench (*Tinca tinca*) 219
flats, intertidal 183–4
flax, fairy (*Linum catharticum*) 46
fleabane, common (*Pulicaria
    dysenterica*) 52
flooding
  nutrient-rich soils 28
  wetland 207, 221, 229
floodplains 223–32
flora, *see* plants
flowers, *see* wildflowers
footpath, *see* trampling
forage harvester for seed collection
    143
forest, reinstating heathland
    formerly occupying site of
    133; *see also* timber;
    woodland
Forestry Commission Bulletin 112
    100
  Research Division, evaluation of
    natural colonization 97

Forestry Screefing TTS 10 machine 157

fox (*Vulpes vulpes*) 182

foxglove (*Digitalis purpurea*) 114, 120

foxtail
marsh (*Alopecurus geniculatus*) 169, 219
meadow (*A. pratensis*) 168

framework habitats 5

freshwaters, *see* wetlands

fungi 53, 105, 121, 124, 195
Amanita spp. 105

gean (*Prunus avium*) 39, 104, 120, 126

Geescroft 39

geese, grassland for 59, 82

genetic stock 9–10
local, using 92, 98–9, 238–41

geographical information systems (GIS) 133

geotextiles
heath/moorland 154, 155
montane/submontane areas 171–2

Gibraltar Point 179

gipsywort (*Lycopus europaeus*) 226

glasswort (*Salicornia* spp.) 182

goldcrest (*Regulus regulus*) 94, 117

golden-rod (*Solidago* spp.) 42, 118, 120

gorse (*Ulex* spp.) 120, 122, 123, 142, 148, 239

grants, farmland 193–4
hedge planting 129

grass baulks 196–7

grass(es)
commercial, survival in boreal conditions 169–71
nurse, *see* nurse species
in seed mix 55

grassland 54–91, 187–8
for animals 79–83

design 239
farm 83, 84, 188, 199–201
maritime cliff 52, 187–8
by natural succession 57–9
kick starting succession 44–6
natural reversion 47
wet 221–3

gravel workings, heathland on 134

grazing (herbivory)
on grassland (farm) 83, 84, 199–201
on heathland/montane areas, unwanted 147–8, 171
rough
heath creation on 201
scrub creation on 201
on woodland 115–16

Grime's stress-tolerance model 22, 23, 69

ground
bare, heathland creation from 146–55
open, in woodland 94
preparation 31–3
grassland 65–7
hedgerow 125
woodland 107

ground flora/herbs
hedgerows 127–8
woodland
fauna supported by 118–21
introducing 111–15
poor dispersal ability 49

ground ivy (*Glechoma hederacea*) 39

groundwater, wetland 206, 207

growth, plant
grassland, retardants 91
heathland 138–40

guelder rose (*Viburnum opulus*) 124, 230

gull, black-headed (*Larus ridibundus*) 197

habitat creation/restoration (general references only)
achievements to date 13–15
benefits 245
European and N. American concepts compared 3
planning and design, *see* designing
problems 9–13
role 3–5
strategic 7–9
types 5–7
hairgrass
tufted (*Deschampsia cespitosa*) 39, 163
wavy (*D. flexuosa*) 53, 149, 151, 152, 157, 158, 201
Ham Wall project 234
hare (*Lepus europeaus*) 192
harebell (*Campanula rotundifolia*) 60, 168
harrier, marsh (*Circus aeruginosus*) 220
harvester, forage, for seed collection 143
hawkbit
autumn (*Leontodon autumnalis*) 179
rough (*L. hispidus*) 41, 60, 90–1
hawthorn (*Crataegus monogyna*) 10, 39, 97, 100, 104, 120, 124
midland (*C. laevigata*) 100
hay field mixes 76–7
hazel (*Corylus avellana*) 34, 94, 100, 104, 120, 124
heath and moor 130–59, 188–9
for animals 156
coastal 188–9
design 239
dwarf-shrubs, *see* dwarf-shrubs
ecological issues 134–45
establishment, *see* establishment
grazing and, *see* grazing
lowland 133–4

management 157–9
seed collection from existing 141–3
upland 130–2
heath, cross-leaved (*Erica tetralix*) 140, 142, 145
heather (*Calluna vulgaris*) 42, 47, 130, 133, 139, 148, 150, 155, 157, 166
at Holme Moss, nurse grass and 150
seed collection 142–3
heath-grass (*Danthonia decumbens*) 47, 53
heavy metals 210
hedges (and hedgerows) 124–9, 202–3
field margin between crop and, *see* field
helleborine
broad-leaved (*Epipactis helleborine*) 105
white (*Cephalanthera damasonium*) 105
hemp-nettle, red (*Galeopsis angustifolia*) 195
herb paris (*Paris quadrifolia*) 115
herb(s), woodland, *see* ground flora
herbicide
slot seeding using 88, 89
weed control with planted trees 109–10
herbivory, *see* grazing
herb-robert (*Geranium robertianum*) 49
Heteroptera 79–82
high altitudes and latitudes, *see* montane/submontane habitats
Highways Agency, grasslands and 65, 79
hills, *see* montane habitats; heath and moor

hogweed (*Heracleum sphondylium*) 24

holly (*Ilex aquifolium*) 39, 100, 111, 120, 125, 126

Holme Moss
  nurse grass 149, 150
  stabilizing bare peat 154, 155

hornbeam (*Carpinus betulus*) 34, 99, 120

hoverfly 217

hydrology 21, 26, 30–1
  wetland 206–8

immigration of new species from surrounding areas 41–2

in-channel restoration 228

insects 11
  in grassland 79–82
  in farmland 194, 196, 199
  in heathland 144
  in hedgerows 128
  in woodland 118–21
  see also invertebrates

interpretation 243

intertidal sand/mudflats 183–4

invertebrates 11, 13, 31
  in farmland 196–7
  in grassland 46–7, 57, 79, 80–2
  in heathland 144, 156
  in hedgerows 128
  in wetlands 212–4, 234–5
  in woodland 117–21
    species supporting 118–21

iris
  yellow (*Iris pseudacorus*) 28, 226
  stinking (*I. foetidissima*) 39

Isle of Man, montane/submontane areas 166–9

ivy (*Hedera helix*) 39, 49, 121

jay (*Garrulus glandarius*) 94, 116

Jersey, Les Blanches Banques 179

Joint Nature Conservation Committee, saline lagoons 186

juniper (*Juniperus communis*) 99, 120

jute/sisal mesh netting
  heathland 154, 155
  montane/submontane areas 171–2

kestrel (*Falco tinnunculus*) 57, 78, 197, 200

kick starting natural succession, nurse species 44–7, 73

kingfisher (*Alcedo atthis*) 207, 218

knapweed (*Centaurea nigra*) 60, 63, 91

Koge Bay Seaside Park 176–7

lady's mantle (*Alchemilla xanthochlora*) 168
  alpine (*A. alpina*) 165

lady's smock (*Cardamine pratensis*) 91

lagoons, saline 185–7

lakes and ponds 214–19
  design 216–19
  trophic status 26, 27

Landlife 62, 74

landscape, surrounding (relationship to) 20
  scrub communities 123
  woodland 92–3

lapwing (*Vanellus vanellus*) 191–2, 197, 200, 221

legumes in grassland seed mixes 72–3

Les Blanches Banques 179

lichen 53, 165–6, 184

lime 120
  large-leaved (*Tilia platyphyllos*) 100
  small-leaved (*T. cordata*) 99–100

limestone quarry 50–2

liming 29
  grassland 61–2
  heathland 138, 139, 151, 152
linnet (*Carduelis cannabina*) 197
Lizard peninsula
  cliff-top grassland 52, 187–8
  heaths 189
lizard, sand (*Lacerta agilis*) 6, 144,
    189
local authorities 4–5
long-term management 37
loosestrife
  dotted (*Lysimachia punctata*) 62
  purple (*Lythrum salicaria*) 28,
    121, 226
lupin (*Lupinus polyphyllus*) 42, 62
lyme-grass (*Leymus arenarius*) 177

Maghull Brook 231–2
magnesium 25, 135–6
  grassland and 62, 65
mammals, woodland 115–16
management 243
  grassland 83–7
  heathland 157–9
  long-term 37
  whole environment 244
  woodland 111, 244
maple (*Acer* spp.) 9, 110
  field (*A. campestre*) 39, 104, 120,
    124, 126
  Norway (*A. platanoides*) 104,
    105
marigold, corn (*Chrysanthemum
    segetum*) 195
marjoram (*Origanum vulgare*) 43,
    60
marram (*Ammophila arenaria*) 140,
    176–7, 178, 179, 237
marshes, *see* duck marsh;
    saltmarshes; wetlands
martin, sand (*Riparia riparia*)
    207–8, 218

mat-grass (*Nardus stricta*) 47, 53, 95,
    141, 163, 165, 171, 201
meadowgrass (*Poa* spp.) 60, 165–6,
    168, 173
  annual (*Poa annua*) 47, 48, 52
meadows 199–201
  'spring' and 'summer' 87
meadow-sweet (*Filipendula ulmaria*)
    28
meanders, recreation 229
melick, wood (*Melica uniflora*) 115
meshes
  heathland 154, 155
  montane/submontane areas 171–2
mesotrophic water 209
Michaelmas daisy (*Aster nova-
    belgii*) 62
migration of new species from
    surrounding areas 41–2
milkwort (*Polygala vulgaris*) 46
  heath (*P. serpyllifolia*) 47
Milton Keynes Parks Trust 111–12
mineral workings
  grassland on 58
  heathland on 134
  natural succession 40–1, 41, 50–2,
    58
    by default rather than design
    53, 58
  opencast, *see* opencast mines
Ministry of Agriculture and Fisheries
  Countryside Stewardship
    Schemes, *see* Countryside
    Stewardship Schemes
  Water Fringe Management
    Scheme 193
Minsmere 29, 137–8, 187, 220
mires 149; *see also* wetlands
mites associated with woodland
    plants 120
mix and match mixtures, grassland
    71–2
mole (*Talpa europaea*) 40

monitoring 37, 238, 243
  grassland 91
  heath/moorland 159
  montane areas 168
  wetland areas 235
montane/submontane habitats (and
    high latitudes) 160–73
  bare root transplants 163–4
  potted plants 164
  seed bank 163
  seeding 164–71
  turves 163
  vegetation/soil reinforcement
    171–2
  see also heath and moor
moor, *see* heath and moor
moor-grass, purple (*Molinia
    caerulea*) 145, 157
moorhen (*Gallinula chloropus*) 226,
    234
moschatel (*Adoxa moschatellina*)
    114
moss 165, 184
mould, grey (*Botrytis*) 36
mountains, *see* montane habitats
mouse
  harvest (*Micromys minutus*) 200,
    234
  wood (*Apodemus sylvaticus*) 115
  yellow-necked (*A. flavicollis*) 115
mouse-ear, sea (*Cerastium diffusum*)
    178
mouse-tail (*Myosurus minimus*)
    195
mudflats, intertidal 183–4

National Rivers Authority 223
National Trust
  cliff-top grassland 52, 187–8
  whole environment management
    244
National Vegetation Classification
  coastal areas 189

communities
  *Agrostis capillaris–Festuca
    ovina–Carex arenaria* 137
  *Alopecurus pratensis–
    Sanguisorba officinalis* 78
  *Anthoxanthum odoratum–
    Geranium sylvaticum* 67–8
  Calluna vulgaris–Scilla verna
    189
  Calluna vulgaris–Ulex gallii 189
  *Crataegus monogyna–Hedera
    helix* 121
  *Cynosurus cristatus–Centaurea
    nigra* 64, 71, 77
  *Erica vagans–Schoenus
    nigricans* 189
  Erica vagans–Ulex europaeus
    189
  *Festuca ovina–Agrostis
    capillaris–Rumex acetostella*
    47
  *Festuca ovina–Agrostis
    capillaris–Thymus praecox* 47
  *Juncus trifidus–Racomitrium
    lanuginosum* 165–6
  Lolium–Cynosurus 64
  Ulex europaeus–Rubus 122
  grassland 54, 67
  scrub 121–2
  woodland 94, 102–3, 104
    Forestry Commission Bulletin
    112, 100
Native Pinewood Scheme (Scotland)
    240–1
native species, using 33–6, 67–70, 92,
    99–100, 238–41
natural appearance, achieving high
    degree of 236–7
Natural Areas 4, 8, 16, 33, 104, 245
natural colonization/succession
    38–53
  by default/neglect rather than
    design 52–3, 57, 146

grassland, *see* grassland
montane/submontane areas 166,
 172–3
objections 52
principal controlling factors 40–4
promoting 5, 38–53
 kick start 44–7, 73
scrub 122
technique in action 50–3
wetland 213, 218–19
woodland 95–8
natural reversion, *see* reversion
nest boxes, woodland 117
Netherlands, sand dunes 177
netting
 heathland 154, 155
 montane/submontane areas 171–2
nettle, stinging (*Urtica dioica*) 28,
 49, 107, 112, 118, 120
newt, great crested (*Triturus
 cristatus*) 18–20, 238
nightingale (*Luscinia
 megarhynchos*) 94, 116
nightjar (*Caprimulgus europaeus*)
 133, 144
nitrogen 25, 26, 28
 farmland 191
 grassland and 62, 64, 73
 heathland and 134–6
 succession and 44
 wetland and 208–9, 233
non-native/exotic species, using
 9–11
 in arctic/alpine areas 173
 trees 104
North America 169–71
 European concepts of habitat
 creation/restoration
 compared with 3
 montane/submontane areas
 169–71
North York Moors 131
Northey Island 182

nudation 40–1
nurse species 36–7
 heathland 149–51, 152
 montane/submontane areas 166,
 167
 in natural succession 59
 for kick starting succession
 44–7
nuthatch (*Sitta europaea*) 94, 116
nutrient(s), soil/water 22–30
 levels (and their alteration)
 22–30
 grassland 62–4, 66
 heath/moorland 134–8
 wetland 26, 30, 208–9
 woodland 107
 see also specific nutrients
nutrient-rich areas 28–30
 grasses in 57, 59, 62–5
 reducing fertility 63–5, 66
 seed mixes for 71
 heathland creation 137–8
 trees in 107

oak (*Quercus* spp.) 39, 120, 126, 238,
 242
 holm (*Q. ilex*) 104, 105, 120
 natural succession by 39–40
 non-native species 9–10
 Turkey (*Q. cerris*) 104, 105
 weed control 110
oat, wild (*Avena fatua*) 192
oat-grass, false (*Arrhenatherum
 elatius*) 63, 64
objectives, setting (in habitat design)
 16–18, 238
 coastal areas 174–5, 180
 farmland 192–4, 203
 montane areas 173
 wetlands 205, 233–4
 rivers and floodplains 224–8,
 231
 woodland 93–4

off-the-shelf seed mixes, grassland 70–1

oil exploration site, abandoned (northern Canada) 169–70

oligotrophic water 209

open ground in woodland 94

opencast mines 239
  grasslands, natural succession 53
  woodlands, nest box study 117

orchid 41, 58
  bee (*Ophrys apifera*) 238
  bird's-nest (*Neottia nidus-avis*) 105
  common (*Dactylorhiza fuchsii*) 88

Ouse Washes 222

oversowing existing dull grassland 88

owl
  barn (*Tyto alba*) 57, 197, 200
  short-eared 57 (*Asio flammeus*)

ox-eye daisy 11, 60, 78, 91

Oxleas Wood 2

oxygen demand, biological, effluent with high levels of 233

Parish Quarry 50–2

parsley
  cow (*Anthriscus sylvestris*) 62–3
  hedge (*Torilis japonica*) 128

partridge, grey (*Perdix perdix*) 86, 192, 197, 199

pastures 199–201

patches, habitat, adding new 18–20

Payne Knight, Richard 14–15

pea, sea (*Lathyrus japonicus*) 177, 184–5

Peak District moorland 131, 155
  Holme Moss, *see* Holme Moss
  soil 138, 139

peat erosion 155
  stabilizers preventing 152–5

Pennines 166–9, 171

decision guide for Pennine Way 172, 173

pennywort, marsh (*Hydrocotyle vulgaris*) 213

Peterborough initiative (Environment City Trust) 4–5, 14, 50

pH (soils/water) 21, 26, 30, 47
  altering 29
  grassland 61–2
  heathland 135–8
  montane areas 168
  species distribution 36

pheasant (*Phasianus colchicus*) 197

pheasant's eye (*Adonis annua*) 195

phosphorus 23–30 *passim*
  grassland and 62, 64–5, 73
  heathland and 134–6
  wetland and 209, 210, 233

pignut (*Conopodium majus*) 78

pine (*Pinus* spp.) 120, 159
  heather invaded by 159
  Scots (*Pinus sylvestris*) 99, 240–1

pink, sea (*Armeria maritima*) 187

planning, *see* designing

plant(s)/vegetation
  contractor errors or duplicity with 242
  ground, *see* ground flora
  growth, *see* growth
  for heathlands 148–9
  high altitude/latitude, reinforcement 171–2
  plug 89–91
  potted, *see* potted plants
  species, *see* species
  for wetland 213
    submerged 219

plantain (*Plantago* spp.) 52, 60
  buck's horn (*Plantago coronopus*) 52, 187

planting
  grassland 89–91

heathland 140–1
hedges 125
    grants 129
scrub 122–3
shingle beach 185, 186
trees 98–9, 105–7, 107–8
    methods 108
    patterns 105–7
    stock 107–8
wetland 213, 218–19
plastic meshes,
        montane/submontane areas
        171
plovers (*Charadrius* spp.) 214
plug plants 89–91
    heathland 140
Plymouth pear (*Pyrus cordata*)
        100
political habitats 6
ponds, *see* lakes and ponds
pondweed, Canadian (*Elodea
        canadensis*) 219
poplar (*Populus* spp.) 9, 120
    black (*P. nigra* ssp. *betulifolia*) 6,
        100
poppy, common (*Papaver rhoeas*)
        195
    yellow-horned (*Glaucium flavum*)
        184–5
potassium 25
    grassland and 62, 64–5, 73
    heathland and 134–6
potted plants
    grassland 89–91
    heathland 148–9
    montane/submontane areas 164
    shingle beach 185, 186
    woodland 112
Predannack 52, 187
preparation, ground, *see* ground
Price, Uvedale 14–15
primrose (*Primula vulgaris*) 112,
        113, 114, 120

privet (*Ligustrum vulgare*) 104, 120,
        125
project planning and design, *see*
        designing
proprietary seed mixes, grassland
        70–1
protection
    hedges 125–6
    trees 108–9
pygmyweed (*Crassula helmsii*) 219

quaking grass (*Briza media*) 42, 60
quarries
    grassland on 58
    heathland on 134
    natural succession 40–1, 41, 50–2,
        58

rabbits causing damage
    heathland 147–8
    woodland 108, 109
radar stations, high-altitude 162, 168
ragged robin (*Lychnis flos-cuculi*)
        88
ragwort (*Senecio jacobaea*) 41, 67
ramsons (*Allium ursinum*) 112
redshank (*Tringa totanus*) 200, 221
reed canary-grass (*Phalaris
        arundinacea*) 209, 242
reed sweet-grass (*Glyceria maxima*)
        209–10
reed, common (*Phragmites australis*)
        209
reed-beds 220–1
    wildlife 220–1, 234
reed-mace (*Typha angustifolia*) 210,
        217, 226, 239
rest-harrow (*Ononis repens*) 178
reversion, natural 47–50
    comparative rates 48–50
rhizomes, planting, heathland 140–1
rides, woodland 116, 118, 119
ripping 32

woodland 107
river channels 207
  creation 231
  nutrient levels 26
  restoration 228
river(s) 223–32
rocket, sea (*Cakile maritima*) 177
rockrose (*Helianthemum
  nummularium*) 35, 36, 41, 60,
  69
Romaulbach Stream 230
root system, tree planting and 108
rooted fragments for transplanting
  to montane/submontane
  habitats 163–4
Roper's Heath 137
rose
  dog (*Rosa canina*) 125
  Japanese (*R. rugosa*) 177
rotational set-aside for birds 197–8
rotovation 87–8, 141, 195
Rother Valley Country Park 49, 50
Rothiemurchus 241
RSPB reserves 220, 221, 234
rubbish clearance 31, 65
Ruddington 237–8
rue, meadow (*Thalictrum flavum*)
  28
rush (*Juncus* spp.) 52, 71
  conglomerate (*J. conglomeratus*)
   146
  heath (*J. squarrosus*) 146, 171
  soft (*J. effusus*) 146, 163, 171, 209
  three-leaved (*J. trifidus*) 165
rye-grass (*Lolium perenne*) 6, 45,
  47, 59, 75, 166–8, 191, 242

saline lagoons 185–7
sallow (*Salix cinerea*) 230
saltmarshes 180–3
  dredged silt dumped on 183–4
saltwort (*Salsola kali*) 177
sand bank construction 207, 208

sand dunes 175–9
sand, intertidal 183–4
sand-shrimp, lagoon (*Gammarus
  insensibilis*) 185
sandwort, sea (*Honkenya peploides*)
  177, 185
sanfoin (*Onobrychis vicifolia*) 11
saxifrage, meadow (*Saxifraga
  granulata*) 88
scabious, devil's bit (*Succisa
  pratensis*) 95
Schleswig-Holstein (S-H) and the
  S-H method 180–2
Scholes Lane opencast site 53
Scoliocentra caesia 79
Scotland
  montane/submontane areas 160,
   164–6
  Native Pinewood Scheme 240–1
screefing 157
scrub 121–4
  grazing 201
sea-anemone, starlet (*Nematostella
  vectensis*) 185
seablite (*Suaeda maritima*) 182
sea-coast, *see* coast
sea-holly (*Eryngium maritimum*)
  178, 185
sea-kale (*Crambe maritima*) 184–5
sea-lavender (*Limonium*) 182
sea-mat, trembling (*Victorella
  pavida*) 185
sedge (*Carex* spp.) 71, 137, 141,
  226
  carnation (*C. flacca*) 74, 78–9
  common (*C. nigra*) 171
  hairy (*C. hirta*) 71
  lesser pond (*C. acutiformis*) 209
  pendulous (*C. pendula*) 114
  pill-headed (*C. pilulifera*) 53
  sand (*C. arenaria*) 178
  stiff (*C. bigelowii*) 164
  yellow (*C. demissa*) 169

sediments, wetland water source 210
seed bank (as donor sites)
   heath/moorland, tests 142, 143,
      145, 146
      results 145
   montane/submontane 163
seed(s) 59–79
   collection from existing
      heaths/moors 141–3
   cost, for different grassland types
      56
   dispersal, *see* dispersal
   dwarf-shrub (for heathlands) 148
   nurse grass (for heathland),
      quantity 151, 152
   sources (natural and commercial
      e.g. mixes) 70–8
      contractor's errors or duplicity
         242
      for heathland 140
      for montane/submontane areas
         165, 166, 173
      non-native species in 10–11
      for wet grassland 222
      for wildflower grassland 55,
         70–8
      for woodland ground flora 115
      see also seed bank
seeding/sowing 59–79
   grassland 59–79
      for diversifying existing dull
         areas 87–9
   heathland 140–1
   high altitude/latitude 160
   for kick starting succession 44–7
   scrub 122
   soil preparation for 32–3
   wetland 213
   woodland
      ground flora 112, 114, 115
      trees 98
self heal (*Prunella vulgaris*) 60, 90
service-tree (*Sorbus torminalis*) 100

set-aside for birds
   non-rotational 199
   rotational 197–8
shade-tolerant ground flora in
      woodland, introducing 112,
      113
Shannon Weiner diversity index
      49–50
shape
   pond/lake 216
   wood 94–5
Sheffield Development Corporation
      8–9
shepherd's needle (*Scandix pecten-
      veneris*) 192, 195
shingle structures 184–5
shore
   pond/lake, profiles 215, 216
   sea, *see* coast
shrew (*Sorex* spp.) 115
shrubs
   dwarf-, *see* dwarf-shrubs
   fauna supported by 118–21
silt, dredged, dumping on
      saltmarshes/mudflats 183–4
sinuous edges to water bodies
      218
sisal, *see* jute/sisal mesh netting
site
   context analysis 18–20
   modification (reaction) in natural
      succession 43–4
   survey 21–31
Site of Special Scientific Interest
      (SSSI) 4
   farmland involving 193, 196
   grassland 11
   natural colonization 38, 52, 53
   saline lagoons 186
Sizewell B power station
   sand dunes 177–8
   shingle beach 185
ski facilities 160, 164–6

skylark (*Alauda arvensis*) 57, 86,
    197–9
slacks, dune 179
slot seeding 88–9
slugs 88
small-reed, purple (*Calamagrostis
    canescens*) 57
snapdragon (*Antirrhinum majus*) 42
snipe (*Gallinago gallinago*) 221
soil
    grassland 60–5
    heath/moorland 134–8
    high altitude/latitude, bare,
        revegetation, *see*
        montane/submontane
        habitats
    seed bank, *see* seed bank
    site survey considering
        characteristics 22–31
    wetland 210
sowing seeds, *see* seeding
sparrowhawk (*Accipiter nisus*) 116,
    197
species (of plant)
    diversity, *see* diversity
    establishment, *see* establishment
    grassland, selection 67–78
    immigration from surrounding
        areas 41–2
    native, importance of using
        238–41
    non-native/introduced/exotic
        species, *see* non-native
        species
    nurse, *see* nurse species
    richness 22, 23, 24
    selection/choosing (principles)
        33–7
    single, repair involving 6–7
    woodland 96, 99–104
        selection 99–104
speedwell (*Veronica* spp.) 196
    germander (*V. chamaedrys*) 46

Sphagnum (*Sphagnum* spp.) 53
spiders 79, 184
spindle (*Euonymus europaeus*) 120,
    124–5, 202
'spring' meadow 87
squill (*Scilla verna*) 52
SSSI, *see* Site of Special Scientific
    Interest
St Boniface Down 104, 105
St John's-wort
    hairy (*Hypericum hirsutum*) 52,
        113
    perforate (*H. perforatum*) 128
stabilizers, heathland 152–5
Stansted Airport
    grassland 64, 65
    non-native buckthorn 242
    woodland 34, 99
starwort, water (*Callitriche
    platycarpa*) 229
stitchwort, greater (*Stellaria
    holostea*) 113, 120, 128
stone picking 32, 65
stonecrop, English (*Sedum
    anglicum*) 184
stonewort (*Chara*) 186
    foxtail (*Lamprothamnium
    papulosum*) 185
strategic habitat creation 7–9
strawberry, wild (*Fragaria vesca*)
    118, 120
stress tolerance 22, 23, 69
    heath/moorlands 140
stripping, *see* topsoil
submerged plants 219
submontane habitats, *see*
    montane/submontane
    habitats
substrate, wetland 210–11
succession, natural, *see* natural
    colonization/succession
'summer' meadow 87
surface water, wetland 206–7

survey, site 21–31
swards, *see* grasses; grassland
sweet vernal-grass (*Anthoxanthum odoratum*) 60
sycamore (*Acer pseudoplatanus*) 39, 104, 105, 120

tassleweed (*Ruppia*) 186
teasel (*Dipsacus fullonum*) 121
temperature fluctuations, cultivars tolerant of large 167
terns (*Sterna* spp.) 214
thinning, trees 111
thistle
  carline (*Carlina vulgaris*) 45
  creeping (*Cirsium arvense*) 49, 67, 140
  spear (*C. vulgare*) 67, 140
  stemless (*C. acaule*) 34
thyme (*Thymus* spp.) 69, 74
  wild (*T. polytrichus*) 41, 46
tidal zone, sand/mudflats 183–4
timber 201
Tinsley Park Opencast scheme 239
tit 117 (*Parus* spp.)
  bearded (*Panurus biarmicus*) 220, 234
  blue (*Parus caeruleus*) 117
  coal (*P. ater*) 117
  marsh (*P. palustris*) 94, 116
  willow (*P. montanus*) 116
toad, natterjack (*Bufo calamita*) 6, 179, 203
Tollesbury fleet 182–3
topography 21
topsoil removal/stripping 29–30
  grassland 63
  heathland 137, 141
tormentil (*Potentilla erecta*) 47, 95, 145
toxic chemicals, wetland water source 210

trampling (footpath) 160–1
  dispersing grazing away from path 171
  species resistant to 167
traveller's joy (*Clematis vitalba*) 71
treecreeper (*Certhia familiaris*) 94, 116
trees 202–3
  farm 202–3
  fauna supported by 118–21
  hedgerow 126–7
  planting, *see* planting
  protection 108–9
  seeding 98
  species
    introduced 104
    selection 99–104
  thinning 111
  see also forest; timber; woodland
trophic status of lakes 26, 27
tundra soil, revegetation 170–1
turfing
  heathland 149
  montane/submontane areas 163
turtle dove (*Streptopelia turtur*) 94, 116

urban areas 8–9, 11, 41–2, 46, 225–6

vegetation, *see* plants
Venus' looking glass (*Legousia hybrida*) 59
vertebrates 13; *see also* specific species
vetch
  bitter (*Lathyrus montanus*) 118
  horseshoe (*Hippocrepis comosa*) 36, 41
  kidney (*Anthylis vulneraria* subsp. *carpathica*) 11, 60, 89
  tufted (*Vicia cracca*) 128
violet, dog (*Viola riviniana*) 113

vole
  bank (*Clethrionomys glareosus*)
    115
  short-tailed (Microtus agrestis)
    234

warbler
  reed (*Acrocephalus scirpaceus*)
    220, 234
  Savi's (*Locustella luscinoides*)
    220
  sedge (*A. scirpaceus*) 234
Warrington New Town, woodland
    ground flora 114–15
waste ground, natural colonization
    42, 58
waste water, wetlands used to treat
    232–3
water
  site survey considering
    characteristics 22–31
  wetland
    balance/levels (and its control)
      206–7, 212–13
    depth/profiles 216
    sources/supply (and its quality)
      206–7, 208–10
    waste 232–3
  see also hydrology
Water Fringe Management Scheme
    193
waterlogging, wetland 207
water-milfoil (*Myriophyllum* spp.)
    231
waterproofing 211–12
wayfaring tree (*Viburnum lantana*)
    104, 124
weasel's snout (*Misopates oronitum*)
    195
weeds 98
  field margins and 195–6
  tree planting and control of
    109–11

wet woodlands, species selection for
    100, 101
wetlands 180–4, 184–5, 185–7,
    204–35
  coastal 180–4, 184–5, 185–7
  freshwater 204–35
    constructed 232–5
    construction 205–14
    design, *see* design
    issues 204–5
    nutrient levels 26, 30, 208–9
wheat (*Triticum* sp.) 38–9
whinchat (*Saxicola rubetra*) 197,
    239
whitebeam (*Sorbus aria*) 99
  Swedish (*S. intermedia*) 42
whitethroat (*Sylvia communis*) 197
wildflowers (in grassland) 54–79
  for diversifying ecologically dull
    grassland 87–9
  species in seed mix 55
    quantities/types 72–3, 73–5
Wildfowl and Wetlands Trust
    Reserve at Barn Elms 214,
    215
wildlife, *see* animals
willow (*Salix* spp.) 120, 126
  dwarf (*S. herbacea*) 165
  goat (*S. caprea*) 9, 97, 125
willowherb
  American (*Epilobium ciliatum*)
    49
  rosebay (*Chamerion
    angustifolium*) 28, 107
winter cereal, birds on 197, 198
wintergreen, roundleaved (*Pyrola
    rotundifolia*) 42
Wolverhampton, woodland ground
    flora 112–14
wood avens (*Geum urbanum*) 112,
    113, 114, 120, 128
wood millet (*Milium effusum*) 113,
    114

woodcock (*Scolopax rusticola*) 116
woodland 92–121
  cowslips sown beside new 82
  designing 93–5, 239
  farm 201–2
  ground flora, poor dispersal
    ability 49
  herb introduction 111–15
  in landscape, role played by 92–3
  management 111, 244
  Stansted Airport 34, 99
  see also forest; timber; trees
woodlark (*Lullula arborea*) 133, 137
woodpecker 94, 116
woodruff (*Galium odoratum*) 112
woodrush (*Luzula* spp.) 71, 145
  field (*L. campestris*) 47, 71, 145
  greater (*L. sylvatica*) 115, 164
  spiked (*L. spicata*) 165
woundwort
  field (*Stachys arvensis*) 88

hedge (*S. sylvatica*) 49, 128
wren (*Troglodytes troglodytes*) 234
Wye college, woodland ground flora
    114–15

yarrow (*Achillea millefolium*) 60,
    63, 91
yellow archangel (*Lamiastrum
    galeobdolon*) 112
yellow bird's-nest (*Monotropa
    hypopitys*) 105
yellow rattle (*Rhinanthus minor*)
    44, 76, 88
yellowhammer (*Emberiza citrinella*)
    199
yellow-wort (*Blackstonia perfoliata*)
    44
yew (*Taxus baccata*) 100, 104, 111,
    120
Yorkshire-fog (*Holcus lanatus*) 41,
    52, 112, 139, 167, 197